DOCUMENTS
ON ART AND TASTE
IN AUSTRALIA

DOCUMENTS
ON ART AND TASTE
IN AUSTRALIA

The Colonial Period
1770-1914

EDITED BY

BERNARD SMITH

MELBOURNE
OXFORD UNIVERSITY PRESS
LONDON   WELLINGTON   NEW YORK

Oxford University Press

OXFORD LONDON GLASGOW NEW YORK
TORONTO MELBOURNE WELLINGTON CAPE TOWN
DELHI BOMBAY CALCUTTA MADRAS KARACHI LAHORE DACCA
KUALA LUMPUR SINGAPORE JAKARTA HONG KONG TOKYO
NAIROBI DAR ES SALAAM LUSAKA ADDIS ABABA
IBADAN ZARIA ACCRA BEIRUT

First published 1975

Smith, Bernard William, 1916-, ed.
Documents on art and taste in Australia: the colonial period, 1770-1914/ edited by Bernard Smith.—Melbourne: Oxford University Press, 1975.
Index.
Bibliography.
ISBN 0 19 550473 9.
ISBN 0 19 550476 3 *Paperback.*
1. Art—Australia—History—Addresses, essays, lectures. I. Title.
700.994

PRINTED IN AUSTRALIA BY BROWN PRIOR ANDERSON PTY LTD

Contents

Contents

Foreword

This book brings together, in the form of a critical anthology, a selection of texts most of which were written either by artists or about artists who lived and worked in Australia between 1770 and 1914. Some of these artists, such as Sydney Parkinson, the first of them all, were in Australia for only a few months, and one of them, Charles Darwin, was a scientist whose text is concerned with his personal reactions to nature in Australia. But Darwin's reactions to nature became so influential for nineteenth-century thought, both in art and in science, that it seemed not only advisable but indeed necessary in this case to break the guiding rule.

The intention of the book is to make better known the existence of a number of documents which are of importance for the study of art, the study of the aesthetic point of view, and of theory about art, in their relationship to the more general study of Australian colonial culture. It may also serve as an introduction to contemporary source material relevant to the study of art and taste in colonial Australia.

The texts have been selected to draw attention to both changing interests and continuing concerns. Possibly a different selection of texts would reveal a different set of interests and different concerns. But those who are inclined to adopt this view from a general belief that all anthologies are to a large extent personal selections must be warned that, for the first half of the nineteenth century at least, the number of texts concerned either directly or indirectly with art and with aesthetic attitudes to nature are few in number, and that even during the second half of the century, where more documents do exist, the broad currents of interest flow in fairly well defined channels. I suspect that, although we need to know more than we do about them, the formation of aesthetic views about nature in Australia, the creation of the first art collections, the interaction of English taste and the colonial social and geographical environment, the moral preoccupations and aspirations of Victorian Evangelists and Utilitarians, the growing concern about art education, and, finally, the triumph of nationalism in art and taste, will continue to be seen as among the major interests and preoccupations of the colonial culture so far as the visual arts are concerned.

The texts are arranged in, for the most part, a chronological order but they are also brought together by topic, in order to illustrate the current preoccupations of a period. Occasionally it has appeared sensible to abandon a strict chronology in order to preserve thematic unity. For whilst it is true that each historical period does reveal its special concerns it is also true that the concerns of earlier periods continue into later periods, especially where relatively constant factors such as the geographical environment or the philistinism of colonial society are active. It is my hope that the publication of these texts will lead to a more sympathetic understanding of the aspirations, ambitions and ideals of that minority who strove, under conditions of extreme cultural poverty and personal isolation, for a more civilized Australia.

Each chapter begins with an introduction, followed by a brief biographical account of the author of each text, then the text succeeded by related notes. These latter are comprehensive in order to make the book useful and self-contained either for group discussion or private study.

I am greatly indebted to a large number of people who have helped me to gain information either about the little-known authors of some of the texts published here or about references and allusions in the texts. Miss Joyce McGrath, the Fine Arts Librarian of the State Library of Victoria, voluntarily undertook considerable research into the hitherto obscure activities of Sidney Dickinson, one of the most colourful characters to appear in these pages; Miss Jean Dyce, the Mitchell Reference Librarian of the Library of New South Wales, was most helpful in providing information concerning the lives of Thomas Shepherd and William Woolls. Mrs Ann Quinn provided invaluable help on several matters concerned with John Peter Russell. Mr Noel Hutchison drew my attention to the article by Lucien Henry. I owe a special debt to two of my research assistants, firstly to Mrs H. M. Taylor who provided typescripts of most of the texts from the originals, and assisted me to edit them. I have adopted the general practice of reproducing the original text as it was written or printed. Where I have departed from this practice, as in the selections from Duterrau and some others, the alterations are made clear in the text. My second research assistant, Miss Gail Newton, has helped to find explanations for many of the less obvious references and allusions. In this regard also, however, I must acknowledge the great value of the London Library, during a year of study leave in the United Kingdom, for research of this kind.

I must also acknowledge the assistance of Professor James Kinsley, of the University of Nottingham; Professor H. D. Jocelyn;

Professor D. Armstrong, Professor J. J. Nicholls and Dr A. W. James, all of the University of Sydney; Professor Emeritus A. D. Trendall, La Trobe University, Victoria; Mr Gordon Phillips, the archivist of the *Times*, London; Dr Jaynie Anderson, St Hugh's College, Oxford; Miss Mary McCrae, the Principal Archivist, State Library of Tasmania; Miss Jacqueline Menzies; Mr John Morris, the Director of the National Trust (N.S.W.); and Miss Frances McCarthy, the Assistant Curator of Australian Art of the Art Gallery of New South Wales, Miss Eve Buscombe and Miss Ann Watson; Mr Edward Comstock (for his work on the life of Eugen von Guerard); Mr Michael Saclier, Archivist, Australian National University; and Dr Rainer Lübbren, Director of the Goethe Institut, Sydney.

🔲🔲🔲🔲🔲🔲🔲🔲🔲🔲🔲🔲🔲🔲🔲🔲🔲🔲

ONE

In a New Land

INTRODUCTION

How did the first European artists to visit Australia see the country? How did they interpret it and reconcile it with what they knew and what they had been taught? These questions are of abiding interest to anyone who wishes to understand the development of the arts and civilization in Australia since the beginnings of European occupation. The first four selected passages have been chosen to illustrate four kinds of response to nature in Australia. The extract from Sydney Parkinson's *Journal of a Voyage to the South Seas* was compiled from notes he made in his manuscript journal when he visited Botany Bay as a member of Joseph Banks's scientific party on H.M.S. *Endeavour* in April and May 1770. Parkinson is objective. He observes carefully, describing in detail the physical features, weapons and canoes of the Aboriginals which Captain Cook's party encountered. He is keenly and personally interested in the kinds of fish found in the bay, the nature of the trees, plants and animals, the general character of the countryside. His prose is a lucid and candid vehicle of communication designed to convey facts accurately. His was a style of writing, that 'close, natural, naked way of speaking', which the Royal Society had done its best to encourage its own correspondents and travellers 'bound for far voyages' to adopt. James Cook and Joseph Banks wrote in a similar style, though Cook's style — he was a self-educated man of unusual ability — is more terse and abrupt, more limited and less flexible than either that of Banks or Parkinson. Fortunately we have descriptions of the visit to Botany Bay by all three men. But since this anthology is built around the writings and opinions of practising artists it is Parkinson's that I have included here.

The second passage is also by a young Scot. But the circumstances were markedly different. Parkinson was a respected and cherished member of a scientific company. Watling was a man in disgrace; a convict sentenced to fourteen years transportation for forgery. Feelings of shame, a prevailing melancholy, and a smouldering resentment are present in his letters to his aunt in Dumfries. We do not know to what extent these letters were edited for publication, but a distinctive personality — and not a particularly attractive one — comes through. Between Parkinson and Watling, however, we may discern not only differences of temperament and circumstance but also the different intellectual temper and sensibility of two generations. Sydney Parkinson was a product of the Scottish Enlightenment. Born in 1745 his attitude of mind was moulded by the generation that produced David Hume, Adam Smith, and Adam Ferguson — a time of intellectual brilliance second to none in Europe. Watling was born seventeen years after Parkinson — a wayward child, not of the Enlightenment but of early Romanticism in Scotland with its cult of sentiment, rhetoric and the picturesque. There is something stagey and artificial about Watling's writing. It is full of literary allusion that is designed to show his betters that he is no mere convict but a true man of feeling who has fallen, through a moment of thoughtlessness, among criminals. True, much of what he has to say about the Aboriginals is of great interest, for he has inherited some of the curiosity of the Enlightenment. But now the observations are coloured by feeling. They lack Parkinson's impersonality. Watling developed a clearly expressed dislike for the natives whom his hateful masters were inclined to idealize as noble savages. In him we may witness the emergence of Australian attitudes to Aboriginals with its incipient racism.

Surprisingly his melancholy, for all its artificiality, can hold us in a way that the bright clarity of Parkinson's prose cannot. For we can, in the light of history and through the experience of so many who came after him and were in their way so like him, enter more fully into his situation. It is the tragedy of a weak and shifty young man, with a high opinion of himself, suddenly cut off from his roots, and forced to endure a life of brutish, unmitigated wretchedness, 'burthened by cruelty, hunger and the most laborious of employment'. We may compare him with that other victim of over-refined sensibility, the forger and poisoner, Thomas Griffiths Wainewright. Both felt that the world owed them a living; and our own more indulgent and permissive world might have given them a better start in life and in the end quite a good living. But eighteenth-century England — eighteenth-century Europe for that matter — was not like that. Beneath the thin crust of tolerant and liberal behaviour that the Enlightenment brought to the few who were privileged enough to benefit from it lay a cesspool of cruelty, violence and archaic law. Those who transgressed were banished from the small and rather closed society of civilized man and were to be reminded constantly in their continuing state of shame and humiliation of their transgressions. Hence the mood of guilt, alienation and exile evoked by Watling's letters and, though to a lesser degree, for these were executed for his masters, by his paintings and drawings of the natives and landscapes of New South Wales. Many others, both transportees and free immigrants, who came after Watling were to find themselves the unwilling occupants of his gloomy terrain, exiled in a country where beauty was a kind of sorcery and deceit a principle of nature. Watling was the first to express the love-hate relationship to Australian nature, the expression, internalization and transcendance of which has done so much to form the texture of Australian sensibility in its struggle for identity and a sense of place. Watling was, we might say, the first of the wounded ones, crying out in self-pity and anguish at a land that did not seem to want them.

To pass from Thomas Watling, painting Australian scenery through the eyes of James Thomson and William Gilpin, to John William Lewin chasing grubs and butterflies with a tomahawk and saw is a breath of fresh air: a jolt from culture to reality. Less well-educated than Parkinson or Watling, as revealed here by his highly personal spelling (far too enjoyable and characteristic to be tinkered with) he was, like Parkinson, concerned with the facts and the systematics of natural science; one of the many little men to be found in far-flung parts of the world at the opening of the nineteenth century, who were assiduously collecting their specimens for Sir Joseph Banks and for Sir Joseph's friends in the Royal Society and the Linnean Society; a quite unimportant and almost anonymous member of that new international brotherhood of science which was extending its dominion throughout the world even while Napoleon was closing off the ports of Europe. That Lewin, too, had his troubles he makes clear to his employer. 'Those few insects that I have sent you was collected at the imminent hazed [*sic*] of my life . . .'. But he does not indulge his miseries; a practical, inventive man, he tries new dodges when old ones fail. He improvises and gets along, joins exploring expeditions to find new grubs for Drury, opens a shop and inn with his wife to make ends meet, paints transparencies for the Queen's Birthday Ball at Government House. This pragmatism, this insensitivity, meant that he did not allow his feelings to affect unduly the way he saw things. So that when, in a great moment of his life, he came to make the journey over the Blue Mountains as a member of the Governor's party Lewin, in a 'close natural, naked, way' of seeing that the Royal Society would have approved of (had they been seeking a report not of a new plant or animal, but upon the colour, atmosphere and light of a new environment), succeeded in becoming the first artist to depict the Australian landscape with an eye unfettered by the aesthetics of the picturesque or the melancholy of romanticism and stands also at the beginning of a tradition. One can almost hear him muttering, like some Delphic oracle, as he busied himself with his superb painting of a platypus, *ornithorhynchus paradoxus,* now in the Mitchell Library, Sydney, 'she'll be right, mate'.

The last extract sounds a note different from all the others. In the advertisement which served as preface to Joseph Lycett's *Views in Australia,* the convict is not speaking for himself as Watling was, but for his masters. Now we are no longer confronted with Parkinson's innocent wonder and curiosity at the strange and the new; nor with the alienated, neurotic sensibility of Watling; nor with Lewin, that archetypal Australian improvising his way through his troubles. Joseph Lycett (or his ghost, for one must wonder how much is truly his and how much was written for him) sounds a rhetorical and confident note. He records not only the scenes of savage nature but also the first steps in the growth of a new civilization in the South Seas; and he does not hesitate to reveal how much he, and all sane men, prefer the latter to the former. Thrice a forger and an inveterate drunk, he manages nevertheless to do his masters proud: to declare in confident words and cleanly finished drawings the triumph of progress in the wilderness, of the British Empire as one of the principal catalysts of human progress. Lewin, in short, speaks for the developers, for the men who believed in the inevitability and sanctity of progress, for that new wave of moral self-assurance and utilitarian confidence that swept across Britain in the years after Waterloo.

Four artists. Four voices. Parkinson, Watling, Lewin, Lycett. The voice of science, the voice of feeling, the voice of common sense, and the voice of progress. They will be heard again and again, appropriately varied, intricately interwoven and blended, all through the nineteenth century as others came to terms, to the extent that their personality and their education allowed them, with the new land.

Sydney Parkinson (1745–71)

Parkinson was typical of many a young man of modest means who responded passionately to the new scientific enthusiasms of the Enlightenment during the later decades of the eighteenth century. They developed their talents for drawing and painting and their knowledge of natural history, and sought their patrons among men of means, gentlemen-travellers and explorers, equally imbued with the scientific spirit, and eager to unravel the mysteries of nature in distant lands among primitive peoples.

Parkinson was the son of an Edinburgh brewer and the family were Quakers. He was possessed, according to his elder brother Stanfield Parkinson, of 'singular simplicity of conduct, sincere desire for the truth, an ardent thirst after knowledge and indefatigable industry to obtain it'. All of which no doubt encouraged him to forsake his apprenticeship to a wool-draper and develop his talent for drawing. In 1765 and 1766 he exhibited paintings of flowers on silk in the exhibitions of the Society of Arts, a Society formed in 1754 to encourage closer links between art, technology and commerce. The prizes awarded at the annual art exhibitions were designed to encourage young men like Parkinson.

In 1767 he had come to the attention of James Lee, a nurseryman of Hammersmith (who had translated Linnaeus and introduced the cultivation of the fuchsia into England) and painted plants on vellum for him. And he had also come to the attention of Joseph Banks.

Banks was only two years older than Parkinson but belonged to a different order of society. Educated at Harrow and Eton, Oxford and Cambridge, Banks entered into his fortune and the estate of Revesby Abbey, Lincolnshire, upon the death of his father in 1761. His tutor at Cambridge fostered Banks's early passion for botany and he soon became an inveterate traveller and botanizer — eager to publish, by means of drawings and engravings, his new finds and those of his friends for the advantage of the world of science. In 1766, quite early in his life, he became a member of the Royal Society, and travelled to Newfoundland and Labrador on H.M.S. *Niger,* employing the famous botanical illustrator Georg Ehret to draw the collection when the voyage returned to England. But Ehret died in 1770, and Parkinson became Banks's leading botanical artist.

One of his first tasks was the production of water-colour drawings of mammals and birds from specimens and sketches

B

brought from Ceylon. Then, when Banks decided to join Lieutenant Cook on H.M.S. *Endeavour* in 1768 on its voyage to the
South Seas, he invited Parkinson to accompany him as his
botanical draughtsman, at a salary of £80 *per annum*.

Sydney Parkinson undertook the commission with enthusiasm.
When Alexander Buchan, the young artist Banks had employed
to draw landscapes and peoples for him on the voyage, died at
Tahiti, the whole burden of artist to the expedition fell largely
on Parkinson. During the voyage he made over 1,300 drawings
of plants, animals, birds, peoples and landscapes. But on the way
home Parkinson contracted dysentery at Batavia and died — like
so many of the crew — at sea, in January 1771.

When the expedition returned a dispute arose between Banks
and Sydney Parkinson's brother Stanfield over the possession of
Sydney's papers and drawings. Banks paid Stanfield £500 for
the material and the balance of the salary owing. He later lent
Stanfield his brother's papers and drawings. Contrary to their
agreement, Stanfield transcribed them for publication. He was,
however, forbidden to publish them until after the official account
of the voyage by John Hawkesworth appeared in 1773. Stanfield
then published *A Journal of a Voyage to the South Seas* later
in the year; and an enlarged edition in 1784, from which the
following account of Botany Bay, the first account by an artist
of an Australian landscape, is taken.

[THE FIRST ENCOUNTER]

On the 28th, we got into a fine bay, and some of our people
went on shore on one side of it, where we saw some houses. On
our approaching the shore, two men, with different kinds of
weapons, came out and made toward us. Their countenance
bespoke displeasure; they threatened us, and discovered hostile
intentions, often crying to us, Warra warra wai. We made signs
to them to be peaceable, and threw them some trinkets; but
they kept aloof, and dared us to come on shore. We attempted
to frighten them by firing off a gun loaded with small shot;
but attempted it in vain. One of them repaired to a house
immediately, and brought out a shield, of an oval figure, painted
white in the middle, with two holes in it to see through, and
also a wooden sword, and then they advanced boldly, gathering
up stones as they came along, which they threw at us. After we
had landed, they threw two of their lances at us; one of which
fell between my feet. Our people fired again, and wounded one

of them; at which they took the alarm and were very frantic
and furious, shouting for assistance, calling Hala, hala, mae; that
is, (as we afterwards learned,) Come hither; while their wives
and children set up a most horrid howl. We endeavoured to
pacify them, but to no purpose, for they seemed implacable,
and, at length, ran howling away, leaving their wives and
children, who hid themselves in one of the huts behind a piece
of bark. After looking about us a little while, we left some
nails upon the spot and embarked, taking with us their weapons;
and then proceeded to the other side of the bay, where we had
seen a number of people, as we came in, round a fire, some of
whom were painted white, having a streak round their thighs,
two below their knees, one like a sash over their shoulders, which
ran diagonally downwards, and another across their foreheads.
Both men and women were quite naked, very lean and raw-
boned; their complexion was dark, their hair black and frizzled,
their heads unadorned, and the beards of the men bushy. Their
canoes were made of one piece of bark, gathered at the two ends,
and extended in the middle by two sticks. Their paddles were
very small, two of which they used at one time; and we found
a large lump of yellow gum in their gigs which seemed to be for
striking fish. Some of their weapons had a kind of chisel fixed
at their ends, but of what substance they were formed we could
not learn.

The natives often reconnoitred us, but we could not prevail
on them to come near us or to be social; for, as soon as we
advanced, they fled as nimbly as deer, excepting at one time,
when they seemed determined to face us: then they came armed
with spears, having their breasts painted white; but, as soon as
they saw our boat go off from the ship, they retreated. Con-
strained by hunger, they often came into the bay to fish; but they
kept in the shallows, and as near as possible to the shore. In one
of their houses, at the top of the bay, we had laid some nails,
pieces of cloth, and various trinkets; and though the natives had
been there in our absence, yet they had not taken any of them.

This bay is in latitude 34°6', and makes a good harbour, being
only two or three points open to the eastward; but the water
is in general shallow; and it has several arms extending from it,
which are also shallow. On these shallows we found a great
number of rays, some shell-fish, and a few sharks. The rays are
of an enormous size: one of them which we caught weighed
two hundred and thirty-nine pounds, and another three hundred
and twenty-six. They tasted very much like the European rays,

and the viscera had an agreeable flavour, not unlike stewed turtle. These rays, and shell-fish, are the natives chief food.

The country is very level and fertile; the soil, a kind of grey sand; and the climate mild: and though it was the beginning of winter when we arrived, every thing seemed in perfection. There is a variety of flowering shrubs; a tree that yields gum;[1] and a species of palm, [*Borasus flabellifer,*][2] the berries of which are of two sorts; one small, eaten by the hogs, and the other, as large as a cherry, has a stone in it; it is of a pale crimson colour, and has the taste of a sweet acid. We also found a species of Salvia Fortea.[3]

We met with but one quadruped on the island, which was about the size of a hare:[4] we found also the skin of a snake, and saw a great number of birds of a beautiful plumage; among which were two sorts of parroquets, and a beautiful loriquet: we shot a few of them, which we made into a pie, and they ate very well. We also met with a black bird, very much like our crow, and shot some of them too, which also tasted agreeably. From the number of curious plants we met with on shore, we called the bay Botany-Bay.

> [From Sydney Parkinson, *A Journal of a Voyage*
> *to the South Seas,* 1773, pp. 134-6]

NOTES—THE FIRST ENCOUNTER

[1] The tree may be either *Eucalyptus gummifera* (Gaertn.) Hochr., 'Red Bloodwood', or *Angophora costata*, 'Smooth-barked Apple', both of which were collected at Botany Bay during Cook's stay, and in manuscripts are referred to as gum bearers *(gummifera)*.

[2] Now classified as *Livistonia australis* (R. Br.) Mart. The pale crimson, cherry-like fruits mentioned by Parkinson are from another plant *Syzygium paniculatum* Gaertn., 'Brush Cherry'.

[3] Possibly *Plectranthus paryiflorus* Willd., which was collected by Banks and Solander at Botany Bay.

[4] Probably a bandicoot or kangaroo rat.

Thomas Watling (b. 1762)

Both New South Wales (1788) and Tasmania (1803) were established as convict settlements; about 80,000 convicts were transported to New South Wales from Britain, and about 32,000 to Tasmania, between 1788 and 1840. Not surprisingly, some of these men were draughtsmen, engravers and painters; most of such men were transported for forgery.

Thomas Watling was one of the first and one of the most interesting of the convict artists. Convicted of forging guinea notes on the Bank of Scotland in November 1788 at the Circuit Court of Dumfries, the town where he was born in 1762, he arrived in the settlement on 7 October 1792.

The son of a soldier, his parents had died in his infancy, and he was brought up by a devoted aunt, Marion Kirkpatrick, who had seen that he obtained a decent education. He began life as a coach and chaise painter, but aspired to become a teacher of drawing, for he sought to establish a drawing school, 'Watling's Academy' which undertook to teach ladies and gentlemen drawing at a cost of one guinea per month. Such schools had begun to flourish in Britain because of the impact of the new taste for the picturesque, which promoted water-colour drawing and painting as an elegant accomplishment among gentlefolk.

Watling had probably read of William Gilpin's travels and knew his methods of drawing, for his manner of composing and painting landscapes in monochrome washes is similar to that of Gilpin; and his letters to his aunt reveal that he had known Gilpin's theory of the picturesque, had read Macpherson's *Ossian,* and cultivated an early romantic and somewhat affected prose style in the manner of Henry Mackenzie (1741-1831), whose *Man of Feeling* (1771), or something like it, he may well have read.

Watling arrived in Sydney in October 1792, and remained until he gained an absolute pardon from Governor Hunter in April 1797, having served eight of his fourteen years sentence from the time of conviction. He appears then to have travelled to India, for there is evidence that Thomas Watling, a miniature painter, lived in Calcutta from 1801 to 1803. In 1804 there is melancholy evidence of his having arrived back home in Dumfries, for in January 1806 Watling was arraigned before an Edinburgh Court and once again charged with forging promissory notes. But the prosecution's case was weak, a verdict of 'not proven' returned, and Watling discharged.

The last piece of evidence concerning the life of this unhappy man is contained in a pathetic letter which he wrote to Hunter, from whom he had obtained his pardon in 1797. It was conveyed to Hunter by Watling's son, whom he described as 'the only living offspring from the connection I formed in N.S. Wales'. He told the Governor that he had but a few years to live, having contracted a cancer in the left breast, and begged 'a slender pecuniary relief'.

The greater part of the work executed by Thomas Watling in New South Wales is now contained in the zoological library of the British Museum (Natural History). It is bound in a large folio volume, and contains 512 drawings mostly in water-colour, with some pencil and some wash drawings. They include charts, landscapes, coastal profiles, illustrations of contemporary events, drawings of natives and native life, animals, birds, fishes, insects, reptiles, plants and shells. There are almost three hundred water-colour drawings of birds; and most of the material depicted is from the Port Jackson neighbourhood.

Watling's only surviving oil painting *Sydney in 1794* is in the Dixson Gallery of the Library of New South Wales. It is probable that Watling executed the painting for John White, the surgeon-general of the Colony, to whom he appears to have been assigned shortly after his arrival in Sydney. Many of the engravings which appear in David Collins's *Account of the English Colony in New South Wales* (1798-1802), appear to have been based upon Watling's drawings.

The extract printed below is taken from *Letters from an Exile at Botany Bay, to his Aunt in Dumfries*, published by a printer of Penrith, Scotland, in or about 1794. It consists of some letters which Watling wrote to his aunt, Marion Kirkpatrick, during his exile. Only a very few copies of the original book exist today.

[A LAND OF ROMANTIC ENCHANTMENT]

The flattering appearance of nature may be offered as the best apology for those mistaken eulogiums lavished by a late eminent circumnavigator upon this place.[1] Perhaps nothing can surpass the circumambient windings, and romantic banks of a narrow arm of the sea, that leads from this to *Parramatta,* another settlement about fourteen miles off. The Poet may there descry numberless beauties; nor can there be fitter haunts for his imagination. The elysian scenery of a Telemachus;[2] — the secret recesses for a Thomson's musidora;[3] — arcadian shades, or classic bowers, present themselves at every winding to the ravished eye. Overhead the most grotesque foliage yields a shade, where cooling zephyrs breathe every perfume. Mangrove avenues, and picturesque rocks, entwined with non-descript flowers: — in short, were the benefits in the least equal to the specious external, this country need hardly give place to any other on earth . . .

My worthy friend, Mr. H———,[4] may reasonably conclude, that these romantic scenes will much amuse my pencil; though therein he is mistaken. The landscape painter, may in vain seek here for that beauty which arises from happy-opposed off-scapes.[5] Bold rising hills, or azure distances would be a kind of phaenomena. The principal traits of the country are extensive woods, spread over a little-varied plain. I however confess, that were I to select and combine, I might avoid that sameness, and find engaging employment. Trees wreathing their old fantastic roots on high; dissimilar in tint and foliage; cumbent, upright, fallen, or shattered by lightning, may be found at every step; whilst sympathetic glooms of twilight glimmering groves, and wildest nature lulled in sound repose, might much inspire the soul — all this I confess; but all this, if I possibly can, shall be considered of hereafter.

In the warmer season, the thunder very frequently rolls tremendous, accompanied by a scorching wind, so intolerable as almost to obstruct respiration; — whilst the surrounding horizon looks one entire sheet of uninterupted [*sic*] flame. The air, notwithstanding, is in general dry. Fifteen months have been known to elapse without a single shower; but though thus dry, the transitions of hot and cold are often surprisingly quick and contrasted without any discernable [*sic*] injury to the human system. I have felt one hour as intensely warm as if immediately under the line, when the next has made me shiver with cold, yet have I not experienced any harm therefrom; owing, without a doubt to the dryness and salubrity of the atmosphere.

The vast number of green frogs, reptiles, and large insects, among the grass and on the trees, during the spring, summer, and fall, make an incessant noise and clamour. They cannot fail to surprise the stranger exceedingly, as he will hear their discordant croaking just by, and sometimes all around him, though he is unable to discover whence it proceeds:—nor can he perceive the animals from whence the sounds in the trees issue, they being most effectually hid among the leaves and branches.

Should the curious Ornothologist [*sic*], or the prying Botanist, emigrate here, they could not fail of deriving ample gratification in their favorite pursuits in this luxuriant museum. Birds, flowers, shrubs, and plants; of these, many are tinged with hues that must baffle the happiest efforts of the pencil. — Quadrupeds are by no means various: but we have a variety of fishes, the greater part of which, are dropped and spangled with gold and silver, and stained with dyes transparent and brralliant [*sic*] as the arch of heaven.

One great error in many of our voyagers, is the giving prematurely a decided opinion of what falls within the circle of their observation. That the inhabitants of N.S.Wales, are centuries behind some other savage nations, in point of useful knowledge, may be fact; but in this there is no criterion of judging mental ability. Their huts and canoes, it is true, are extremely rude and ill formed; but when we consider their non-acquaintance with iron tools, and the hardness of their wood, it is more surprising that they can use it at all. — It being so ponderous as to sink immediately in water, renders it entirely useless that way; — consequently no succedaneum here can be so easily moulded, or so fit for the purposes of forming their little vessels as the bark — and this, both as builders and sailors they manage with a very singular dexterity.

The people are in general very straight and slim, but extremely ill featured; and in my opinion the women more so than the men. Irascibility, ferocity, cunning, treachery, revenge, filth, and immodesty, are strikingly their dark characteristics — their virtues are so far from conspicuous, that I have not, as yet, been able to discern them.

One thing I may adduce to their credit, that they are not cannibals. They burn and bury their dead, but from what motive it is hard to conceive; immolation it cannot be; as they have not apparently the smallest idea of a Deity, much less of religion.

In imitation they are extremely apt, particularly in mimicry; and they seem also in many other respects to be capable of much improvement; but they are so very unsteady and indolent, that it would be almost next to a miracle to bring them to any degree of assiduity or perseverance. Here I cannot help making what may appear rather an ill-natured remark; our governors, for they are all of such, have carried philosophy, I do not say religion, to such a pitch of refinement as is surprising. Many of these savages are allowed, what is termed, a freeman's ratio of provision for their idleness. They are bedecked at times, with dress which they make away with the first opportunity, preferring the originality of naked nature; and they are treated with the most singular tenderness. This you will suppose not more than laudable; but is there one spark of charity exhibited to poor wretches, who are at least denominated christians? No, they are frequently denied the common necessaries of life! wrought to death under the oppressive heat of a burning sun; or barbarously afflicted with often little merited arbitrary punishment — this may be philo-sophy, according to the calculation of our rigid dictators; but I think it is the falsest species of it I have ever known or heard of.

The men and women, at any early age, devote to their chieftain, the former, one of the upper fore-teeth; and the latter, the first joint of the little finger of the left hand, as a token of their fidelity. — This is one of their public ceremonies, and is performed in the most bungling manner; but it is impossible to descend to particulars in the limits of a narrow letter.

A canoe, spear, wooden sword, and shield, short bludgeon, stone hatchet, fishing tackle, and a rude basket formed of bark, comprize the whole of their domestic or offensive implements. Their substitute for knives is ever at hand; the first shell that occurs fully answering that purpose.

They are very quick eyed, and dexterous in the striking of fish or aiming of the spear; but they are neither so atheletic or nimble as might reasonably be expected in a savage race.

Bedaubing, or streaking themselves in various forms with red or white earth, they would prefer to the most tawdry birth-day suit whatever. The same want of taste keeps them honest this way — but victuals, knives, or hatchets, vanish with them in a twinkling.

It pays no small compliment to poesy and painting, that they are affected by the most unenlightened as well as the most refined countries. The natives are extremely fond of painting, and often sit hours by me when at work. Several rocks round us have outre figures engraven in them; and some of their utensils and weapons are curiously carved, considering the materials they have to work with.

Their Poets neither having the advantage of writing or printing, are necessitated to travel as the hedge-preachers in *Britain,* to extend their reputation. It is but lately that an itinerant sable Ossian[6] called this way, and held forth to some hundreds of his countrymen, who after kindly entreating, escorted him to some other bourne, to further promulgate his composition.

Whatever may be their merits in this department, I confess that I am not connoisseur enough to guess at them. Of their music, however, I may aver that nothing can be more disagreeable, unless it be their other favorite amusement, dancing; for if harmony be the foundation of the one, and grace of the other, these aborigines have not, as yet, the smallest idea of either.

The hair smeared with gum, and forked as the porcupine; a bone or straw stuck horizontally through the middle cartilage of the nose; and the body streaked over with red or white earth, completes the *ton* of dress of the inhabitants of *N.S.Wales,* either for war, love, or festivity.

Many of them are tatowed [*sic*] over the arms, back, and breast, in a very irregular manner, which seems to have been done at an early period of life, for which they can assign no other reason than that of ornament.

It were presumption in me to speak of their language, with which I am but little acquainted. Glossaries have been attempted by some of our pretending and aspiring gentry, who, I am conscious, are as much ignorant of it as myself. I think it is by no means copious, but rather confined to a few simple sounds; but whether this is, or is not a beauty, I leave to the learned to determine. To an European ear the articulation seems uncommonly wild and barbarous; owing, very likely, to those national prejudices every man imbibes, and perhaps cannot entirely divest himself of. One thing they have in common with more refined communities, that marks a clannish propinquity of kindred; which is a similarity in the termination of their sir-names: Terribi-long, Benna-long, Bye-gong, Wye-gong, Cole-bree, Nan-bree, &c. &c. are full as striking as Thomson, Johnson, and Robson.

As it is impossible for me to be so particular as I could wish, the barbarian *New Hollander* must give place to a few other remarks, I would inform you of ere I finish my letter.

Returning then back to general observation; and supposing you to have heard something of the swiftness, meekness, and singular formation of the Kangaroo, of the Opposum, Guanoe, Lizards, &c. I may say, that not only these, but the whole appearance of nature must be striking in the extreme to the adventurer, and at first this will seem to him to be a country of enchantments. The generality of the birds and the beasts sleeping by day, and singing or catering in the night, is such an inversion in nature as is hitherto unknown.

The air, the sky, the land are objects entirely different from all that a Briton has been accustomed to see before. The sky clear and warm; in the summer very seldom overcast, or any haze discernable [*sic*] in the azure; the rains, when we have them, falling in torrents, & the clouds immediately dispersing. Thunder, as said, in loud contending peals, happening often daily, & always within every two or three days, at this season of the year. Eruscations and flashes of lightning, constantly succeeding each other in quick and rapid succession. The land, an immense forest, extended over a plain country, the maritime parts of which, are interspersed with rocks, yet covered with venerable majestic trees, hoary with age, or torn with tempests. — In a word, the easy, liberal mind, will be here filled with astonishment, and find much entertainment from the various novel objects that every where present themselves.

To sum up natural reflection for the present; — though there are a variety of objects to exercise the imagination, yet such a sameness runs through the whole of the animal and vegetable creation of New South-Wales, that I think it would be no hard matter for the discerning naturalist to at once distinguish them from those of every other country, by their peculiarity. The various Banksias do not more appear to belong to one common family, than the Kangaroo, Opposum, and Kangaroo-rat, to that of the Kangaroo. The fruit and feed of the trees, and most of the underwood, ligneous and scarce penetrable to the hardest instrument, have all of them something of resemblance to each other. In short, from the savage native in the animal, and the towering red gum in the vegetable, every thing indigenous to this colony, approaches or recedes by a very striking and singular gradation of proximity.

[From Thomas Watling, *Letters from an Exile
at Botany Bay, to his Aunt in Dumfries*,
Penrith (Scotland), [1794], pp. 7-16]

[A PROSPECTUS FOR A SET OF PICTURESQUE DRAWINGS]
Sydney-Cove, Port Jackson,
New South Wales, May 20th, 1793.

THOMAS   WATLING
Principal Limner in New South Wales,
Extremely anxious to deserve better of his Country, proposes, with due Deference, under the Patronage of an
impartial Public,

The Execution of a
PICTURESQUE DESCRIPTION of that COLONY;
In an highly-finished Set of Drawings, done faithfully upon the
Spott, from Nature, in Mezzo, Aqua-tinta, or Water Colours.

That the subjects attempted, shall be partial and general views of *Sydney, Parramatta*, and *Toongabbe*; romantic groves, or native groupes, and that, if possible, in the course of the work, curiosities in ornothology [*sic*] and botany shall be interwoven.

Though the fabricator, with deep confusion, confesses him-self a prisoner, he would, nevertheless flatter himself, that a philantrophic [*sic*] and liberal minded nation, would not render that an insuperable barrier; nor from so melancholy a circumstance, deny him any claim to merit. He would modestly insinuate, that he rates his abilities equal to the task proposed; and flatters himself, that his performances shall be the most accurate and elegant that have, as yet, been received in *Britain,* from the new world.

Those gentlemen inclined to encourage a work attempted by an unfortunate being, that possibly may not be utterly destitute of genius, are humbly requested to transmit their names (post paying) to Mrs. M. K——,⁷ nigh, &c.

No emolument is expected until the paintings or drawings shall arrive in *Britain,* and be submitted to the subscribers for engraving; when, should they be found worthy the indulgence and protection of the really unbiassed friends of lowly distressed merit — the author, shall gratefully thank his patrons for what they may think him deserving for his labours.

> [From Thomas Watling, *Letters from an Exile at*
> *Botany Bay, to his Aunt in Dumfries* [1794]
> pp. 26-7]

NOTES—WATLING

¹ i.e. Captain James Cook. Watling is probably referring to remarks attributed to Cook in John Hawkesworth's *Account of the Voyages Undertaken by ... Byron, Wallis, Carteret and Cook,* London, 1773, iii, 504 ff. Cook did not enter Port Jackson and so did not see the Parramatta River. Nor can his descriptions of either Botany Bay or of New South Wales as a whole as published by Hawkesworth be described as 'eulogiums', mistaken or otherwise.

² The reference is to François de Salignac de la Mothe-Fénelon's didactic romance Télémaque, written for the edification of his pupil the Duc de Burgogne and later published surreptitiously in 1699. This book, much used as an educational text in the eighteenth century, expressed many of the ideals of the Enlightenment. John Hawkesworth published an English translation of *Télémaque* in 1769. The romance recounts the imaginary adventures of Telemachus, the son of Ulysses, after he set out from Ithaca in search of his father. He is accompanied by Mentor who is the goddess Minerva in disguise and also the model of a good and faithful tutor. Watling remembered the opening scene of the book where Telemachus is delighted by the beauty of Calypso's grotto but is warned by Mentor to beware of the sorceress and the beguiling scenes with which she surrounded herself.

³ A reference to the tale of Damon and Musidora which James Thomson (1700-48) introduced into his poem *Summer* (1727), the second of his four *Seasons* (1726-30).

⁴ An unidentified Scottish friend.

⁵ Off-scapes: a distant scene or prospect. The word was current in the eighteenth and early nineteenth centuries, but is now obsolete.

6 The name commonly given to Oisin, a legendary Gaelic bard who is the hero of the spurious Celtic poems *Fingal* (1762) and *Temora* (1763) by James Macpherson (1736-96).
7 i.e. Marion Kirkpatrick, Watling's aunt in Dumfries.

John William Lewin (1770–1819)

Australia's first artists were either convicts or amateurs, such as naval or military draughtsmen. The first professional artist to arrive as a free immigrant was John William Lewin. He was, like Sydney Parkinson, a naturalist and an artist. His father, William Lewin, was a fellow of the Linnean Society and the author of *Birds of Great Britain,* published in seven volumes between 1789 and 1794. It was a family affair, for his two sons, John William and Thomas, helped their father to prepare drawings of specimens, engrave plates, and assist to some extent in the compilation of the text.

It was possibly through his father's connections that John William gained the patronage of the Duke of Portland and Lady Arden, for both helped him when he decided to migrate to New South Wales. A third patron was Dru Drury, a London gold-smith who had retired in 1789 to devote himself to his passion, entomology. Drury made contact with travellers embarking for distant and little-known lands, provided them with nets and other implements for catching insects, and promised to pay for specimens posted back to him. As a result he had collectors scattered in many lands. The letter reproduced here from Lewin to Drury tells of his difficulties in the new land, and of the strange habits of its insects.

Lewin's first book, *Prodromus Entomology: Natural History of Lepidopterous Insects of New South Wales,* was published in London in 1805, and dedicated to Lady Arden 'in grateful remembrance of that goodness which gave the Author an oppor-tunity of employing his talents... in a new world'. Lewin en-graved the eighteen plates himself. It appeared in a second edition in 1822. In 1808 he published *Birds of New Holland with their Natural History,* two further editions appearing in 1822 and 1838, and also a variant edition published in Sydney in 1813.

Although not trained, Lewin turned to occasional landscape painting, and in some of his later work, such as that executed when he accompanied Governor Macquarie over the Blue Mountains in 1815, he succeeded in capturing something of the character of Australian vegetation and scenery. Being the one free artist resident in Sydney in Macquarie's time he was called upon, from time to time, to embellish the vice-regal ballroom for special occasions.

Governor King granted Lewin and his wife a hundred-acre farm near Parramatta, where he did much of his work collecting specimens and engraving plates for his books. He was one of the settlers who supported Bligh, and was a signatory to the petition which expressed alarm at the Governor's deposition in May 1808. Governor Macquarie made use of his services and helped both Lewin and his wife; and granted them two hundred acres in Airds. Lewin died on 27 August 1819 and his wife returned to England, where she appears to have assisted in the publication of the later editions of his two books. His brother Thomas wrote the introduction to his *Prodromus Entomology*.

Collections of Lewin's paintings are to be found in the Mitchell Library, the Dixson Gallery, and the Nan Kivell Collection of the National Library of Australia.

The letter which follows was written by Lewin to Dru Drury in connection with his undertaking to collect insects for him. It provides us with a fascinating glimpse of the many problems which confronted an artist in the early days of settlement.

[THE TROUBLES OF AN INSECT COLLECTOR]

> Per favour of Captain Law,
> Commander of the *Greenwich,*
> a whaler homeward bound.
> Farm Cove, Sydney, the 7th
> of March, 1803.

I have tak[en] this opportunity to send you a box of insects marked D. Drury, Strand, London, some of which are the produce of Otaheite, collected by myself.

The reason that I have not wrote before I must candidly acknowledge and if it will not excuse it will at least palliate some of the neglect is this — When the ship *Royall Admirall,* commanded by Captain Wilson, came into this Harbour in 1801 I went on board to enquire for a letter etc., from you and received for answer that there was none. And after some enquiry I found that Captain Wilson had a number of Boxes etc., for collecting Insects which he shewed me and telling me at the same time that Mr. D. Drury had commission[ed] him to purchase all the Insects that I had collected for you[rself] at which I was not a

little surprized, but on his shewing me the papers &c., on collecting I was satisfied that they came from yourself but could not
immagine the reason that there was no letter with them and was
accordingly hurt at it but however I thought it best to send the
Insects by him and stay till I received a letter from you before
I sent any more. Those Insects that I sent [were] packed in one
of those square Boxes that he told me he had from you. I think
to the best of my remembrance [were] upwards of 4 hundred in
[480] Number for which he paid me and I gave him a receipt,
since which time I have not sent home a single Insect, being
determined not to do it till I had received a letter from you, and
my not being in this country when your last Letter &c. came
has been the reason of my not writing to you before; but I rest
in hope you have got the Insects as I should [not want them to?]
fall into other hands . . .

I see by your letter dated Saturday June 6 1801 that you
complain of the little information that I gave you in the letter
I sent by Governor Hunter, but you may rest assured that I
never will give you that cause to complain for the future as I
am really ashamed of my past negligence in that particular and
I hope that this letter will give you some satisfaction on that head
if not all the pleasure you [are] [anxious?] to receive.

In the same letter [you] inquire if I have a beating Sheet,
in answer to which I must inform you about this country, and
you will find that Insects [are] not to be got here as att home, for
in all my trialls with the Sheet by beating I never could get
Ither [i.e. either] Catterpillars or full-Boddyed Moths for the
trees are so exceedingly high that it is but few that you can
reach with a long pole, and I have not found it answer by
beating the Shrubs or underwood, and I was at [a] loss to know
where to look for the larvia of the moths for a great while after
that I came here, for I never could find any in all my differant
travils into this country; but now my surprise is at an end and
dare to say yours will be the same when I inform you, and I
[doubt] not but will be greatly pleased to hear that I have twenty
drawings with the larvia and crysalis and moths, compleat for
engraving, which feed by night and secret themselfs by knawing
a hole ither in the Body of the tree, or else the branches and
there lie hide all the day and sometimes for severall days together,
for when they want to feed they come out at night and knaw of[f]
a small twig and drag it to their hideing place to feed upon at
[their] leisure. They cover [their] hole with a web in a verry
artfull manner so that it requires a carefull person to find [their]

hideing places, [so] that a beating sheet is little or of no use here in this country; instead of which I have adopted a Tomyhawk and saw, by which I expect to get a most interesting and beautifull work. I have not the least doubt but before this letter arrives at home that the first volume will be on its way to England. And I am not in the least affraid but it will meet with a rapid sail for there is a number of beautifull moths and [they] are all new, which together with the plants they feed uppon will make not onely a beautifull but interresting work and as a specimen I have sent you a drawing of the manner and execution which I am sure will give you both pleasure and satisfaction. I have not sent any of the moths that I have painted nor shall, till the first volume gos home and then shall send you a pair of each of thos I have figured, god willing, I shall do my utmost to compleat as soon as possible.

In regard to publishing the Insects of this Country I most heartily join with you, and of course will exzert my utmost to get finished the first volume that I have begun. As I have mentioned in the above, some of the drawings [were] made nearly two years ago so that I had made great progress before I was informed [of] your Ideas on making a Supplement to your work on Insects so that it will be best to finish my work as I have begun but you will be [a] better Judge when you see the first volume which I am [sure] will give you every satisfaction.

I thank you [sincerely] for your advice and shall act accordingly, and of course I shall publish with your [kind?] assistance the Insects first and I intend to print fifty [copies?] of the Insects and send them home and while [they are] on the [passage] to you I shall go about the Birds which you [would] have had long before this, as I had engraved a number of plates but was unfortunately forced to lay it aside until I could get some printing Ink from England as that [I?] had brought with me was all spoiled and I could not get [none] here. I wrote home to my Brother to send me both printing Ink and copper plates by Captain Bunker a whaler which I hope to get by the first ship that comes from England.

You kindly mention in your letter your [design?] of getting 20 or 30 advanced by some gentleman to [be laid?] out in Haberdashery of which you are in hopes of making a deal of money by them but, alas, the times [are] strangely altered since I gave you that information, for there [has] been so many Ships in this port since I wrote to you that the market is over stocked with those Articalls. As for my imploying them in paying a man for collecting catterpillars [for] me, it is not so easy a matter as you may [think] for every thing in Naturall History is contrary to our known knowledge in England and in fact I was greatly puzzled to find any myself for a great while, not knowing their manners and [various] methods of secreting [themselves] that the larvia of moths [in] this country have, but I have got such an insight into their manners that I have no doubt but that I shall procure you some of the most Beautifull and rare moths. I hope you will not mention any more in your letters about gold &c. Sorry enough I am that ever such a thought entered into my head but enough of that subject for I am really sick of it for had it not have been for those Ideas or rather dreams I never should have gone to Otaheite in search of pearls where I very nigh lost my life for the vessel that I went in¹ was stranded on the Beach on Point Venus where she was intirely lost in a heavy gale of wind which lasted five Days and that was not the only misfortune for after we got on shore we had the natives to fight for they were at war with the party* that were our friends so that for the nine months that we was on the Island we were continually alarmed with the Dreadfull Ideas of haveing our throats cut and I have not the least doubt but we should have been all marooned and the missionary intirely distroyed or at least forced to fligh to the other Island at the risk of being drowned only [for] a few of us who well new the use of fire arms. As for thos dastards called missionary they would have run and hid themself rather than fight or protect there property and wife &c.

Thos few Insects† that I have sent you was collected at the imminent hazed of my life so that all the time I was forced to stop on the Island was lost. For a History of that nation I must refer you to Cook, who is very correct in is Discription of that Island and its inhabitants.

You may be sure we where all glad when the Porpois a Ship that came on the same errand as we did which was to cure pork for the Use of the Colony came in to the bay of Mativia,⁵ where after a few weeks we embarked on board her without our losing any lives and after a fine passage I arrived safe in Sydney the latter end of December 1802 and with a firm resolution to set down to my pencell and never to go any more in search of gold pearls or anything but Insects and that not out of sight of land.

* The King's name is Otto², who was our friend and his party was at war with two chiefs named Rooā and Tartir rè³.
† Many of those were collected at Emio⁴, an Island about thirty miles from Otaheite.

C

Among the instruments you sent was a bras frame intended to be used in killing moths and Butterflies which I find of great use and am infinitly obliged to you for the discovery and the Boiling watter is the Best way I ever met with to kill all sorts of Insects.

I know must return my sinscer thanks for all your kindnesses but particular that of your getting me made an associate of the Linnean Society[6] and rest in hope that your most sanguin Ideas will not be [deceived?] in the confidence you have placed in me notwithstanding the many slanderous and malicious things as been [said?] of me and that I shall have it in my power to return all the many Obligations that you have laid me under to your worthy self and it will give me the most heartfelt satisfaction to hear that this will find you in Health which I hope god in is infinate mercy may grant for a few years longer so that I may have it in my power both in word and actions to shew you how sencible I am of your valuble friendship.

I am extremely sorry to inform you that the Box of Clothes that you sent by the Atlas[7] where all damaged with the salt water. The coat I have sent to you as a specimen of the state they came in but I hope you insured them. If you did you can make? the Captain pay for this as it was intirely neglect through bad [stoage?].

The Box of Haberdashery came safe as well as the other Articalls that you sent. The Coper plates are most all engraved. Some of the proff prints I have sent with this letter under the care of Lieutenant Thompson of the glattan[8] who is a very worthy young man and he will be able to give you a great deal of information. I intended to have sent this by another Ship as you may see at the beginning but the glattan a king ship[9] come in to port before she sailed and on which the grenwich[10] was detained untill the glattan was ready to saill with her and thinking it would be better to send thos Insects with Mr. T. who as promised to deliever this letter in person together with the print of insects and Birds that I have sent you as a specimen of the manner and likewise to shew you that I have surmounted most of the dificulty, that I laboured under for I have found a meathod of making printing Ink so that there is nothing now to stop me from going on both with the Insects and Birds as I almost filled thos last Copper plates that you sent me and as soon as I have engrave the plates of Insects I shall print of fifty Coppy, and send them home by the next conveyance. I wish you had sent a enough for a volume as then you would have been able to have published The volume at once but as it you must publish them in numbers which you can bring out a number every three month untill I can get more Copper and paper an articall I am much in want of. I trust you will send me a good quantity by the next conveyance for the sooner I get it the better. When you get the paper you will have a draw Back[11] allowed to you which will be a great saving of expence to us it will be best to cut it up in quarters and pack it in small double cases well pitched Both inside and out which will prevent it from spoiling by the salt water and brown paper laid on the seam while it is hot The same casses will serve to send the print home again so that there will be nothing lost by getting them well made.

I am exceedingly obliged to you for Edwards[12] work on bird which came safe and should a bean expressly pleased if you had sent me your own work of Insects[13] as It would have bean of great service to me as I do not no in what manner these are done if we should make a supplement it would be necessary for me to have it. I think that the Beatles locust mantis [libellerium?] would make a good [suplement?] as thos Insects loos so much of there beauty when they are dry for any length of time it will be best to paint and [etch?] them as they would be sure to [be entertaining] as the [colours?] are so various and pleasing when living but turn black as soon as dead. Your Ideas of this subject I will pay the greatest attention to. The mantis of [this] Country and [that] will alone make a volume. They all Insects of prey feeding on Catterpillars and other Insects which I think is the reason that the larvia are so scarce as nature as so contrived it that most of them have some perculiar method of hiding themselfs as the mantis are continualy on the [search?] for them and there verry voracious for I have seen a mantis feeding on a larvia above [four] inches in length just treble it one size.

I wish if you possible can that you will send any of thos undermentioned articalls as they will ennable me to employ people to colect for me as they pass for mony an [therefore?] pay away as such:

Spirrits of any kind that you think best and cheapest
Tea
Sugar moist
Soap
A good patent lamp would be very acceptable as we have nothing but oile.

I must conclude and hope that this will find you in good

Health and Spirrit which god willing I hope you will enjoy for many years and may God preserve and keep you in safety and happiness.

I am yours
Truly
J. W. Lewin

Mrs. Lewin desires her kind remembrance to you.

P.S. Pray send a few good pairs of Shoes?
a little
and small cask of molasses will be very acceptable.

N.B.

I have sent 3 specimens of the plates of Insects coloured and [1?] of Birds to shew you the manner in which they will be done. They are not so delicate as I could wish owing to the prints being the first proof. There in a square deal Box in which ther is a letter for Mr. Heathcote and a parcell of drawings for him and a small Chip Box with loos Beatles which I hope you will get safe. I hop by the next ship to send you some chois moths together with 50 Copies of thos 10 plates you sent me last and? the glatton would have shipped but one month longer I should have bean able to send you proff of all the plates.

[Letter from J. W. Lewin to Dru Drury, 7 March 1803]

[THE EXTRAORDINARY INSECTS OF NEW SOUTH WALES]

PREFACE

The contents of this little Volume are Lepidopterous Insects, indigenous of New South Wales, were there collected, painted, and engraved, by the Author; and sent to London by him for publication, to furnish him with the means of returning to England, his native country, after an absence of near eight years, which he has spent almost solely in the pursuit of natural history, principally in the branches, Ornithology and Entomology; in which he has in New South Wales, and in Otaheite, made some hundred of original paintings; from which it is hoped he may, by the profits of this little first effort, be enabled to return and reap an honourable benefit, as their publication, under his ingenious hand, we flatter ourselves, would somewhat redound to the honour reputation, and increase of those branches of the sciences in Britain. The insects here figured are new, and some of them extraordinary in their natural history, the singularity of which, with the correctness of the figures, must render this Work, we conceive, peculiarly valuable. For till this author, none has discovered, or expected to find lepidopterous insects of the families here figured, as the destroyers of timber, or the depredators of massy and hardest trees, in the way which is here made known. And it should be observed also, that the natural history, as well as the engraving, was done on the spot, and not from dry specimens, or notes still more abstruse. And all that was left for us to do was merely to define the genus, and name the individual in some cases, which we have done sometimes from the plant on which the insect was found; and for the names of those plants we make our acknowledments to the learned President of the Linnean Society, Dr. Smith,[14] and also acknowledge the kind observations of the Secretary of the Society, Alexander Mac Leay,[15] Esq. for whose abilities, as an Entomologist, we have the highest respect, though we cannot avoid differing greatly from him in some points.

Of the style of the publication, and the arrangement of the subject, we can only say, being well instructed in the Field of Nature, we have endeavoured to render the book useful.

[Thomas Lewin's Preface to J. W. Lewin's
Prodromus Entomology, 1805]

NOTES—J. W. LEWIN

[1] The *Norfolk,* commanded by Lt James Grant, which sailed for Tahiti on 8 November 1801.

[2] i.e. Otoo, Tu or Pomare II. An account of the conflict in which Lewin found himself involved is contained in John Turnbull, *A Voyage Round the World*, London, 1813. Turnbull describes Lewin as 'a landscape painter, sent hither from Botany Bay, for the purpose of taking views, and making drawings of objects in this island' (p. 131).

[3] Rua and Taatarii, see W. Ellis, *Polynesian Researches*, 1, 115, and Vincendon-Doumoulin and Degraz, *Iles Taiti*, I, 468.

[4] i.e. Eimeo or Moorea.

[5] i.e. Matavai Bay, Tahiti.

[6] Named after Carl von Linne (Linnaeus), 1707-78, the famous Swedish biologist and pioneer taxonomist. The Society was founded in 1788.

[7] The *Atlas* arrived in Sydney on 30 October 1802.

[8] H.M.S. *Glatton* left for England on 17 or 18 May 1803.

[9] i.e. a ship of the Royal Navy.

[10] The *Greenwich* arrived in Sydney on 14 February and sailed for London on 18 May 1803.

[11] i.e. 'an amount paid back from a charge previously made *esp.* a certain amount of excise or import duty remitted after the commodities on which it has been paid are exported' (*O.E.D.*).

12 George Edwards, F.R.S. (1694-1773) who published a *History of Birds* (1743-64).

13 Lewin is probably referring to Drury's *Illustrations of Natural History*, exhibiting upwards of 240 figures of Exotic Insects, 3 vols, London, 1770-82.

14 i.e. Sir James Edwards Smith (1759-1828), botanist and founder of the Linnaean Society (1788).

15 Alexander McLeay (1767-1828)—the name was spelt variously—public servant and entomologist, later Colonial Secretary of New South Wales (1825-37).

Joseph Lycett (b. 1774)

Lycett is said to have been a portrait and miniature painter. Born in Staffordshire, he was convicted of forgery at Salop in 1811, and sentenced to transportation for fourteen years. He reached Sydney in February 1814, and was made a clerk in the Police Office. In May 1815 he was convicted of forgery a second time (of 5s bills drawn on the postmaster) and sent to Newcastle, a place of secondary punishment. Here he assisted with plans for the church, built in 1818, and painted the altar-piece. He is believed also to have designed the three-light window now in the bishop's vestry of Newcastle Cathedral. Captain James Wallis, the Commandant at Newcastle who helped Lycett (they had travelled out to Sydney together in 1814 on the *General Hewitt*) secured a conditional pardon for him, and during 1819 and 1820 he travelled widely about New South Wales and Van Diemen's Land drawing picturesque views for a projected book. Governor Macquarie, too, helped him. Three drawings sent by the Governor to Lord Bathurst in February 1820 were probably instrumental in gaining Lycett's absolute pardon in November 1821. He sailed with his two daughters to England in September 1822 and began to prepare his material for publication. It first appeared in serial form, monthly: two views of New South Wales and two of Van Diemen's Land in each part (7s in plain and 10s 6d in coloured aquatint) — commencing from July 1824. When all the parts had appeared the remaining plates with their accompanying texts were bound and sold as *Views in Australia* (London, 1825).

[PICTURESQUE VIEWS IN AUSTRALIA]

Among all the various occurrences which constitute the history of human affairs, there are perhaps none calculated to excite such universal interest as the DISCOVERY OF UNKNOWN

COUNTRIES, and the progress of ART upon the soil and people, which NATURE, on such occasions, resigns from her own creative hand to the care and culture of their civilized discoverers.

In the noble and beneficent enterprises of discovery and civilization, no modern nation has surpassed Great Britain; and, when we look at the present state of AUSTRALIA, it seems probable that the most recent of her glories of this description will prove the brightest and most valuable.

It is, indeed, impossible to contemplate the scenes of natural grandeur, beauty, richness, and variety, with which the Colonies of NEW SOUTH WALES and VAN DIEMEN'S LAND abound, without impressions of mingled delight and wonder at such magnificent specimens of the stupendous power of Nature, as they burst upon our view in all the freshness of a new Creation! Or, if we turn from the wild scenery of Australia in her pristine state, to view the benign changes which the arts and sciences of Britain, aided by the liberal policy of her government, and the enterprising spirit of her merchants, manufacturers, and traders, have pro-duced upon this new theatre of Nature, we shall have before us one of the most pleasing studies which can engage the mind of the philosopher or the philanthropist. We behold the gloomy grandeur of solitary woods and forests exchanged for the noise and bustle of thronged marts of commerce; while the dens of savage animals, and the hiding places of yet more savage men, have become transformed into peaceful villages or cheerful towns.

> 'Here SYDNEY* gazes from the mountain's side,
> Narcissus-like, upon the glassy tide;
> There HOBART† stretches, where the Derwent sees
> Her yellow harvests tremble in the breeze.'‡

When the interesting origin and the rapidly increasing importance of these Colonies are considered, it may seem sur-prising that the present should be the first attempt to give the British public any adequate idea of the grandeur and beauty of their natural scenery, or any correct representation of their chief settlements. But it must be recollected how extremely remote Australia is from Great Britain,— how very limited have been the opportunities of communication between them, — and how numerous, and almost insurmountable, are the obstacles which

---

* The Capital of New South Wales.
† The Capital of Van Diemen's Land.
‡ 'Australia,' a Poem, by THOMAS H. HERVEY. [London, 1824].

in these regions are opposed to the labourers of the most enthusiastic disciple of the Arts.

The Work now submitted to the Public, under the title of

VIEWS IN AUSTRALIA,

Or, New South Wales and Van Diemen's Land Delineated,
is designed to be at the same time a HISTORY of the Discovery,
Settlement, and Progress, of these Colonies, and a GRAPHIC
DELINEATION of the principal Scenery, and of every object of
interest in that part of the New World.

The VIEWS may be regarded, with implicit confidence, as
absolute *fac-similes* of scenes and places, having been taken from
nature on the spot by Mr. LYCETT, who resided more than ten
years in the country, in the especial employ of the Governor as
an Artist. The peculiar privilege which he thus enjoyed of
selecting the most picturesque, as well as the most important,
subjects for his pencil, have enabled him to enrich the present
work by those truly original Views, which no other Artist could
possibly have obtained the same favourable opportunities of
drawing. In the compass of twelve Monthly Parts, the first of
which will appear on the 1st July, will be contained twenty-four
Views of Scenes in New South Wales, and twenty-four of Scenes
in Van Diemen's Land, including the principal Settlements of
each Colony, with their Public Buildings; and also the Mountains,
Plains, Forests, Rivers, Lakes, and, in short, every object which
meets the eye of a spectator of the actual scenes, whether they
be such as the rude hand of Nature formed, or such as the arts
of civilization have fabricated for the use of social man.

Each Plate will be accompanied with two pages of Letter-
press, containing a clear and ample description of the subject, and
such further information as may be necessary for its complete
elucidation; and with the twelfth Part will be given a brief
HISTORY OF AUSTRALIA from the earliest period of discovery to the
present times.

Upon the completion of this Work, it is intended to publish,
in the same size and manner, the NATURAL HISTORY of Australia,
comprising specimens of the Animals, Birds, Fishes, Insects,
Trees, Botanical and other Productions of Nature, from Drawings
carefully taken by the same artist, and which will be executed
in the same style of elegance and correctness. The several subjects
will be scientifically explained in the accompanying pages of
Letter-press; and the two Works together will form one of the
most valuable and curious collections of the Graphic Art which

has appeared in modern times, and which, for many years to come, cannot be rivalled by any similar production.
London; June, 1824.

[Advertisement for Joseph Lycett, *Views in Australia,* first published in June 1824]

🔲🔲🔲🔲🔲🔲🔲🔲🔲🔲🔲🔲🔲🔲🔲🔲🔲🔲

Some Early Reflections on Nature in Australia

INTRODUCTION

The four extracts included in this chapter develop themes introduced in the first. But in this case they are not drawn from the writings of artists — with the important exception of Thomas Shepherd the landscape gardener, the first artist of his kind in the country. They are, however, observations of men with some claim to cultivation and taste. They reveal a desire to generalize and reflect upon the aesthetic problems, and in Charles Darwin's case at least, upon the scientific implications raised by the nature of nature in Australia.

During the 1830s, within which most of the observations were written, occupation and settlement west of the Dividing Range developed apace. It was a period of pastoral expansion, of optimism for the future. The point of view expressed by Thomas Watling that Australian beauty is a superficial cheat is heard little. Nor is there, on the other hand, any ready acceptance of the Australian scene. The discussion is conducted largely within the terms of the picturesque. Barron Field begins with a brilliant essay called forth by his journey across the Blue Mountains. He admits readily and with some enthusiasm that Australian shrubs and flowers are remarkably beautiful — New South Wales is 'a perpetual flower garden'. Indeed the first poem of this first Australian poet, his *Botany Bay Flowers,* a pleasant conceit garnished with Shakespearian allusions, testifies to his civilized delight in *epacris grandiflora* and the fringed violet. But for Field the landscape as a whole is unpicturesque and he goes to some lengths to find a reason. Building his case upon a suggestion gleaned from Robert Brown — Flinders's botanist and the best of his generation in England — about the orientation of eucalyptus leaves to the sun. Field proceeds to write a panegyric to the deciduous landscape of northern Europe as fine as anything of its kind in English. His style seems to be modelled, on this occasion, upon Joseph Addison. The deciduous landscape, he assures us, is the perennial source of inspiration for European poets and painters, and essential to European culture. Eighteenth-century writers like the Abbé Dubos, Montesquieu, and Winckelmann, who developed the theory that geographical position determines the nature of a culture, would probably have agreed with him. So too, indeed, would that arch-priest of High Victorian taste, John Ruskin. But whether his theory linking the deciduous with the European is valid or not, Barron Field certainly expressed the antipathy which many immigrants felt and still feel at the first encounter with eucalyptus forest; and for many, as for Field, the first encounter was the deciding one. Yet he does not, it is to be noted, express the brooding resentment of Watling. A Supreme Court judge had less reason. He took things as they came. With an amused, supercilious authority, and William Gilpin's picturesque precepts to guide him, he rode through the land passing judgement upon God's antipodean handiwork at every new prospect he encountered. With the same self-confidence he expresses, as did Joseph Lycett, pleasure at the signs of progress and government spreading into the antipodean wilderness — 'the very sleeping grooms beneath me had been thieves and robbers . . .; but our persons and property were inviolate'.

Eleven years separate the publication of Field's *Geographical Memoirs* and Thomas Shepherd's *Lectures in Landscape Gardening in Australia,* a period in which the colony of New South Wales grew rapidly in population and wealth. Shepherd, a professional landscape gardener, was well versed in theory of the picturesque and the practice of picturesque landscape gardening developed in England by William Kent, Capability Brown, Uvedale Price, Richard Payne Knight and Humphrey Repton. In our present context, however, the most important point Shepherd makes is his advice, constantly repeated, to prospective improvers not to destroy needlessly the indigenous vegetation when clearing their grounds. He notes with approval the example set by Alexander McLeay when laying out the gardens of Elizabeth Bay: 'From the first commencement he never suffered a tree of any kind to be destroyed, until he saw distinctly the necessity for doing so' and he speaks with strong disapproval of those 'proprietors of residences at Woolloomooloo' who ignorantly set the murderous hoe and grubbing axe to work' upon the native trees. McLeay and Shepherd were the pioneers of nature conservation in Australia. Having found, unlike Field, ways in which the indigenous vegetation contributes to a pleasing and picturesque landscape, they proceeded to recommend its judicious conservation. It was an answer also to the naive enthusiasm for the 'progress of Art upon the soil and people' expressed by Joseph Lycett twelve years before.

The clerical botanist and essayist, William Woolls, takes the discussion a stage further. He concedes, in the first place, that Australia lacks those material reminders of antiquity that 'enliven and dignify the histories of other countries'. There are no pyramids, no castles. John Ruskin was to make a similar point some years later about America. Yet, argues Woolls, the Australian landscape can arouse, in those with some feeling for history, associations even more primal and basic. Its great treeless plains and numerous flocks can remind him of the days of the patriarchs; its vines and figs; its cicadas screeching away happily in the summer sun, of the poets of Greece in its golden age.

Woolls, of course, mixes it. He reacts warmly, positively, to the new scenery, the new ecology we might say of the 1830s, the blend between the Mediterranean and Antipodean which the pastoral extension was bringing with it. 'William Kent', said Horace Walpole, in a much quoted phrase, 'leapt the fence and saw that all nature was a garden'. William Woolls in his essay, and many were later to adopt his point of view, leapt the fence of picturesque taste, which prevented Field and many of his compatriots from seeing the peculiar beauties of Australia, to find, in the 1830s at least, a kind of primitive arcadia inhabited by squatters with their flocks and families re-enacting the story of Abraham. If that too was but a vision affected by a point of view, it had more going for it in reality than the romantic melancholy of Thomas Watling or the picturesque one-upmanship of Barron Field.

But Charles Darwin was more cautious. When he wrote his account of his journey over the Blue Mountains (that crossing was almost archetypal for establishing attitudes to Australian nature) he echoed many of the reservations of Field. The mountains were 'most disappointing', really no more than the 'inconsiderable front' of a 'sloping plain' and the scenery was 'monotonous'. But unlike Field, who had no stomach for the sublime, Darwin was moved by the great gorges of the Jamieson and Grose valleys and wrote memorably about them. His prose possesses the same tone of cool but committed curiosity and balanced judgement that we have already met with in Sydney Parkinson. Both were about the same age when they visited Australia, Darwin twenty-six, Parkinson twenty-five. But Parkinson had only a few months to live; Darwin lived to become one of the greatest of all scientists. In the passage selected we may gain a glimpse of his insatiable curiosity at work, his warm interest in everything about him, and at the end of the passage we may observe also that subtle interplay between reflection and observation which characterized his mind (as he watches a struggle to the death between a lion ant and a common ant) and led him many years later to the enunciation of the theory of natural selection.

Barron Field (1786–1846)

Barron Field was the son of a London surgeon who was also apothecary to Christ's Hospital, where the boy was educated. Field read law at the Inner Temple and was called to the Bar in June 1814. In May 1816 he was appointed Supreme Court Judge in New South Wales. Field possessed a firm grasp of legal principles and Governor Macquarie held, at first, a high opinion of him until it became clear that he was opposed to the Governor's emancipist policies, siding strongly with the 'exclusives' led by Samuel Marsden and the Macarthurs.

The Report of Commissioner Bigge on the *Judicial Establishments of New South Wales and Van Diemen's Land* (1823) had the effect of terminating Field's appointment, and he returned to England in 1824. In 1827 he resumed practice at the bar in Liverpool, and in March 1829 became the first Chief Justice of Gibraltar, where he remained — despite strained relations with the Governor, Sir William Houston — until his retirement in 1841, due to ill health.

Throughout his life Field cultivated his scientific and literary interests. As a schoolboy at Christ's Hospital he became an intimate friend of Leigh Hunt, to whose *Examiner* he contributed poems and essays, and moved in the circle which included Coleridge, Wordsworth, Henry Crabb Robinson, and Charles Lamb. Field acted for a time as drama critic for the *Times,* and also contributed to the *London Magazine.*

In 1816, shortly before he left London, Field married Jane Cairncross, to whom Charles Lamb addressed some verses. The Fields set up house in Macquarie Place, Sydney, where they entertained many of the notables of the Colony, such as the

Blaxlands, Pipers, Macarthurs and Marsdens, and encouraged the development of some of the early cultural institutions of the Colony. Field was an active Foundation member of the Philosophical Society of Australasia (est. June 1821); an early President of the Agricultural Society (est. 1822); a founder of the Society for Promoting Christian Knowledge among the Aborigines; a generous supporter of the Benevolent Society (est. 1813); active on the Committee for the Establishment of Public Schools; the first President of the New South Wales Savings Bank; and a founder of the Sydney Institution, where newspapers and periodicals were made available to the general public.

In 1819 Field wrote a preface to the *Memoirs of James Hardy Vaux,* and published his *First Fruits of Australian Poetry,* the first book of verse to be published in Australia. It consisted of two poems, and was issued for private circulation. In 1825 he edited the *Geographical Memoirs on New South Wales* which included a number of his own papers. They reveal his interest in natural history, and his wide-ranging curiosity. After he had left Australia Field published *Spanish Sketches,* another book of verse printed privately in Gibraltar in 1841, the year of his retirement. Field also wrote memoirs of Coleridge (in 1835) and of Lamb (in 1836) for the *Annual Register.* In his retirement he edited five of the plays of Thomas Heyward for the Shakespeare Society; his favourite love having long been the Elizabethan drama. He died at Torquay in 1846.

[FIELD ON CROSSING THE BLUE MOUNTAINS]

Monday, 7th October, 1822. This spring month is the fittest to make this excursion in. The winter nights are too cold, and the summer days too hot. In the autumn the flowers are not in bloom.

The difficulties of the travel commence at Emu Ford[1] over the river Nepean, a branch of the Hawkesbury. Crossing this stream is always a work of such time and trouble, and sometimes of such difficulty and danger, that the traveller should send forward his cart ar baggage-horses, to overcome it, half a day before he rides or rows through it himself. The ferry is the property of government, who have hitherto delayed* either to provide a punt themselves, or to suffer the stockholders of the colony to build one by subscription. The consequences are frequent losses of cattle in swimming, and injury of sheep in boating, over.

* Since this was written, a punt has been established by government at Emu Ferry.

Although the river was not unusually high, we were obliged to
unload our cart before it could be drawn through the ford; and
thus lost several hours in transporting the baggage by one small
boat, and in reloading the cart.

On the banks of the Nepean, I saw almost the only deciduous
native tree in the territory, namely, the white cedar (melia aze-
darach), the common bead-tree of India*,[2] beautiful in itself, and
congenial to me from that singularity. All the other indigenous
trees and shrubs, that I have seen, are evergreens; the eternal
eucalyptus, with its white bark and its scanty tin-like foliage, or
the dark casuarina tall, and exocarpus funeral; all as unpicturesque as the shrubs and flowers are beautiful: — the various,
justly called proteaceous, banksia, and the hesperidean mimosa†,
the exquisite epacris, the curious grevillea, xanthorrhoea, the
sceptre of Flora, telopea the magnificent, and thysanotus the
lovely. New South Wales is a perpetual flower-garden, but there
is not a single scene in it of which a painter could make a landscape, without greatly disguising the true character of the trees.
They have no lateral boughs, and cast no masses of shade; but,
in return, it is to this circumstance, which causes so little vegetable putrefaction, that the healthiness of the climate is mainly
to be attributed. 'A part of their economy (says Mr. Brown the
botanist),[3] which contributes somewhat to the peculiar character
of the Australian forests, is, that the leaves both of the eucalyptus
and acacia, by far the most common genera in Terra Australis,
and, if taken together, and considered with respect to the mass
of vegetable matter they contain (calculated from the size, as
well as the number of individuals), nearly equal to all the other
plants of that country, are vertical, or present their margin and
not either surface towards the stem, both surfaces having consequently the same relation to light‡.' Can this circumstance be
partly the cause of their unpicturesqueness — of the monotony of
their leaf? Or is it merely their evergreenness? 'In the Indies
(says Linnæus), almost all the trees are evergreen, and have
broad leaves; but in our cold regions, most trees cast their
foliage every year, and such as do not, bear acerose, that is,
narrow and acute, leaves. If they were broader, the snow which
falls during winter would collect among them, and break the

---

* I met with this tree also in the Brazils.
† I do not mean that the mimosa belongs to Linnaeus's natural order
  hesperideae, though the eucalyptus does: my epithet is merely classical: I
  would say *golden*.
‡ Flinders's Voyage, vol. ii. p. 578.

branches by its weight. Their great slenderness prevents any
such effect, and allows the snow to pass between them*.' But
snow is not unknown to the eucalypti and acaciæ of New Holland;
and may not the verticalness of the broad leaves of some of them
answer the same snow-diverting purpose as the acerose-leavedness
of European evergreens? Yet the foliage of the eucalypti is always
scanty; that of the acaciæ acerose; and the snow of Australia is
apt to melt. Be this as it may, no tree, to my taste, can be beautiful
that is not deciduous. What can a painter do with one cold
olive-green? There is a dry harshness about the perennial leaf,
that does not savour of humanity in my eyes. There is no flesh
and blood in it: it is not of us, and is nothing to us. Dryden
says of the laurel

> 'From winter winds it suffers no decay;
> For ever fresh and fair, and every month is May.'[4]

Now it may be the fault of the cold climate in which I was bred,
but this is just what I complain of in an evergreen. 'For ever
fresh' is a contradiction in terms; what is 'for ever fair' is never
fair; and without January, in my mind, there can be no May.
All the dearest allegories of human life are bound up in the
infant and slender green of spring, the dark redundance of
summer, and the sere and yellow leaf of autumn. These are as
essential to the poet as emblems, as they are to the painter as
picturesque objects; and the common consent and immemorial
custom of European poetry have made the change of seasons,
and its effect upon vegetation, a part, as it were, of our very
nature. I can therefore hold no fellowship with Australian foliage,
but will cleave to the British oak through all the bareness of
winter. It is a dear sight to an European to see his young
compatriot trees in an Indian climate, telling of their native
country by the fall of their leaf, and, in due time, becoming a
spring unto themselves, although no winter has passed over them,
just as their fellow-countrymen keep Christmas though in the
hottest weather, and, with fresh fruits about them, affect the
fare and sometimes the fireside of Old England. 'New Holland
(says Sir James Smith) seems no very beautiful or picturesque
country, such as is likely to form, or to inspire, a poet. Indeed
the dregs of the community, which we have poured upon its
shores, must probably subside and purge themselves, before anything like a poet, or a disinterested lover of nature, can arise

* Sup. to Encyc. Brit., *Art.* Botany.

from so foul a source. There seems, however, to be no transition of seasons in the climate itself, to excite hope, or to expand the heart and fancy*.' . . .

Tuesday, 8th October . . . The timber now became more dwarf, and we were actually crossing the Blue Mountains. We found the pass very alpine and difficult, rocky, sandy, stony, flowery. The views were very grand. The night was stormy, but little rainy — all in the sublime. "The power of hills was on me," as Wordsworth says. I could not sleep for thinking of our situation, and walked forth from my tent. The air was refreshing. All were asleep from fatigue, with large fires of piled wood at their feet, the gleams on which (for they had been suffered to go down) gave a picturesque effect to the tent and cart, and to the tethered horses, which were patiently standing on the bleak and bare hill. A little more than thirty years ago, this land was inhabited by savages only, and these hills had, from the beginning of time, formed an impassable barrier between their tribes. The spirit of British government had now come from the antipodes, and, with nothing but a colony of convicts, had, in that short time, penetrated upwards of a hundred miles into the interior of the country, and established a township there, to which the unarmed might travel as safely as from London to Bristol. The very sleeping grooms beneath me had been thieves and robbers, and the blasted heath looked like New Hounslow; but our persons and property were inviolate.

Wednesday, 9th October. Moved at $8\frac{1}{2}$ a.m., and arrived at the bottom of Cox's Pass down Mount York at $5\frac{1}{2}$ p.m. (twenty-one miles and a half). The ridge of mountains (or rather rocks), along which this passage could alone be effected, is very difficult and desolate. The trees (still eucalyptus) are stunted and burnt, with the exception of one light species called the ash, of which good white-coopers' work might be made, and perhaps ships' smaller spars. The King's Table-land is as anarchical and untabular as any His Majesty possesses. The Prince Regent's Glen below it (if it be the glen that I saw) is not very romantic. Jamison's Valley we found by no means a happy one. Blackheath is a wretched misnomer. Not to mention its awful contrast to the beautiful place of that name in England, *heath* it is none. *Black* it may be when the shrubs are burnt, as they often are. Pitt's Amphitheatre disappointed me. The hills are thrown together in a monotonous manner, and their clothing is very unpicturesque

---

* Sup. to Encyc. Brit., *Art.* Botany.

D

— a mere sea of harsh trees; but Mr. Pitt was no particular connoisseur either in mountain scenery or in amphitheatres. Mount York (as Governor Macquarie named it) redeems the journey across the Blue Mountains, for it leads you to the first green valley. The earliest burst of the Christian transalpine country, as seen from the beginning of this mountain, is very beautiful. The sight of grass again is lovely. The view from the commencement of Cox's Pass down to it, is finer still. This *Big Hill*, as it is alone called, should have been named Mount Pisgah,[5] for it affords the first view of the promised land of Australia, after the wilderness of the Blue Mountains. In Van Diemen's Land they have a river Jordan, and plains of Jericho; but the river is so called (I suppose) because it may be occasionally passed over on dry ground; and the plains are not equal to Bathurst Plains. After three days' starving among the mountains, your cattle now get plenty of green grass. Encamp then at the first bite; . . .

[From Barron Field, *Geographical Memoirs on New South Wales,* 1825, pp. 421-30]

NOTES—BARRON FIELD

1 The ford on the Nepean River, N.S.W. thirty-six miles from Sydney, from which William Cox's road across the Blue Mountains (built in 1814-15) began. The present town of Emu Plains grew up at the Ford.
2 *melia azederach* L.; *Toona australis* (F. Muell.) Harris 'Red Cedar', another native species of the family *Melia Ceae,* is also deciduous.
3 Robert Brown (1773-1858), naturalist to Flinders on the *Investigator* voyage.
4 From 'The Flower and the Leaf', a medieval English poem translated by Dryden in *Fables Ancient and Modern* (1700).
5 A mountain in Moab (the biblical name of the region east of the Dead Sea) with a commanding view over the desert and Western Palestine, said to have been the scene of Moses' vision of the Promised Land (*Deut.* 3.27; 34.1).

Thomas Shepherd (1780–1835)

Thomas Shepherd was born in 1780, on the estate of the Earl of Crawford, in Balcarres, Colinsburgh, Fifeshire, Scotland, where his father was the head gardener, the family having been tenants of the Earl for almost a century. He was educated at a local school and on the estate acquired a sound knowledge of landscape gardening and the rudiments of architecture. In his first lecture in the series, from which the extract printed below is drawn, he wrote:

A gardener's lodge in a first rate place in Scotland, was more like a school than a lodge. In the evening, the young gardeners would study, principally from books, by their own exertions, grammar, arithmetic, geometry, trigonometry, land surveying and mapping; mensuration, horticulture, botany, garden architecture, and geography. It was customary for the head gardener to attend in the lodge for an hour or two in the evening to teach the apprentices and junior men.

Shepherd worked first with a Mr White, a Scottish landscape gardener, and later undertook commissions on his own account. He laid out a number of gardens in Scotland before establishing himself in London. Near Hackney he opened a nursery and designed many parks, pleasure grounds and gardens. The Hackney nursery, however, did not prosper and Shepherd became interested in emigrating from England, having come into contact with the New Zealand Company shortly after its formation in 1825. Shepherd joined the company as Principal Agricultural Superintendent, part of his work being to engage suitable farmers and mechanics for the proposed settlement in New Zealand. The contingent, which consisted of seventy-two settlers, sailed from England in 1826 in the *Rosanna* and *Lambton* under Captain James Herd. On reaching New Zealand, Stewart Island in the far south and then Otago Harbour were surveyed, after which they proceeded to the Thames River where the party was to form a settlement. Captain Herd, however, found conditions for settlement unfavourable and in January 1827 set sail for Sydney, which he reached on 12 February.

Shepherd had obtained a grant of land in Tasmania prior to leaving England, and he exchanged this, following a successful request to Governor Darling, for a grant in New South Wales. The Governor, however, stipulated that Shepherd should establish a fruit garden and nursery upon the new land grant, which consisted of twenty-eight acres in the parish of Petersham (in the present suburb of Chippendale) two miles from the centre of Sydney. In gratitude, Shepherd called his nursery the Darling Nursery. Darling Street, Chippendale, is today his sole memorial. The Darling Nursery was later transferred to Waterloo.

Shepherd worked hard on his grant. After the arduous task of clearing had been completed he first grew vegetables in order to bring in ready money and then planted an orchard. Both Alexander McLeay and William Macarthur helped him to establish his nursery. Shepherd's nursery prospered. He claimed that he had sold 30,000 fruit trees in four years, and that he had grafted 10,000 fruit trees in one season, chiefly by candlelight, with his own hands. Shepherd died on 31 August 1835, his business being carried on by two of his sons. In its best days Shepherd and Co's Darling Nursery at Waterloo possessed branches at Rydalmere of forty-four acres and at Rooty Hill of 1,300 acres.

[ON PLANNING THE GARDENS OF THE MARINE VILLAS OF PORT JACKSON]

Gentlemen,

To establish correct principles and rules for the general embellishment of Marine Villas is what I shall endeavour to aim at in this Lecture, which I hope will be attended to by such of you as are interested in the subject. It is more particularly to such persons I shall address myself; and as the possession of such residences may be in the reach of most of us or our friends, and requires less outlay than the splendid park and mansion, I may be excused should I dwell upon them.

This description of residence will in a few years become the admiration of the lovers of Landscape Scenery. A spirit in favour of this sort of residence has been already evinced by numerous persons who have saved money by their industry, and by gentlemen who have had the means of retiring from town to their marine villas or country cottages. Numerous villas and cottages of this description have been already built, and others are in progress of erection. Many small estates have been purchased of late years, which are kept in reserve for this purpose. Rural scenery and water views seem to be the favourite subjects of taste with most persons of capital at present. But I am sorry to say there is a great lack of knowledge exists among them, of the principles and rules which have been established by Landscape Gardeners for their construction and improvement. Instead of choosing the middle elevation for a site to build upon, the highest situation is chosen, which makes the newly erected villa appear as if it were suspended in the air, as there is no back ground either in land or in trees. Some persons, however, have adopted the modern style, and these are worthy of imitation.

The branches, bays, inlets, headlands, and shores of the river of Port Jackson, between the Heads and Parramatta, present many fine situations for houses. The fantastic rocks, covered with trees and shrubs, forming its outline, and the islands in the stream cannot be exceeded in picturesque beauty and grandeur. Thousands of sites may be found in this tract. I picture in imagination the time when all the land on each side of this splendid river, together with its branches and bays, will — and that at no distant date — be ornamented with beautiful marine villas and cottages at short distances from each other, forming most pleasing parts of the landscape. I picture to myself these residences placed upon the middle elevation, the richly picturesque and wooded hills forming a back ground, each with a carriage and garden front, with lawns, walks, and shrubberies. I picture in my own mind, these villas furnished with wings, surmounted by luxuriant foliage, the trees spreading their magnificent branches over the tops of the edifices. Were such villas placed on the commanding situations I have pointed out, the effect would far exceed imagination itself.

It is only within the last few years that attention has been paid to this kind of residence; and notwithstanding the want of taste in general, yet a great improvement has taken place, in this respect, within a very short period. If this spirit of embellishment continues, I hope this Country will present no common figure in a few years.

In place of giving you a repetition of what I have already laid down at great length, in reference to cottages, I think it will be preferable to give you a detailed description of improvements made on two of the most highly finished places of residence and ground to which I have had access in this Colony. These are *Elizabeth Bay*, the intended seat of the Hon. Alexander McLeay, Esq., and *Lyndhurst*, the residence of Dr. Bowman,[1] both on the banks of the river, and I am happy to add, that I have received permission to do so for the information of such gentlemen as may be inclined to take these places as specimens of what may be effected by taste, wealth, and perseverance.

The estate of Elizabeth Bay is situated within the town boundary of Sydney, in a delightful situation, and bounded on its north side by the river and harbour of Port Jackson. On one side is a circular bay half a mile in extent, in a commanding style, between rocky promontories of lofty elevation, branching off to the right and left. Between these promontories the ground sweeps round, by a grand and gradual descent into a low and fertile flat of about ten acres, which has been cleared from the natural woods. The outline of this flat ground is also circular terminating in an abrupt slope, beautifully furnished with rocks, trees, and bushes, forming a splendid amphitheatre. A range of luxuriant woods and precipitous rocks follows the boundary of the water on the north side, till it reaches the boundary line of the estate, forming a straight line by the side of a new road,

about a mile in length, to a corner of an angle where the main
entrance gate is placed. A similar range of beautiful woods and
rocks extends from the other promontory for half a mile, by the
side of the water of a large bay, ending in a flat of several acres,
and thence running up to a fence forming the south-east corner
of the boundary. Thus, this estate has the entire command of one
bay on the north, and one side of a bay on the east, and part of
the south side ends in a flat of good land of several acres in
extent.

The high lands and slopes of this property are composed of
rocks, richly ornamented with beautiful indigenous trees and
shrubs. About ten acres have been cleared for pasture, which
space has been laid off in two paddocks into two enclosures. The
deficiency of pasture is a fault common with every other estate
near Sydney, and prevents them from being laid off in the
useful and ornamental style on a scale of magnitude. Sensible
that his land is not calculated for pasture, Mr. McLeay has very
judiciously applied but a small space of it for that purpose, and
has preserved his native trees and shrubs to extend his Landscape
Gardening. From the first commencement he never suffered a
tree of any kind to be destroyed, until he saw distinctly the necessity for doing so. He thus retained the advantage of embellishment from his native trees, and harmonised them with foreign
trees now growing. He has also obtained the benefit of a standing
plantation which it might otherwise have taken twenty or thirty
years to bring to maturity. The moment the improvements are
finished they will be furnished with full grown trees. The proprietor has certainly gone to great expense in general improvements. His botanic, flower, landscape, fruit, and kitchen gardens,
are all on the first scale, and he has also expended large sums
in digging out rocks, filling up hollows, making approaches, and
walks, grass plats, basins, &c., and in the purchase of foreign
trees and plants, which have been arranged with great skill and
taste. He has also planned a vineyard of considerable extent
upon terraces, which has answered every expectation. The coach
house and stables, with other buildings, have been erected upon
an eligible site, entirely out of sight of his intended mansion and
principal walks. About twenty men have been engaged in these
general improvements which have been going on, in a moderate
and judicious manner, for several years, and it will require a few
more years to complete the work; but when completed the place
will probably not be surpassed by any garden in New South
Wales.

I must now point out the nature of the whole design of the improvements on the ground. Great taste has been employed in choosing the site of the mansion. In my opinion, it is so correct according to the principles of Landscape Gardening, that if one had studied for a century he could not have selected a better. The mansion is placed upon a flat piece of land, in the bosom of a gentle elevation, furnished with beautiful trees, branching off in thick masses to the right and left. A splendid open lawn is placed in the main centre front of the house, leaving to view from the adjoining grounds and windows one of the most interesting prospects of the harbour and shores of Port Jackson. To remove a few touches of nature's harshness, a dwarf ornamental stone wall, having at two extreme points corners of ornamental scroll work, has been raised, surmounted by a curvilateral coping with a few inches of projection. This wall forms an elegant sweep, and is bordered by a broad gravel walk. The ground outside of this wall towards the bay falls abruptly down a slope, which is richly furnished with healthy and beautiful trees, not in thick masses, but sufficiently so to form a proper foreground to intercept the over-magnificence of the light reflected from the beautiful expanse of water which forms the front of the background on the opposite shore,[2] and which becomes the second distance[3] in the landscape. All the polished scenery below will be in connexion with this situation, branching off to the right and left through ornamental lawns and polished shrubberies, furnished with choice trees and plants from England, China, the Mauritius, the East Indies, North and South America, and from Moreton Bay, Norfolk Island, the Cape of Good Hope, and other places. In a few years, therefore, the beauties of Elizabeth Bay will appear unrivalled.

At the extremity of this beautiful shubbery and mowed-grass lawn, wood walks will commence, winding through thickets of trees naturally grouped among picturesque rocks. Here also rustic chairs and rustic caves are placed, and the river is seen from them through a rich foreground of natural trees and beautiful creepers. Walks descend from the dwarf wall to a carriage road, which leads to the river, where a convenient wharf has been constructed for enjoying marine excursions.

Crossing the coach-road you enter through a lattice-work bower, covered with the passion flower, into the botanic garden, laid out in beds and borders of exotic flowers, with elegant sweeping walls and bowers of lattice-work. These are tastefully arranged, imitating Nature in her loveliest forms, and creating sensations of exquisite delight in the mind. In walking among these lovely trees, you view on the one side an amphitheatre of lofty woods; and on the other you view a large expanse of water with ships, small vessels, and boats, passing up and down the harbour. The kitchen garden, pits for producing pine apples without fire heat, gardener's cottage, vineyard, and terraces sloping to the north, sheltered from the south, and bearing abundance of grapes, follow in succession, and require no particular description.

This description, which I have given, to show gentlemen how much may be made out of the roughest materials nature furnishes, will teach them what may be done on ground favourable for the purpose. If I might be allowed to make any suggestion, it is, that to complete Elizabeth Bay in a style of the first magnificence, there should be an *Aviary* erected, and particularly a Conservatory at a little distance from the house, close to the hill which backs in the mansion; and a good *Pinery*[4] with grape vines to produce early grapes. I would recommend an ornamental *Summer house,* to be placed at the most conspicuous point upon the promontory, on the right hand side of the bay, with a covered-in summer house, to preserve parties from excessive heat or from rain. These improvements, which probably it is the intention of the respected proprietor to make, would, in my opinion, render Elizabeth Bay one of the most finished residences to be met with in any Country.

Before I leave the neighbourhood of this mansion, I must address a few words to the proprietors of residences at Woolloomoolloo and other places in the Colony, who have fallen into an error, which I have in these Lectures spoken of with some regret. I must address myself to them on this interesting point to prevent other gentlemen from falling into the same error. When you, gentlemen, first got your estates, your ground was well furnished with beautiful shrubs. You ignorantly set the murderous hoe and grubbing axe to work to destroy them, and the ground that had been full of luxuriant verdure, was laid bare and desolate, and the prospect was ruined. I have no wish to find fault personally with any one, but I must give my advice as a practical Landscape Gardener, that when a gentleman obtains a piece of ground near the sea, or on a river, where he intends to build a mansion, let nothing be done until a plan has been first made, or approved of by a professional man; he will then know where every compartment requisite should be placed before any work is commenced. You will know by this plan where the trees and shrubs should be rooted out, and where they should be left standing for ornaments. You will know where your various gardens should be placed, as well as lawns and walks. You will have a selection of grown wood without expense upon your ground. But by grubbing up the trees, dislike and distaste follow, and the proprietor must beg, borrow, buy, or exchange trees and plants to make some figure, and take off the appearance of poverty and sterility. The only profit to be got from the practice hitherto pursued, is that a few peas, cabbages, and turnips are grown. This, however, is as much out of character, with a splendid villa, as if a gentleman should change coats with a labourer. I maintain, therefore, that the fine houses near Sydney and in other districts of the Colony, would have looked much better than they now do, if advantage had been taken of the natural state in which these grounds were, when they came into the possession of the proprietors; and that they will not recover their position for many years. These observations are given in perfect sincerity, and without the least desire to give offence, and may probably be of use to other proprietors.

There is another first-rate edifice, the grounds of which have been laid off with great attention to the principles of Landscape Gardening, Lyndhurst, the seat of Dr. Bowman, to which I shall direct your attention, with a view to enlighten the proprietors of land, on the capabilities of their estates.

This residence is situated on the south side of a branch of the river of Port Jackson; the ground contains fifty acres of land, and is bounded by Church land, a new road, and the estate of John Betts, Esq. This estate will have an imposing effect, both internally and externally. The house has three fronts open to a mowed-grass lawn of considerable extent. The site is placed upon a flat piece of land about two hundred yards from the river; the situation is commanding. The offices are enclosed within a high wall at the back of the house, and are well arranged. A tank of large dimensions has been sunk in the back yard, supplied by pipes from the roof of the house; and is built with brick and covered with cement, with a drain at the bottom. The coach house and stables are built out of sight of the house, park, and pleasure grounds. A road will lead from them with a bold sweep through part of the park to the house, and also from them to a small wharf. The kitchen garden is in a valley behind the stables; it is composed of rich loam, and has been laid out in straight walks, and planted with fruit trees. The approach of the mansion enters at the south-east corner; it is seen for several hundred yards, and then takes a bold turn towards the coach sweep in front of the house without any reverse turn, which adds to its beauty. The coach sweep will form an exact oval, the whole width of the front of the house, convex in the centre, and covered with mowed grass. No clumps will be placed in the centre of the lawn, as that would lessen its breadth, but the lawn will be surrounded by a shrubbery, except on the side next the paddock, from which it will be divided by an invisible fence of iron, or posts and chains. The shubbery which borders the terrace at the bottom of the paddock, will be enclosed by a post and chain fence. The shubbery walks will branch off from the approach in front of the house, into shrubberies extending to the right and left. These will be considered parts of the Landscape Garden, and will darken the glow of light which is produced by the expansion of the water. The opposite shore has a fine effect from this residence being richly furnished with beautiful trees disposed with much natural taste amongst picturesque rocks. At a distance the landscape is heightened by gentle elevations conveying the idea of broken ground divided by water.

This estate commands about a mile of frontage to the bay. It is beautifully wooded, and has a considerable extent of glade or lawn within thriving forest scenery. The house is the principal feature in the landscape. Thick masses of wood branch off from the back part of the house. This estate will present a splendid instance of what may be effected by knowledge, taste, and wealth, upon ground to all appearance unfit for improvements. It will be a model for a genteel marine residence. The indigenous trees have been preserved, and are as pleasing as if a new assortment of trees had been planted, and had grown up in their place.

Before I conclude these Lectures, I propose to point out to you a proceeding that will enable any gentleman to judge for himself, what openings it may be necessary to make in his natural woods to give effect to the landscape. Making the supposition that the site for the house has been chosen, I would advise that two or more strong stakes be driven into the ground as near as can be in the centre of the dining room, or other public room where the principal windows are to be placed, so that from them you may have the advantage of the best views. Upon one of those strong stakes place a compass, and view the distant surrounding scenery; set your compass in a direct line with the first object preferred, and note down the number of degrees it bears from the fixed station. Do the same with the second, and, if necessary, with a third and a fourth stake. You have thus ascertained the bearings of the best views. Set your compass agreeably to some fixed bearing, and commence a line of direction to the object until you have arrived at the outer boundary of the park; and in the direction of this line let all, or the greater part, of the trees be cut down, without reservation, wherever they obstruct the view, so as to form an irregular expanse, in width agreeable to the extent of the landscape, and at irregular distances from ten to a thousand yards. This being done set your compass agreeably to some other bearing, commencing with another line of direction, and cut down the trees as before directed. Do the same in other directions, taking the utmost care not to spoil the prospect by the destruction of trees, that, standing out of the line of view, are an embellishment rather than an obstruction to the prospect.

When the principal openings from the house, or fixed stakes representing the site of the house, are completed, go in search of another station, not less than a quarter of a mile, nor more than a mile from the house, and take a similar line of direction as before. Driving a stake into the ground, and taking your lines by the compass, mark out the trees proper to be destroyed, and also those that do not interfere with, but embellish the view, and leave them standing for future consideration. Take a third station and do the same as before. When your stations have been completed, as well as the openings you think necessary to be made in the park, proceed no further in your work of destruction, except by thinning out the low brush and scrub, and otherwise ornamenting the ground, till you discover how the whole harmonises, and till you have discovered how the house and grounds will appear from the distant stations to which you have directed your bearings, and from which the house will be seen. You then form the best judgment you can on the point, and apply such other means as you think advisable for improving the view. But should you have only a very few, or perhaps no distant surrounding landscapes of value, make artificial openings through the park, so that the best possible natural objects within the park itself may be left open to view, suitable to the ground. It is here that the taste, judgment, experience, and ready perceptions of the Landscape Gardener come into action; and if the Proprietor has any hesitation in deciding on the situation of the house, and openings, and walks, he should take the opinion of a professional man, as his ground may be ruined for many years by an error in judgment or taste.

But after all that can be said on this subject, some will be disposed to say — Why do you treat us with dissertations on natural and relative beauty, or the imitative art of laying out grounds, when alas! many of us have not yet got a foot of ground in possession? nor have we any hopes of it in reversion, except the six feet square we must all occupy at last. There may be some truth and propriety in this question; but you must admit, that all knowledge is useful, and that knowledge of this kind in particular can never do any harm — it is amusing and instructive; it is pleasing to acquire it; and it may be useful, and certainly will be advantageous, if we can assist and persuade them that have land and money to expend some of their funds in this manner. Moreover, if we have not yet acquired land on which to try these experiments, it is not impossible that we may at some future time obtain it; and if we do not obtain it, we can console ourselves in the happy reflection that we deserve it. If we think that the beautiful lawns, and pleasure grounds of others, are as much ours when we are delighted with them, as they are the property of the owners, who feel no more from them than we do, we have the word of the *Spectator* for it, that they are our own by adoption, and we are pleased with them accordingly. At all events in this country we can obtain one hundred acres of good land by the side of some river or murmuring rill, for £25, and it is our own faults if we do not become *Lairds* and *Land-Owners.*

If the directions, therefore, which I have given are followed up, a handsome profit may, at very small cost, be realised, by disposing of an improved portion of ground, fit for a mansion of large size, to other persons, who either do not know how to improve it, or prefer an estate already improved, to the trouble and expense of clearing it. In either case we should make the best bargain we can for our property; and perhaps the only evil any of us is subjected to, is that our means to sell on such advantageous terms, are inferior to our wishes. I hope, however, that my Lectures on Landscape Gardening will not be un-attended with benefit to the resident settlers, in clearing away or opening up the thickets of misconception that exist, on this subject, and in giving correctness to our ideas by placing limits to the wildness of unregulated taste, and directing it with pro-priety in the varied objects connected with Landscape Gardening — an art in which I admit I am enthusiastic, in common with others who have indulged in it; and which I am confident is qualified to make this Colony present an appearance altogether unlike that it has hitherto presented, and that must be attended in other respects with advantageous consequences to the Colonists.

I cannot conclude these Lectures, which have been written within a very short period, and without reference to books, without craving your indulgence for their imperfections; nor can I refrain from quoting the words of Lord Bacon — 'A garden is the purest of human pleasures. It is the greatest refreshment to the spirits of man, without which buildings and palaces are but gross handyworks, and a man shall ever see that when ages grow to civility, and clemency, men come to build stately, sooner than to garden finely, — as if gardening were the greater perfection.'[5]

> Long was the night of error, nor dispell'd
> By him that rose at learning's earliest dawn,
> Prophet of unborn Science. On thy realm,
> Philosophy! his sovereign lustre spread;
> Yet did he deign to light with casual glance
> The wilds of taste. Yes, sagest Verulam
> 'Twas thine to banish from the royal groves
> Each childish vanity of crisped knot
> And sculptur'd foliage; to the lawn restore
> Its ample space, and bid it feast the sight
> With verdure pure, unbroken, unabridged:
> For verdure soothes the eye, as roseate sweets
> The smell, or music's melting strains the ear.

—*Mason's English Garden*[6]

[From Thomas Shepherd, *Lectures in Landscape Gardening in Australia*, 1836, pp. 86-95]

NOTES—THOMAS SHEPHERD

1 James Bowman (1784-1846), surgeon and pastoralist, son-in-law of John Macarthur, the pioneer of sheep-breeding in Australia. The Lyndhurst Estate in Glebe, Sydney, was subdivided in the 1870s and 1880s. Today (1974) only the central block of the house remains in a sadly neglected condition. See Bernard and Kate Smith, *The Architectural Character of Glebe, Sydney*, Sydney, 1973, pp. 17-20.

2 Compare Shepherd's dislike of 'an over-magnificence of the light reflected from the beautiful expanse of water' with Uvedale Price's comment: 'Objects of reflection are peculiarly required for beside their distinct beauty, they soften the cold white glare, of what is usually called a fine sheet of water . . .', *Essays on the Picturesque*, 1810, i, 315.

3 The term 'second distance' belongs to the special vocabulary of the picturesque. Compare Jane Austen's account of Henry Tilney's wooing of Catherine Morland in chapter xiv of *Northanger Abbey* 'He talked of foregrounds, distances, and second distances—side-screens and perspectives—lights and shades; and Catherine was so hopeful a scholar, that when they gained the top of Beechen Cliff, she voluntarily rejected the whole city of Bath, as unworthy to make part of a landscape'. Catherine's picturesque dismissal of Bath may be compared with Barron Field's dismissal, for similar reasons, of the Blue Mountains.

⁴ i.e. a place in which pineapples are grown. Shepherd is here recommending the practice common in Europe in the eighteenth and nineteenth centuries of growing pineapples in hot houses.

⁵ Francis Bacon, *On Gardens*. But Bacon wrote 'when ages grow to civility, and elegancy'.

⁶ Book 1, ll. 407-19.

William Woolls (1814–93)

William Woolls was born in Winchester, England, in March 1814, being the nineteenth child of Edward Woolls, a merchant of that city. He was given a good classical education, first from a private tutor and later at the Grammar School at Bishop's Waltham in Hampshire. By the time he was sixteen, however, both his parents had died and he decided to emigrate. At first he sought a cadetship with the East India Company but, failing, he decided on Australia. Some friends were able to procure a letter of introduction for him from Viscount Goderich, the Secretary of State for the Colonies, to Sir Richard Bourke, the Governor of New South Wales, and armed with it he left England in 1831.

Woolls had already written some occasional poems and on the trip out occupied himself writing a poem based on his thoughts and experiences during the voyage which he was able to publish, shortly after arriving in Sydney in 1832. It is called *The Voyage: a moral poem written during, and descriptive of, a Voyage from England to New South Wales* (1833).

Governor Bourke found a place for Woolls as a clerk at the Government Factory, Parramatta, but he was looking for a post closer to his taste and interests. This he found as an assistant teacher under the Reverend Robert Forrest at the recently-established King's School, Parramatta. Later he became classics master at the Sydney College (now Sydney Grammar School) under W. T. Cape. Woolls proved himself an able and conscientious teacher and in the early 1840s set up his own school at Parramatta, which he conducted successfully until 1865.

Almost from the time of his arrival in the Colony, Woolls contributed frequently to the local press; and as a result of his friendship with Louisa Atkinson, developed a keen interest in the local Parramatta flora, from which there grew a passionate love of Australian botany. For many years he worked in close contact with some of the most famous botanists of the day, including George Bentham and Baron Ferdinand von Müller. Indeed it is reported that he wrote more than one thousand letters to von Müller between 1857 and his own death in 1893.

Woolls' botanical publications were considerable. Among the most important are 'Plants which have become Naturalised in New South Wales' which gained for him a Fellowship of the Linnean Society of London (1865); and *Species Plantarum Parramattaensum,* which was published in Göttingen and gained him a doctorate from Göttingen University. His botanical observations included the discovery of several new plants, some of which bear his name.

In Parramatta Woolls became a close friend of the Reverend Samuel Marsden who encouraged him to seek Holy Orders, a step he did not take until 1873, when he was ordained deacon by Bishop Barker. In 1874 he was appointed Rector of Richmond and in 1877 became rural dean. In 1883 he resigned from that position and was granted a general licence in the Sydney Diocese. He died at Richmond on 14 March 1873, and a stained glass window in St Johns, Parramatta, commemorates his ministry in the Anglican Church.

The extract printed below is taken from a small book, *Miscellanies in Prose and Verse,* which William Woolls published in Sydney in 1838 in which he brought together several of his essays and poems, some of which had been previously published separately.

[THE BEAUTIES OF AUSTRALIA]

It is a remark frequently made by persons who have immigrated to New South Wales, that this colony is not only devoid of any venerable remains of antiquity, but that it also is deficient in those interesting scenes which contribute so much to enliven and dignify the histories of other countries. To a certain extent, we must admit the truth of this assertion. It is true that we cannot boast of the massive structures which have been raised by the piety of our forefathers, and which are now the sacred storehouses of our predecessors, and guardians of their bones: we cannot pride ourselves upon the triumphal arch, the high-raised battlement, the moated tower, and the mouldered grandeur of days gone by; nor can we lead the traveller to the contemplation of those glorious fields on which tyranny and oppression fell beneath the sword of patriotism. We are not famous for the gigantic pyramids which were reared by kings whose names are now unknown. The lofty column and the lengthened aisle do not grace our shores. We have no plains of Marathon,[1] no pass of Thermopylae,[2] on which we may feel an honest pride; nor are our towns decorated with the trophies of ancient victories, and the headless busts of heroes long forgotten. But, nevertheless, Australia is not uninteresting to the lover of antiquity, for we may truly say that many of its scenes are calculated to awaken the most pleasing recollections. Can the admirer of classic lore survey the numerous flocks, which now are seen sporting over our plains, and be forgetful of those primitive ages when kings and queens tended their flocks, and valued them as their chief possessions? Can he behold the vine and the fig spreading luxuriantly over the land, and be unmindful of the beautiful passages in ancient writings which speak of them as the attendants of peace and plenty? And can he traverse the wide-spreading plain, climb the summit of the lofty range, or wander 'by gushing fount, wild wood, and shadowy dell', without calling to mind the inimitable descriptions of the ancient poets? In Australia, indeed, he may ponder with increased interest and delight on the wandering lives of the patriachs, and the sublime language of the prophets. Homer affords new beauties to him, and he appreciates many of those excellencies and eastern allusions, which are almost unintelligible in the cold and ungenial regions of the north. Nor is the Roman bard[3] lost upon him, for the Eclogues and the Georgics, in sweet melodious numbers, instil into his breast a fondness for rural pleasures and agricultural pursuits. The man of observation, as he wends his lonely way through the woods of Australia, often recognises some object on which the poets of former days loved to dwell. Even the locust — which glorying in the scorching rays of the summer's sun — pours, far and wide, its deafening strains, reminds him of the τέττιξ, or cicada, and he recollects with satisfaction the beautiful ode of Anacreon[4] addressed to it:—

Μακαρίζομεν σε, τέττιξ,
ὅτι δένδρεων ἐπ᾽ ἄκρων,
ὀλίγην δρόσον πεπωκῶς,
βασιλεὺς ὅπως, ἀείδεις. [5]

Thus it is manifest that Australia is by no means deficient in objects of interest to persons of a refined taste. She may, indeed, be poor in works of art, but she is rich in those of nature. Instead of splendid piles and victorious triumphs, she can boast of her clear Italian sky, her woolly flocks, her vine and fig; while her stupendous mountains and awful glens are far superior to all the paltry works of human skill.

[From William Woolls, *Miscellanies in Prose and Verse*, 1838, pp. 86-8]

NOTES—WOOLLS

1 A plain situated about twenty-five miles from Athens on the eastern coast
of Attica, where the celebrated victory of the Athenians over the Persians
took place in 490 B.C.
2 i.e. 'the Hot Gates', (Hot Springs) a celebrated pass in Greece leading from
Thessaly in Locris. It was the only pass by which an enemy could penetrate
in ancient times from northern into southern Greece; and is specially celebrated on account of the heroic defence of Leonidas and 300 Spartans against
the hosts of Xerxes, King of Persia (485-465 B.C.), in 480 B.C.
3 i.e. Virgil (Publius Vergilius Maro) (70-19 B.C.). His most famous poems are
the *Aeneid*, the epic poem of the Roman people; the *Georgics*, a didactic
poem on the cultivation of the soil and the raising of cattle; and the
Eclogues, which imitate the pastoral poems of Theocritus, the Greek poet,
who lived in the third century B.C.
4 A Greek poet who lived on the island of Teos in Ionia in the sixth century
B.C., the author of poems in praise of love and wine.
5 We pronounce thee happy, O Cicada!
because having sipped a little dew,
thou singest on the tops of trees, like a king. Ode 43, On the Cicada.
T. Gilpin, *The Odes of Anacreon of Teos*, London, 1806.

Charles Darwin (1809–82)

Charles Darwin, the famous scientist who first enunciated a
convincing theory of evolution by means of natural selection,
visited Sydney in 1836 as the naturalist aboard H.M.S. *Beagle*,
which had been engaged upon a survey of the southern coasts of
South America. Darwin embarked on the voyage at the invitation
of Captain Robert Fitzroy in 1831 and during the voyage
befriended Conrad Martens (see p. 96) who joined the *Beagle* at
Montevideo in November 1833.

The passage quoted here is taken from *Journal of Researches
into the Geology and Natural History of the Various Countries
visited by H.M.S. 'Beagle' under the command of Captain
Fitzroy, R.N., from 1832-1836.* The same volume appeared as
volume III of *Narrative of the Surveying Voyages of His
Majesty's Ships Adventure and Beagle* between 1826 and 1836,
describing their *examination of the Southern shores of South
America, and the Beagle's circumnavigation of the Globe,* 1839.

The *Beagle* was anchored at Sydney from 12 to 30 January
during which time Darwin made the journey to Bathurst, part
of which is described here. The passage illustrates Darwin's
remarkable powers of observation, his insatiable scientific curiosity, and his command of English.

A young man of twenty-seven at the time, the extract also
reveals his youthful capacity for aesthetic enjoyment, a faculty

E

which, to his own expressed regret, he later lost with age and immersion in the problems of natural history. We find him here expressing a keen pleasure at the sight of a flock of white cockatoos in a cornfield and the pretty park-like valleys around Wallerawang. It is obvious, too, that he enjoyed the excitements of a kangaroo hunt. But even in his enjoyment he is also to be found reflecting upon what seemed to him to be the inevitable extermination of the indigenous animals and Aboriginal inhabitants of Australia. Such deterministic pessimism is typical of much nineteenth-century thought about primitive peoples and exotic flora and fauna.

[DARWIN ON CROSSING THE BLUE MOUNTAINS]

JANUARY 17th.—Early in the morning we passed the Nepean in a ferry-boat. The river, although at this spot both broad and deep, had a very small body of running water. Having crossed a low piece of land on the opposite side, we reached the slope of the Blue Mountains. The ascent is not steep, the road having been cut with much care on the side of a sandstone cliff. At no great elevation an almost level plain extends, which, rising imperceptibly to the westward, at last attains a height of more than three thousand feet. From so grand a title as Blue Mountains, and from their absolute altitude, I expected to have seen a bold chain of mountains crossing the country; but instead of this, a sloping plain presents merely an inconsiderable front to the low land of the coast. From this first slope, the view of the extensive woodland to the eastward, was striking, and the surrounding trees grew bold and lofty. But when once on the sandstone platform, the scenery becomes exceedingly monotonous; each side of the road is bordered by scrubby trees of the never-failing Eucalyptus family; and with the exception of two or three small inns, there are no houses, or cultivated land: the road, moreover, is solitary; the most frequent object being a bullock-waggon, piled up with bales of wool.

In the middle of the day we baited our horses at a little inn, called the Weatherboard. The country here is elevated 2800 feet above the sea. About a mile and a half from this place, there is a view exceedingly well worth visiting. By following down a little valley and its tiny rill of water, an immense gulf is unexpectedly seen through the trees which border the pathway, at the depth of perhaps 1500 feet. Walking on a few yards one stands on the brink of a vast precipice, and below is the grand bay or gulf (for I know not what other name to give it), thickly covered with forest.

The point of view is situated as if at the head of a bay, the line of cliff diverging on each side, and showing headland behind headland, as on a bold sea-coast. These cliffs are composed of horizontal strata of whitish sandstone; and so absolutely vertical are they, that in many places, a person standing on the edge, and throwing down a stone, can see it strike the trees in the abyss below. So unbroken is the line, that it is said, in order to reach the foot of the waterfall, formed by this little stream, it is necessary to go a distance of sixteen miles round. About five miles distant in front, another line of cliffs extends, which thus appears completely to encircle the valley; and hence the name of bay is justified, as applied to this grand amphitheatrical depression. If we imagine a winding harbour, with its deep water surrounded by bold cliff-like shores, laid dry, and a forest sprung up on its sandy bottom, we should then have the appearance and structure here exhibited. This kind of view was to me quite novel, and extremely magnificent.

In the evening, we reached the Blackheath. The sandstone plateau has here attained the elevation of 3400 feet; and is covered, as before, with the same kind of scrubby wood. From the road there were occasional glimpses into a profound valley, of the same character as the one described; but from the steepness and depth of its sides, the bottom was scarcely ever to be seen. The Blackheath is a very comfortable inn, kept by an old soldier; and it reminded me of the small inns in North Wales. I was surprised to find that here, at the distance of more than seventy miles from Sydney, fifteen beds could be made up for travellers.

JANUARY 18th.—Very early in the morning, I walked about three miles to see Govett's Leap: a view of a similar but even perhaps more stupendous character than that near the Weather-board. So early in the day the gulf was filled with a thin blue haze, which, although destroying the general effect, added to the apparent depth at which the forest was stretched below the country on which we were standing. Soon after leaving the Blackheath, we descended from the sandstone platform by the pass of Mount Victoria. To effect this pass, an enormous quantity of stone has been cut through; the design, and its manner of execution, would have been worthy of any line of road in England, — even that of Holyhead.[1] We now entered upon a country less elevated by nearly a thousand feet, and consisting of granite. With the change of rock, the vegetation improved; the trees were both finer, and stood further apart; and the pasture between them was a little greener, and more plentiful.

At Hassan's Walls, I left the high road, and made a short detour to a farm called Walerawang [*sic*]; to the superintendent of which, I had a letter of introduction from the owner in Sydney. Mr. Browne had the kindness to ask me to stay the ensuing day, which I had much pleasure in doing. This place offers an example of one of the large farming, or rather sheep-grazing, establishments of the colony. Cattle and horses are, however, in this case, rather more numerous than usual, owing to some of the valleys being swampy, and producing a coarser pasture. The sheep were 15,000 in number, of which the greater part were feeding under the care of different shepherds, on unoccupied ground, at the distance of more than a hundred miles, and beyond the limits of the colony. Mr. Browne had just finished, this day, the last of the shearing of seven thousand sheep; the rest being sheared in another place. I believe the profit of the average produce of wool from 15,000 sheep, would be more than 5000*l.* sterling. Two or three flat pieces of ground near the house were cleared and cultivated with corn, which the harvest men were now reaping: but no more wheat is sown than sufficient for the annual support of the labourers employed on the establishment. The usual number of assigned convict servants here is about forty, but at the present time there were rather more. Although the farm was well stocked with every requisite, there was an apparent absence of comfort; and not even a single woman resided here. The sunset of a fine day will generally cast an air of happy contentment on any scene; but here, at this retired farm-house, the brightest tints on the surrounding woods could not make me forget that forty hardened, profligate men, were ceasing from their daily labours, like the slaves from Africa, yet without their just claim for compassion.

Early on the next morning, Mr. Archer, the joint superintendent, had the kindness to take me out Kangaroo-hunting. We continued riding the greater part of the day, but had very bad sport, not seeing a kangaroo, or even a wild dog. The greyhounds pursued a kangaroo rat into a hollow tree, out of which we dragged it: it is an animal as big as a rabbit, but with the figure of a kangaroo. A few years since, this country abounded with wild animals; but now the emu is banished to a long distance, and the kangaroo is become scarce; to both, the English greyhound is utterly destructive. It may be long before these animals are altogether exterminated, but their doom is fixed. The natives are always anxious to borrow the dogs from the farm-houses: the use of them, the offal when an animal is killed, and milk from

the cows, are the peace-offerings of the settlers, who push further
and further towards the interior. The thoughtless aboriginal,
blinded by these trifling advantages, is delighted at the approach
of the white man, who seems predestined to inherit the country
of his children.

Although having bad sport, we enjoyed a pleasant ride. The
woodland is generally so open that a person on horseback can
gallop through it. It is traversed by a few flat-bottomed valleys,
which are green and free from trees: in such spots the scenery
was like that of a park, and pretty. In the whole country I
scarcely saw a place without the marks of fire; whether these had
been more or less recent — whether the stumps were more or
less black, was the greatest change which varied the uniformity,
so wearisome to the traveller's eye. In these woods there are not
many birds; I saw, however, some large flocks of the white
cockatoo feeding in a corn-field, and a few most beautiful
parrots; crows like our jackdaws were not uncommon, and
another bird something like the magpie. The English have not
been very particular in giving names to the productions of Australia; trees of one genus (Casuarina) are called oaks for no one
reason that I can discover, without it is that there is no one point
of resemblance. Some quadrupeds are called tigers and hyenas,
simply because they are carnivorous, and so on in many other
cases.

In the dusk of the evening I took a stroll along a chain of
ponds, which in this dry country represented the course of a
river, and had the good fortune to see several of the famous
Platypus, or *Ornithorhyncus paradoxus*. They were diving and
playing about the surface of the water, but showed so little of
their bodies that they might easily have been mistaken for water-
rats. Mr. Browne shot one: certainly it is a most extraordinary
animal; the stuffed specimens do not at all give a good idea
of the recent appearance of its head and beak; the latter becoming
hard and contracted.

A little time before this I had been lying on a sunny bank
and was reflecting on the strange character of the animals of
this country as compared with the rest of the world. An unbeliever
in every thing beyond his own reason might exclaim, 'Two
distinct Creators must have been at work; their object, however,
has been the same, and certainly the end in each case is complete.'
While thus thinking, I observed the hollow conical pitfall of
the lion-ant: first a fly fell down the treacherous slope and immediately disappeared; then came a large but unwary ant; its

struggles to escape being very violent, those curious little jets of sand, described by Kirby* as being flirted by the insect's tail, were promptly directed against the expected victim. But the ant enjoyed a better fate than the fly, and escaped the fatal jaws which lay concealed at the base of the conical hollow. There can be no doubt but that this predacious larva belongs to the same genus with the European kind, though to a different species. Now what would the sceptic say to this? Would any two workmen ever have hit upon so beautiful, so simple, and yet so artificial a contrivance? It cannot be thought so: one Hand has surely worked throughout the universe.

[Charles Darwin, from '*The Voyage of the Beagle'*,
London, 1839, pp. 522-7]

FOOTNOTES—DARWIN.

1 The Holyhead road built from 1815 to 1830 was designed and constructed by the famous engineer Thomas Telford (1757-1834). It has been described as 'the most famous in the history of British road construction' by J. W. Gregory in his *Story of the Road*, London, 1931.

* Kirby's Entomology, vol. i., p. 425. The Australian pitfall is only about half the size of the one made by the European species.

🎑🎑🎑🎑🎑🎑🎑🎑🎑🎑🎑🎑🎑🎑🎑🎑🎑🎑

THREE

Some Early Reflections on Art in Australia

INTRODUCTION

The first two chapters have been concerned with the reactions of some artists and writers to nature in Australia in the early years of colonization. The present chapter contains a selection of early comments on art. The first two report on the ways in which an interest in the arts began to reveal itself in New South Wales. They are of interest not only for the information they contain concerning the first art exhibitions and the first art collectors in Australia but also for their more general reflections on the emergence of art and patronage in a colonial situation.

John McGarvie may well have been the first person to publish a critical comment about art in Australia. From the onset he strikes that note of happy utilitarian optimism which we have already noticed in Joseph Lycett's preface to his *Views in Australia*. As a result of trade and British initiative civilization is progressing well in New South Wales. McGarvie is convinced of it. He points to the small but growing scientific circle which had been encouraged by Sir Thomas Brisbane, the former Governor, and by Alexander McLeay, the Colonial Secretary; he points to the circle of taste and fashion centred about Mrs Darling, the Governor's wife; and then to Augustus Earle, 'the wandering artist' who found support from Mrs Darling and her circle of friends. Earle's exhibition of work in Sydney, perhaps the first one-man show ever held in Australia, stimulated local interest in portrait and landscape painting. McGarvie records it all with the slightly jocular air of a man somewhat embarrassed at the company circumstances have forced upon him. It is characteristic of the tone of much of the journalism of the *Sydney Gazette* and other early colonial newspapers. The model no doubt was the wit and elegance of essayists such as Joseph Addison and Sidney Smith, but the tone is that of a club-man of Pall Mall reporting surprising events at Newgate prison.

Dr John Lhotsky writes in a more serious vein about the beginnings of art in a convict colony. Art, he assured his readers, begins 'in distant zones' only when the material needs of life have been satisfied; and proceeds to cite the problems of cultural isolation experienced by the colonists who first became collectors of art in New South Wales. Lhotsky was a sensitive observer and a trained naturalist. His exploratory travels in the south-east made him a keen champion of Australian nature. He was writing from direct experience when he concluded that 'Australian sky and nature awaits . . . a whole system of landscape painting of the most striking character'. Fifty years later the painters of the Heidelberg School began to embody in their work something of the vision Lhotsky had foreshadowed.

As we turn from John Lhotsky to the studied rhetoric of John West we become aware immediately of a striking change of tone. It is like leaving the eighteenth and entering the nineteenth century. Both men were widely read and of liberal outlook. But Lhotsky was a volatile and radical Pole in whom the values of the Enlightenment still lingered; John West was a congregational clergyman for whom all values were, ultimately, moral values — reflections of the inscrutable ways of God. West brought to his consideration of art a mixture of utilitarian philosophy and a belief in progress, under the watching eye of the Deity, which was to prevail in ecclesiastical circles and polite society throughout the second half of the nineteenth century in Australia, as in most Anglo-Saxon countries. This meaty and formidable blend of the useful and the good determined the taste within which art was cautiously savoured, art societies formed and, finally, art museums established.

Though addressed to a small and rather select group of Launceston citizens West's voice was a new and powerful one in the colonial community. For he was a good man not easily corrupted by his *milieu*. He justified art largely on the grounds that it would effect some moral improvement among the young; public loan exhibitions gave the privileged members of society a chance to share their treasures with the common folk who could not afford art. His lecture, considering the place, occasion and the audience, was indeed ambitious; for West undertook to survey nothing less than the role of art in the history of human society. First he considered primitive art, which was for him, as it was for most of his generation, an example of a defective attempt at representation by men who had not yet been granted spiritual light. For the true model of art was nature — God's handiwork. Only by his light can it be seen as it truly is. But the imagination of the pagan 'teems with hideous combinations' out of which monstrous distortions of nature in the form of idols are created. The artist should endeavour to depict only the finest subjects, and these are to be found in the sacred events of the Bible, or, failing that, in narrative paintings which point a moral. In asserting such a view West was, of course, proclaiming to the citizens of Launceston the academic belief in the supremacy of *istoria* (paintings of events from the scriptures or the classics) first asserted by Alberti in the fifteenth century. His secular moral paintings had found their first great champion in Diderot, the Encyclopaedist. It is suitable that the first man to thus assert academic doctrine so confidently in Australia should pay tribute to Michelangelo, though he makes it clear that he had never seen one of the master's original works. Yet even the sublimities of Michelangelo are not to be compared to the sublimities of nature. Art for West is always the handmaiden of a nobler master: God, or morality, or nature, or utility. He constantly stresses the utility of art. Artists convey information precisely, by means of diagrams; by them we can understand intricate mechanisms, the costumes and manners of foreign nations, the truths of natural history. It is of interest to note that West still sees the artist as man's best graphic recorder, though photography had been invented ten years before and photographers were already active in Tasmania.

Although West provides at best but a qualified justification for art as a human activity, he is certainly no philistine. Although educated in a puritan tradition he rejects John Calvin's view that art is a tempter, distracting men from their devotion to God. His lecture concludes on a fine note of High Victorian rhetoric. If created in conditions of luxury, West warned his audience, art invariably declines. But it is nurtured by liberty. Australia perhaps will one day achieve her 'day of opulence' but West would clearly prefer to put it off for as long as possible; for his mind was obviously filled with grandiose images of declining empires which he had gathered from Milton, Gibbon and Macaulay. For the moment it is to 'a vigorous intellect, a robust constitution, and industrious habits' that Australia must look for her prosperity.

Benjamin Duterrau's lecture, though smaller in scale and learning, is cast in a mould similar to West's. But the stress is all upon education and utility. He was, after all, an artist not an evangelist. Duterrau took for his theme Plato's academy as Raphael interpreted it in his *School of Athens* in the papal apartments of the Vatican. Duterrau had seen a copy of the painting believed to be by Giulio Romano, Raphael's pupil, at the University of Oxford. In a condition which can only be described as visionary euphoria Duterrau based his lecture upon a comparison of Plato's Athens Academy and the Mechanics' Institute of Hobart Town. Are not, he proclaimed (pointing first to his lantern slide of the *School of Athens* and then to the interior of the lecture hall) even the very buildings similar. It is all too easy, of course, to see the comic aspect of Duterrau's theme today; but in those days the inhabitants of Tasmania, despite the smallness of their numbers, had a high vision of human destiny. It called forth, for example, Lady Franklin's little classic temple at Acanthe built for the support of the arts and sciences.

Duterrau's lecture is rambling and repetitious. It obviously gave him little pleasure. But it does provide us with a curious insight into the minds of those public-spirited citizens of Van Diemen's Land who entertained such high hopes for the Mechanics' Institute movement as a means by which, through education, the young colony might overcome the banality and depravity, as they saw it, of its convict heritage. So far as the Schools of Art and Mechanics' Institute movements were concerned that was a forlorn and unfulfilled aspiration. Country folk absorbed the Institutes as dance halls and snooker pools; in the cities they were forgotten. Kenneth Slessor wrote their epitaph fittingly in his poem 'Country Towns':

> In the School of Arts a broadsheet lies,
> Stained with the sarcasm of flies.

Benjamin Duterrau appears to have been overawed a little by the occasion and spoke out of role; not as artist but as social moralist. Conrad Martens, when asked to lecture by the 'Club', made no such mistake. His Lecture Upon Landscape Painting is the earliest account which has survived in which a professional artist at work in Australia chose to discuss the technical aspects of his art. Nothing is known of the Club to which he spoke and of which he appears to have been a member. But there need be little doubt that it was similar to the small groups of amateur painters which had sprung up in Tasmania some years earlier, as a result of the stimulus provided by such visitors as John Skinner Prout.

Martens himself gave private lessons for many years and it is likely that the club he addressed contained some of his pupils.

Although a pious man, Martens did not stress the moral value of art. He discusses painting as an aid to perception and the enjoyment of natural beauty. Though a social art, painting promoted conviviality rather than social amelioration. It is a kind of training in perception; for it is only through art that we come to see nature correctly. This being so, anyone who endeavours to learn the rudiments of art whilst residing in Australia — where so little art exists — suffers a grave disadvantage. For Martens the mental side of painting was of greater importance than the physical, executive side.

In his technical discussion he distinguishes the sketch from the study: the sketch serves to provide a general idea of the subject, the study is concerned with individual details that might become part of a painting. Much of his lecture was given to a discussion of breadth; of which a correct understanding was crucial for landscape painting, for by it an artist achieved unity. In this regard landscape is to be distinguished from still-life painting; for it is not an art concerned with the imitation of objects but one concerned with imitating *effects* of nature that are themselves produced by means far beyond those which an artist can command. Martens proceeds to argue the case for classical naturalism quoting Sir Joshua Reynolds in support. But he does not linger on generalities, proceeding instead to show how a useful range of pigments may be set out in preparing a painting, how to treat dark tonal masses, how to deal with problems of middle distance, the size of the cone of vision, aerial perspective, of composition, gradation and contrast. Little was said about colour for on that subject he planned to give a second lecture. If he did, neither the manuscript nor any other evidence that the lecture was given, survives.

During the first half of the eighteenth century a very large number of books appeared in England on the theory and practice of water-colour painting and landscape painting. Martens was well versed in this literature. He knew John Burnet's publications, had a good knowledge of Reynolds's *Discourses* and a deep admiration of Turner's methods, having taken the trouble to compare many of Turner's paintings with the actual scenes that he represented.

John McGarvie (1795–1853)

A Presbyterian minister and writer, John McGarvie was born in Glasgow, Scotland, and graduated at Glasgow University. The Reverend John Dunmore Lang selected him as minister for the church at Portland Head on the Hawkesbury River in New South Wales in 1825, McGarvie arrived in the Colony the following year and immediately took up his appointment as the first Presbyterian minister at Ebenezer Church on the Hawkesbury River, remaining there until 1830. In 1829 he contributed biographical articles and some poems to the *Sydney Herald* under such pseudonyms as 'M, Ananbaba, A.B. Marramatta, and C.D. Warrambamba'. He was one of the three original proprietors of the *Sydney Herald* and contributed editorials for some years. McGarvie was also a founder of the Sydney School of Arts. After the Australian College was founded in 1831 he conducted the mathematics department, and also lectured in natural history and chemistry. He played a prominent part in the early history of the Presbyterian Church of Australia and in 1838 and 1848 was Moderator of the Church. In 1840 the University of Glasgow awarded him an honorary Doctorate. McGarvie was widely read and took a sympathetic interest in the beginnings of cultural activity in the Colony. He died on 12 April 1853 and was buried at Gore Hill cemetery.

The extract printed below is taken from the *Sydney Gazette* for 20 July 1829 and appears in the form of a letter to the editor, signed with the pseudonym 'A.B., Marramatta', a name he used also in publishing some of his poems in the *Sydney Gazette*.

On the State of the Fine Arts in New South Wales

Sir,

From a perusal of some recent English and Scots newspapers, we are glad to perceive, that this Colony is drawing the attention of the inhabitants of the Mother Country more forcibly to it every revolving year. Many circumstances tend to produce this effect. Our commercial relations are upon the increase; and the indisputable fact, that not long ago forty square rigged vessels lay at one time in our harbour, is a proof that the Colony is qualified to furnish a respectable profit to so many 'wanderers o'er the vasty deep,' is not undeserving of all the attention the members of the Home Government can bestow upon it. The yearly transportation of from three to four thousand males and females; the residence of three regiments amongst us; and the interest taken in their welfare by fathers, mothers, brothers, sisters, and cousins, to the tenth generation, gives importance to every statement made respecting its population or its products. The scientific observations made by Sir Thomas Brisbane,[1] Mr. James Dunlop,[2] Mr. Christian Rumker,[3] Captain King,[4] Mr. Cunningham[5] and the French[6] and Russian naturalists,[7] and the expectations formed from the long residence of our scientific Colonial Secretary,[8] have tended to increase, or keep alive, the interest excited regarding every thing connected with New South Wales.

These circumstances have been heightened in their influence by a very powerful source of attraction, at present operating in the principal towns in Britain, the 'Panorama of Sydney,' painted by Mr. Earle, and the beautiful lythographic [*sic*] sketches and paintings in various parts of the Colony, produced by the graphic pencil of the same distinguished artist.[9] You have inserted, in your valuable Journal, several notices regarding these productions; but as you have never taken any notice of the collection of pictures formed by Mr. Earle while resident in the Colony, and which, though on a small scale, formed the first picture gallery ever presented for the inspection of our young Colinists [*sic*], you may, perhaps, in the absence of a more appropriate means of communication, permit me to make a few observations on the state of this branch of the fine arts, and to furnish you with a list of the paintings of which it was composed, as interesting matters of Colonial history.

The idea of fine arts in New South Wales may excite surprise in those not acquainted with the merits of the case; and some may suppose, that we who talk of fine arts are in the habit of indulging in that favourite figure of speech not found in the 'Philosophy of Rhetoric,' the 'Bounce of a Botany Bay swell.' The fine arts may seem a misnomer for foul arts, when applied to this Colony. Nevertheless, it gives us pleasure to undeceive the patrons of so preposterous a sentiment. Forty years is a period in which Britons can work wonders. The Muses and Graces are not inimical to our southern climes; and we have no doubt that they will take up their residence amongst us, and that the 'Lucus et ara Dianaë [*sic*]',[10] will also be established in this our adopted Country.

It is not our intention to bring to your recollection the beautiful drawings made in an early period of the Colony by the indefatigable Dr. White,[11] and which engaged the benefit of the delicate Burin of Angelica Kauffman;[12] [*sic*] nor is it necessary to remind your readers of the beautiful and interesting drawings of Colonial scenery made by Westall,[13] in his professional capacity, with Captain Flinders; nor of those published by Captain Wallis.[14] These paved the way for the spirited productions of Mr. Earle, and subsequently of Mr. Carmichael,[15] both of which have been engraved with considerable success. The late Mr. Liewen [*sic*][16] was for many years our Apelles.[17] His views in New South Wales have the merit of accuracy; but the Sydney of 1817 can scarcely be recognised in the Sydney of 1829. The coarse daubs in Collins' New South Wales[18] merely indicate that there were huts and houses around Sydney cove, and that a mill or two were perched on windmill hill; but they give no idea whatever of the present state of this flourishing settlement.

Your readers must be aware that there are several very good painters and engravers in Sydney, and that bank plates, shop bills, silver plate arms, lettering, cards, &c. and all that is technically named job work may be executed here with as much beauty and accuracy as in any provincial town in Britain. One of the oldest teachers of the pleasing art of painting was a pupil of Sir Joshua Reynolds, and has transferred to the canvas the charms of not a few of our young scions of Colonial growth.[19] A gentleman well acquainted with the art, and whose talents were more than once called into exercise to gratify Mrs. M'Quarie, a true patroness of the arts, has forsworn the pencil and pallet, and cleaves to the brush hook rather than the brush.[20] The arrival of Mr. Earle, a professional painter, gave a fresh impulse to the public taste, and a direction to its energies which we trust will not be lost upon us but will render it fashionable to patronise the arts and their meritorious professors. Besides the paintings executed for private individuals, his lythographic [*sic*] press threw off many fine specimens of Colonial art, embellished with great taste and judgment, though much inferior to the splendid specimens that have issued from the presses of London and Paris. With great liberality, he collected his private pictures, and devoted an apartment for the purposes of a picture gallery, which was much visited by the youths of the Colony, and must have had considerable influence in promoting good taste amongst the rising generation. A portrait of General Darling was engraved in copper, under his inspection, which is allowed to be a most striking likeness.[21] Mr. Earle's representations also of romantic scenery in Tristan D'Acuuha [*sic*],[22] where he resided nine months with Governor Glass, were much admired here, as they partook of the Manner of Wilkie,[23] and had something congenial to colonial taste in their character and execution. When Sir Thomas Brisbane dined with the Emancipists, Mr. Earle painted for them a transparency, representing Diogenes with a lanthorn in his hand, searching through 'this varsal worlde' for an honest man, and at length finding one in the person of Sir Thomas. The representation was too childish to have been the offspring of Mr. Earle's refined taste, though it may of his sportive fancy. But even the execution of it was not worthy of him in consequence, perhaps, of the hurried manner in which it was got up. It bore no resemblance to a great philosopher and honest man: Sir Thomas's infant daughter screamed with horror when told that 'the honest man' was her father. It seemed rather a caricature representation of an honest guardian of the hours, in the height of his zeal to preserve the peace, slapping his lanthorn to the face of a drunken pickpocket.

In these respects, therefore, it must be admitted that Mr. Earle had considerable influence in keeping alive the public taste of the Colony. To this was subsequently added another cause, in alluding to which, we trust, we shall not be accused of saying more, though we justly may, of saying less than the truth. While his Excellency General Darling discountenanced speculation and oppression, the besetting sins of the Colony in all ranks, his inestimable family, without the least parade, did much to foster and fan the flame of pure taste. Mrs. Darling draws with great beauty and effect; and is besides deeply skilled in the minutive [*sic*] of architectural embellishment. Three premiums were offered some time ago for plans of a new Government house to be erected in Sydney, and in the midst of much competition that of Mrs. Darling was approved as most commodious, most classical in the exterior, and least expensive to the Colony. Colonel Dumaresq[24] sketches with great beauty in black lead and Indian ink; while Captain Dumaresq[25] is well versed in the drawing of working models, &c, for the Engineering department which he has lately quitted. These and other causes have operated with great effect in enlightening the minds and improving the taste of the community. We leave it to any man of common candour to say whether within the last three years there has not been a decided improvement in the exterior of the buildings erected during that period, and in the ornamental decorations of our new public structures. 'Show me,' said a critic, 'the knocker on a man's door, or the letters on his brass plate, if selected by himself, and I will tell you his taste.' If such improvements have taken place amongst us, all we demand is, 'to give honor to whom honor is due.'

Mr. Earle, to whom we now return, has acquired considerable distinction as a portrait painter. In his portraits, the contour and general resemblance of features are certainly well preserved; but we cannot help thinking that the colouring is sometimes sombre and heavy. In his own portrait, which is a surprising likeness, this has been avoided. It is admirably correct, and presents the spectator with a full view of the fire of genius that animates the countenance of the original. But in many other portraits painted by him, there is a deadness and rawness that make you think the portrait is a patchwork daubing, the colours being laid on at random with a tar brush. From this charge we must except the fine full length (as well as the small portrait) of Sir Thomas Brisbane, which has the merit of correctness in drawing in a surprising degree. It is a perfect resemblance of the amiable original, and cannot but strike an experienced eye as a most elaborate and highly wrought picture. It is not moulded indeed in the school of Vandyke, but the Colony may be proud of it as a genuine colonial production of the first class.

The humble effort made by Mr. Earle to present to the Colonists a small collection of paintings as a nucleus for a larger, was an attempt worthy of every degree of praise, even though it is no longer in existence. It served for a time to recall the noble picture galleries in the mother country, endowed by Government, or the wealth of private individuals, and had it been permanent, might have preserved the public taste from the risk of torpor, or of falling back into barbarism. We are sure your readers will ask no apology for presenting them with a list of the pictures that adorned the first miniature gallery in their adopted country. They will thus see how much a man of talent and industry may do by his individual exertions for the public interest, in subserviency to his own, and that to whatever clime Britons penetrate, they carry their national vigour, activity, and attainments along with them. Had any man, sixty years ago, declared to Captain Cook or Sir Joseph Banks, that such a collection of paintings should be exhibited in this place, in less than half a century after a Colony was founded, and that, too in the midst of European luxuries and British institutions, they would have called in question the soundness of his intellect, for indulging in the supposition of its possibility.

Yours faithfully,
A.B., Marramatta, July, 1829   [*Sydney Gazette,* 20 July 1829]

NOTES—McGARVIE

1 Sir Thomas Brisbane (1773-1860), the Governor of New South Wales from 1821 to 1825, was greatly interested in astronomy. He built an observatory at Parramatta and made extensive observations of the stars of the southern hemisphere and appointed two excellent astronomers James Dunlop and Christian Rumker to assist him. When he departed from New South Wales he left his astronomical instruments and 349 volumes of his scientific library to encourage the growth of science in the young colony.

2 James Dunlop (1793-1848), the assistant astronomer appointed by Brisbane to his Parramatta observatory. His interests included poetry, geology and zoology. Dunlop's most important scientific work was his Catalogue of 7,385 stars from the *Observations made at the Observatory at Parramatta* (1822-26) for which he was awarded the gold medal of the Royal Astronomical Society.

3 Christian Carl Ludwig Rumker (1788-1862), the assistant appointed by Brisbane, together with Dunlop, to man the Parramatta observatory. In December 1827 Governor Darling appointed him geometrical astronomer. Rumker quarrelled with both Brisbane and Dunlop but was an able and indefatigable scientist. In 1854 he received the gold medal of the Royal Astronomical Society in recognition of his work.

4 Captain Phillip Parker King (1791-1856), the son of P. G. King (1758-1808), the third Governor of New South Wales (1800-06), was the first native-born Australian to achieve fame beyond the Australian colonies. He has been described as 'the greatest of the early Australian marine surveyors'.

5 Allan Cunningham (1791-1839) botanist and explorer.

6 McGarvie is referring to the visit of Dumont D'Urville and his party of scientists in the *Astrolabe* to Sydney (from 2 to 19 December 1826) during their voyage to the Pacific and the Antarctic. Dumont D'Urville has been described 'as the man who made the greatest single contribution to the perfecting of the map of the Pacific', see J. Dunmore, *French Explorers in the Pacific*, Oxford, 1969, ii, 383.

7 Probably a reference to the scientific voyage of exploration to the Antarctic of the *Vostok* and *Mirnyi* under the command of Thaddeus von Bellingshausen (1778-1852). They put in briefly at Sydney on their way south and returned to Sydney on 9 September 1820, spending seven weeks there. Bellingshausen wrote in his journal for 31 October 1820: 'with great regret we left this town where during the whole of our stay we had passed so pleasant a time'.

8 i.e. Alexander McLeay (1767-1848) see note 15, p. 26.

9 Augustus Earle (1793-1838), artist and traveller, resided in Sydney from October 1825 until October 1827, where he painted portraits of notable colonists and travelled about New South Wales making landscape sketches in pencil and water-colour. Earle's *Panorama of Sydney* consisted of eight views which he painted from the top of Palmer's hill, Sydney, and sent to Robert Burford, the London entrepreneur of mechanical panoramas. Burford was assisted by Lieutenant-Colonel Dumaresq (see note 24) in producing the panorama and naming the buildings. Earle also painted scenes for a panorama of Hobart.

10 *lucus et ara Dianae* lit. 'the grove and temple of Diana'.

11 John White, the naval surgeon to whom Thomas Watling was assigned for two years (see p. 10).

12 Angelica Kauffmann (1741-1807), the historical and portrait painter whose

F

work was highly fashionable in England and Italy during the second half of the eighteenth century. She was not as McGarvie implies ('the delicate Burin of') an engraver but her work, highly suited to engraving, was engraved by many of the most famous engravers of England and became much better known in engraved reproduction than in the original.

13 William Westall (1781-1850) travelled with Matthew Flinders in the *Investigator* on its circumnavigation of Australia (1801-03) as topographical draughtsman. Several of his drawings were reproduced as line-engravings in Flinders's *Voyage to Terra Australis*, published in 1814. The original drawings which Westall made on the voyage are reproduced in *Westall's Drawings* edited by T. Perry and D. H. Simpson, London, 1962.

14 James Wallis (1785-1858), commandant at Newcastle, N.S.W. from 1816 to 1819. Here as in the case of John White, Wallis's reputation as a draughtsman is probably largely erroneous, due to the practice of masters making use of the drawings and paintings executed by convicts assigned to them without making any published acknowledgement.

15 John Carmichael, a Scottish engraver, who had been apprenticed to John Horsburgh (1791-1869) prior to his arrival in Sydney. It is probably to Carmichael that McGarvie refers in the next paragraph for he was responsible for most of the engraved commercial work of the kind described. He also engraved portraits of Aboriginals.

16 i.e. J. W. Lewin.

17 Apelles, the court painter to Alexander the Great, lived during the late 4th century B.C. He was widely regarded in antiquity as the greatest of the Greek painters but no originals by his hand have survived, his reputation depending entirely upon literary sources.

18 David Collins (1756-1810), the Deputy-Judge-Advocate and Lieutenant-Governor of New South Wales, author of *An Account of the English Colony in New South Wales*, 2 volumes (1798, I; 1802, II). It is illustrated with engravings by Edward Dayes, some after drawings (again unacknowledged) by Thomas Watling.

19 Probably a reference to Richard Read (b. 1765) and usually known as Richard Read senior to distinguish him from another artist of the same name living and working contemporaneously in Sydney. Read senior had been sentenced to fourteen years transportation in 1812. In November 1814 he established a drawing school at 37 Pitt Street, Sydney. The claim that he was a pupil of Sir Joshua Reynolds has not been substantiated but his age at the time of conviction (forty-seven) allows for the possibility of his having worked as an assistant in Reynolds's studio.

20 Probably a reference to J. W. Lewin to whom Macquarie granted 200 acres at Airds, New South Wales (see p .18).

21 The original portrait by Earle is at Government House, Sydney.

22 These paintings are now located in the Nan Kivell Collection of the Australian National Library, Canberra.

23 Sir David Wilkie (1785-1841), painter of genre scenes and portraiture.

24 Colonel Henry Dumaresq (1792-1838), military secretary to Governor Darling. His estates at St. Helier's (named after his ancestral home in Jersey) near Muswellbrook, New South Wales, covered approximately 13,000 acres.

25 Captain John Dumaresq (1793-1868), a military engineer, provisionally appointed by Darling as inspector of roads and bridges. His estates at St. Aubins (named after his ancestral home in Jersey) near Scone, New South Wales, amounted to approximately 13,000 acres.

John Lhotsky (1800–?)

John Lhotsky was born in 1800 in Lemberg (Lvov), Galicia, of Czech parents. Educated in Prague and Berlin, he practised for a time as a doctor of medicine in Vienna. A member of the Bavarian Botanical Society, he succeeded in obtaining a grant from Louis I of Bavaria (1786-1868), an enlightened patron of the arts and sciences, to assist research into natural history in South America and Australia. Lhotsky arrived in Sydney from Brazil in 1832. In 1834, with some government assistance, he explored the Monaro district, publishing his experiences and findings in his *Journey from Sydney to the Australian Alps*, in 1834-35. Disappointed at his inability to obtain preferment in New South Wales he sailed for Hobart in 1836 where, after some fruitless efforts to gain suitable employment, Governor Sir John Franklin appointed him to develop coal mines near Port Arthur, by means of convict labour. About this time he made a geological map of the Tasman Peninsula. But deeply disappointed with his reception in Australia, Lhotsky sailed for London in 1838.

In London Lhotsky continued to live precariously by lecturing and writing. He contributed widely to European scientific journals, and wrote for newspapers over a wide field, which included natural history, anthropology, geology, botany, art, politics and revolution. His name is commemorated in a genus of plants (*Lhotskia*) and of fishes (*Lhotskya*). The date of his death is not known.

[THE STATE OF ARTS IN NEW SOUTH WALES AND VAN DIEMEN'S LAND]

The assertion of Goethe, that 'man cannot live without poetry and art', has been no where so fully understood by me, as in Australia, when I saw a country, which only a few years back had been reclaimed from a primaeval, nay savage state, already occupied by the works of the architect; when I saw the mansion, and the cottage, around which the shrill tones of the cockatoo still resound, filled in a few cases with the works even of first rate artists, in many with respectable pictures and engravings. The most important object of art in Australia, is undoubtedly the Catholic Cathedral[1] in Sydney, a building, which with the exception of the old gothic churches in London, outbids in its style all other places of public worship, I have seen even in this metropolis. It is entirely built of hewn stone (freestone), occupies a commanding position, and the climate, like that of Italy, having given a yellow hue to the surface of the slabs, it presents, especially in the brilliancy of Australian evenings, from many parts of the town, nay, the many bays of the gorgeous harbour, a charming and grand sight. Although its portal is somewhat contracted, yet taken altogether, it is a grand edifice, the interior graced by splendid gothic columns, and although I am not aware of its exact dimensions, I am confident it will contain at least 3000 people. Since the arrival of Bishop Paulding [i.e. Polding],[2] its interior decorations have much advanced; he has also so arranged that some of Haydn's Oratorios are therein annually performed, which as the tide of emigration sets so strongly towards these shores, count nearly 150 performers, and evidence the great acoustic qualities of the building. The only other structure that may be ranged amongst objects of art, is the Villa at Cambden [*sic*],[3] in the Cowpastures, New South Wales, belonging to Mr. H. McArthur,[4] one of the largest sheep farmers in the colony. Emerging, as the traveller does, from a forest of gum trees (Eucalyptus), reminding him with their particularly coloured foliage of the distant country he is in, he finds himself at once upon a small plain or parterre, but shortly redeemed from nature, and he views with astonishment the extensive and elegant Villa, built in the best and chastest Italian style, with a large and graceful colonnade, the columns of which are made of a very hard and ornamental freestone. There are other fine buildings in the colony, but this certainly reflects the greatest credit on the architect. Even architectural antiquities are to be met with in Sydney, for as such I must mention a store of Robert Campbell Esq.,[5] on the doorway of which the figure of 1802 is inscribed upon a slab. This is the most ancient date, I ever saw cut in stone at the Antipodes, and it will no doubt hereafter be an object of some interest.

Proceeding, as I now do to painting and pictures in Australia, I will shortly state the manner how, independently of higher sentiment, arts are intruding as it were, upon the settler in distant zones. After the first years of struggle are over, he perceives, when lounging leisurely on his sofa, that the walls of his house are bare and empty. It would afford him and his family satisfaction, to have something to fill up this emptiness, and the vacuum, which he, freed from material cares, begins to feel in his mind. This certainly is the beginning of art, and of the patronizing of arts in distant zones. But it will surprise many of our readers, if they are informed to what a high degree this art-instinct, if I shall call it so, has been satisfied in such a young colony. There is even a first-rate picture of Van Dyke [*sic*], which has penetrated to Botany Bay. It is a full length figure of a female, with a beautiful form of body and limbs. The owner is Sir John Jamieson [*sic*], and it adorns one of the tasteful rooms in his fine mansion at Penrith Emu-Plains.[6] How this jewel came to New South Wales is half a mystery; but I believe it proceeded direct from Holland, and Sir John purchased it from a Captain, going to, or coming from the Cape of Good Hope. From the same place came a smaller, yet equally valuable picture of Rembrandt, for which the price demanded was 50*l*. But the most important event in the artistical world of Sydney, was the importation of a whole collection of oil pictures, by C. H. Ebden Esq.;[7] but as I was absent when they arrived, I have not seen them, yet know, that among them were several pieces of ancient and first-rate masters. In fact, art speaks to men under all zones and climates, and the really *good* is appreciated every where. I recollect a dozen of Mr. Martin's[8] mystic dramas, as I would call them, arriving in Sydney, and although they were in very indifferent frames and charged 10*l*. a piece, they sold rapidly. In Hobart Town is a Canaletti [*sic*],[9] which I consider equal, if not superior to any of this master's pictures in the National Gallery; this picture was exchanged for a house in Hobart Town. A very respectable piece of Julio Romano,[10] representing the Forum at Rome, was sold at the same time.

But it is impossible that arts should be appreciated anywhere, unless men endeavour also to cultivate them. Not only drawing, but oil painting is cultivated in Australia to a considerable extent. The drawings of Van Diemen's Land, by Thomas Glover [*sic*],[11] are known to the public.* Although this gentleman is an eminent artist, yet his pictures are deficient in two respects. First, he has not endeavoured to select really primitive and original Australian nature; and besides, being not a sufficient observer of nature, has given to his pictures neither that hue of light, characteristic of those countries, nor do they possess that detail of genius, as I would call it, so much praised by Goethe in the works of Hackert,[13] whose foliage (Baumschlag) is so true, that it is possible to distinguish, at the first glance, what sort of trees is represented. Sculpture also has found its votaries in Aus-

---

* In speaking of Australian artists, I cannot omit mentioning Mr. Ferdinand Bauer[12], who strongly combined the two qualities of an artist and naturalist. A biography of him, containing some remarks on his paintings, written by me, has been read lately before the Linnean Society.

tralia; and Mr Low,[14] in Hobart Town, has modelled a number of natives of Van Diemen's Land, of which a specimen is to be seen in the United Service Museum. They are of full size, perfect likenesses; in fact, altogether a respectable work. As the race of the natives of this island is nearly extinguished, these casts will retain a constant historical value. Sydney also possesses an artist of some note, we mean Mr. Rhodius,[15] who had been occupied by the French Government in engraving some of the edifices of Paris. Mr. R. is very efficient in water-colour, and his portraits of Natives and Scenery are much sought for by travellers.

As, from my first arrival in Australia, I perceived, that it would afford a rich scope for the landscape painter, I had some drawings executed, most of them on a large scale. Amongst them were several studies of trees of unique appearance: Xantorrhea Arborea, Eucalyptus, Casuarina, &c. In the Australian Alps I took a sketch of a great mountain panorama; and in Tasman's peninsula I had a virginal forest drawn, which breathes all the mysterious and silent majesty of such scenery. One of my most cheerful sketches, is the spot where Captain Cook first landed, and where a brass tablet, commemorating this historical event, has been erected by Sir Thomas Brisbane, G.C.B., when Governor of New South Wales.[16]

Yet, Australian sky and nature awaits, and merits real artists to pourtray it. Its gigantic gum and acacia trees, 40 feet in girt, some of them covered with a most smooth bark, externally as white as chalk; the enchantment-like appearance of forests, the foliage of which is pruinous and mellow, in a way defying description — mornings and evenings so pure and serene, that the eye is absorbed as it were, in the depth of the azure of the horizon — miles covered with the most ornamental shrubs and flowers (Hovea, Epacris, Boronia &c.) — scenery, the foliage of which possesses all varieties of colours, from brown-red through orange and yellow into the most tender light green; all this and more, unnecessary to be broached on the present occasion, will produce a Daniell,[17] and in succession a Salvator Rosa,[18] and perhaps, such as will even exceed them. It has been said, that 'there is nothing new under the sun;' still, if we see, that amongst many others, there is a whole system of landscape painting of the most striking character, yet available for human art, it seems to have been rather pre-ordained, that our mind shall never lack objects worthy of its attention and exertion.

[From a manuscript on 'Australia, in its historical evolution' by Dr John Lhotsky, *The Art Union*, July 1839, pp. 99-100]

NOTES—LHOTSKY

1 The foundation stone of the cathedral was laid on 29 October 1821 by Governor Macquarie. It was probably designed by Father J. J. Thierry (the roof by Henry Cooper). It was extended from 1848 to 1862 probably from the designs of William Munro. The Cathedral was burnt down in 1865.

2 John Bede Polding (1794-1877), the Catholic Archbishop of New Holland and Van Diemen's Land from 1834 to 1877.

3 Camden Park (1831-6), designed by John Verge (1782-1861).

4 Hannibal Macarthur (1788-1861), a nephew of John Macarthur (1767-1834). But Lhotsky's statement is inaccurate. Hannibal's brother William lived at Camden Park, he himself at the Vineyard, Rydalmere.

5 Robert Campbell (1769-1846), the pioneer Sydney merchant and pastoralist.

6 Sir John Jamison (1776-1844). Neither of the paintings said to be owned by Jamison have been traced and the ascriptions to Van Dyck and Rembrandt must remain highly questionable.

7 Charles Hotson Ebden (1811-67), a pastoralist, business man and politician, was born at the Cape of Good Hope and settled in Sydney in 1832. He developed large pastoral interests and was the first man to settle in the Port Phillip District north of the Dividing Range. 'He was' says Geoffrey Serle 'something of a dandy who fancied himself a Beau Brummel', *ADB*, i, 351.

8 John Martin (1789-1854), an English painter of religious history pictures in grandiose landscape settings.

9 Canale, Antonio, called Canaletto (1697-1768), famous Venetian painter of *vedute*, i.e. views—mainly of Venice.

10 Giulio Romano (1499-1546), famous Italian architect and painter, the chief pupil of Raphael.

11 i.e. John Glover (1767-1849), the successful English landscape painter and art teacher who settled in northern Tasmania to paint and farm at the age of sixty in 1831.

12 Ferdinand Bauer (1760-1826), the Austrian botanical painter employed by Banks, and later worked with Robert Brown on Flinders's Voyage on the *Investigator*.

13 Jacob Phillippe Hackert (1737-1807), a German landscape painter. He lived mostly in Italy and worked both for Ferdinand, King of Naples and Catherine the Great of Russia.

14 The reference is to Benjamin Law who arrived in Hobart on 14 February 1835 and is described in Henry Melville's *Van Diemen's Land Annual* for 1836 as a sculptor. In the *Hobart Town Courier*, 7 October 1836, he offers busts of Truganini for sale. Both busts were illustrated in Dumont, d'Urville, *Voyage au Pole Sud, Anthropologie* (Atlas), 1842-7, pl. 13. He also made busts of Woureddy, the chief of the central tribe of Aboriginals. According to William Moore, about thirty casts were taken from it and published at four guineas each (*Story of Australian Art*, 11-71).

15 Charles Rodius (also Rhodius) (1802-60), an artist born in Cologne who spent some years in France. In 1829 he was convicted at Westminster on a charge of stealing a reticule and was sentenced to transportation for seven years.

16 This was an inscribed plate placed on the face of the cliffs at Kurnell by the Philosophical Society of Australasia in 1821. A facsimile is in the Mitchell Library, Sydney.

17 Lhotsky is referring here to one or both of the Daniells: Thomas Daniell

(1749-1840) and his nephew William (1769-1837), whom he took to India where they both practised as topographical and landscape painters for ten years prior to returning to England. There they published *Oriental Scenery* (1808) in which they sought to render with accuracy the landscapes, architecture, customs and manners of India. They are among the best-known of the picturesque topographers of the nineteenth century.

18 Salvator Rosa (1615-73), the Italian painter born near Naples, best-known for his painting of wild mountainous scenery inhabited by banditti. Lhotsky was probably thinking of the mountainous country he had explored in the Southern Alps of New South Wales and its suitability to treatment by an artist like Salvator Rosa.

John West (1809–73)

John West was a Congregational minister, historian and newspaper editor. After serving in several ministries in England he was accepted by the Colonial Missionary Society for service in Van Diemen's Land. In 1842 he became minister of St John's Square Chapel, Launceston, and made his home at Windmill Hill.

In Launceston West made many friends and became one of the moving spirits of the town. He was a founder of the Launceston *Examiner* (1842), the City Mission, the public hospital, the general cemetery, the Launceston Mechanics' Institute, the Cornwall Insurance Company, and the Hobart High School (1847).

West became one of the most vigorous leaders in Australia's first national political movement, the campaign to abolish the transportation of convicts to Australia. He later achieved fame for his *History of Tasmania*, 2 vols (Launceston, 1852), written when the colony was only forty-seven years old. This history, though inspired by the abolitionist cause, was written with 'fairness and detachment' and has won the respect of later Australian historians. West was also one of the first journalists of influence to advocate a union of the Australian colonies, and occupies therefore an important place in the development of the idea of Federation. In 1854 West became the editor of the *Sydney Morning Herald,* its owner John Fairfax being a fellow-Congregationalist and a leading Abolitionist. Towards the end of his life West helped to found and govern Camden College, for the training of evangelists.

[THE FINE ARTS IN THEIR INTELLECTUAL AND
SOCIAL RELATIONS]

We owe our thanks to the committee of the Launceston
Mechanics' Institution, for a display of art so pleasing to all,
and especially so useful to the junior members of society.[1] These
exhibitions are subservient to the cause of virtue. Such pleasures
diminish the power of meaner gratifications: every addition to
the intellectual amusement of the day is a new guarantee for the
morrow. The youthful visitor will return with his views increased,
and his notions more distinct; he will feel a new interest in his
race, and a fuller consciousness of its mental dignity; dissipation
will be resisted, not only by the warnings of authority, but by
the instinct of taste. These objects are worth pursuing; and if he
who increases the subsistence of mankind by the exercise of his
skill, makes society his debtor, shall not they be deemed bene-
factors, who propagate noble thoughts, and sow the moral
harvest of the future.

Nor should we forget our obligations to those gentlemen, who
for a season have parted with the ornaments of their dwellings, to
supplement the stock of public enjoyments. The illiberal spirit
of a former period is happily declining: works of art are thrown
open to the world, and men of humble stations are permitted to
share in gratifications, once reserved to a privileged few. It is now
admitted, that the pleasures which may circulate without loss,
rise in value as they flow. This advance in the sentiments of the
opulent, is followed by its natural consequence: it has abated the
stupid wish to handle and destroy. The excluded classes are ever
dangerous: but even hordes of savages who stab the canvas, and
shiver the marble, whose curiosity is ruthless, when better taught
gather up with veneration the relics of their former devastations.
Those who extend the knowledge of genius, enrol a guard to
defend it; and time will shortly extinguish that meddling
barbarism which far less generous nations have long ago abjured.

To the collection it is no small honour to contain original
works — works which might grace a palace, and gratify a royal
taste. The artist has fixed on the canvas, scenes which have often
delighted the colonist, when surveying the landscape arrayed in
the beauties of spring and smiling in the beams of the morning. Happy will that era be when the moralist shall rival the
sweet delineations of the pencil; when this region of surpassing
loveliness shall be studded with the dwellings of industry and
innocence; when the appalling contrast of hutted crime shall for
ever disappear.

The object of this lecture is not to expound the material mysteries of the studio, or to catalogue its works. We propose to view the arts in relation to our intellectual and social being; our eyes will be less on the picture than the spectator — to watch his countenance, and to estimate his emotions. It is deeply interesting to retrace the progressive steps in the history of art, by which the rude sketch expands into the forms, and glows with the colouring of life; nor less to observe the artist through all the developments of his plan, and the delicacies of its execution. But perhaps a higher kind of interest leads the mind to observe the arts in their symptomatic aspects, to pursue them through their relations to the intellectual and moral perceptions of our nature; to see how they illustrate the history, refine the luxury, and embellish the intercourse of nations; how they indicate their corruption, and enervate their spirit; and how, at length, they swell and precipitate the perdition of their overthrow.

The gradual development of the human powers is illustrated by the relics of art which have been recovered from the ashes of nations. Among all, the imitative faculties have been early displayed. Ignorant of letters as the symbols of thought, they have endeavoured to perpetuate the memory of events, by copying the objects and actions which interested their passions. Even the natives of this country left a few rude exemplifications of this primitive practice. In this town, many years ago, an example was exhibited.* In a pamphlet lately published at Port Phillip, several coloured figures are given drawn by the Australian blacks on stone.[3] A recent traveller in North America, saw an Indian rapidly complete a sketch on the sub-bark of a tree, which expressed the time, the direction, and the companions of his journey. But of all barbarous nations, the Mexicans carried this system of pictorial writing to the greatest extent. Dr. Robertson thinks their attainments exaggerated by their conquerors, but still admits that they sometimes exhibited considerable skill and intelligence.[4] They contrived to record affairs of much complexity with clearness and detail: they also blended the various plumage of their birds into imitative forms with wonderful nicety and harmony. The fantastic gods of India are pictured on their walls. In Egypt, too, they are the great subject of the artist. But in Egypt, not only their mythology — every circumstance of domestic life is exhibited on their temples and their tombs. Thus every people for the purposes of utility, ostentation, or devotion, have exerted

* At a lecture delivered by the late Mr. Headlam.[2]

their imitative powers; and an enquiry which should range through the forests of America, through Egypt and Greece, — to Italy, might ascertain the gradations of imitation and invention, from the outline which a child might rival, to those amazing combinations which delight the most scrupulous taste, and hold the loftiest intellect in astonishment and admiration.

From these facts it would appear that a natural impulse prompts the human race to attempt artificial resemblances; that when you see a child endeavour to copy the objects around him, you behold the workings of a natural passion. If you believe the phrenologists, the very conformation of the head exhibits a physical cause for this common disposition. But whatever its origin, its existence cannot be doubted; or, that less or more, it is innate and universal. We need not closely enquire whether the idea of beauty is equally innate and uniform. A wide difference of opinion has existed among speculative men. It is scarcely, however, conclusive to infer from the powers of execution, which depend on the state of congenial science and continuous effort, in what degree conception may anticipate artistic skill. But who can look abroad and behold the works of the creator, and doubt that from the Great Teacher our impressions are collected and refined. On every hand he has constructed models of symmetry and elegance, and diffused the tints of loveliness. It is needless to ask if that taste is founded on reason which prefers a Grecian statue, or an Italian painting, to the stiff outline of the Egyptian artist, or the patches of colouring mapped out on the gaudy pictures of China. Hogarth delineated the line of beauty;[5] but nature prescribed the rule after which he drew. Our ideas of human beauty are doubtless determined by our social affections: we prefer a particular style of countenance because it is associated with domestic endearments. A sentiment stronger than abstract taste, resolves our choice; but where the natural predilections no longer dictate, broad varieties of idea also disappear. The progress of civilisation assimilates the standard of nations; and following one guide their preferences resemble each other. The works of art most valued by the people, are such as exhibit least violent departures from the divine original. The Hindoo and Egyptian artists have indeed set these maxims at naught. Their imagination teems with hideous combinations of the brute and human forms; but it must be remembered that these were the sacred symbols of the priesthood, and probably embodied the mysterious terrors of their faith. They saw in the monstrous distortion the delineation of a power, or the incarnation of a deity. The presence of

monstrous idols would affect the common arts of life; their ornaments were talismanic, and bore the image of their gods.

Thus the perception of beauty and propriety is not confined
to the judges of art. The phrases of criticism may be all unknown,
the contrivance of the artist may be quite disguised in the general
effect, but the responses of the heart demonstrate that the original
teacher has given one common impulse alike to the spectator and
the designer. The great French dramatist first read his pieces to
his foster-mother, and caught from her countenance the felicitous
omens of his fame. The artist is not to be regarded as an eccentric
prodigy, but as a ministering priest — the passions of his age
embodied — the representative of the imaginations of his race . . .

The subjects of the christian faith have given wide scope to
the most felicitous combinations. On such topics, poetry must
often yield to the pencil in its power to satisfy the imagination.
The touches of sacred history are so brief and passionate, that
in a word they call up a scene; but when the poet attempts to
dilate and illustrate, he becomes poor and tame; for human
society presents no equal analogies and similitudes. It is here
the painter shines. Thus, at The Last Supper, the enquiry 'Is it
I?' — soon expressed in words — calls up a panorama of thought;
surprise, grief, conscious guilt, hesitation, indignation: every
line and every countenance expresses a sentiment or delineates
a passion.

You could not walk through this exhibition without being
conscious of the intellectual and moral power of art. The contrast between 'Health and Sickness' is a sweet commentary on
domestic love — on that providence which hallows affliction with
a thousand smiles. There is the young wandering musician who
looks on with pensive sympathy; the joyful little dancer tripping
in ruddy health; the languid pleasure of the sick one, who
struggles with her sickness, and seems exhilarated with the effort.
The tale of 'Domestic Tenderness' charms beyond the glories of
a 'Coronation.'

'The Daughter reading to her aged Parents:' — we accommo-
date the language of Johnson — 'life has among its soothing and
quiet comforts, few things better to give than such a child.'

Beneath the gorgeous prints of Martin,[6] — the riot and
dismay, the splendour and ruin, — you write — 'Surely thou has
set them in slippery places;' 'as a dream when one awaketh, so,
O Lord, when thou awakest, wilt thou despise their image.' But
the representation of divine compassion moves all the soul. A
crowd of various misery is gathered at his feet. He looks with the

calm confidence of power, and with benevolence which cannot weary:- 'Jesus healing the Broken-hearted.' The penitent weeps, but not with despair; she hangs upon his arm and confides in his compassion; the laborer stretches out his hand for help; the bereaved for consolation; the oppressed for deliverance: all forms of human sadness, destitution, and woe implore the succour of his mercy, and none plead in vain: his pity, like a sunbeam glancing through a cloud and mantling all beneath it, relieves the melancholy band with the assurance of hope.

In another place, you have the personification of the spirit of evil — the sad meditative air of the man; the malignant certainty of the demon. So men hazard love, duty, and happiness; so they obtain wretchedness in recompense. Miserable gamester! a few more moves, and all is lost!

Those who have seen the original works of the masters of the pencil, must have a strong recollection of their magical power. Their works are disposed so that they arrest the eye before it can be guarded from illusion. The canvas is annihilated by the shade. Take the Crucifixion as depicted by a master-hand. Everything enlarges the catastrophe: the sufferer heaves with more than mortal pain; the spectators gaze in every attitude of wonder and grief; the crowd shrink back; nature envelops that dread sight with darkness: for the first and last time, death has smitten the guiltless.

Every traveller tells of the majesty of Angelo.[7] His scenes are tremendous: they fill the beholder with amazement; he is borne on the wings of genius beyond the regions of this life, and mingles with the shadows of eternity.

But the immortal Angelo, the Homer of arts, was a wonder in the mastery of the hand. When he painted, his pencil swept the canvas, as if to disperse an envious covering; when he smote the marble, say his contemporaries, his vehemence was sublime; his blows fell with the rapidity which threatened to shatter; 'he drew out from the unshapen rock the hidden symmetry and beauty:' ten thousand thoughts dropped from his pencil: his works were heroics on canvas or stone.

Yet in the presence of nature, the glories of art are as tinsel and mimicry. The works of man illude when most successful; but nature invites the microscope, and defies the scrutiny; her vast and glorious combinations lose no part of their strength by analysis. Sometimes the artists of Pompeii with curious skill drew portraits of nature and life; but when the spectator, charmed by the prospect, came nearer to the picture, its design at once withdrew, and rough lines and senseless colours, disappointed his gaze, — just as the mimic river of the desert cheats the traveller with unreal waters, and vanishes in sand. How glorious that Divine Artist, whose plans comprehend systems of worlds; and, yet, who softens off the tints of the flower beyond the scope of vision! Thus, while we are attracted by genius whose powers a few years developed and extinguished, we may turn with new reverence to that glorious being, to whom the concentrated skill of all minds and all ages, is but as a drop to the ocean — the finite to the infinite!

We do not pretend to condense within the limits of a lecture a perfect view of the benefits conferred on mankind by artistic achievements. We cannot, however, fail to observe how greatly our knowledge of the world is assisted by such labours. A person born in this country could know imperfectly by verbal description what art enables him to comprehend. No richness, no point, or circumlocution of language, could display those wondrous engines of intellectual and material strength, before which time and distance seem to evaporate. But the artist exposes alike the secrets of gigantic mechanism, the splendour of architecture, and the pomp of ceremony. The costume, the habits, the visage of nations grow familiar to the eye; foreigners speak a language which requires no interpreter, and prejudices melt away. The hostile sentiments of nations are supported on the basis of ignorance. The alien is ferocious, meagre, and miserable; but the delineations of the pencil, guided by fidelity, enlarge the sympathies of mankind. Virgil has availed himself of this truth in one of his choicest passages:- the anxious Trojan finds himself on a foreign shore: he wanders to the temple, and sees on its walls the history of his misfortunes, — and thus the pledge of hospitality.[8] How far this feeling may extend it is hard to tell; but you would expect, like the hero, kindness where you should see the relations of humanity recognised in the dwelling.

Without the artist, the many could know little of natural history; for ages the fancy teemed with animal monsters. The testimonies of the pen, even when read, can hardly subdue credulity. It is the pencil which is irresistible.

The artist represents those regions of nature which few can investigate: the riches of the earth, the order of the heavens, and the treasures of the deep. He assists the astronomer in his researches, and helps the physician and surgeon to propagate their cures. Neither trade or profession is quit of obligation. The highest efforts of the artist are demanded to facilitate the comfort and preservation of life. The psalmist celebrates the dread knowledge of the mariner:- 'These see the works of the Lord.'[9] But a people centered in the bosom of a continent can only know the world of waters by the aid of the pencil; and if to witness the elemental war,

'Where the Almighty's form glasses itself in tempest,'[10]

is subservient to piety, and promotes a reverence for Deity, even the faint image of the ocean may not be in vain.

The denunciation of luxury can only have weight with the moralist as luxury is defined, and the specific indulgence is proved incompatible with manly and christian virtue. The questions of time and expense must be settled by a view of society, and the relation of a particular art to common gratification and instruction. It has been held by some that art is a tax on the body politic; that it generates novel wants and new temptations. In this view the Genevan sophist[11] contemplated the arts; and so the anchorite[12] estimated its endless varieties. According to the first, the blissful simplicity of nature is forfeited; in the view of the second, the soul is endangered. But these sentiments are both erroneous, though not equally respectable. The most devout abstraction will not be diverted from its great concerns by familiar elegance; nor does it follow that pride will be promoted. The tub of Diogenes is not the model of moral architecture. 'Thus,' said the cynic, striding over the philosopher's carpet, 'thus I trample on the pride of Plato;' 'and with more pride,' was the reply — as true as it was cutting.[13] The cabinets of the rich have doubtless often shone at the expense of social virtues; and amidst the splendour of their dwellings the soul has remained unadorned with moral sentiments and kindly affections. It is not, however, in this form that selfishness chiefly displays its temper. It is in the riot of debauch, in grasping gold, in tasteless magnificence. It is rare that a genuine love of art in the middle classes is divorced from a perception of moral worth. The time devoted to the arts is small indeed, compared with that exacted by animal wants, and devoured by sensual pleasures. The luxuries of the eye are cheap compared with the epicureanism of the table. Consider how small a portion of mankind are employed in the arts distinct from immediate utility. The bulk labour with ceaseless toil, from youth to decrepitude, to replace their daily consumption: they retract all they produce, and leave nothing to add to the accumulations of time. Surely society can well spare a few of her brightest spirits, who, while they indulge the yearnings of their own genius, when they have completed its aspirations, offer to thousands the fruit of their toil ...

The decline of the arts has hitherto always attended the luxury and enervation of society: the specimens are multiplied, but the inspiration ceases. The artist labours at a trade, and seeks his success by dexterous accommodation to a vulgar patronage: pictures are sold by the measure, and statues by the ton. When art is valued by the markets, and the indefinable and ideal worth is abandoned for a mercantile appreciation, the decline is rapid. It was thus with Athens and Rome. Nor is liberty unimportant to the perfection of art. It was during the age of freedom, or before its momentum was spent, that the choicest models of antiquity were produced. It was during the era when mental liberty was revived, and ancient literature regained the ascendant, that the arts recovered their lost graces and power. Angelo was contemporary with Luther and Erasmus. Mental independence is indispensable to intellectual grandeur. Taste flies from the presence of despotism, or languishes under its capricious favour. One while the monarch revels in the dull pomp of rude magnificence, and another the rough warrior builds his ramparts with rifled Parian marble.

Reasoning from the past, the growth of luxury multiplies the works of art, debases their merit, and prepares for their destruction.

What gold is to the midnight thief, a splendid and enervated capital is to demi-civilized and warlike invaders. The languid patriotism and intense selfishness of an opulent empire, allures attack and abates the means of defence. The affections of the heart are corrupted: principles are diverted by the love of individual ease; and ultimately those household words which roused and rallied all affections, and united all hands, are unmeaning sounds. The city is the empire: nationality is confounded; the constitution of freedom dies; and the capital becomes a theatre of intrigue and pleasure, where vice and folly provoke the contempt and encourage the aggression of barbarous but valiant foes. Then comes the tide of ruin. Torn by civil convulsions, shivered by massive violence, the picture becomes a target, the statue a broken stone, and the accumulating wrecks hide a few remains to testify to another age how glorious the magnificence, and how terrible the overthrow.

Such has been the history — such the ruins of empires! A long line of catastrophies palls the memory of nations past! Is it reserved to add another to the mournful train? It was so that

Scipio, the representative of Rome triumphant, reflected and feared, when sitting amidst the ruins of Carthage he remembered Troy, and contemplated Italy. With a prophetic eye, he saw the terrible example, and wept at the prospect of a more prodigious ruin.[14] Will another age behold another Rome perish, and see the empires of the west again a prey to athletic destroyers? Is there a conservative principle which will neutralise the influence of wealth and luxury, and preserve the virtues of primitive times? True, Rome became magnificent by conquest; her capitol was rich with Grecian spoils; her labour was performed by slaves; her pleasures were the bloodshed of the amphitheatre; her heroes at length were but hirelings. The disgusting egotism of her nobles, and the vices of her people, distained her soil and shook her glory to the dust.

But whatever may be the fate of nations now most adorned with genius, art has received from the graver's hand the pledge of immortality. Never again, until books shall perish, can the power of reproduction be lost: commerce will diffuse her dominion beyond the reach of imperial devastation. Perhaps Australia has in reserve her day of opulence, and will open her bosom to receive the fugitives.

But it is not to art, at least in its most luxurious form, that the people of these lands will look for prosperity. While with a liberal discrimination they prize the modest embellishments of life, they need not envy the gilded couch of decaying nations. The vigorous intellect, the robust constitution, and the industrious habits of her children will be the best presages that their country shall be great. The plough — not the pencil — must be the crest of infant empires.

Such indeed are the ornaments we covet for our homes — chiefly freedom! Long may England be permitted to exhibit the graces of art embossed on her shield — never glittering on her chains. It is for her freedom, not her wealth, we remember her with admiration. If that survives, she may be fresh and lovely as in days of yore; as when Addison[15] sung what crowds of patriots have repeated, and we may hope hereafter to appropriate:—

Others with towering piles may fill the sight,
And in their proud, aspiring domes delight;
A warmer hue to the cold canvas give,
And teach the animated rock to live.
'Tis LIBERTY that crowns Britannia's isle,
And makes her barren rocks, and her bleak hills to smile.

> [Sections from a lecture by John West delivered at the
> Launceston Mechanics' Institute in 1848]

NOTES—WEST

1 The art exhibition was held in the Cornwall Assembly Rooms, Launceston, in January 1848. John Glover was among the exhibitors. The result of the exhibition was a deficit of 5s 9d.

2 Probably John Headlam (*c.* 1776-1843) who arrived at Hobart on the *Skelton*, 27 November 1820, and conducted a boarding and day school at Hobart until 1823, when he removed to a 700-acre grant on the Macquarie River, which he called 'Egglestone'. He later purchased 'Lomont' on the Salt Pan Plains. During his time in Hobart he also acted as an advocate in the Lieutenant Governor's Court. He died on his property on 11 March 1843.

3 Most probably 'Remarks on the Probable Origin and Antiquity of the Aboriginal Natives of New South Wales. Deduced from certain of their customs, superstitions, and existing caves and drawings, in connection with those of the nations of antiquity.' By a colonial Magistrate. Melbourne. 1846. The author was probably William Hull, see J. A. Ferguson, *Bibliography of Australia*, Sydney, 1955, iv, 1846-1850.

4 i.e. William Robertson (1721-93) the Scottish historian whose *History of America* (1777), Book IV, discusses the condition of life, character and attainments of the American Indians. West's summary of Roberton's views however, appears to be at fault, since it was not the Spaniards, but the systematic philosophers, Rousseau particularly who, in his view, exaggerated the attainments of the Indians.

5 See his *Analysis of Beauty* (ed. Burke) London, 1955.

6 i.e. John Martin (1789-1854) see p. 75, n. 8.

7 i.e. Michelangelo Buonarotti (1475-1564), the renowned Italian sculptor, painter, architect and poet.

8 The *Aeneid*, Book I, 11, 453-493.

9 *Psalms* 107, 24.

10 Lord Byron, *Childe Harold's Pilgrimage*, Stanza 183.

11 i.e. Jean Jacques Rousseau (1712-78) a native of Geneva, who in his *Essay on the Origins of Inequality among Men* (1754) argued that man was happier in a 'state of nature' than when living in societies corrupted by man's arts and artfulness.

12 'the anchorite': literally a person who retired into solitude (in medieval times usually a cell adjacent to a religious community) to live a contemplative and religious life. They regarded the arts and most other things as temptations and diversions from personal sanctity.

13 The ultimate source of West's story is Diogenes Laertius, vi, 26 (*vita Diogenes*).

14 The reference is to Aemilianus Africanus Numantinus Scipio (185-129 B.C.) the famous Roman commander who destroyed Carthage in 146 B.C. The story is told in *Polybius*, Book 38, Ch. 21 and beginning of Ch. 22; and *Appian*, Pun., 132.

15 West appears to be quoting Addison from memory: the original reads:
'Tis Liberty that crowns Britannia's isle
And makes her barren rocks and her bleak mountain's smile.
Others with tow'ring piles may please the sight
And in their proud aspiring domes delight:
A nicer touch to the stretch'd canvass give
Or teach their animated rocks to live.'

Benjamin Duterrau (1767–1851)

Benjamin Duterrau was born in London, his parents being of French descent. He was apprenticed to an engraver but developed an aptitude for painting and exhibited six portraits at the Royal Academy between 1817 and 1823, and three genre paintings at the British Institute. At the age of sixty-five he emigrated to Van Diemen's Land to take up a position as a drawing master and music teacher but the position was filled before he arrived in Hobart. Here Duterrau set up a studio in Campbell Street, exhibited paintings brought from London and sought commissions for portraits. He began lecturing at the Hobart Mechanics' Institute on 16 July 1833 on the importance of cultivating the Fine Arts in the development of colonial society, the same theme which he chose for the lecture, extracts of which are printed below.

In 1833 Duterrau painted a series of portraits of Tasmanian Aboriginals brought to Hobart by G. A. Robinson and in 1836 modelled the head of Robinson and twelve Aboriginals in bas-relief. He also made etchings (1835-36) of Aboriginals and painted topographical views of Hobart.

In the extract from his 1849 lecture, printed below, Duterrau refers to Raphael's famous fresco painting 'The School of Athens' in the Stanza della Segnatura (the seat of the ecclesiastical tribunal) in the Vatican Rome. The painting depicts the philosophers of antiquity gathered about the two central figures of Plato (the philosopher of the spirit who points toward Heaven) and Aristotle (the philosopher of the material world who points to the earth). As a whole the painting symbolizes the rational search for Truth through philosophy and science, and forms one of a pair with Raphael's *Disputa* in which the supreme Truth is proclaimed, again in two ways: in heaven, in a celestial vision of the Church Triumphant, and on earth by the Church Militant — the fathers, doctors, saints, popes and faithful.

Duterrau is concerned, however, not so much with the Christian symbolism of Raphael's painting as with the original character of Plato's Academy in Athens as the first home of philosophical education devoted to the distinterested pursuit of knowledge. By means of a comparison which we might call brave and visionary, or absurd and ludicrous, according to our own point of view, Duterrau compares Plato's Academy and Raphael's Christian interpretation of it to the Hobart Mechanics' Institute, which he claims was established for a similar purpose '. . . the school of Hobart Town may do as much in proportion for our little happy community, as the School of Athens has done for the world'.

Duterrau informs us that he had seen and studied the copy of the School of Athens which in the early nineteenth century was in the possession of the Bodleian Library, Oxford, and was then believed to be painted by Giulio Romano, Raphael's most famous pupil. It is now considered to be an eighteenth century copy. Duterrau had also read the pamphlet published in Oxford in several editions, entitled 'The History of the Celebrated Painting in the Picture Gallery, Oxford; called "The School of Athens" supposed to be painted by Giulio Romano', for he begins his commentary on the painting, as does the author of the pamphlet, by justifying Raphael's contravention of the Aristotelian unities of time, place and action; and in some other respects he follows, though not closely, the explanation of the painting given in the pamphlet.

Duterrau's lecture provides us with contemporary evidence of the influence of the Greek Revival upon the taste of the small, but cultivated, colonial society of Van Diemen's Land, a style that was expressed in Tasmania most notably by James Blackburn in his Lady Franklin Museum (1842-43), and in the Public Offices, Hobart (1842-43).

[THE SCHOOL OF ATHENS, AS IT ASSIMILATES
WITH THE MECHANICS' INSTITUTION]

LADIES AND GENTLEMEN — The subject of the Lecture, is the School of Athens (which is nothing more than one single picture), but as it assimilates with the Mechanics' Institute, an explanation of it we hope will prove interesting.

I regret having to observe that lectures on the subject of painting have not been interesting, which proves a supineness, in this part of the world, respecting the fine arts, *owing* very much to that false and pitiful phrase — *The Infancy of the Colony.* Consequently I have not confined myself to that subject of late, but have introduced some diversity.

When I look round and see many notaries to Art and Science, with whom at present the Lecture Hall with honour abounds, it seems that babbling about the infancy of the colony should be treated with contempt.

That poor pitiful suterfuge [*sic*] must not be hawked about till the colony has arrived at a mature age, and allowed wantonly to impede the charming effect of civilization; it is time to have done with such paltry means and adhere to common sense; then we shall wash away foul barbarism, which obtrudes itself more or less, according to the amount of refinement, which is always beautifully implanted in the human breast by the gentle hand of valuable knowledge.

The absurdity of the phrase is now proved by this assemblage of a very respectable auditory, who are not to be lulled into a stupor by any fictitious representation.

The lecture I shall deliver this evening is not on painting, but on the advantage of arts and sciences in general, as they tend to our happiness — our plan of conduct — and our search of truth.

The School of Athens, which I shall describe (not only as a picture), but because it bears a great similitude with all institutions established for the promulgation of useful and ornamental knowledge.

Then, again, the similitude it bears to this our Lecture Hall, besides being denominated the School of Athens, it has been denominated the Temple of Philosophy. May not this Lecture Hall be deemed the Temple of Philosophy? Have not subjects been introduced of a nature sufficiently exalted to bear a comparison with the ancient Temple of Philosophy.

I humbly submit, that as a question for discussion, trusting to the event, our business is, to point out the advantages that may accrue from this — our Temple of Philosophy.

In the first place, it must be allowed that the fine arts form a considerable branch of civilization, therefore, the more they are studied the more the mind is furnished with new and good ideas both of art and nature: then follows the transcendent pleasure of transmitting those ideas to others, and, as in proportion, one branch of knowledge may add to that pleasure — how much that pleasure must be enhanced by combining a knowledge of various arts and sciences as they are set forth in this Institution . . .

I have engaged to describe the picture as regards mere rule, which is generally attended to in the contriving of most pictures — that of introducing one subject, one time, and one place; but according to that rule, the source and progress of philosophy from age to age, and by such elevated powers as were not always contemporary could not be accomplished. Rafaello, therefore, has set aside common rule to satisfy the imagination when it rises and floats on the regions of true grandeur.

As too much apology cannot be made for setting aside established rule, I beg leave to make a short digression in order to reconcile us to the deviation — it may pave the way in pursuing our course and we shall travel smoothly.

Let it be noticed, that we have no objection to see the first budding of a tender plant represented by the pencil, and likewise to see the same plant depicted at the full growth and ripeness, and though they may be delineated on the same sheet of paper,[1] we shall not confuse the time of budding with the time that brings the plant to maturity and ripeness, this will help to reconcile us to the deviation from common rule and lead to an admiration of a supposed noble Temple at Athens, where Socrates, and Plato were born; although some others who were not born at Athens are exhibited here, namely — Pythagoras and Archimedes were not born at Athens, yet, as highly illustrious characters, demand a place in this renowned company of philosophers.

This celebrated picture, called the School of Athens, which is at Oxford University,[2] where I have spent much time in studying it and examining every minute part, was painted by Julio Romano from the original picture in the Vatican at Rome, which was painted by Rafaelle.

The more I bring this grand work to my mind, the more it appears to be a subject that should be spoken of in this room, when we consider that this School of Hobart Town was instituted to disseminate useful knowledge,[3] and in that point of view closely resembles the School of Athens.[4]

The Temple of Philosophy, as this picture is sometimes called, represents the most illustrious schools of philosophy, distinguished by their rendering the study of nature subservient to moral precept; they taught that nothing was useful but what was honourable — that the honourable was inseparable from justice, and that justice was the support of all good order and felicity; therefore, the Epecurean[5] and all the Atheistic and licentious sects are excluded.

It represents a record of transactions, which embrace several ages, and are all brought together in one magnificent building.

Rafaelle has placed the schools in very regular order. The school of Pythagoras being the most ancient is on the foreground, for being the first in point of time, should be the first in point of sight. The next, immediately behind, is the school of Socrates. The next is the school of Plato, the most eminent of all the disciples of Socrates; then follows the school of Aristotle, the most illustrious of the disciples of Plato.

These few philosophers are sufficient to shew the purport of the picture.

The next we find, and in good order placed, is the mathematical school, which proves the valuable connection of that school with all the others.

Two figures may be discerned — one holding a terrestrial, and the other a celestial globe — which point out the value of the mathematics, as concerns geography and astronomy.

Rafaelle has adopted a plan worthy of observation, he has totally excluded those philosophers that should be regarded with execration, he has brought in none but original investigators of truth, whose instructions made great impressions on those who heard them.

Socrates, Plato, and Aristotle are names that must recall great ideas and engage most noble sentiments in the enlightened and well disposed mind.

The great ideas and noble sentiments which Alcibiades[6] possessed were gathered from the philosophical wisdom of Socrates, therefore may have been learnt in the school of Athens; this leads us to contemplate the benefits which must arise from this school of Hobart Town.

The lectures are strenuously bound to moral precept, while teaching moral and natural philosophy, we firmly believe that many who attend the lectures here are equal in noble character to Alcibiades, and equally prompt in gaining wisdom; to doubt it, would be to cast a libel on a respectable audience. Let us do everything that will increase the number of hearers, and the blessing of useful knowledge will shew itself in proportion.

Besides the celebrated Alcibiades being made conspicuous in this picture, a young Prince may be observed holding the terrestrial globe in his hands, to shew that geography should be studied by Princes to assist them in the extension of commerce and civilizing the barbarous parts of the world . . .

When this picture, the School of Athens, was painted, America was a late discovery, which recommended the study of Science so necessary to a complete knowledge of navigation.

It was not the happy increase of Arts and Sciences (which in those days was beginning to spread) that lead to the abuses made in valuable discoveries, but the great deficiency of useful knowledge; 'tis useful knowledge alone, which can lessen the amount of crime, and thereby renders the attainment of it invaluable.

We will, as we go on, take a view of the pleasant means that naturally must incite an emulation while pursuing an enquiry into those points which we generally consider elevate the mental character of man.

My observations, I humbly submit to an audience ever ready to promote arts and sciences.

The original picture by Rafaelle being in the Vatican at Rome, may have promoted much emulation in the study of philosophy in that quarter.

The copy of the picture by Julio Romano, is capable of producing the same effect at Oxford.

And we have good reason to believe that a beneficial result would accrue, if a print from the same subject could be seen in some conspicuous part of the Mechanics' Institute, where free access could be allowed to its members . . .

There is a caution necessary to be taken in the development of the peculiar management displayed by Rafaelle, particularly where he represents Plato very young, as a scholar, to Socrates, and in another part of the picture old, and the master of scholars; the circumstance would certainly appear absurd if not viewed in chronological order, that is why I mentioned the first budding of a plant, and its time of maturity being drawn together, and, though on the same paper, yet they denote progression. Such humble means may help us to a full understanding of the picture.

And from that one step, let us take another step of great importance, which is to fully comprehend that the Mechanics' Institution is a very amiable forerunner of civilization, where all knowledge worthy of attainment is set forth in an honourable manner; and the School of Hobart Town may do as much in proportion for our little happy community, as the School of Athens has done for the wide world . . .

Let us now take a general view of the valuable result that a Temple of universal instruction leads to in every department where mental power is required.

The best architects in the world were among the Greeks; they added beauty to magnificence, and eloquence to grandeur — in short, they raised the first monuments of good taste.

Phidias, the Athenian, who lived between four and five hundred years before the Christian era, was the first sculptor whose works have been immortal.

I must here remark that the immortal perfection in the works of Phidias and Cleomenes[7] was not the result of imagination or any thing so flighty, for imagination would only expose to ridicule its own sterility, in presuming to amend any masterpiece in the Creation.

All the beauties in the Venus de Medicis, and the Apollo of

Belvidere [*sic*] were borrowed from nature — the wisdom of nature is the only source from which such excellence could be derived.

If one model in the performance of their work did not possess all the parts they required, they would study 10 or 20, or any number of models rather than venture to assert what was not authorised by the Creator.

To view such wonderful works in any other light, would be to allow that, human puny power would go a step higher than sacred Divine power.

Zeuxis,[8] during the same age, discovered the power of the pencil, and all the magic art of painting.

Composition, by the beauty of cadence and harmony, reached perfection in the Greek language, at that period of time; but it was Demosthenes who improved its full force and power.

It was not only in the Fine Arts that the Greeks excelled, but in every species of Philosophy, which was cultivated with the same success. Solon and Lycurgus established wise laws in Greece.

We must approach their merit as near as we can. That sculptor, has but a narrow soul who would give up his favourite art, because he cannot rival Phidias — he is the greatest man (in his own time) whose mental productions pronounce that he is nearest to perfection.

It is very true that many centuries of time have taught us numberless valuable secrets in the wisdom of nature, which those philosophers were unacquainted with; yet, men of learning and genius have been glad to adopt their turn of thinking and manner of expression.

It will be necessary to make a division in the different great characters thus depicted. That is to say, we will name those that Rafaelle has made it certain are in the picture — namely, Pythagoras, Socrates, Plato, Aristotle, Zenophon, Alcibiades.

Now we will mention a few that conjecture tells us who they are, for Rafaelle did not leave a catalogue of all he represented. They are — Zoroaster, Archimedes, Euclid, Diogenes, Zeno, Hippocrates.

Such characters may be in the picture, but the identity of persons is only supposed.

As we arrive at a full understanding of the picture, we must keep in mind a very material circumstance, which is that painting, like poetry, is not confined to strict historical truth — a plausible or probable appearance is sufficient, and frequently gives great force to the effect . . .

Next to Pythagoras we ascend to the school of Socrates. The first figure that strikes the eye, is a young man remarkably handsome, in a rich military dress, with a helmet on his head . . . This is the celebrated Alcibiades . . .

Socrates is near Alcibiades and is directing his discourse to him, the attitude and gesture of Socrates in his discourse seems suitable to exact reasoning on subjects, and bringing the person step by step to acknowledge the truth — he spreads his left hand open, with the palm upwards, and takes hold of the fore-finger of his left hand with the fore-finger and thumb of his right hand, which gives the appearance of intense thinking.

We next come to the school of Plato, who stands in the open air, with his disciples round about him. There we see Aristotle.

We now come to the last school of universal philosophy. The school of Aristotle.

The Painter has given him his book of Ethics, which he holds in his left hand, and his right hand is spread out agreeing with his calm persuasive eloquence.

There are four figures employed in learning mathematics. The master, who is teaching them is delineating a scheme on a slate, with his compasses. Some appear joyous and satisfied with understanding the scheme clearly, others very anxiously investigating the subject profoundly, while others are writing, with their slates or boards to show the master what they had been doing.

Civilization is increasing daily in Van Diemen's Land, and that is made apparent by the number of subscribers to the Art Union, who are not deaf to the calls that the Fine Arts are making upon those who are endowed with clear and bright faculties, suitable for the enjoyment of the highest degree of mental attainment. The number of subscribers in Hobart Town and its vicinity were ninety persons in the year 1848, and are still increasing, which proves how many there are willing to promote refinement, while others are misled by specious impediments put in their way by low-minded people, who are apt to think themslves very cunning, and would keep the colony in swaddling cloths, and talk of infancy, for forty or fifty years, as an *excuse* for the enjoyment of *brutality,* which to them is infinite delight. Such vermin are execrable.

Together with the happiness such auspicious views afford us, we may expect that the Mechanics' Institute (by liberal support) will be actively instrumental in conveying every noble, useful and enviable attainment that raises the mental character to its highest order of human perfection . . .

The object of the Mechanics' Institute is to increase the number of enlightened characters, which will not only lessen the number of loose and wanton characters, but will eventually sink them into nothingness. Shame can do much. 'Tis shame that makes a barbarous savage turn to be a good Christian, when the difference is clearly pointed out to him. The Missionary duty has proved that good effect completely.

Many who have changed from vicious habits, and cling to virtue, are well pleased with their new life, which is an ineffable proof that virtue is happiness.

I have now come to the goal I wished to arrive at, which is the opportunity of urging an unabating warmth in the zeal necessary for the acquirement of what is truly useful, by setting forth what has been done in former days, and may be done again, by rallying the same good spirit, which the comparisons we have made this evening may probably bring about and forcibly recommend.

As the School of Athens has proved much in the great world, so may the school of Hobart Town do much in the little world where our happy community subsist, by honest industry and cheerful contentment.

With such a pleasing prospect before us, I beg leave to conclude.

[Sections from a lecture by Benjamin Duterrau delivered at the Hobart Town Mechanics' Institute on Friday 29 June 1899]

NOTES—DUTERRAU

1 Duterrau is referring to the practice among botanical illustrators to depict on one page various sections of a plant, root, bud, blossom, and foliage at various stages of its growth in one page—a neat comparison considering the general interest in botany which was a cultural manifestation of the time.

2 It was presented to the Bodleian Library by Sir Francis Page in 1804, and transferred to the Ashmolean Museum, probably between 1845 and 1847, where it now is.

3 The Hobart Mechanics' Institute, the oldest in Australia, was established in 1827, only a few years after George Birkbeck had established the first Mechanics' Institute in Glasgow in 1823.

4 The comparison is not as far-fetched as it sounds. Both Plato's Academy and the Hobart Mechanics' Institute were modest enough: Plato's a park in Athens where he and his pupils foregathered; the Hobart Institute met in a small Georgian building which was built in 1827, and doubled as a Wesleyan Hall and Mechanics' Institute almost from the time of its completion. Plato would certainly have recognized the style of the Greek Revival facade which was probably added during the extensions of 1845. (*Hobart Courier*, 7 February 1846). But there was, of course, a considerable difference in quality between the originality of mind which Plato and his

pupils displayed and the educational aspirations of the 'philosophical' citizens of Hobart Town.

5 i.e. the followers of Epicurus (341-270 B.C.), the Greek philosopher who held that the senses provide the sole criteria of truth, and that pleasure was the natural goal of human conduct. Since he denied immortality he has been much reviled by theologians.

6 Alcibiades (450-404), the mercurial and devious general of the Athenians. The parallel is an unfortunate one, however, since Alcibiades completely lacked moral scruples.

7 Cleomenes, the Greek Sculptor described by Pliny the Elder (XXXVI. 33) as excelling in the human form. Reynolds refers to Cleomenes in his translation of de Piles, *Parallel between Poetry and Painting*. The Venus de Medici was attributed to Cleomenes on the strength of an inscription on the base which is now believed to be of seventeenth-century origin.

8 Zeuxis, who lived in the latter part of the fifth century B.C. was one of the most famous painters of ancient Greece, but none of his original paintings have survived.

Conrad Martens (1801–78)

Conrad Martens, born in London, was the son of a Hamburg merchant who had been appointed Austrian Consul in London, and whose three sons were painters. Conrad studied drawing and water-colour painting under Copley Fielding, who also taught John Ruskin, and was the most popular teacher of his day. After the father's death Martens' family moved to Exeter from whence Conrad painted many Devonshire landscapes.

In 1832 Martens accepted an offer of a voyage to India, but whilst at Rio obtained the position of artist on H.M.S. *Beagle*, when Augustus Earle left the expedition due to ill health. On the *Beagle*, Martens made a lasting friend of its naturalist, Charles Darwin. Martens left the ship at Valparaiso in October 1834, and later sailed for Tahiti, where he spent some time sketching, before sailing on to New Zealand in March 1835. Six weeks later he arrived in Sydney where he remained for the rest of his life.

During his first months in New South Wales Martens travelled widely in the Illawarra, the Blue Mountains and Broken Bay. He settled in Cumberland Street, in the Rocks area of Sydney, and opened a studio in Pitt Street where he gave lessons in drawing and painting. In 1837 he married Jane Carter, the daughter of William Carter, who later became Master in Equity and Registrar of the Supreme Court. In 1844 he built himself a house at St Leonards on the north shore of Sydney Harbour and settled there with his wife and daughters, Rebecca (born 1838) and Elizabeth (born 1839).

During the 1840s, when the colonial economy was depressed, Martens produced a lithographic view of Sydney from the North Shore, which was hand-coloured and sold for a guinea. In 1850 he issued *Sketches in the Environs of Sydney,* consisting of twenty lithographs in five parts. He also continued to paint water-colour paintings of the houses and villas scattered about Sydney Harbour or upon country holdings. For the latter he sometimes travelled far afield, and in 1851 made an extensive tour through the Darling Downs. At the age of sixty-two Martens obtained, by the help of his friend Alexander Berry, the post of Parliamentary Librarian in the New South Wales Parliament. He continued to paint, however, and during the later years of his life developed an interest in astronomy. He died in 1878 and was buried at St Thomas's Church, North Sydney, where the rest of his family were also buried. The font in the church was the work of Martens.

On 21 July 1856 Martens delivered a lecture on landscape painting, accompanied by illustrations, at the Australian Library to members of a recently-formed club of amateur painters. The manuscript of the lecture is printed below in full.

[A LECTURE UPON LANDSCAPE PAINTING]

July 21, 1856

Gentlemen,

In accordance with the rules of the Club, I have now the honor of addressing you upon the subject of Landscape Painting. But before I proceed, allow me to bear testimony to the great progress which has already been made by some of its members; and I trust that the occasion which has now brought us together may be the means of advancing you still farther in that *delightful but difficult Art.*

I must beg leave also to say that I feel much flattered by so great an addition to my audience, and only hope that if the inducement has been *instruction* rather than *mere amusement* they also will not find themselves disappointed. It cannot however be expected that I shall have anything very new to say upon the *general principals* [*sic*] of art. Yet as those precepts and maxims which do not immediately bear upon our practice are apt to be forgotten, or but lightly regarded, it is highly necessary from time to time as we advance in our practice that they should be *repeated.*

Presuming therefore on this occasion that most of my hearers are devoting more or less of their time to the practice of the art, I shall endeavour to keep that object in view and shall do so with more confidence, being able to refer to notes which I have made relative to my own practice during a period of more than thirty years.

Painting would be worthy of study were it only for the increased perception and enjoyment of the beauties of nature which is sure to arrive from it, but this is only one of its many recommendations. It is a social art, and can only thrive amidst social intercourse, and while congratulating you and myself also upon the formation of this society, I shall shew how essentially this is the case, for by attending to the remarks of others, we get not only new ideas but that also which is of the *utmost importance* a *fresh eye* to our work. The eye becomes unable to appreciate the exact force of a color upon which, in the *execution* of a *picture,* it has long dwelt; and will frequently from the same cause lose its power of detecting awkwardness in form and composition; and then it is that our friends' eyes will be so useful in bringing us back to the right use of our own; without which we shall frequently waste both time and labor.

Note. This assertion which I have not made without due consideration, I am well aware requires explanation, but as it would lead me far into the subject of color, I must beg to reserve for a future occasion —

Burnett[1] and I am backed [*sic*]   I can add however from high authority by way of *consolation,* that the eye which is soonest put out in this way is the most sensitive to a nice distinction of color, and will, all other things equal, *assuredly make* the best painter.

And here I cannot but express my perfect conviction of the many and great disadvantages under which all labor who aspire to art in this distant country for it is through the *medium* of *art only* that we *learn to see nature correctly.* To the unpractised eye, a green leaf is a green leaf and nothing more, and a white flower is but a white flower — whereas the leaf may have upon its polished surface, all the colors of the rainbow, and the white flower but one single spot of white upon it. — How much more difficult then must it be to judge of the *true color* of *familiar* objects *seen through* the *intervention* of *atmosphere,* a faculty of *all others* the *most* to be *desired* by a landscape painter.

Note. Knowing *what to do* in painting may be compared to knowing what *to say* in writing — and the mere dexterity in the use of the pencil, to that of the pen. — A person may write a very learned and elegant letter in a very indifferent hand, and a very foolish and nonsensical one, may be a beautiful specimen of penmanship.

In its proper place I think I shall be able to shew, how, in the absence of others of a similar taste we may, by certain rules, sit in judgment upon ourselves and arrive at right conclusions. I shall however in this discourse mainly endeavour to describe in what manner the *head* as well as the *hand,* is to be *employed* in painting a picture; the *mental operation* being by far the most important.

Only let us know what to do, and we shall soon find some way or another of doing it:—

The *sketch* then being the first part of the business; and as the term is frequently misapplied, let us clearly understand its nature, and how it differs from a *study*.

Now the sketch should be slight as it is for the purpose only of giving a general idea of the subject to be painted, and the beginning of a work is not the time for details. It may be made in pencil only, in order to shew how the forms will combine, or it may be made in black and white for the purpose of arranging the light and shade, or, it may be just blotted down in color, as a guide to *that* important part of the picture, or lastly it may be composed of all together but on too small a scale to define objects or to enter into any details. —

The principal difficulty in sketching with the pencil out of doors, is to avoid confusion, and at the same time to get your paper full of forms. This can only be done by different degrees of force of outline according to the distances of the principal masses, and if these are got in first with a firm and unbroken line, all that is included by them will keep its place; a much greater variety of distances can be thus obtained than would at first be imagined. A common pencil will produce in good hands at least four different degrees of strength, *viz*: a light clear but thin line, the same with a broader point, then a second degree of pressure with its sharp and soft line.

What is termed Hatching, should be avoided as much as possible, in a *sketch*. Rapidity is very desirable and we all know that *Hatching is a slow process.*

To have this command of the pencil however it must be held with a *firm* grasp and on *no account be allowed to turn in the fingers* except for the express purpose of altering the touch. You will thus always have a face as it were to the lead, as well as the power to give by the least turn of it a sharper line than can be obtained by the most careful scraping. One pencil thus managed will generally be sufficient and the sketch will have a better appearance than if more are used.

This then I submit is the proper definition of a sketch —

The *means* to *an end.*

Now, a drawing on the spot — called by the contradictory term 'a finished sketch' — having in fact no further object than a topographical illustration is another thing, of which we have some fine examples in Roberts' 'Sketches in the Holy Land',[2] in doing which it may be supposed that in most cases he had no other purpose in view. However, the 'Liber Studiorum' of Turner[3] is I should say a book *to be studied* with the *greatest advantage.* Here will be found *breadth, grandeur,* and a total absence of all petty details and yet notwithstanding these high qualities it is from the general simplicity of the subjects, particularly well suited for, and easily to be understood by, the young student.

Now a *study* on the other hand must be made with *all possible care,* or it is useless; it is not done for any other purpose than that of obtaining a more perfect knowledge of certain *objects* (of their character; whether of form, color, or texture) *of which a picture is composed.* It tells no story, it appeals not to the feelings, it is close matter of fact (observe I confine myself to Claxton[4] cast his *landscape*) and for obtaining which the draperies and then daguerreotype apparatus will often be found daguerreotyped them. exceedingly useful. It consists only of *parts* such as *trees, rocks, foliage, water, clouds,* and *sky* at different times of day, in short whatever objects enter into the composition of a picture. All these should be done with the *highest possible finish,* and much *patient drugery* [*sic*] *is required.* But this *is not* (This kind of practice *a picture,* otherwise than in a very *confined* is above all the most *sense* of *the word.* (Practice is above all the necessary for *the student*). most necessary for *the student.*)

Sir Joshua Reynolds says, 'The highest *finish is labor in vain',*[5] (that is to say, it will not make a picture) 'unless there is at the properly so *called* for all same time preserved a *breadth* of *light and* these terms have generally *shade'.* This breadth of light and shade the same meaning then it would seem is the making of the picture; all the others are but studies and sketches.

Now let us go a little further into this matter of light and shade, or breadth, or chiaro scuro as it is called and, if we can understand *that thoroughly* and put it in *practice,* we shall go very far beyond the *mere immitator* [*sic*], he who with the least *feeling will succeed the best.* Now breadth is an *extension,* either of light or of shade, *over and above* that which is required for giving objects their *proper* form or roundness. It is the art of uniting light objects, or dark objects together, so as to form masses of either, — the masses themselves also taking agreeable forms, so that the picture when seen at such a distance that the subject is not intelligible shall yet have an agreeable effect upon the eye.

If on the other hand the picture has not this quality, it will, when seen near, be rather a representation of certain objects, separate and complete in themselves, but quite independent of each other, and the higher they are finished the more complete will this be. Thus each will be contending for observation, and each perhaps admired in turn — while at a distance, the appearance will be that of a confused mixture of lights and darks, without principal, subordination, or harmony.

Now some one perhaps would like to put the question, Has nature this breadth? Then why not copy it! I answer, so she has, and we do copy it as near as our means will allow, but let me tell you that if you hope to *succeed* (that is, in producing breadth), you must drop the aforesaid high finish and detail. Only let the uninstructed aspirants to *the art* attempt an open daylight scene, and then the closer his attempts at imitation, and the more patient drugery he bestows, the greater will be his disappointment and his failure; for this simple reason, that by closely copying shade after shade, and tint after tint, in their different and almost numberless gradations, he will have exhausted the whole strength of his palette long before the completion of his work. The brightness of light, and the depth of shade, will be left out, and his work *as a picture* will be weak, vapid, and unsatisfactory. *Herein then* lies in a great measure the *art* of *landscape painting,* not in that of imitating individual objects, but the art of imitating an effect which nature has produced with means far beyond anything *we* have at command. It is true that in order to represent the scene before us we must imitate the objects of which it is composed; but the excellence of the picture will by no means depend upon the care with which these are painted. Observe, I am not speaking of 'still life', or a picture representing bread and cheese, or a piece of bacon, but I would direct your attention to pictures by such men as Danby,[6] Turner, Stanfield,[7] Cox,[8] Cattermole[9] and Copley Fielding.[10] Of Cox above all for his wonderful faithfulness in color, form, and texture, accompanied by what might be termed a contempt for all petty detail and *finish* as that word is usually

allowing him all skill in copying

H

understood. The sight of such works as these must give rise to feelings far above, and very different from, what we should experience by that of a *mackerel upon a deal board*,[11] even though we might fancy we could take it up with our fingers.

Professor Hart R.A.[12] in one of his lectures delivered at the Royal Academy this year, says, 'Because an essential element in painting is *imitation,* the painter's art has by many been mis-apprehended, and narrowed down into one in which imitation is at once the means and the end.'

Now if this were the case I, for one would never venture to shew pictures with a *china man*, for they are allowed to be the best hands at imitation in the world.

But once more let us just refresh our memories with what Sir Joshua Reynolds says. In one of his discourses he says, 'If our judgment is to be directed by narrow, vulgar, untaught, or rather *illtaught, reason,* we must prefer a portrait by Denner[13] or any other high finisher, to those of Titian[14] or Vandyke,[15] (observe he applies the principal to portrait painters also) and a landscape by Vanderheyden[16] to those of Titian or Rubens[17] for they are certainly more exact representations. If we suppose (he continues) a view of nature represented with *all the truth* of the *Camera Obscura*,[18] and the same scene represented by a great artist how little and mean will the one appear in comparison with the other.'[19]

Again he says, 'Amongst the painters and the writers on painting, there is one maxim universally admitted and continually inculcated: *Imitate nature,* is the invariable rule; but I know none who have explained in what way this is to be understood. The consequence is that every body takes it in the most simple and obvious sense . . . It may appear strange perhaps to hear this sense of the rule disputed, but it must be seen that if the excellence of a picture consists only in this kind of imitation, *painting must lose its rank* and be no longer considered a liberal art, and sister to poetry, this imitation being merely mechanical, in which the *slowest intellect* is always *sure to succeed the best,* for the painter of genius cannot stoop to drudgery in which the understanding has no part, and what pretence has the art to claim kindred with poetry, but by its powers over the imagination?

'To this power the painter of genius directs *his* aim; in this sense *he* studies nature, and often arrives at his end, even by being *unnatural* in the *confined* sense of the word.'[20]

The painter then imitates nature in the main by an abbreviation as it were of what is before him. He takes the top and the bottom, the two extremes, as strong as his palette will give him, and many of those numberless middle tones, which he cannot afford to put in, he very wisely leaves out. Now if along with this mode of treatment a judicious *selection* of nature's effects be made, success will follow and that often beyond expectation. As a guide to such selections, then, and a proper treatment of them, I should recommend to those who are seeking assistance in this part of the art a few simple rules.

First. In choosing your subject, take care that there is some principal object on which to concentrate your effect, and attract attention, and let the highest light and the largest mass of dark assist each other at this *point by their contrast.* If however this mass of dark be at any considerable distance from the foreground it must not contain or receive the very strongest touches of dark, otherwise its distance will not be preserved, for the intervention *Rule*   of atmosphere always lightens the darks, altho it does not necessarily reduce the brilliancy of the lights. The *strongest touches* of *dark must always* therefore be reserved for the foreground *even tho it be a light one.* The effect of air in your picture must on no account be lost sight of, and it is upon the proper observance of this very simple and well known rule that this effect mainly depends.

Secondly. I venture strongly to recommend that this mass of dark be detached more or less from the side of the picture and not to form a part of the frame, for in that case it would lose much of its force; but if on the contrary, it is surrounded by middle tint at those parts where the high light does not come in contact with it, it will have its utmost forms and effect. — See *Stanfield.*

'Wreckers'. Stanfield.

As far then as an engraving will permit — this 'Of Wreckers off Fort Rouge,' after Stanfield, is *an apt illustration of what I have advanced.* I say, as far as an engraving will permit, because in a painting we can produce relief by opposition of color alone, without any alteration in the amount of Light and Shade. But without color, that is to say, in black and white only, *that alteration of tone must take place,* and thus in a greater or less degree the breadth will be disturbed.

Another useful hint may be given on the selection of a subject, and that is to place yourself in such a position that much of the middle distance may be hidden, and some considerable portion of your foreground thus brought into *immediate opposition to the extreme distance.*

If a rule is to be given for the quantity to be taken in, 55 deg. of the circle is the most that should be included from left to right of the subject we are about to sketch; this can always be found with sufficient accuracy by holding up the paper before your eyes at a distance equal to the width of it. (*Note.* This I need scarcely say will give the same *angle, whatever may be the* dimensions of the paper.) This attention to the quantity of subject taken in, is of far greater consequence than at first might be imagined. A smaller angle may be taken with perfect propriety and great advantage will sometimes be derived from so doing, but by taking into your picture *more* than can be conveniently seen without turning the head, everything will appear smaller than it really is, for it will naturally be supposed that all which is seen in the picture at one glance, can be so seen in nature, and every one looking at a picture *will so place himself as to do so.*

This then will convey an impression the very opposite to space and grandeur, a quality much to be desired, especially in mountain scenery. — Taking now the converse of what I have just said, namely, a smaller angle, say 40 deg. for the extent of the picture; grandeur and magnitude will be the result, without in the least departing from the truth, for we are only then drawing things upon a larger scale; and I may here take the opportunity to add that this was one of the first practical lessons which I myself learnt by carefully comparing the drawings of Turner with the scenes which he represented. I am supposing, of course, that a proper amount of aerial perspective is maintained — and as the true appearance of a *distant* object depends much more upon this quality than upon mere drawing, it will be right in this place to take some notice of it.

For example, a distant mountain may be quite correctly drawn as to form, but if through want of aerial perspective it only appears to be 5 miles off when its true distance is *10* it will be recognized as the mountain, but robbed of its elevation by just one half.

In *most* instances therefore, if not *always*, I advise that distant mountains should be drawn higher than *strict linear* perspective would allow, because of the *impossibility* of giving their *full* amount of *aerial* perspective, and as the only means by which a correct idea of their magnitude can be given.

(*Note.* That the eye, when objects are seen perfectly clear, will sometimes return a wrong impression, can be proved in many instances, and as the subject before us presents a remarkable one, it may scarcely be considered a digression if I allude to it:—It is the diminution in magnitude and elevation of all distant objects when seen with the *eye inverted.*

This experiment can be best made by turning your head to the scene, stooping down and looking between your legs. Now that objects seen thus, are, as to *linear* perspective quite correct, can also be proved. (Of course I do not wish you to sketch in that position) but raise your head and up jump the mountains again. Now can there be a question as to which way they should be pointed. I think not, unless we adopt the fashion said to exist on the moon in Baron Munchausen's time[21]—that of carrying the head under the arm ---)

Respecting the horizontal line there is a rule generally insisted upon, which is, 'That it must never be placed at half the height of the picture because it would *divide it in two equal parts'*. Now if the horizontal line *must* necessarily divide the picture into two parts, it would I think be a matter of little moment whether these two parts were equal or unequal. I would however give the painter but little credit for good composition who allows his horizontal line to *cut the picture in two,* under any circumstances; moreover if in taking a subject from a considerable elevation, say the top of a mountain, we are to make the line above the middle of the picture, and if, on descending to the level plain below we are desired to have a low horizon, surely there must be some place by this same reasoning half way up where it would be right to make the line also between the two extremes, at which place it might probably turn out was the best point of view after all. The truth is that a proper management of light and shade will wholly prevent the eye from being in the least offended, even tho it should be half way up the picture. Objects may break it, clouds, or a diagonal line of shadow may effectually lead the eye in a different direction. Excepting therefore the single case of a much extended sea line, this rule need not in my opinion be insisted upon.

Rules are necessary as guides to beginners and plenty of them there are; but pictures painted according to a written receipt would I fear be no great things after all. Constable was asked where he intended to have his *brown trees,*[22] and another occasion, 'I see two of your lights Mr. Constable but where is the third?'

(The principal [*sic*] of the three lights is one upon which indeed Sir Joshua insists, but as it is certainly not founded upon nature I am at a loss to conceive where he got it from, unless it was from the Old Masters.)

There is a diagram in a book I have somewhere seen professing to teach the art, something like a gridiron, shewing where all the *principal objects of the picture are to be placed.*

The rule also which forbids one object from being placed over another is a guide for the purpose of keeping them at their proper relative distances, but if at the same time the upper object so placed (a boat sail for instance) is by the proper treatment of *aerial perspective* made to appear a mile off while the lower object is in its place in the foreground, the eye would no more be offended, or even be made sensible of the circumstance, than it would if the same thing took place in nature, which of course it often does.

Note. Illustrations Rogers' Poems page 36 *J. M. W. Turner* distant cascade over boat in the foreground[23]

There is a rule however respecting the gradation of light and shade, which, as it is strictly and universally observed by nature herself under all circumstances, must surely be a safe one, and I will venture moreover to assert that the violation of it in a picture is always as injurious, as the observance of it is beneficial.

In nature, the sun being the source and concentration of light, a gradation must of necessity be the consequence, whether we look towards the sun itself or whether our attention is directed to any object receiving its light, for the angle of reflection of the sun's place will in that case be the *concentration* of light. This

Note. All other objects receiving the light less directly will be in subordination.

then proves the soundness of the rule, and a judicious selection of the subject will prevent confusion. I allude to the choice of one principal mass, made so either by its brilliancy or its extent.

This principal of gradation is also one of great latitude, for as it is ever to be found in nature, it is equally applicable to a light effect as to a dark one, to a battle scene where all is confusion or to the quiet repose of evening. It regulates the treatment of the picture from its first commencement to the *last touch upon a leaf or a stone!* In short if I were required to reduce the whole art of light and shade to its simple elementary principals, I should sum up all in the two words Gradation and Contrast.

The theory of the universal gradation of light then is true but it cannot be *properly carried out* without the application of another rule which is, 'That no object or mass shall be equally relieved on both sides', for that side of an object, in itself equally light throughout, *will appear brightest* which is relieved by the darkest background. Hence then you will perceive a *gradation* is obtained, *the most delicate and refined,* by contrast alone. Begin then, your picture at once by a gradation of light and shade and cover all down but the highest lights. Other lights will be sure to come as you proceed with your work but they will always be in proper subordination to the principal.

In finishing your picture, let your highest lights be confined to the smallest possible surface. They may sparkle in great profusion about the picture; but the most laboured details will fail to give an appearance of *finish,* unless this be attended to.

I may take occasion to remark that what I have here said respecting *contrast* of light and shade is equally applicable to color: that is, if for instance we take green and oppose to it on the one side, *red,* and on the other *yellow* or *blue,* it will have a gradation and intensity towards the red and will fade as it approaches the yellow; but more of this when we come to the subject of color.

Altho the term light and shade is generally made use of when speaking of this branch of the art, it is by no means explanatory in itself, inasmuch as the mass of light may contain within itself objects in shade, and the mass of shade, on the other hand, may embrace objects in light — trees for instance may have much light upon them and yet not disturb or break up the mass of shade, and a light object may be in shadow and yet not break up the mass of light.

The forms of these masses of light and shade as well as the quantity of each are left in a great measure to our own choice and thus we have it in our power to excite corresponding ideas in the mind of the spectator of stillness and repose, gloom and grandeur, or vivacity and cheerfulness.

Now the subject, and the time of day which is to be represented, will always suggest one or the other of these modes of treatment. If an open daylight scene is required, with the sun high, a breadth of light with the darks sharp and cutting will best represent it. The shadows cast by the different objects being *short,* and not uniting into masses, will do no more than connect each object with its ground, and being treated at the same time *Example*   with much tenderness, and in some cases distinguished more by their color than strength, will still partake of the all-pervading light and sunny atmosphere. Strong and rich color will stand for the darks while their cast shadows will shew that the light is at the same time falling upon them. Middle tint will be of a light tone, and but sparingly used, and the whole picture will thus be made up of clear light tints, interspersed with a few strong darks.

Now let us suppose the reverse; the sky shall be dark and lowering, and the lengthened shadows of evening falling horizontally upon one another increase the gloom, objects in distance are unmarked, vague and uncertain forms make up the mass, while a single gleam of light glancing upon the nearest objects, bring them out in strong relief.

Example   This picture therefore is made up of low toned middle tint and *half* dark, the small bright lights, taking the place of the *strong darks* in that previously described, thus the whole picture is completely reversed, for middle tint *prevails,* to the exclusion as much as possible of half light. Let me here remind you that in the case of a *dark* picture, such as just described, no *strong darks* to tell as such are required, and in delineating whatever forms may be necessary in the masses of shade, they are best done by leaving them while deepening the tone of the surrounding parts; in short, by carrying throughout the picture the principal of *lights* upon a dark ground for a dark picture, in contradistinction to *darks* upon a light ground for a light one. It is necessary here however to remark that a picture may and ought to contain somewhat of both these principals either in the larger masses or in the details. The examples just now described are treated broadly in order that they may be more clearly understood.

In examining your picture, while in progress, observe whether the dark masses, either large or small, are terminated by a sharp cutting line; if so, let them be softened in almost every instance. It is often very injurious to the picture and induces you to take down the whole mass, when it is only the edge which requires softening.

Again while in your solicitude to obtain breadth, see that you do not degenerate into flatness, and on the other hand, *beware* lest by too much *relief* a dry hard effect is the result.

Remember that a strong dark will come best off half light, as that has a more retiring quality than high light. The smallest possible quantity is sufficient for the two extremes.

Take care that your darks are not too much detached from each other, if in a light picture, by which a spotty effect will be produced, and that your lights, if in a dark picture, have a sufficient quantity of half light to connect them.

Use the full force of the palette for it is weak at the *best* when compared with nature. As your work sometimes appears too heavy, and at others too weak, think of Sir Joshua's proportions, viz., $\frac{1}{4}$ light, $\frac{1}{4}$ dark, and the remainder, middle tint.

It is very good to have the sun in the picture, for besides its being of necessity either morning or afternoon, which are always the most picturesque times, it at once gives a focus of light.

It was a favorite effect, both with Claude[24] and Turner, than whom it must be acknowledged there are no higher authority in landscape. It however imposes restraint, because, if the source of light is anywhere out of the picture, no one can dispute the truth of any cast shadows you may choose to introduce for the purpose of uniting the darks or assisting the breadth of effect.

Never make use of cast shadows for your *darks,* but on the contrary keep them as light as possible, which will preserve the breadth, as well give the appearance of air and sunshine. Let your darks therefore be where there is *dark, local color,* and your effect will then be more powerful as well as more natural.

In copying nature there are three things to be closely observed, viz.: the forms of objects; their true color; and effect as to light and shade, by which will be understood the expansive look and brightness of a midday sky, the gloom of an approaching storm, or the sombre hue of twilight, which things I will venture to affirm are only to be obtained by departing in some instances from the exact imitation of nature, that is with respect to the depth of tone or shade. For instance, how is sunshine upon a white building to be represented when the white paper is only equal in lightness to the shadowed side of it? If the shadowed side is given, it must of course be considerably lower in tone. And again, how can that same building be properly relieved if the scale is not kept up and the back ground made darker than nature? It might in reality be no lower in tone than that which you are obliged to give to the shade side of the building. Variety of color cannot always be substituted for variety of tone. For the same reason those who practice will find that strong darks can only be given their proper value by making the ground on which they are placed of a lighter tone than nature, or in other words, by giving more *breadth* to the light.

This practice might at first appear to lead to difficulties but it must be remembered that strong darks are not wanted *to tell as such,* when a *breadth* of *shadow* is to be given, but on the contrary, *bright lights;* and on the other hand, where a breadth of light is to be given, it is then and then only that the darks should have their greatest force.

Those therefore who are such sticklers for the exact imitation of nature in every particular must not attempt her grand and striking effects, nor must they be surprised if their picture look poor and insipid.

In concluding these remarks, in which while aiming at brevity I have taken much pains to be clear and intelligible, I will only add that he who can freely adopt them in his practice needs no further instruction upon the subject, but will be fully prepared to follow up the more difficult subject of color, which on some future occasion I will endeavour to explain as far as lies in my power.

[A lecture delivered by Conrad Martens to a sketching club at the Australian Library, Sydney, 21 July 1856]

FOOTNOTES—MARTENS

1 The reference is to John Burnet (1784-1868), painter, engraver and influential writer on art. Among his most important books are: *Practical Hints on Composition* (1822); *Practical Hints on Light and Shade* (1826); and *Practical Hints on Colour* (1827) which were published together as a *Practical Treatise on Painting* in (1827). In 1837 he published *An Essay on the Education of the Eye.*

2 David Roberts (1796-1864), a Scottish painter who began life as a scene painter for the theatre, but turned later to architectural and picturesque topography, visiting Europe and later Egypt and Syria in search of suitable subject matter. His *Sketches in the Holy Land and Syria* (1842) are among his most famous productions.

3 J. M. W. Turner (1775-1851), the famous English landscape painter, published in 1807 a 'Liber Studiorum' or book of studies which illustrated the various *classes* of landscape: pastoral, marine, historical etc. within which Turner worked. It was published at irregular intervals between 1807 and 1819. The first plate was in aquatint, but the remainder consisted of a combination of etching and mezzotint. The idea was suggested to Turner by Claude's *Liber Veritatis*, lit. 'book of truth' which was intended by the artist as a means for identifying his true works. Turner employed many of the best engravers of the time and supervised the execution of each plate with the greatest care.

4 Marshall Claxton (1813-81), the portrait and history painter. He was a prolific painter and, finding that by 1850 he had more works than he could dispose of, hit upon the plan of taking 200 paintings (by himself and others) to Australia with the intention of selling the paintings and starting an art school. But he met with little success (he arrived at the height of the gold fever in Sydney and this may have made things more difficult than usual for artists in the colony) so he decided to leave for India where he was much more successful in selling his paintings.

5 The quotation is from Reynolds's *Notes on Du Fresnoy:* 'The highest finishing is labour in vain, unless at the same time be preserved a breadth of light and shadow'. John Burnet used the quotation as a motto on the title page of his *Practical Hints on Light and Shade in Painting* (1826), and Martens probably derived it from this source.

6 Francis Danby (1793-1861), an English painter who specialized in romantic and biblical subject matter akin to that of John Martin, but turned later to effects of morning and evening light.

7 Clarkson Stanfield (1793-1867), a marine and landscape painter, greatly admired by Ruskin who called him 'the leader of the English realists' and the noblest master of 'cloud form'.

8 David Cox (1783-1859), an English landscape painter whose work is well described here by Martens himself.

9 George Cattermole (1800-68), a water-colour painter who specialized in romantic subject matter featuring the manners and customs, and chivalric and religious sentiment of medieval times. His work may be compared in style and taste to that of Delacroix and Bonington.

10 Anthony Vandyke Copley Fielding (1787-1855), the water-colour painter and art teacher who taught Conrad Martens and John Ruskin. He was celebrated for his storms at sea, and for his pictures of lake and mountain scenery in Wales, Scotland and the North of England. Subtle tonal gradations and delicate effects of light and mist are a feature of his work.

11 i.e. the *trompe-l'oeil* type of subject matter favoured by artists whose main interest is a meticulous realism.

12 Solomon Alexander Hart (1806-81), a painter of historical and biblical subjects, often upon a very large scale. He was elected R.A. in 1840 and in 1855 succeeded C. R. Leslie as a teacher of painting at the Royal Academy schools. He later became the Librarian of the Royal Academy.

13 Balthazar Denner (1685-1749), a German portrait painter and miniaturist famous for the meticulous realism of his work.

14 Titian (Tiziano Vecellio) (*c.* 1487-1576) one of the greatest of the Italian painters whose style dominated Venetian painting during its finest period.

15 Sir Anthony van Dyck (1599-1641), the Flemish painter who studied under Rubens and became famous for the beauty and elegance of his portraiture.

16 Jan van der Heyden (1637-1712), the Dutch painter, illustrator and engraver mainly of genre scenes and landscape. Like Denner he became known for the meticulous realism of his work.

17 Sir Peter Paul Rubens (1577-1640), the greatest of the Flemish painters and one of the greatest of his age, equally famed for his history paintings, portraits and landscapes.

18 lit. 'dark chamber'. An apparatus which projects the image of an object or scene on to a sheet of paper or ground glass so that the image can be traced. It consists of a shuttered box or room with a small hole in one side through which the light from a brightly lit exterior scene penetrates and forms an image (inverted) on a screen opposite the hole.

19 Reynolds, *Discourse*, XIII, (ed. R. Wark) p. 237.

20 Reynolds, *Letters to the Idler* (no. 79) *see* H. W. Beechey, *The Literary Works of Sir Joshua Reynolds*, vol. II, 1835.

21 The famous teller of tall tales, as recounted in *Baron Munchausen, Narrative of his Marvellous Tales* by Rudolph Erich Rospe (1785).

22 Sir George Beaumont, Constable's friend and patron, is reported by C. R. Leslie to have asked him, 'Do you not find it very difficult to determine where to place your brown tree?' and the reply was, 'Not in the least, for I never put such a thing into a picture'. C. R. Leslie, *Memoirs of John Constable* (ed. J. Mayne), London, 1951, p. 114.

23 Martens is referring to Turner's vignette illustration of the Lake of Como in Samuel Rogers' *Italy* (1822-28). It was engraved by Edward Goodall.

24 Claude Gellée or Lorraine, the French landscape painter who was born in Lorraine, but spent most of his life in Italy. The most famous exponent of classical landscape painting, his work continued to exercise a considerable influence on landscape painting throughout the eighteenth and nineteenth centuries.

🮣🮣🮣🮣🮣🮣🮣🮣🮣🮣🮣🮣🮣🮣🮣🮣🮣🮣🮣🮣

Artists in Search of Gold

INTRODUCTION

The discovery of gold in payable quantities in New South Wales and Victoria in 1851 resulted, not surprisingly, in a rapid increase in immigration. The growth of population which occurred during the next two decades in consequence of the discovery changed the whole pace and tone of colonial development. New political issues emerged such as the right of imposing compulsory licences upon the diggers (which led to the Eureka Stockade), or the increasing scarcity of good pasture land due to the extension of squatter holdings in the 1830s and 1840s (which led to the Robertson Land Acts of the 1860s). The conflicting economic and social interests of different classes of free citizens became a major factor in the development of society. Artists now began to turn their attention to the observation of colonial life where before most of their attention had been given to the observation of the plants, animals and Aboriginals.

The two extracts included in this chapter are taken from the diaries of Eugen von Guerard and Thomas Woolner, and both record experiences on the Victorian gold diggings. They are of interest not only because they provide fascinating first-hand impressions of life on the gold diggings when alluvial digging prevailed but also becaues they are records of initiations into a colonial way of life — a life radically different from anything Eugen von Guerard had experienced in his native Austria or Thomas Woolner had left behind him in England.

The first extract is from Eugen von Guerard's *Journal* in the Dixson Library, Sydney. It is, almost certainly, an English translation from a German original for it is clear from the letter which von Guerard wrote to the editor of the *Argus* twenty years later (see p. 166) that his command of English was not in 1851 of the quality revealed in the manuscript. It is probably a fair copy of a journal written in German kept on the diggings and translated into English much later in life by either von Guerard himself or a friend. The *Journal* provides a fresh, lively account of his experiences on the diggings. There is, for example, an excellent account of the diggers' reactions to the attempt by mounted troopers to collect licences by force on the spot.

The second extract is taken from the manuscript diary of Thomas Woolner in the Australian National Library, Canberra. Whereas von Guerard was a man who seemed to be able to cope with things as they came, Thomas Woolner felt the gulf acutely between his education and cultural values on the one hand, and the raw life which confronted him on the diggings on the other. He found, too, the necessary accommodation more difficult to make. On the Victorian diggings his rough companions continuously offended him, the flies persecuted him, the trees made him feel 'shut up in a basket' and the diggings at Reid's Creek looked like the meeting place of 'all the gypsies on the earth'. He found it difficult even to think in Australia. As Australians came increasingly to pride themselves on their toughness, their physical stamina, and their capacity to make a culture out of their lack of one, others who came after Woolner during the next hundred years were to experience frequently a similar sense of repulsion.

Eugen von Guerard (1811–1901)

Johann Joseph Eugen von Guerard was born in Vienna, the son of Bernard von Guerard, a miniature painter who had been made court painter to the Emperor Franz I a few years before. At the age of fifteen he travelled with his father to Italy, visiting Venice, Milan and Florence. In 1831 Bernard von Guerard exhibited in Rome and Eugen came into contact with northern expatriates working in Rome such as the sculptor, Thorwaldsen, and the painter, Koch. In 1832 father and son arrived in Naples where Bernard painted miniatures and landscapes for the Neapolitan concert. Both artists travelled extensively through southern Italy and Sicily; but in 1836 Bernard died in a cholera epidemic at Naples. In 1838 Eugen returned to Germany and enrolled in the Academy of Art, Dusseldorf, under the landscape painter J. W. Schirmer; he made frequent sketching trips in the Rhineland, and toured Belgium and Holland. For a period in the 1840s he lived in London, and it was there that he joined a party of Frenchmen preparing to depart for the goldfields of Victoria. They sailed from London in August 1852 and arrived in Geelong on 24 December. The party immediately set off for Ballarat where they arrived on 18 January 1853.

The extracts from the Von Guerard diary printed below record his entries for sixteen days of the ensuing twelve months. They provide a glimpse of his experiences on the gold diggings. After sixteen unsuccessful months seeking gold, von Guerard settled in Melbourne and in 1854 married Louise Arnz, a native of Dusseldorf. From Melbourne he made painting excursions to Tasmania, South Australia and New South Wales. He exhibited with the Victorian Society of Fine Arts (1857); and works of his were sent from Australia for the Paris Exhibition (1855) and the International Exhibition, London (1862). He joined A. W. Howitt's government survey in Gippsland (1860) and G. B. von Neumayer's meteorological expedition in Western Australia. In 1862 von Guerard and his family settled in 'Little Parndon', Gipps Street, East Melbourne, where they lived for nearly twenty years. In 1870 von Guerard was appointed Master of the Painting School and Curator of the National Gallery of Victoria. During the 1870s he exhibited with the Victorian Academy of Arts and at international exhibitions in London (1872), Philadelphia (1876), Paris (1878), Sydney (1879) and Melbourne (1880). In 1881 he resigned from his post at the National Gallery of Victoria and sailed for Europe in January 1882. The family settled first in Dusseldorf, but in 1891 he went to live with his married daughter in England. In 1901 von Guerard died and was buried in Brompton Cemetery, Chelsea.

[VON GUERARD AT THE BALLARAT GOLD DIGGINGS]

Jan. 18th. [1853]

After travelling for a week, we arrived at Ballarat. The journey has been interesting in many ways. The forests of immense gum-trees, the waterholes by which we camped at night, the unpleasant discovery of a scorpion as a bedfellow, the intolerable flies, etc. were all new experiences. We occasionally passed human habitations, and one day met a poor young fellow who had been attacked by bushrangers, robbed of his horse, and all the money he possessed, and then tied to a tree. When we saw him he was in a cart with a man and a woman, who had heard his cries and rescued him. The poor fellow's arms and legs were terribly swollen from the tight ropes with which he had been bound to the tree. Ballarat consists of a camp of tents, and some buildings constructed of boards. One building, made of the trunks of trees, constitutes the prison, and is often the temporary abode of bush-rangers, and also of diggers who can't — or won't — pay their licence.

Jan. 23rd.

The last five days have been spent in seeing the gold-commissioner, Mr Green, to ascertain the laws for diggers, and in obtaining our licences. And further to prepare our encampment. This necessitated the felling of trees, for the purpose of constructing a work-shop and store for our possessions, our tents being barely roomy enough for our personal shelter. The work, to which we were all new, was somewhat arduous at first, and caused much backache and blistering of hands. The evenings are a delight after the day's work, being both novel and picturesque. From every direction weary diggers are to be seen returning to their canvas homesteads, hundreds of fires are kindled and illuminate the scene, and at each tea is made and mutton roasted. The evening meal finished, the air is filled with the sound of firearms being fired, in order to be reloaded anew before the night. A Frenchman, named Fougery, with his wife, and several others has arrived from California — they have rigged up their tent close to ours, and make a pleasant addition to our party. Have had the very painful experience of being bitten by one of the gigantic black ants that are to be met with out here. The pain and swelling lasted several days. Received our licences, for which we pay 30/- per month. An encampment of police here, both mounted and on foot, have a quite military appearance.

Jan. 25th.

Yesterday we went to peg out our claims at Eureka Hill. Our nearest neighbours are Chinamen, Englishmen, and Americans. We afterwards went on towards Gravelpit, and repeated our pegging...

March 13th.

Have done a wonderful walk to Warrenheip Hill, through miles of forest. Saw many magpies, black cockatoos, parrots, etc. Much relished the exquisite clear water of Leigh Creek, the first I had tasted for a long time, such a thing being unobtainable at the diggings.

April 3rd.

Some days ago a large tent was put up close to mine by some

very undesirable-looking people. A man with a wife and daughter, and several young men, seem to share it. They possess carts and horses, and seem to be carrying on an illicit sale of spirits. The gambling at night invariably ends in loud quarrelling and fighting. Very unpleasant neighbours.

April 15th.

Yesterday a party of armed police raided the tent of my neighbours, and carried off a cartload of barrels, bottles, and jugs, as well as the two women. The men were all away at the time. To-day the whole lot have disappeared. Only in certain parts of the township public-houses are allowed, and for these the licence is very heavy. Spirits, however, are sold illegally at most of the little stores, and this is often known and winked at by the police. We are subject to periodical unexpected requests to produce our diggers' licences. As in every gully there are a number of men who have evaded taking out a licence, one is quite accustomed on these occasions to hear the signal passed along, giving warning of approaching police. The latter usually arrive to the number of twelve to sixteen men, armed with bayonets, and headed by a mounted officer. They pass from one shaft to another to examine these licences. On hearing of their approach many of the miners disappear rapidly into either mine, or into the bush, and so succeed in evading the law. Those who are not so nimble, and are caught, are roped together in pairs and taken prisoner. I have seen as many as thirty or forty at a time, taken off like this. They are then imprisoned with robbers and other criminals. This method is causing a good deal of bad blood.

April 18th.

I and the mate I have taken on, Bagot by name, have had some hard work putting planks into our shaft, as it showed signs of collapsing. It has paid, however. After B. had gone to-day and I still worked on, I was surprised by a drunken Englishman of huge dimensions, who descended to where I was at work. I begged him to remove himself, which he refused to do, whereupon I climbed up out of the shaft, pulling the rope up after me, hoping to give him a wholesome lesson by keeping him prisoner down below for a time. To my astonishment he managed to climb up out of the shaft and approached me in a perfect fury, and most anxious to have a boxing match. I told him that he'd find my boxing done with a pistol, whereupon he moved off. I hear this evening that he has pronounced me to be 'a true gentleman!'

A circus has arrived, and is doing a roaring business.

April 25th.

To our unspeakable disgust we discovered on going to work, a day or two ago, that our neighbouring diggers had worked through into our shaft, partly destroying our timbering. This naturally led to considerable unpleasantness, which however we ended as amicably as possible. In order to repair the damage as quickly as we could, we have taken on another mate, a Yorkshireman, George Griffiths by name. He has the commendable and rare distinction, out here, of being a teetotaler, and is moreover an experienced and good worker, though like ourselves he has, so far, not met with any luck.

May 7th.

We have had a week of incessant rain. I had already taken some precautions against the coming winter, having put a hoarding round part of my tent, and also built a chimney of earth and beams, so as to avoid the discomfort of cooking in the rain. Everywhere chimneys of this kind are being built up.

Rheumatism in my right arm is giving me much trouble. This is very usual out here, resulting from being exposed to wet and cold winds, after working oneself into a perspiration down in the mine . . .

August 4th.

This morning my mate James and I again shouldered our picks and spades to join a new rush to the neighbourhood of Black Swamp, there to peg out some claims. We found some seventy diggers there, at work, surface-digging at a depth of one and a half to two feet with very poor results.

August 14th.

Have had a good walk with Guibert to the Bald Hills, which lie some eight or ten miles from Ballarat. We passed a great swamp with a quantity of wild fowl. We also came upon a large sheep station — green fields, fences, shepherd's huts, and the squatter's house with a pretty garden. At the shepherd's hut we had some delicious milk and bread. We had our guns and got some snipe and a kind of quail. The hills, which we reached the foot of a little further on, are three to four hundred feet in height, and are most certainly of volcanic origin. The view from

J

the top is grand. To the east Buninyong and Warrenheip Hill,
to the north Mount Alexander, to the north-west the crest of the
Pyrenees and Mount Cole, Lake Burrumbeet, Mount Etna, and
part of the Grampians, etc. — The forests through which we
went are magnificent, the wattle in full bloom. I shot a snake,
measuring at least six feet in length, a horrible-looking reptile,
black and yellow spotted, commonly known as the tiger-snake.

August 20th.

Am at the moment storekeeper for some of the men of my late
French Company. They begged me to undertake the job as
Armand (their storekeeper) had to go to Geelong. I agreed,
thinking I might as well add another to my various experiences.
I find it quite amusing. Have brought all my belongings with me,
leaving James to look after my tent. Before departing, Armand
initiated me into all the workings of the business. The Store
and my habitat are some twenty paces in length, and about
half that in width. In front are displayed a vast variety of goods,
such as butter, cheese, flour, candles, boots and other wearing
apparel, shovels, picks, rope, etc. etc. In the back part — hidden
— there is a small barrel of beer, spirits, and an assortment of
French wines in bottle, and the necessary glasses with which to
regale friends and old customers. These leave corresponding
cadeaux on departing! On first hearing of this I demurred about
following this illegal custom, but was assured that a number of
members of the Commissioner's Camp were among the 'friends'.

Have come across several sailors from the 'Windermere', and
hear that nearly all bolted to the diggings shortly after our
arrival in Melbourne.

August 25th.

A number of us met, and celebrated the anniversary of our
departure from Europe with huge bonfires, and much firing of
guns. All around, people not belonging to our party were of
course ignorant of the reason of our festivity, and soon the false
rumour spread, that we were celebrating Governor La Trobe's
consent to all the diggers' demands. The excitement for all now
grew intense.

Jan. 4th. [1854]

The Guillerot ménage is coming to an end. G., and Catherine
with him, are preparing to return to France.

For some time news has reached us here of the wonderful
gold mines in Peru, and there has been quite an exodus to that

part of the world, several of my old mates going to try their luck there.

Jan. 9th.

Going to Ballarat Flat to-day, I saw cricket being played for the first time out here. Heavy rains and thunder-storms have cooled the air, after a long spell of intense heat.

Jan. 17th.

Just a year since my arrival at Ballarat, and how changed it all is in that short time. Stretches of fine forest transformed into desolate-looking bare spaces, worked over and abandoned. In many parts, where a year ago all was life and activity, there now is a scene of desolation. At the same time the population has enormously increased, and there is less and less chance of having a lucky find, as at every new place that shows any promise, swarms of diggers settle down like flies on a midden.

> [Selection from the typescript of a section of a journal
> (18 August-16 March 1854) kept by Eugen Von Guerard,
> in the Dixson Library, Public Library of
> New South Wales]

Thomas Woolner (1825–92)

Thomas Woolner was born at Hadleigh, Suffolk. He studied sculpture under William Behnes, a prolific early Victorian sculptor. After four years with Behnes, Woolner joined the Royal Academy Schools in 1842, though he continued to carve for his old master. In 1843 he exhibited 'Eleanor Sucking Poison from Prince Edward's Wounds' at the Royal Academy and in 1845 won the Silver Medal from the Society of Arts for a bas-relief, entitled 'Affection'. Two years later he met Dante Gabriel Rossetti and joined the Pre-Raphaelite Brotherhood as a sculptor-member. In 1848 following upon an unfavourable reception of his 'Titania and the Indian Boy' at the British Institution he turned from idealistic sculpture to portrait medallions. In 1850 he made a medallion of Mrs Coventry Patmore, the wife of the poet, in 1851 a medallion of Thomas Carlyle and, having already carved a medallion of Wordsworth, entered the competition held to choose a sculptor for the poet's memorial. His disappointment at not gaining this commission together with an unfortunate love affair led him to seek his fortune elsewhere.

Consequently, in 1852 he set sail, accompanied by Bernhard Smith (1820-85) a sculptor friend and associate of the Pre-

Raphaelites, from Gravesend, bound for the Victorian gold fields. Among the Pre-Raphaelite group who saw them off was Ford Madox-Brown whose painting the *Last of England* (1855) (Birmingham Art Gallery) was inspired by emigrants farewelling their friends as the vessel departed.

The extract printed below is taken from a fair copy of a diary which Woolner kept of his experiences on the gold fields. Disappointed at his lack of success he turned to sculpting portrait medallions of notable colonists, such as Sir Charles Fitzroy, Sir John Nicholson, and others. But it is clear from his diary that Australia did not appeal to him, and he found the state of society incapable of supporting a professional sculptor, so he returned to England in 1854.

On his return he made a bust of Tennyson and in 1856 a popular medallion of Browning. Thenceforth his success as a popular sculptor of busts, medallions and full-length statues of men of letters and other worthies was assured. He was elected an Associate of the Royal Academy in 1871, and a full member three years later.

Although Woolner found Australia an undesirable place to live and work in, several important commissions came to him as a result of his Australian connections: the monumental statue in Hyde Park, Sydney, of Captain James Cook (1879); busts of Edward Wilson (1869) and Sir Redmond Barry (1880), both in the Public Library, Melbourne, and Sir Thomas Elder (1890) for Adelaide University.

[LIFE ON THE DIGGINGS]

Sat. Nov. 13. [1852]

We have camped by a creek 4 m. the Melbourne side of the Broken river, a placid spot. Mr. Palmer and Cook fell in with us just now had some tea and scran and are gone; they missed their dray yesterday but expect to fall in with them tonight. The day has been very warm and of course chokingly dusty: this is bad, but the greatest pest we have to withstand is the common domestic fly; these pernicious wretches torment the day from dawn to sundown and make it essential to wear a veil, but that affects me more than the pesty brutes themselves, rendering the senses smothered with closeness. There is a constant grumbling among our fellows concerning provisions; no one is satisfied and few fail to show it; Josh. Pinchin is the best disciplinarian we have, he beats me: the truth is we came not stocked with the best food and feel its want; we brought biscuits in large quantity instead of much flour; and after a day's dusty, dry marching nothing compensates for something in the cake way: biscuit is hard fare: I detest it. Our marksmen often shoot parrots of lovely plumage, principally of the rosella kind, young Pinchin shot a white cockatoo last night and he is now cooking it for supper. It is growing dark. I was resting under a gumtree today when a set of rough fellows sat beside, and after jabbering to each other some time one began to quote Tennyson, mocking some person he heard quote 'The May Queen'.

Sunday Nov. 14.

We have not moved from our camp yet and it is mid-day; our driver wishes to give his team a rest and nothing is ever got, he says by travelling on a sunday: this is not a pious sentiment, for he indulges but minutely in that, and the people about seem but little troubled with religiosity or psalm-singing. The day is dry and hot; the air cursed with flies. What would this country do without the great fires that spread over the country, burning up vermin, reptiles, etcetera with the grass and scrub, and above checking those spots of vivid detestation, flies? the wretches! they weave a net of hellish irritation around one's face. I do hate a bush life as I am now; I know not how it would be if I were perfectly well, but unfortunately there is no chance of that for no food that agrees with one is attainable; I am doomed to be unwell while I remain here, which shall be as short as I can cut it conveniently. I scarcely ever felt so dull, gloomy, pained, weak and generally wretched as now amidst air pure and fresh as if it came from the hill of paradise, and sights beautiful for beauty and thought. I shall be glad when we reach the diggings that I may try and work this misery off me, or at least try for gold that I may soon return to England: by St. George! how I shall respect my England when I once touch it again. I hate colonial life and would not remain here a year longer than necessary if they would make me Emperor of Australia: a land lovely to look at, loathesome to be in; that is to me. The accounts from the Ovens improve as we draw near, most say they are doing very well there, tho somewhat troubled with the quantity of water. I hope Mr. Howitt's party will soon catch up.

Mon. Nov. 15.

We started early this morning after our sabbath rest and passed the Broken river; we halted at a tavern called the Black

Swan, the drivers wanted their nobblers I suppose; I saw there a black man attiring himself, performing toilet duties with grimaces of fastidious self-admiration; he combed his thick shock of wool with some pain to himself, then gaumed it with grease and rubbed some fat over his visage, then combed again twisting his delight into hideous leers; after he had finished I told him he had made himself look very pretty, he grinned at me in ecstasy and asked if I wanted a light for my pipe. At the township of Broken-river I obtained a pint of milk just warm from the cow; it was a soothing draught to thirsting fatigue. At our midday halt I yarned with an Adelaide man, found he knew Mrs. Orme's brothers settled there, at least he knew one, had heard of the other; he described Mr. F. G. Andrews as a mild, soft spoken man, dark hair and eyes, roundish nose, rather a long face, and has been very well educated. I saw several little hills today for a wonder, the grass was a trifle greener and the shadows somewhat cooler. We are camped in a dampish place, plenty of water; the air strikes chill and raw.

Tues. Nov. 16.

We struck tent and started in good time this morning, and are now taking the usual noon rest after dinner. My cold has not oppressed me so much today, and I have enjoyed the walk more than heretofore, which has been this country where the flat is considerably broken by variety of broken ground: it is tedious travelling, a dead level, trees everywhere, trees right and left, trees before and trees behind, boxed in with trees; I feel as if I were travelling shut up in a basket. A camp scene has a busy and wild effect, the fires blazing, meal frying, bullocks being unyoked, snapping of whips, people getting their traps from the drays, dogs barking, guns banging away in all directions &c.

Wed. Nov. 17.

We have just crossed the Ovens river and are making the midday halt. The country has been a trifle more shady that we passed thro today, but very serpentine. I saw a herd of oxen cross the river, they huddled together, snorted and did it very well; I also saw two blacks cross, they did it with uncommon neatness. While I was bathing in the river where we camped last night a leech bit the side of my foot, but I soon pulled the creature off and no harm came of it tho it bled freely. Old men complain sadly of the changes in this country, one said to our driver the other day, 'When I was young men were men; now boys are men, and men are damned old fools.' Drink some say is the ruin; it helps no doubt, but I think the constant eating of flesh with no vegetable whatever but flour also aids. Books say here people are never troubled with coughs or colds, this is false for I scarcely meet any who are not troubled with them, settlers, newcomers and natives. The township where we halted at midday was called Wangaretta; just after we started I saw a group of loobras and just beyond them a group of black men; they asked for smoke. I gave one well-made fellow a piece of tobacco, he was gnawing at a mutton bone, and asked which he preferred, mutton, or kangaroo flesh; he said 'This no kangaroo now for the black man.' They were all stretched about in the sun looking as if the place was theirs but they were there only on sufferance; they had the aspect of an old race who felt their power had passed from them, but they were born and would eat and live at as little trouble as possible. We have heard no news of the Howitts yet. People are swarming to the diggings like folks go to a fair: I notice some women among them, hideous looking creatures, more frightful to my eyes than the black gins.

Thurs. Nov. 18.

We are at noon-halt in a pretty spot beside a river, still the Wangaratta I believe. I walked a few minutes ago along the dried bed of a swamp and a delicious odor rose up from minute lilac star-flowers; this I thought extraordinary for such an un-poetic country; a land where the birds cannot sing nor flowers give perfume, scarcely; a land without fruit or vegetable. It rained pretty hard last night, grass was very wet this morning and we could see but a short distance for mist, this was a rarity for sight is usually impeded by trees only, so that the mist was rather a relief than otherwise.

We are encamped beside a little creek seven miles from the diggings; there is the battle field close to us and we shall see it tomorrow; soon after discover if it be worth leaving civilisation for and coming 16,000 m. for, and enduring every kind of annoyance for and, in short, if it be a good speculation we have made. The road is well filled with people going and returning from the diggings, most give bad accounts, some middling and a few quite good news. I take but small notice of either, knowing what a vague and dishonest thing rumor is. We shall soon know what gold seeking is, and will need no tongues upon the matter. I hate flies and human bullocks.

Friday, Nov. 19.

We started late this morning, it rained hard. I saw the

diggings this afternoon, a vigorous scene, bustle [?   ] the earth looks as if an earthquake had torn it up. I cannot see well for I am writing by dull moonlight. The mountain country we passed thro today is very fine.

Sat. Nov. 20.

We are camped on the Reid's Creek diggings.

Sunday, Nov. 21.

It is early morning, the place is quiet as yet except a few barkings of dogs and axes cutting wood. There was a great settling of accounts among our fellows last night: none of them are in a brilliant state as to hope, some are down low. The numerous tents scattered everywhere give me the notion of this place being the grand meeting place of all the gipsies on the earth, all the men look like gipsies. I am obliged to leave off writing to fetch a sheep's liver for the dogs.

We went this afternoon and selected two spots for digging, to commence upon tomorrow: there will be plenty of water to take out as they are just beside the creek. The country round here is magnificent in scenery, much the best I have seen. One great gully a gigantic gorge between broken granite masses with water rushing from crag to crag, has an aspect of tremendous force, and opens upon with surprise. Yesterday we passed thro a forest where a storm had gone; trees of great size were thrown down as if they had been dry reeds, and great boles were wrenched and splintered, twisted like ropes; a fire also had swept thro; trees were left as charred posts merely, without bark or branches, a scene of fierce desolation. Sunday is a peaceful day at these diggings; men walk leisurely prospecting, others drive about on horses, some are washing clothes before their tents, where the perpetual camp-fire is burning, some are barking, others felling trees that fall every now and then with a shaking crash: nearly all diggers smoke, they go to anyone's fire to light the pipe, they seem a tolerably friendly set, rough enough, coarse as brickdust, but nothing more; I see none one has any need to fear, they are civil to me if I have occasion to ask questions, what does one want more from strangers? This digging will be anything but dreaming on a couch of down; standing up to and over our knees in water, and aching with labor in each joint; the strongest and most accustomed are thus, so that beginners need not expect it will be better with them. It is entirely or nearly chance if a man make enough to repay the trouble; he may work his hardest and scarcely live thereby, or he may work lightly and touch lucky spots; almost not quite a lottery: I feel anxious for the result. I have heard nothing of Bateman, I hope to see him soon.

Monday Nov. 22.

It is now close to sundown, we have been at work since soon after sunrise. Digging for gold is not play. My hand trembles so much I can scarcely write. I have been digging, felling trees, barking and carrying bark, baling water the whole day. We have sunk our hole 5 ft. deep; the water comes in fast upon us. The Pinchins are admirable workers, first rate fellows. This has been the hardest day's mere labor I ever did. The creek fills with people fast.

Wed. Nov. 24.

I wrote nothing yesterday, I was too tired, for we were baling out water and barking or digging till after washing several dishfuls, the holes proved of no worth, only two or three specks in a dishful. We gave them up. Most of our fellows are down flat in their hopes. We heard the commissioner had been taking many people off for digging without a license; we went this morning over to the old diggings to see the commissioner, he told us we had better not take a license till next month. I have something like news of Bateman, but nothing certain. We met a party of people from the Windade, among them the 'Bucktoothed 'un' and the Sucking-Butcher. Trees, or shrubs rather, grow in this country with two kinds of leaves. Unusual to my eye.

Thurs. Nov. 25.

I have been fossicking and prospecting all day. Last night a great meeting of miners, as they call themselves, was held near our tent to discuss and resolve regarding the license, whether the miners would allow their mates to be taken by a few police; it was agreed all should take licenses the beginning of next month, but for lack of it the few remaining days of this no man should be taken off these diggings, they would resist to a man and use force if it were employed against themselves; immense hurrahs, chuckling and a general dispersion. Today the police were driven from the ground; the commissioner ditto, tho he came and said he meant not to enforce a license till next month: he was chased up the hills with hoots, sticks, stones and pistol firings. We begin a hole tomorrow.

Friday, Nov. 26.

We have been working hard at our hole all day, and I think it contains promise; it has one advantage, dryness: the wet is making many ill with violent colds. Our hole is a round one, and some old miners were looking at it just before we knocked off work, and praised it: if the result equal the striving for it we shall be satisfied. The two Pinchins are our bulwarks and contain our chief strength: famous workmen. The commissioners have been riding over the grounds and nothing more. I have heard nothing of Bateman. A set of fellows on horseback came on the diggings today, and pretended to want tools &c. for digging; I like not their aspects and think they mean no good. We are preparing for supper, some washing, others wishing it ready, changing clothes, lounging: The indefatigable Kipping is busy broiling mutton.

Sat. Nov. 27.

We have been hard at work all day; some washed clay and gravel stuff mixed with quartz; we got as much gold as would half fill the shell of a small hazel nut: a minute quantity to satisfy six greedy fellows as we are. We are more than 12 ft. down, much lower than any around us; experienced diggers think it a likely hole; we intend following it to the bare rock if possible. I begin to use the pick with some freedom and not so much labor to myself as at first, the spade and shovel are easy to me, comparatively. The great advantage I find in hard work — it keeps me from thinking; thoughts here in this country are not always shining resplendently, they do not ever wave white arms of welcome; I cannot see the certainty of solid attainment even afar, or maybe not until the Sun has quite sunk in ghostly twilight.

Sunday, Nov. 28.

This morning I took a walk and looked for promising places; after rambling nearly the whole morning I saw a spot which seemed to my eye the most likely of any among the hills: it is the deposit from an immense succession of waterfalls, where the stuff became caught in the fissures and roughness of granite crags: H. Pinchin and I mean to cut into it tomorrow morning. Several came with me this afternoon to see it and are well pleased with its aspect. Last night another great meeting of miners was held near our tent; much talk; the orator wanted to do away with licenses altogether in consequence of a duty, they say, having been put on gold halfcrown per oz. The meeting was held again this afternoon to a similar end; they mean to go to the commissioners on Wednesday to state their important resolutions. The chief speaker was a very ugly, bragging fellow.

Mon. Nov. 29. [1852]

We have been hard at work among the rocks, we must have moved tons of them: our fellows are short-seers and expect every day if they work a few hours to clutch reward, — expect a harvest in the evening if they sow in the morning. I could only give half my attention to work for the other half was employed in sustaining the drooping spirits of the mopers. Nonentities —.

> [From the manuscript diary of a Journey to the gold diggings at Fryer's Creek and Bendigo kept by Thomas Woolner from 31 October 1852 to 18 May 1853, with a final entry for 26 May 1854, National Library, Canberra]

◙◙◙◙◙◙◙◙◙◙◙◙◙◙◙◙◙◙◙◙◙◙

FIVE

Hardship and Weird Melancholy

INTRODUCTION

During the second half of the nineteenth century an image of Australia as a country that taxed human endurance to the limit developed and spread. It had been forming, as we have seen, since the first days of settlement in the views disseminated by Thomas Watling, Barron Field and others in their writings and illustrations. By 1850 most of the good land had been taken up, and settlement was forced into the more marginal, drier areas. The great explorations into the interior undertaken during the 1860s and 1870s brought back countless tales of hostile Aboriginals and of harsh, dry, inhospitable country. The dangers attendant upon pioneering life was yet another factor which helped to promote an image of Australia as a hard country — a land that could dry out the body and the spirit of a man, and no place for women.

The first extract is taken from the diary of William Strutt, an English artist who studied in Paris where he was trained in the *Beaux Arts* tradition of history painting but mingled it with the sharp precision of line of the Pre-Raphaelites. Whereas von Guerard was an exponent of the Germanic form of Pre-Raphaelitism and stressed the infinitude of space in a sharp-focus naturalism of detail, Strutt sought instead to present the drama of pioneering life under difficult social and natural conditions. He came to Australia for the sake of his health and decided to try his luck on the diggings. Once there he drew constantly and assiduously, with his eye open for subjects that were typical of colonial life, in order to provide himself with material for contemporary paintings.

Strutt's first great chance came with his personal experiences of Black Thursday, a day in February 1851 when the whole State of Victoria seemed to turn into a dull red blaze of fire. The large painting which he made to record the disaster now hangs in the Public Library of Victoria. From such paintings as this, and from the many drawings which appeared in the illustrated press of the time recording natural disasters such as floods, fires and famine, the stereotype of Australia as a land of hardship and privation was fashioned.

Strutt recorded facts: Marcus Clarke often records a mood. Like Barron Field and William Woolls, Clarke noted that Australia lacked the human associations of an historic past; that it held man and nature in a timeless present. Nature, it seemed to him, played a sinister role in Australia, alienated from man. He became a stranger in a place which reached blindly out against him.

Yet Clarke, it must be stressed, did not turn away in distaste and with a sense of repulsion in the way that Watling and Woolner did. In Clarke we glimpse, perhaps for the first time, a deep sense of emotional involvement, a commitment to his adopted country that is almost involuntary. He did not speak for those who came to exploit the country, to make their fortune or, not making it, leave with their curse on the land. He spoke for those who found themselves bound to the country in their failure. For Clarke, by the values of the prevailing philistinism of his day, was undoubtedly a failure. Although a gifted and highly imaginative writer he was melancholic by temperament and had little capacity to manage his private affairs. He drank heavily, was continuously in the grip of money-lenders and on more than one occasion contemplated suicide. He died of pleurisy at the age of thirty-five; his work was largely forgotten and his grave neglected, while the politicians and the brave explorers wrote their names importantly all over the map of Australia. Yet it was perhaps Clarke more than anyone who first began to experience what it was to be an Australian; to internalize for himself and the new men of his adopted country a dark vision of Australian nature which contained in its kernel the pain and guilt of the colonial experience.

William Strutt (1825–1915)

William Strutt came of a family long interested in the arts, being the son of William Thomas Strutt, a miniature painter, and the grandson of Joseph Strutt, a writer and artist. He received his first training from his father, and later studied under

Michael Drölling, in Paris. He immigrated to Australia in 1850 and remained in Victoria for eleven years before returning to England to continue his career as a painter. Strutt began working in Melbourne as a lithographer, but his great ambition was to paint history pictures of colonial life. Important collections of his drawings are held by the Parliamentary Library of Victoria, the Dixson Gallery of the Library of New South Wales and the Alexander Turnbull Library, Wellington. He worked on his painting 'Black Thursday' for three years. It was shown first at the Royal Academy and then at the Crystal Palace, London, later being taken on a tour of the capital cities of Australia.

[THE BUSHFIRES OF BLACK THURSDAY]

It was on a Thursday morning, 6th February 1851, that the sun rose lurid and red and the wind increased with stifling heat, producing such a deadly languor that it must be felt to be realized. The unextinguished little fire spread in the dry grass, and soon got too fierce to beat out in the usual way with green boughs and altogether beyond control. Thus it spread and coursed down the ranges into the more level country, the burning patch widening with the furious wind, till eventually it became one mighty, irresistible wave of flames about fifty miles broad, sweeping on! on! on!! It leaped over the creeks, burnt fences, huts, stations; seemed to spring into the trees, and with two or three whirls blazed up and enveloped the whole mass of foliage, which roared and crackled till consumed: then sped on to another tree to serve it in like manner. The flocks of sheep were burnt up by thousands, also the cattle and horses.

The terrified squatters and settlers hastily made their escape, leaving everything. The sick, put into drays, were hurried off; it was now a stampede for life, as represented in my picture of Black Thursday. Kangaroos and other animals, immense flocks of birds of all kinds, mingled in mid air, amidst the flying sparks, and in the stifling smoke making for the south. Numbers dropped dead from terror and exhaustion; even flying out far to sea and settling on the vessels. Several shepherds were burnt to death, whilst some had to plunge into creeks and just hold their heads out of the water to save themselves. In the town of Kilmore[1] the inhabitants thought the end of the world had come, and clinging to one another bade each other, as they supposed, a last farewell.

The groans of the unfortunate horses and bullocks, half

roasted, in the creeks where they had taken refuge, as one passed where they were after the fire had done its work was quite heart-rending. A company of travelling actors and an actress, *en route* for Sydney, having a cart filled with the necessary paraphernalia of their avocation, which they intended following at the various towns upon the journey, became enveloped in the flames on the Big Hill, and the whole of their wardrobe and effects were destroyed, the only article snatched from the burning being a cornopean and violin. The fire careered along at the speed of a race horse. A traveller who reached Melbourne from the Pyrenees[2] stated that for fifty miles of his route a chain of fire ran along each side of him, even to the margin of the road the grass and scrub was blazing — a fiery ride indeed!

Thus the devouring element continued its course of destruction till, after burning through the Cape Otway[3] forest, it was arrested by the sea.

I can never forget the morning of that scorching Thursday, ever after memorable in the annals of the Colony as 'Black Thursday'. The heat had become so terrific quite early in the day that one felt almost unable to move. At the breakfast table the butter in the butter dish was melted into oil, and bread when just cut turned to rusk. The meat on the table became nearly black, as if burnt before the fire, a few minutes after being cut. Everything felt hot to the touch, even the window panes in the shade. Cold water you could not get, and the dust raised in clouds by the fierce wind was sand which penetrated everywhere. Layer after layer did I brush off from my lithographic stone whilst etching thereon a design for the Anti-Transportation League,[4] at Messrs. Ham's in Collins Street.

Before Black Thursday the flies swarmed everywhere and settled on the black coats of the pedestrians in the streets in hundreds, and walking in the grass outside the town the grass-hoppers sprang up in front of you as you walked in scores. But the fire settled them all on that day.

The sun looked red all day, almost as blood, and the sky the colour of mahogany. We felt in town that something terrible (with the immense volumes of smoke) must be going on up country and sure enough messenger after messenger came flocking in with tales of distress and horror. One unfortunate man, severely burnt, tried in vain to rescue his wife and children, and just managed to escape with his own life.

For years afterwards the traces of this storm were still visible in the Colony, and the charred skeletons of many venerable monarchs of the forest stood gaunt and black against the sky, testifying to the severity of their baptism of fire.

[From William Strutt's Australian *Journal,* 1850-1862]

NOTES—STRUTT

1 A town in Victoria on the Hume Highway about forty-two miles (68 km) north of Melbourne.
2 Part of the Dividing Range lying in western Victoria, north-east of Ararat. It was so named by Sir Thomas Mitchell in 1836, whom it reminded of some hills in the lower Pyrenees of Europe.
3 Cape Otway, a cliffy promontory on the coast of Victoria, approximately seventy miles south-west of Port Phillip heads.
4 The Anti-Transportation League was a body formed in Melbourne in 1851 to agitate against the transportation of convicts from the United Kingdom into Australia. John West (see p. 76) was particularly active in the League, which was the first politically effective movement to emerge in Australia.

Marcus Clarke (1846–81)

Novelist, essayist, journalist and dramatist, Marcus Clarke was born in Kensington, London, on 24 April 1846. After completing his schooling at Cholmeley Grammer, Highgate, he left for Australia at the suggestion of his uncle, James Langton Clarke, A County Court judge in Melbourne, after the death of Marcus's father in 1862.

Clarke first worked in a Melbourne bank but finding the work totally unsuited to his temperament he gained employment on a station at Glenorchy, Victoria. From there he began to write for the *Australian Magazine* under the pseudonym, Mark Scrivener. In 1867 he became a member of the literary staff of the *Argus.* A year later he became the proprietor and editor of the *Colonial Monthly* and also helped to establish the Yorick Club, Melbourne's first literary club. Other members of the club included Adam Lindsay Gordon, Henry Kendall and George Gordon McCrae. The club did much to make the Melbourne of those years the literary centre of Australia.

In July 1869 Clarke married Marion Dixon, an actress, who bore him six children. In June 1870 he gained appointment as Secretary to the trustees of the Melbourne Public Library, but found this work uncongenial also.

Marcus Clarke's best known work, the novel *For the Term of His Natural Life,* was published in 1874 but had appeared previously in instalments in the *Australian* during 1870 and 1871. A shorter novel *Twixt Shadow and Shine* was published in 1875. Clarke also wrote pantomimes, operettas and plays.

In 1873 the Trustees of the Public Library and Museums of Victoria discovered that indifferent photographs of the paintings in the National Gallery of Victoria had been issued and that photographs of students' copies of paintings, purporting to be photographs of the originals, were in circulation. In 1874, therefore, they decided to reproduce a selection of the paintings in the National Gallery collection by photography. A local photographer, Thomas F. Chuck, photographed the paintings under the direction of Eugen von Guerard, who was then master of the School of Painting at the Gallery, and a letterpress (of about four to five folio pages) was written by Marcus Clarke to accompany each photograph. Clarke was at that time Secretary to the Trustees of the Library and Museums. The photographs with their accompanying texts were published in monthly parts. Printed below are the texts which Clarke provided for Louis Buvelot's 'Waterpool near Coleraine' and Nicholas Chevalier's 'The Buffalo Ranges'. Clarke subsequently incorporated large sections from both texts in the preface to the 1876 edition of Adam Lindsay Gordon's *Sea Spray and Smoke Drift*. The preface became famous and was used to introduce later editions of Gordon's poems.

WATERPOOL NEAR COLERAINE

No. VIII.—WATERPOOL NEAR COLERAINE, by LOUIS BUVELÔT. Painted on canvas. Dated 1869. 42 inches by 60 inches. *Purchased by the Trustees of the National Gallery, Melbourne, in the year 1871, for £131 5s.*

The township of Coleraine is situated in the most fertile portion of the West, — the district known as the Garden of Victoria. Twenty years ago, the up-country traveller, soon after leaving Hamilton, or, as it was then called, The Grange, found himself journeying over vast plains raised more than six hundred feet above sea level, well grassed and lightly timbered. These plains, watered by the Wannon and the Glenelg, spread, far as the eye could reach, in a series of undulations broken here and there by clusters of red gum trees growing near the waterpools and along the creeks. Originally settled by the squatters — the shepherd pioneers of our new civilization — this rich province gave pasturage to thousands of sheep and cattle, and the scattered homesteads or 'stations' of the flock-owners were the only signs of human habitation. As population increased, and a revised land law permitted the settlement of the agriculturist and farmer, the character of the country changed. Farm-houses built after English

K

fashion, well-cared for crops, and ever-widening lines of fencing, gave sign of the appearance of a race of independent yeomen, eager to found new homes in the liberal and fertile land of their adoption. The wandering aboriginal, the solitary shepherd, or the travelling stockman, were no longer the sole occupants of the soil. King Cobb and his coaches brought the civilization of the goldfields nearer and nearer. The bends of the rivers and the sheltered nooks of the great prairie began to gather to themselves the elements of villages and towns. Having conquered the sterner difficulties of colonization, the settlers sought for the orderly comfort to be enjoyed in older lands, and commenced to erect around their own dwellings the signs of a civilized prosperity. School-houses and churches arose. The telegraph wire and the newspaper aided to develop social intelligence, and to-day— barely twenty years since the plough of the first farm-owner cut the turf of the Western Plains—there exists in this rural county a civilization as complete in its degree as that of the capital itself.

The painting of M. Buvelôt, however, does not deal altogether with this new order of things. With true artistic instinct, he has selected a subject which at once touches that sense of the poetic which dwells in awakened memories and suggested contrasts of past with present. It is a hot summer evening, and the sun sinking in an unclouded splendour of pure light more dazzling than the crimson glories of a heavier sky, glows already on the rim of the rising pasture land. His beams thus flung over the landscape fill the air with golden splendour, and bathe every tree and herb in soft and vaporous warmth. The scene is a little valley, shut in by the upreaching stretches of the downs. A waterpool in the fore- ground reflects the deeper tints of the upper sky, and from either bank rise into intermingling bewilderment of branches, the reft and splintered trunks of two ancient gum trees. A little herd of cattle rest lazily on the verge of the clearing, and some horses are approaching from the distant timber belt. On the margin of the pool a few ducks, the property of the new lord of the soil, preen their plumage; the axe of the settler rests against a hollow log; and the well trodden path to the water would seem to lead to a home at a little distance. But all the accessories of the scene are subordinated to the prevailing sense of quiet. All is hot, silent, still, and dreamy. The mopokes have not yet begun their wild chattering cries. The air is heavy with the intense hush of the last instant of a dying Australian summer's day, and the old gum trees stand alone with motionless branches and folded leaves beside the solitary pool.

The sight of aged trees must necessarily evoke some thoughts
of the vanished past which saw them bud and blossom — which
witnessed their youth and their prime. Sheer force of association
at such time brings to mind many melancholy imaginings of
scenes of bygone happiness and unthinking enjoyment of present
good, which were all-potent realities to the forgotten folk who
once lived out their little lives beneath the shade of the still living
witness of their hopes and their decay. In historic England, where
every rood of ground is hallowed in legend and in song, the least
imaginative amongst us can find food for sad reflection. In this
young land, which lacks as yet sufficient history of its own to show
by its exampled teachings the littleness of man's ambitions, we
meet with natural writings more sombre in their meaning for the
student, if less plain to the casual glances of the hurried seeker
after worldly fortune. Australasia has been rightly named a Land
of the Dawning. Wrapped in the mists of early morning, her
history looms vague and gigantic. The lonely horseman riding
between the moonlight and the day, sees vast shadows creeping
across the desolate and silent plains, hears strange noises in the
primæval forests, where flourishes a vegetation long dead in other
lands, and feels, despite his fortune, that the trim utilitarian
civilization which bred him, shrinks into insignificance beside the
contemptuous grandeur of forests and ranges coeval with an age
where European scientists have cradled his own race. There is a
poem in every form of tree or flower, but the poetry which lives
in the trees and flowers of Australia differs from that of other
countries. Europe is the home of knightly song, of bright deeds
and clear morning thoughts. Asia sinks beneath the weighty
recollections of her past magnificence, as the Suttee[1] sinks jewel-
burdened upon the corpse of dead grandeur, destructive even in
its death. America swiftly hurries on her way, rapid, glittering,
impetuous, insatiable as one of her own giant waterfalls. From
the forests of Africa, and the creeper-tangled groves of the Islands
of the South, arise from the glowing hearts of a thousand flowers,
heavy and intoxicating odours, the fabled upas[2] poison which
dwells in barbaric sensuality. In Australia alone is to be found
the Grotesque, the Weird, — the strange scribblings of Nature
learning how to write. Some see no beauty in our trees without
shade, our flowers without perfume, our birds who cannot fly,
and our beasts who have not yet learned to walk on all fours.
But the dweller in the wilderness acknowledges the subtle charm
of this fantastic land of monstrosities. He becomes familiar with
the beauty of loneliness. Whispered to by the myriad tongues of

the wilderness, he learns the language of the barren and the uncouth, and can read the hieroglyphs of haggard gum-trees blown into odd shapes, distorted with fierce hot winds, or cramped with cold nights, when the Southern Cross freezes in a cloudless sky of icy blue. The phantasmagoria of that wild dreamland called the Bush interprets itself, and he begins to understand why free Esau loved his heritage of desert-sand better than all the bountiful richness of Egypt.

If I interpret the spirit of this poetic painting rightly, M. Buvelôt did not unwittingly, or from mere love of colour, choose the sunset hour for the contemplation of this lonely pool and its aged guardians. Behind each true work of art lies the poetic thought which inspired it, and the influence of the distant and almost-forgotten past was surely with our artist when he committed to canvas the scene which the accompanying photograph feebly renders. The time-worn gums shadowing the melancholy water tinged with the light of fast-dying day seem fit emblems of the departed grandeur of the wilderness, and may appear to poetic fancy to uprear in the still evening a monument of the glories of that barbaric empire upon whose ruins the ever-restless European has founded his new kingdom. Glorified for a last instant by the warm rays of the sinking sun, the lonely trees droop and shiver as though in expectation of the chill night which will soon fall alike on the land they have surveyed so long and the memory of the savage people who once possessed it.

M. Buvelôt is an artist who has made Victoria his home, and is it unnecessary to refer to the position which he occupies in the small artistic world which the thoughtful friendship of a few men of taste has created in this city. He has laboured among us for eight years, and the best testimony of the rank he holds in his profession is doubtless that which he himself would desire to alone advance — the estimation in which he is held by those whose opinion he deems of consequence. He received his art education at Paris, in the studio of Flers,[3] and has contributed to our various exhibitions. Among the best known of his paintings may be mentioned 'The Woodspoint Road,' which obtained the Gold Medal at the International Exhibition, in 1872-73.[4] The 'Waterpool near Coleraine' was painted for the Exhibition of Objects of Art, which was held in March, 1869, at the Great Hall of the Public Library.[5] It was taken from a sketch made on the spot in November, 1867, and was purchased by the Committee of the National Gallery in 1871, for the sum of £131 5s.

MARCUS CLARKE.

THE BUFFALO RANGES

No. XII.—THE BUFFALO RANGES, by NICHOLAS CHEVALIER. Painted on canvas. *Dated* 1864. 52 inches by 72 inches. *Purchased for the National Gallery, Melbourne, by the Fine Arts Commission in the year 1869, for the sum of £200.*

In the year 1863 the Fine Arts Commission[1] resolved that out of the sum of £1,000 placed at their disposal by the Government, the sum of £200 should be *'expended in the purchase of a painting or paintings by an artist or artists resident in Australia, provided that the painting or paintings possess sufficient merit to qualify it or them to compare favourably with the works of eminent living artists in Europe.'* An advertisement to this effect was inserted in the Government Gazettes of Victoria, New South Wales, Queensland, South Australia, and Tasmania, and a period of twelve months was given for the completion of the work. In January, 1865, the competing pictures were viewed, and the painting of the Buffalo Ranges by M. Chevalier,[2] selected for purchase.

The Buffalo Ranges is the name given to a tier of lofty mountains lying to the north-west of Buckland, and running north and south between the Buffalo and Ovens rivers. These ranges may be said to form part of the Great Australian Alps, and were discovered and crossed by Messrs. Hume and Hovell, the first overlanders. These gentlemen started in October, 1823, from the then newly discovered Murrumbidgee river, with the intention of penetrating to Port Phillip. After many hardships they reached and crossed the first great Alpine Chain, and camped upon the banks of a stream now the centre of a populous district, which they named after Major Ovens, the Ovens River. 'Four miles further,' says Mr. Woods, 'they ascended a range coming from the Alpine Chain. One of the snow-topped mountains now in sight was named the Buffalo.' [*Discovery and Exploration of Australia, J. Tennison Woods*]. Mr. Woods gives the following picturesque account of the view which burst upon the explorers of this mountain land:—
Mountains of a peaked shape, and covered with snow, were seen extending in a circle to the southward and eastward in a stupendous chain about twenty miles away. The view was magnificent. Below, the green valley, with its rich undulations, and the clear stream rolling through its pebbly channel. Beyond this the valley-slopes crowned with dark forest; and then far beyond the angular outline of dazzling whiteness, which reflected back the brilliancy of the sun, and showed an awful contrast with the gloomy gullies

beneath. A sight like this was worth all the inconveniences of exploration. To unlock such scenes to the gaze of men was worth a lifetime of labour — almost like the scenes of enchantment, delighting the view of the fairy prince of romance.'

Seen from the pinnacle of some lofty crag, the panorama of the plains is indeed magnificent. But it is rarely to be so viewed. There are few peaks accessible even to the most daring climber, and the mountaineer carries with him the memory of shadow rather than sunshine. Except the Western Tier of Tasmania, and the unapproachable glory of Shasta, which, to use Joaquin Miller's splendid phrase, 'lonely as God and white as a winter moon, towers above the storm-stained tamarack and strong tossing pines' of Northern California, there is no mountain range which can be compared with the Australian Alps — not for magnificence — but for gloom, for greatness of solitude, and for that grandeur which is born of the mysterious and the silent. The Australian mountain forests are funereal, secret, and stern. Their solitude is desolation. They seem to stifle in their black gorges a story of sullen despair. No tender sentiment is nourished in their shade. In other lands the dying year is mourned, and falling leaves drop lightly on his bier. In the Australian forests, no leaves fall. The savage wind shouts among the rock-clefts. From the melancholy gums, strips of white bark hang and rustle. The animal life which exists in the glooms of these frowning hills is either grotesque or ghostly. Great grey kangaroo hop noiselessly over the coarse grass. Flights of white cockatoo stream out shrieking like evil souls. The sun suddenly sinks, and the mopokes burst into horrible peals of human laughter. The natives aver that when night comes, from out of the bottomless depth of one of the huge lagoons the Bunyip rises, and in form like a monstrous sea-calf, drags his loathsome length from out the ooze. From some corner of the silent forest arises a dismal chant, and around a fire, dance natives, painted like skeletons. All is fear inspiring and gloomy. No bright fancies are linked with the memory of the mountains. Despairing explorers have named them out of their sufferings — Mount Misery, Mount Dreadful, Mount Hopeless. The plains below bear titles of ill omen. As when among sylvan scenes, in places

> 'Made green with the running of rivers,
> And gracious with temperate air,'

the soul is soothed and satisfied — so placed before the frightful grandeur of these barren hills, she drinks in their sentiment of defiant ferocity, and is steeped in bitterness. Amid all this sadness there is that weird delight, which Hoffman, Poe, and Hawthorne have expressed in their stories.

In the townships around the Buckland, however, the tide of modern life flows with its customary dulness [*sic*]. A police-station, a road board, a common school, together with the convenient number of public-houses, give evidence of the progress of civilization. The natives have killed themselves with gin, and immigrants from Berkshire pic-nic on the spurs of Mount Despair. The painting by M. Chevalier represents a view taken on the main road leading through the range, and no doubt faithfully represents the local features of the landscape.

M. Nicholas Chevalier is a native of Switzerland. Upon his arrival in Victoria he lent himself readily to satisfy popular taste, and became soon recognized as a rapid and skilful draughtsman. Having drawn successfully for the illustrated periodicals of the day, he found leisure at length to devote himself to the higher branches of his art. A painter of great industry, he sought and obtained the patronage of His Royal Highness the Duke of Edinburgh during that Prince's visit to this colony. He accompanied His Royal Highness to England in the Galatea, and made drawings of objects and places of interest during the voyage. On his arrival in London he was honoured by several commissions from those connected with the Court, and has since achieved for himself a secure position among artists resident in London. M. Chevalier was commissioned to paint the 'Thanksgiving at St. Paul's' on the occasion of the recovery of His Royal Highness the Prince of Wales, and at this time of writing, is understood to be engaged upon a pictorial representation of the marriage of his other Royal Patron.

The picture now under notice is very popular with visitors to the Gallery, and has been highly spoken of by many persons. It was thus criticised by a Melbourne journal upon the occasion of its first exhibition:—

'There is an Alpine Chain, snow-clad, dark as belongs to the sublime and precipitous, and full of the grandest reminiscences of the old world. Clad with verdure to the line of almost eternal snow it affords us a distinguishing feature in the varied beauties of Australia Felix. Mr. Chevalier has not before painted a better or more characteristic picture; the rich foreground surrounding the old water-wheel — especially the rock-work with its fine lichen clothing — is a beautiful piece of painting. In the centre there is a grove, which displays in a very brilliant manner the effect of the sylvan sunlight peculiar to our clime. The mountains are almost verdure-clad to the top, and the scene as a whole almost reminds one of Chamounix. A watercourse, most beautifully introduced, supplies a defect in Australian landscape, and life is given to the picture by the bullock-team in the foreground. — [*Melbourne Argus, December* 28, 1864.]

The 'Buffalo Ranges' became the property of the country for the sum of £200.

MARCUS CLARKE.

NOTES—CLARKE

Waterpool near Coleraine
1 Suttee (an English corruption of the Sanskrit *sati* i.e. 'the good woman' or 'true wife'). It refers to the ritualized burning alive of the widow upon the funeral pyre of her husband, as practised among certain Hindu castes.
2 Upas, an Indonesian word meaning poison, and specially applied to the poison derived from the gum of the anchor tree (*Antiaris toxicaria*) from which poison was obtained to envenom darts.
3 Camille Flers (1802-68), a French landscape painter associated with the Barbizon School.
4 i.e. the London International Exhibition of 1872-73.
5 i.e. the Exhibition of Works of Art, Art Treasures, and Ornamental Decorative Art. It attracted 1,406 exhibitors. 700 oil paintings were lent, and 70,000 visitors attended the exhibition. From the profits of the exhibition the Trustees invested £450 as a nucleus for the establishment of a Travelling Scholarship.

The Buffalo Ranges
1 The Commission was appointed under Sir James McCulloch's Ministry (1863-68) in order to develop an adequate purchasing and educational policy for the new National Gallery of Victoria.
2 Nicholas Chevalier (1828-1902), painter, lithographer and cartoonist, was born in St Petersburg. He was of Swiss descent, studied painting in Paris and architecture in Munich. He was a cartoonist for the Melbourne *Punch*, 1856-61, and is said to have introduced chromolithography to Australia.

🔲🔲🔲🔲🔲🔲🔲🔲🔲🔲🔲🔲🔲🔲🔲🔲🔲

SIX

Education, Taste and Nature

INTRODUCTION

The discovery of gold and the resulting increase in the growth of population in Australia quickened the pace of life. The consequent development of the cities led to new demands for cultural amenities to which the small communities of the pre-gold era had not aspired. One such demand was for art education.

The two articles printed below are taken from the *Month,* a journal current in Sydney, 1857-58. The articles were written by Joseph Sheridan Moore and constitute the first plea for government assistance to the visual arts to be published in Australia. Moore was well informed on recent developments in Great Britain, gained probably through such periodicals as the *Art Journal* and the *Magazine of Art*.

He begins by criticizing the atmosphere of philistinism prevailing among men in Australian public life. It was universally believed that the Australian colonies could not yet afford to cultivate the arts. We have already noticed that such a view was expressed by one so well-informed, socially-responsible and intelligent as John West a few years before. West was no philistine in principle; like so many high-minded Victorians he did see a place for the arts in the good society but he saw it largely through the stained-glass windows of religion, morality and history. For him art is a dangerous luxury that might soften 'the sinews of Empire', an indulgence a young society could barely afford. 'The plough not the pencil must be the crest of infant empires'.

For Moore that kind of talk was but an hypocritical way of doing nothing 'nobly' for the arts. 'What kind of society is it', he asks, 'that with upwards of half-a-million civilized men' cannot confidently provide a decent living for one artist? Was he thinking of Marshall Claxton, the English artist who had come to Sydney with two hundred paintings and high hopes of establishing an art school, only to leave in disillusionment for India in 1853?

Moore quotes Sir Joshua Reynolds and Luigi Lanzi in support of academies of art, claiming that the cultural milieu which they help to create leads to an improvement in the quality of taste and national life. Academies develop patriotic sentiment since, he assures us, it is only as a result of artists and poets responding creatively to the landscape of their birthplace that the general public are made aware of their environment. Whilst there is much to be said for this view in itself, it must be questioned whether academies of art have ever done much to encourage patriotism by means of landscape painting. Landscape as a distinct category of painting came into its own in a period during which the art academies of Europe were in decline. Moore probably had the two finest of all English landscape painters, Turner and Constable, in mind; but the degree to which the Royal Academy assisted their particular visions of the English countryside is, to say the least, questionable.

Academies of art have rarely sought to promote national sentiment overtly. Their explicit loyalty has been to art itself and a particular theory of art at that, the idealist theory of beauty based upon the study of the human body and a belief in human perfection as embodied in perfect form: a theory based ultimately upon Plato's belief in the reality of the *idea* and Aristotle's view of art as *mimesis,* or imitation. To the extent that academies remained faithful to this ideal they were supranational. In their historical development, however, they became powerful institutions of the national state during the seventeenth and eighteenth centuries. Colbert, Louis XIV's great minister of State, established the French Academy in order to establish French pre-eminence in the arts. Sir Joshua Reynolds sought, through the establishment of the Royal Academy of Arts in London, to improve not only the quality of British art but also the social status of British artists. All academies placed history painting (the *istoria* of Alberti) at the top of the ladder of painting. History painting depicted the noble deeds of the heroes of antiquity and the sacred scriptures. During the late eighteenth and nineteenth centuries, however, opinion as to just what was appropriate to history painting changed. *Istoria,* for the new world of the Enlightenment, came to mean increasingly the depiction of the deeds of recently-dead national heroes, such as James Wolfe, the hero of Quebec, or of Captain James Cook, the hero of Pacific exploration. In such ways the academies indeed kindled national sentiment.

Having outlined the importance of academies Moore turns to utilitarian arguments. Art, he stresses, pays. Neglect of art is bad for business. Behind the argument lies a knowledge of the *Parliamentary Report of the Select Committee on Arts and Manufactures*, published in 1836. This *Report* had provided overwhelming evidence as to the adverse effects which the lack of skilled designers in Britain had had upon the quality of, and hence the market for, her exports. Art education in Bavaria, Prussia and France, the *Report* revealed, had outstripped Britain. This, it argued, was the hidden reason for the vulnerability of British products on the international market.

Moore proceeds to argue that if ever Australia is to become a manufacturing nation she will have to face similar problems. It will, however, be absolutely essential to establish schools that will teach the general principles of art, not merely mechanical skills. He proposes that the Mechanics' Institutes, already by 1850 established in many Australian towns, should become the nucleus of a new art education scheme: to each a professionally-trained teacher of drawing and painting should be attached and art classes established.

Sheridan Moore's argument has two faces and they do not look in the same direction. He makes use of arguments that had long been advanced in support of the establishment of academies together with arguments of a quite different kind that had been advanced more recently in Britain in support of the establishment of Schools of Design. The double face of his case becomes explicit in the proposal to establish an 'Australian Academy for Fine Art and Design'. This was a compromise to suit the extremely open Australian situation and make use of all arguments that might conceivably influence a politician. In England, however, the distinction between the Academy and the Schools of Design was sharply drawn. The Academy was concerned exclusively with High Art, the Schools of Design with training artisans to design for industry. Care was taken to ensure that design students did not 'get ideas' about becoming artists. One safeguard was the prohibition on drawing the figure, either from cast or from life, in the Schools of Design.

In his second article Moore develops his case in detail. His desire to establish an academy-type training rather than Schools of Design becomes explicit. So, too, does his ultimate goal: the development of an Australian school of Painting. Unlike John Lhotsky (see p. 74), who envisaged an Australian school arising naturally from the pictorial problems presented by the distinctive character of the Australian vegetation, light and colour, Sheridan Moore, a practical man, realized that institutions had to be created before an Australian school of art could be formed. So he recommended the establishment of a 'few High Art seminaries' and asks that 'some half-dozen respectable European artists' be invited 'to come amongst us' as teachers of drawing and painting.

Ideas take time to fructify. It was not until a quarter of a century after these articles had been written in the *Month* that the ideas championed therein began to bear fruit. During the 1870s the colonial governments of Victoria and New South Wales established technical schools in which art classes were held. As in Britain, the Mechanics' Institutes were ignored and gradually declined as educational instruments. Many 'respectable' and quite a number of radical artists came to the country, encouraged by the news of gold and the growth of an illustrated press in the capital cities that was capable of providing them with a livelihood. Many turned to art teaching. By 1890 there were probably more artists who had been born and trained abroad actively teaching art in Australia proportionate to native-born teachers than there has ever been before or since. In Victoria, as a result of the establishment of Artisans' Schools of Design and a Central School in the form of the National Art Gallery School, the educational prerequisites for the creation of a national school of painting (advocated by Moore) was effectively established. It began to form around Tom Roberts after his return from study in Europe in 1884.

In modern communities, the practice of art is closely associated with criticism published in newspapers and periodicals. Sporadic comment on art appears in Australia from 1829 when McGarvie's article was published in the *Sydney Gazette* (see p. 64). But art criticism as a continuing activity does not become a feature of journalism until the 1870s by which time sufficient work was being exhibited to the public to justify specialized attention. James Smith was the first journalist to work in Australia sufficiently knowledgeable and experienced in the visual arts to present an informed, professional point of view consistently and to maintain it. A journalist of wide, cultural interest, he played a leading role in the development of the arts and gave his active support to institutions that promoted the arts in Melbourne during the second half of the nineteenth century. His work is significant for the emergence of a serious interest in arts and letters in Melbourne, and his life awaits and should repay a detailed study. Unfortunately his inability to appreciate the work of the Heidelberg School in 1889 has given him a reputation for insensitivity which he does not deserve. Greater critics than Smith, John Ruskin among them, failed to appreciate impressionism, but this need not blind us to their positive achievements.

The first example of Smith's criticisms printed below was evoked by the exhibition of Eugen von Guerard's *View of the Grampians.* It is well informed. The comments made: the use of great detail in a subject that also called for sublime treatment, the hardness of colour, the theatricality of the Aboriginal group, are all to the point. Moreover, von Guerard's painting was correctly placed in its context of history and style. What is irritating about the article is the superior and at times supercilious tone with which the criticism is conducted. That von Guerard had recently been appointed to a new, influential post, as Head of the recently-formed National Art Gallery School, may have helped to sharpen Smith's asperity. His reservations on this score, though implicit, do not appear to have been unjustified. Von Guerard was an interesting and sincere painter but he certainly did not make his mark as an inspiring teacher, for he set his young students most of the time to copy pictures in the new National Art Gallery of Victoria.

James Smith's criticism hurt von Guerard's pride and stung him, though possessed of an indifferent command of English, into a reply. It was either not submitted to the *Argus* or, if submitted, never published. The painter's problem with his English was a sufficient reason. It is published here, however, for the insight it provides into von Guerard's method of painting and his relation to the Pre-Raphaelite movement in Europe. He does not, it will be seen, take up the issues raised by Smith but discusses others loosely related.

It is of interest to find, when we compare von Guerard's list of German Pre-Raphaelite painters with James Smith's similar list, that von Guerard has added three landscape painters: von Schadow, Reinhart and Koch. We may assume that von Guerard admired the work of these men and that they had perhaps some effect upon the development of his own manner of landscape painting. The burden of his reply is to stress that he owes nothing to English Pre-Raphaelitism, and like most artists he objected to having his work tagged to a movement. But Smith was certainly correct in noting, as von Guerard himself confirms, that the painter was greatly influenced by the *Lukasbruder* and Nazarenes, first of the nineteenth century Pre-Raphaelite groups of painters. But in our present context it is important also to notice that von Guerard, in his respect for a precise manner of delineating plants and vegetation, was heir to a colonial tradition that reached back to Sydney Parkinson, the first European artist to see and describe the country. The development of botanical science in the nineteenth century lay at the back of both traditions: the new delight in the fresh but meticulous painting of plants by the Italian artists of the fifteenth century, and the special demand of science that artists provide accurate records from distant or outlandish places; requiring them to paint the exotic precisely in order to avoid deceit and the exaggerations associated with travellers' tales.

The latter part of von Guerard's reply consists of ineffective attempts at irony and an elaborate humility which his precarious command of English cannot sustain. The concluding blast at Smith reveals the depth of the painter's feeling. But it all ended pleasantly. Artist and critic became good friends and corresponded for years after von Guerard had returned to Europe.

The natural environment continued to be the most important single influence upon the development of painting in Australia throughout the nineteenth century. In the early years emphasis was placed, as we have seen, upon the accurate portrayal of plants and animals, as an essential part of the classification of the whole world of natural things: a labour which engaged the greatest botanists and zoologists of the century. The gradual penetration of the Australian continent from several points on the coast gradually revealed new types of landscape scenery; mountain and plain, jungle and desert, types that required classification both geographically and aesthetically. We have seen how early writers such as Barron Field and Marcus Clarke had sought to characterize Australian landscape as unpicturesque or melancholic, but the relevance of such categories lay more in the situation of the beholders coming to terms, in their own exile, with a strange country. The process, of course, continued inexorably. Many artists were associated with surveying and exploring the country to be opened up to settlement. Charles

Conder, for example, who ended his life decorating *fin de siecle* fans in London began his life as an up-country surveyor in New South Wales.

Joseph Sheridan Moore (1828–91)

Moore was born in Dublin and educated at the Jesuit College at Stoneyhurst, Lancashire. In 1847 he migrated to Sydney, became a Benedictine lay-brother and the headmaster of Lyndhurst College, Glebe. Moore became the leader of a group opposed to Archbishop Polding and his Secretary, Abbot Gregory. As a result of his conflict with his superiors he was refused ordination and later excommunicated. In April 1856 he left Lyndhurst. In October the following year Moore married Flora MacDonald Harris at the Ashfield District Registry. During 1856 and 1857 he was editor of the *Freeman's Journal,* a periodical addressed to the Catholic laity.

Moore became one of the leading spirits in a small but influential literary group in Sydney during the 1850s. In June 1857 this group of friends established a literary periodical called the *Month*. It was edited first by Frank Fowler, a London journalist, and then by Moore. The main contributors were Richard Rowe ('Peter Possum'), a journalist and teacher who wrote essays and verse; Henry Halloran, a civil servant who enjoyed writing commemorative odes for patriotic and solemn occasions; Edward Reeve, who wrote plays and was also the first Curator of the Nicholson Museum, University of Sydney; James Lionel Michel, a poet and early champion (in England prior to arriving in Australia) of the Pre-Raphaelites; Henry Kendall, the poet; and Nicol Drysdale Stenhouse, the patron of the group.

Moore wrote poetry, essays and articles, prided himself upon his oratorical powers and frequently lectured at the Mechanics' School of Arts, Sydney. His published works include, *The Elements of Elocution* (1855), *The Life and Genius of James Lionel Michel* (1868), and the *Ethics of the Irish under the Pentarchy* (1872). He took a keen interest in the affairs of Sydney University and his students from Lyndhurst College performed well there. In his *University Reform, Its Urgency and Reasonableness* (1865), he criticized the exclusiveness of the University and advocated the introduction of evening and 'external' students, together with the liberalization of courses to include the study of a modern language, and the creation of schools in medicine, civil engineering, and architecture. Moore claimed that it was he who suggested that the motto of Sydney University should be *Sidere Mens Eadem Mutato* and later, in a moment of irritation, translated the motto as 'although we have left the British Isles we still cling to our insular prejudices'. His programme for the development of art education in Australia reveals him as an independent mind, in this field also well ahead of his time. Moore died at his home in Elizabeth Street, Redfern, on 17 October 1891.

[ART EDUCATION IN AUSTRALIA]

If this fifth great division of the earth is ever to be a something more among the nations than a safety-valve to regulate the high pressure of the European money-markets, and is to become celebrated for other than bucolic and mercantile pursuits, it is the duty of her present population to make an effort to lay the foundations of those institutions which not only promote civilization, but win, with the universal consent of enlightened mankind, the brightest and most enduring renown. Few will deny that a vigorous public spirit and generous philanthropy have already in this country accomplished much social and moral good. But while cheerfully admitting our past achievements in these directions — it cannot be denied that we stand condemned of serious short-comings, if not of absolute neglect, in the promotion, protection, and right estimation of that highest sagacity of nature — ART. What in fact has been done to mark our recognition of Art, in any of its departments, as a great element of progressive civilization? What artists, in the great exodus of the past lustrum, have been tempted to visit our shores? What paintings, what sculptures do we possess? Were you, Reader — who, you will permit us to presume, glories in that transcendent and almost mythical quality, yclept 'colonial experience,' — to receive an intimation from some tolerably well-known, second-class European artist, that he was disposed to visit your 'sunny clime', provided you could give him a reasonable assurance of success — such success at least as a good surgeon or musician would probably meet with — what answer would you return? Be honest, Reader, — Would you not strongly (and reasonably enough, too) recommend him to remain at home? Certainly, if you were his friend, you would! Your 'experience,' however impalpable in its nature, has, at all events, confirmed you in the popular creed, *that the time has not yet come for the cultivation of the Fine Arts in*

Australia. Oh! ye votaries of the Good and True, — here are we —
upwards of half-a-million civilized men, — living in a glorious
land, in an age of Art-Revival, and yet the time has not arrived
for our cultivation of the Beautiful! It almost induces one to
believe that there is some foundation for the very profound
observation put into the mouth of an honorable member of our
Parliament, that 'in this country we are *above* painting, sculpture,
and — all that kind of thing!' But let us consider the matter
seriously.

It does not come within the scope of these remarks to dwell
at length on the advantages of the cultivation of Art as an
educational element, nor to comment on the grave duty of the
body politic to encourage and protect it. On the very threshold
surely that much may be assumed. But there are a few considerations which must be urged on the *practical* man before we can
excite his sympathy or secure his co-operation. Art, then, we beg
to tell him, repays the State that encourages it — and not in glory
alone, but in safe and sure returns for the money invested. This
we may show at some length before we conclude. The grand
doctrine of Sir Joshua Reynolds ought not, however, to be
forgotten, that institutions for the cultivation and encouragement
of the *Liberal* Arts should not be recommended upon considerations merely mercantile; for, as he ably maintains, academies,
founded upon such principles only, can never effect even their
own narrow purposes. If they have no higher origin, no pure taste
can ever be formed in manufactures; but if the higher Arts of
Design flourish, their inferior end, he rightly concludes, will of
course be attained. In language, massive and imposing as one of
his own splendid creations, this great Master points out the
advantage of Art Seminaries:—'Every seminary of learning,' he
writes, 'may be said to be surrounded with an atmosphere of
floating knowledge, where each mind may imbibe somewhat
congenial to its original conceptions. Knowledge thus obtained
has always something more popular and useful than that which is
forced upon the mind by private precepts, or solitary meditation.
Besides, it is generally found, that a youth more easily receives
instruction from the companions of his studies, whose minds are
nearly on a level with his own, than from those who are much
his superiors; and it is from his equals only that he can catch the
fire of emulation.'* The distinguished Abbate Lanzi† urges the

---

* Works of Sir Joshua Reynolds, vol. I, pp. 307-8 Bohn's edition.
† Every student of the branch of aesthetics under consideration, should read
and re-read Abbate Lanzi's 'History of Painting.'

L

formation of numerous schools for the simple and cogent reason, that it must be a very ill-starred school that cannot turn out some good artists.[1] There is one advantage, we think, in the formation of these High Art Seminaries, which we do not remember to have seen elsewhere urged, but which cannot fail to strike every enlightened observer. Genuine love of country — the real, joyous, abiding *home*-feeling — is strengthened and preserved by a thorough knowledge of the scenery of one's native land. This knowledge we can never fully, and in its brightest form, acquire without academies of Art. One may wander over a country again and again — be familiar with its most picturesque and romantic spots — and yet, unless he possess the poetic or artistic grasp, there will be no-long-lived impressions left on his mind. He lacks, in fact, the great creating power of Idealization. But let him see these scenes in a series of good paintings. A divine afflatus (and we are not now dealing in mere turgid phrases) seems to emanate from the canvas — his spirit is raised to a loftier and more ennobling contemplation — all commonplace fades from his view, and the scenes, before possessed of so little to awe or charm, suddenly acquire a certain consecration in his enraptured mind. When Guido was asked where he got his models, he summoned a common porter to his studio, and, from a mean original, drew a head of surpassing beauty. 'It resembled the porter,' a judicious and enthusiastic Art-critic* observes, 'but idealized the porter to the hero. It was true but it was not real;'[2] that is to say, — it glorified the commonplace, and even made vulgarity spiritual and precious. And this has ever been the end of the painter. Beneath his touch a snowy twig becomes a rib of crystal. A wreath of smoke from a cottage chimney takes the form of summer clouds, or glistens in the moted atmosphere like fairy robes. A clay bank washed by the sea becomes a field of amethyst and gold. A river ties the curves of a landscape like a zone of steel; and the sun, in burning showers, ravishes the encaverned world until each foot of dusky earth grows pregnant with cool green leaves and glowing blossoms. All things take fresher meaning. A daisy, an oak-cup, a few red leaves, the brown cheek of a pear, a bit of red tile — are each and all full of beauty, purpose, and deep significance.

But, to return a little — Painting, like Music, may be considered as a great means of developing a healthy but refined patriotism. Notwithstanding our limited space, we cannot force ourselves to narrow this consideration. It is, in part, ably sup-

---

* Sir E. Lytton-Bulwer in his charming prose-poem Zanoni 2nd ed. p. 303.

ported by a vigorous writer, in whose estimation the scenery of a
country is nothing less than 'the furniture of a man's temple
home.' Instead of being the circumstances, or conditions, or even
the compliments of the national character, it forms at once its
elements and model. No people has ever been so creative and
independent as to rise above its suggestions and studies. Scenery
has an intellectual import and mission. It is a grand and har-
monious assemblage of substantial symbols, through which the
Almighty instructs men, in the language, traditions, and literature
of the world. Sydney Smith talks of nature like one fresh from a
mountain walk:—'I for one,' says he, 'strongly believe in the
affirmative of the question, that nature speaks to the mind of man
immediately in beautiful and sublime language; that she aston-
ishes him with magnitude, appals him with darkness, cheers him
with splendour, soothes him with harmony, captivates him with
emotion, enchants him with form; she never intended man should
walk among her flowers, and her fields, and her streams, unmoved;
nor did she rear the strength of the hills in vain, or mean that
we should look with a stupid heart on the wild glory of the
torrent, bursting from the darkness of the forest and dashing over
the crumbling rock.' Thus, in sooth, nature talks to the Poet and
the Painter, to the Artist in words and the Artist who transfers
nature's highest and most beautiful manifestations to canvas;
but to make the high thoughts of both enrich the common mind
of mankind, the Poet must embody his conceptions in his songs,
the Painter in his delineations. Pope is characteristically subtle
in his sentiment,

> Art is but nature better understood, —

the apophthegm meaning, nature understood by being studied
from the high point of contemplation on which we have desired
to take our stand.

And now just two words for our utilitarian friends: words that
should have the same effect upon their hearts and pockets as had
Ali Baba's two words on the cavern door in the fable.[3] ART PAYS.
In the several continental countries where it has been more
cherished by government than in England, the results have been
surprising. It almost seems, indeed, that Beauty can vindicate
herself in the market-place. The list of articles, manufactured in
Great Britain, for which continental Artists alone, till within the
last few years, gave designs, would astonish the reader not versed
in such kinds of statistics. Designs for laces, ribbons, embossed
bands, crochets, damasks, and similar light gear, are at the present

moment, all the productions of French and German artists. In fact, the Great (English) Exhibition, of 1851,[4] demonstrated nothing more clearly than the superior grace and precision, and consequently the greater value, of foreign workmanship.[5] Even American designs were pronounced, by competent judges, to be more intelligible, better finished, and generally of a higher order of art, than English. This is a national disgrace, which has ere now been to some extent wiped away by the institution of a Central College of Arts and Design, in London,[6] resembling the celebrated one at Paris, at the Hotel Sale. That Marlborough House[7] will realize the anxious expectations of the nation we cannot reasonably doubt. The decided — the triumphant — success of Art-Education throughout the greater portion of continental Europe, is a fact that should be pressed on the consideration of patriotic capitalists. We shall, for the present, however, content ourselves with a condensed summary of Mr. Dyce's reports,[8] which we find at hand —

> These reports (Mr. Dyce's) prove that schools exist all over Germany affording the highest scientific instruction to all classes: that geometry, with drawing and modelling from the antique, is taught at a merely nominal charge, which in cases of poverty is dispensed with; while pecuniary aid is often given, and the talented transferred to the Art Academies. The great Trade Institute of Berlin is free, and gives a full, scientific, and technical education, with a view to producing a class of skilled and intelligent artizans. Bavaria shows a most complete system of public instruction, in every stage of which, art is combined with science, design for industry included, and drawing made as common as writing. In France, as is well known, attention to art, in its first principles, is promoted in every sphere, and that drawing, especially of the figure, is practised by all. What wonder, then, where art and science so mingle with the most elementary details of instruction, that they should enter into the whole character of a community, and be shaped to the exigence of its commerce? that the metal-work of Nuremburg, the silk-trade of Lyons, the ceramic art of Sevres, should variously illustrate the thorough artistic grounding which continental governments secure to the masses? That England, so great in mechanical appliance, is so wanting in well-assured science and the general expression of artistic feeling, must be attributed to our want of love and faithfulness toward these high graces of the mind. On the part of government and people, a too self-willed contempt of show has led to the grave error of contempt for the great truths of nature, written alike in flower and star; to know which intimately must elevate the individual *and promote general prosperity*.

Did our space permit, we could corroborate these conclusions by a reference to the state of Art Education in the several states of Italy, in Spain, and also in Denmark and Sweden.

Now why should Australia be blind to the importance of Art Institutions? Why should she, with a Chinese-like fidelity, imitate the *great defect* of the fatherland? Shall we never have more than one manufacturer in silk and cotton fabrics? Shall we not work in iron and clay — in gold and silver? And why not possess genuine, accurate, and chaste home designs for these possible, and in fact, very probable manufactures? This, surely, is a good point for the practical man's meditation. We earnestly hope it will secure his attention to the *suggestive* part of our paper, with which alone, for the present, we mean to occupy the reader.

There is no royal road to Art. The laurel crown of honorable distinction or triumphant success, must be won leaf by leaf. Labour, the grand necessity of humanity, is required to *inform* the mind of the Artist in the *habit* of his art. And this is natural: for, as the Royal Academician, Redgrave, at the opening of the session, 1853, at Marlborough House, observes:—

> Executive power, arising from the training of the hand and eye, is so obviously a first requisite of the artist, that its acquisition has, in some degree, obscured the importance of understanding the principles which regulate its successful application, and thus given an undue prominence to the mere executive means. Yet it ought hardly to have been requisite, in the present day, to uphold the necessity there is of imparting to the student rules and principles to guide him, or to maintain that every art and science must be regulated by them. It is no doubt true that rules and principles, however derived, whether from natural laws, or gathered from past practice, should not be fetters to restrain the natural genius (which may and will break through them when intellectual strength renders their support and guidance less necessary): still such rules and principles must always be valuable to the teacher, enabling him to convey to the student a knowledge of those restrictions which the laws of nature impose, and those considerations, which being found consistent with other truths, have governed the practice of the skilled artist in all ages — that cumulative stock of experience, in fact, which, had it been separately gathered by each individual, would waste life in preliminary study. What should we say of the musical composer, who, thinking only of the fingers of his pupils, gave him no insight into the laws of harmonic intervals, or those principles of counterpoint so essential to the agreement arrangement (*sic*) of musical sounds — or of him who should leave his pupil to find out for himself those rules of grammatical construction that regulate the language in which he would have him compose his theme? Would the knowledge of these laws, the enforcing on the

young student such oft-tested rules, restrict the genius of the one, or restrain the other from expressing, in clear language, the results of his mental reflections or his perceptive faculties? or would not the powers of both be more free to exercise themselves from a sense of mastery over all known means — the knowledge of the natural laws, and the past application of them to the practice of their particular Art or Science.*

This quotation contains such sound doctrine, that we should not have been justified in either abridging or paraphrasing it. It will illustrate to young Australians the necessity of acquiring sound rudimental training in every department of Aesthetics.

We have in this paper already mourned over the dreary apathy of our fellow citizens in reference to the cultivation and encouragement of High Art in all its departments;† we have pointed out or referred to some of the most prominent advantages to be derived from its patronage and protection; it, therefore, only remains for us to propose or suggest our scheme for the diffusion of Art Education throughout the country. This, for brevity sake, we condense into the style and form of propositions:—

1st. That there be established, in every Municipal town in the colony, possessing a Mechanics' Institute,[9] in connection with such Institute, a Professorship of Painting and Drawing (including Design).

2nd. That such school be open to all persons of good character, who can read and write.

3rd. That there be a Local Board, consisting of —— members, to superintend and carry out the objects of the Institution.

4th. That there be annual examinations and exhibitions — the exhibitions open to the pupils of all schools, private and public.

5th. That there be prizes awarded once a-year, the principal one of which shall be a Scholarship of £——, tenable for —— years.

6th. That the Sydney branch of the Institution be called the 'Australian Central Academy of Fine Arts and Design.'

Now we come to the home question:— Where are we to find the two or three thousand pounds of 'good British money' necessary to carry out our *scheme*, or something analogous to it?

---

* *Art Journal*, November, 1853, p. 269.
† Not even excepting Music. The patronage which has been extended to this Sister-art is neither healthy nor just, as we shall on another occasion show.

There are three sources from any, or all, of which the money can be procured; namely, the Government Treasury, the Municipal Marsupium, or the purses of private individuals. From one or all of these we must draw; and without trenching on the dangerous, and to us forbidden, ground of political discussion, we shall, in our next number, attempt to show, that it is on the Government we should — and, indeed, must — mainly depend for support. Aristotle, that hearty old king of philosophers, truthfully and powerfully remarks:—

> A Government ruling for the benefit of all, is, of its very nature, anxious for the education of all, not only because intelligence is in itself a good, and the condition of good, but even in order that its subjects may be able to appreciate the benefits of which it is itself the source; whereas, a Government ruling for the profit of its administrators, is naturally willing to debase the mind and character of the governed, to the end that they may be disqualified to understand, and to regard, and to assert their rights.

NOTES—ART EDUCATION IN AUSTRALIA

1 Luigi Lanzi, *History of Painting in Italy* (trans. T. Roscoe), London, 1828, 6 vols. In this historical account of the provincial schools of Italian painting the author speaks continually of the value of academies in raising artistic standards in all the centres in which they were established.

2 Several such stories are told of Guido Reni. Lanzi tells a similar tale: 'I find moreover that he took for the model of one of his magdalens the extremely vulgar head of a colour-grinder; but under Guido's hand every defect disappeared, each part became graceful, the whole a miracle'. *History of Painting in Italy*, v. 144.

3 i.e. 'Open sesame', a reference to the story of Ali Baba and the Forty Thieves in *The Arabian Nights Entertainment*.

4 'The Great Exhibition of the Works of Industry of all Nations', was held on the south side of Hyde Park in a building of iron and glass designed by Joseph Paxton which became known as the Crystal Palace. The two men mainly responsible for the organization were Sir Henry Cole and the Prince Consort.

5 The superiority of French and German design as applied to industry had, however, been made clear in the very thorough investigation undertaken by the Select Committee of the House of Commons on Arts and Manufactures of 1835.

6 This was the school established at Somerset House, London, in 1837 by the Board of Trade and reorganized in 1851.

7 After the reorganization of the School of Design in 1851 the Prince Consort made rooms available at Marlborough House.

8 William Dyce (1806-64), a Scottish painter who had associated with the Nazarenes during his stay in Rome. At that time he also became interested in the problems of art education in an industrial society. He was in consequence asked by the Select Committee on Arts and Manufactures to make an investigation of art education for industry on the Continent. His

extensive Report, published in March 1840, led to an attempt to bring design more closely into relation with industrial processes.

9 Mechanics' Institutes were set up in Britain in the 1820s for teaching science to working-class men as a result of the activities of George Birkbeck (1776-1841), Professor of Natural Philosophy at the Andersonian University, Glasgow. The Glasgow Mechanics' Institute, founded in 1823, developed from Birkbeck's extra-mural classes to artisans. An Institute was set up in London in 1824 and the movement spread into the provinces. The first Mechanics' Institute was established in Australia in 1826 at Hobart and a second at Sydney in 1833, where, as we have seen, they became for a brief period civic centres for lectures related to the arts and sciences, but appealing more to middle-class than working-class interests.

[ART EDUCATION IN AUSTRALIA] (second article)

In our first paper* on this important topic — in which it was attempted to embody a few earnest personal reflections on the subject, rather than build up an elaborate argument — we noted — in a kindly, if somewhat enthusiastic, spirit — the shortcomings of our fellow-citizens in every department of High Art — Painting, Sculpture, and Design in particular; lamented over the dreary apathy which prevents an immediate and united movement in its behalf; urged a few considerations with regard to the most obvious advantages that spring from its cultivation and protection; and offered some suggestions for the initiation of those institutions, by means of which the atmosphere of its humanizing influences may surround and pervade the whole community. Our object was to excite an appreciative taste for Art, and to awaken a strong desire in the public mind for its application as a powerful element of popular education. The subject, although in itself of the highest importance, is one that requires neither the grasp of a peculiar order of mind to seize its spirit and investigate its principles, nor the action of the finest intellect to promulgate and defend its claims. In fact, it is universally admitted among all civilized people, that it is, as the schoolmen have it, a great good *in se* — in its very essence — and also in its results. Our object, then, was rather to arouse the attention of those who, without denying or slighting its real value, neglected or postponed a movement in its favor. We tried to awaken sympathy in the public mind — and to arouse in the heart of our fellow men purer desires than a cold, though feverish, aspiration for mere stock-exchange honours and commercial diplomas. This, we assumed, could not be more safely accomplished than by calling to our assistance the aid of the master-spirits of the world whose inspired voices and lofty doctrines have

* The *Month*, no. 1, pp. 1-6.

enlightened men once as deficient as ourselves in the discipline and knowledge of true Art. From the very outset of our undertaking, we expected little sympathy — and no co-operation — from those who talk and write so illiberally about Aesthetics, without understanding the large significance of the term. Very different are the sentiments of the truly good and wise of all countries and all times in reference to our theme. The ancient Greeks called sculptures and pictures living writings; the books of all classes of men. The severest attack Pliny could make on the Epicurean philosophers was by charging them not so much with a desecration of the temple of Art, as with a neglect of its worship:— 'So it is indeed,' he indignantly exclaims, 'sloth has destroyed the Arts; and because there are no models of souls, those even of bodies are neglected.'* Greek and Roman poetry glorifies art and artists in language of the most impassioned enthusiasm; but we have no doubt with a certain class of persons — those who, like Settle,¹ abuse the classics from an inability to understand Greek — illustrations would be pronounced pedantic. To select, however, one or two expressions of modern opinion on the matter, what admirable philosophy is condensed in the following passage from Père Cahier:—'It is impossible to form an idea of Art without penetrating into a multitude of details, which long study can alone furnish. Never, assuredly, were the forms of matter carried to a degree so near speech, never so many thoughts, and such lofty thoughts, transmitted to the soul by the eyes without the aid of writing; but here was, at the same time, for the intelligence, the abstract and almost boundless range of written language, and for the imagination the magic power of vision. Add to this, what is truly admirable, that this majestic system of expression was continually consecrated, not only to truth, but to the most useful and the grandest truths which man has ever possessed.² Listen, also, to the elder Schlegel:—'The true object of art should be, instead of resting in externals, to lead the mind upward to a more exalted region and a spiritual world.'†
The mission of the artist is beginning to be every day more popularly understood; and, we hope, that ere long the remark of Theocritus, 'that poverty — or rather want — alone excites men to labor in the fine arts,'³ will soon be universally repudiated. The advocate of the true artist contends, — Truth must be his, for he deals with facts; purity, for he is a servant of the All-Pure; reverence in an especial degree, for he, more than other men, is

---

* 'ita est profecto: artes desidia perdidit, et quoniam animorum imagines non sunt, negleguntur etiam corporum.' Pliny, N. H. xxxv, 2.

† Aesthetical Works, Bohn's Ed. p. 145.

brought within the influence of that revelation which is written in the book of nature, and with unsandalled foot, treads close on holy ground. To delight, not by base truckling to the changeful wills of men, but by the enunciation of truths in whose shadow the Great First Cause is dimly veiled; to arrest the fleeting footsteps of the sunbeam on the mountain's side, and bid it tell us somewhat of that home from whence it comes, and to which we are wending on, that the heart may be cheered by hope and anticipation of things unspeakable, greater and more beautiful than ear hath heard, or eye hath seen; to catch the transient glory of tree and flower, and to fix in fairest guise that which is best and purest in the actions of man, who fadeth also, like the flower of the field, and is withered and cut down like its grass; and thus to purge the heart of its dross of passion and leaven of vanity through these moral influences whose plaintive and appealing cry the world's conventionalism would strangle at the birth; — such and so great, to our mind, is the artist's mission among men.

These reflections, however, lead us away from the matter to be considered on the present occasion. We advocate the institution, of a few High Art Seminaries, which it is our sincere hope will one day, and that not a very far distant one, develop themselves into a great Australian School of Art. Our demand is a modest one; for it only asks the country to hold out a sufficient inducement for some half-dozen respectable European Artists to come amongst us — to establish classes of Drawing, Painting, and Design, in our Mechanics' Institutes — to offer to successful pupils some honorary recognition of their ability and merit. The realization of our dream of an Australian School of Art depends mainly on the enlightened liberality of Government. If the matter be not taken up by those who have the means to give it a quick vitality and healthy constitutional vigor, we fear the apathy of the people at large will suffer this high educational element to remain in its present neglected condition. Nor do we anticipate much assistance from municipal liberality, even should we await the organization of corporate towns. So many other exigencies will more imperiously, though not more deservedly, claim the kind consideration of burgesses, that we may despair of seeing anything really encouraging done in behalf of Art Education. If the people would only earnestly desire the Government to establish a Central School in Sydney, and affiliated institutions at Maitland, Bathurst, Goulburn, and other places, we should, before many years, possess the nucleus of that Grand School, which we so ardently wish to see established, and the very hope of which induced us to bring the matter under public consideration.

Let it not be supposed that we violate one of our established rules in the conduct of this journal in thus appealing to Government to inaugurate the seminaries we have suggested. Had we any strong hope of assistance from other quarters, we should perhaps hesitate in making a bold demand on the public Treasury. But since Government is assumed to be always influenced by the sovereign principle of ruling for the benefit of the majority, it would be an affected sensitiveness, if not an absolute dereliction of duty, on our part, to shrink from urging on their attention a matter of such national importance as the support of Art. Without attempting to make an invidious comparison, we contend that the establishment of these academies would be a more immediate and direct good to a community like ours, composed as it principally is of a large working population — carpenters, builders, and similar handicraftsmen, who require instruction in drawing and design more, perhaps, than in any other branch of education — than a University which, from its very nature — embracing as it does a complete course of knowledge, demanding long study and comparatively heavy expenditure — must be limited to particular sections of a population.[4] What examples could be adduced of the liberality of European states for the advancement of Art! The few cited in our first paper may again be referred to by the reader with advantage. The history of the Italian Schools of Art, is full of splendid examples of the generosity of enlightened sovereign princes, and its glorious results; and France at the present moment deserves the highest praise for her noble Art Institutions. It is to be hoped that Australia, growing day by day into more mature prosperity, will not fail to recognise her manifest duty in reference to this subject.

We think there is an imperative obligation on the part of legislators at the present time to lend us their co-operation. There are many young men — law-students, clerks, artizans, etc. — in Sydney and the inland towns, full of noble impulse in this direction, who have absolutely no suitable place for the refined recreations for which they long. Will the utilitarian suggest to us how these young aspirants can best employ their leisure time? Will the practical man deny that many of them would be led away from temptation, if the schools we recommend were established? Will any one assert that among so many high intellects and fine organizations, some few would not distinguish themselves and reflect honor on the country? *We* at all events have sufficient faith in the youth of Australia to dare reply in the affirmative. But we know what we have to encounter in taking this position: even in this sixteenth century after the fall of Rome we have still need to fear the Goths and Vandals.

Full fifteen hundred years ago the great Longinus — the father of all literary criticism — recognised the secret of the decay of genius in his own times on account of the sovereign selfishness and utilitarian spirit of the public mind:—'Upon the whole, then, I have shown,' he confesses, 'that the bane of true genius in the present day is that dissolution of morals, which, with few exceptions, prevails universally among men who, in all they do, or undertake, seek only applause and self-gratification, without a thought of that public utility which cannot be too zealously pursued, or too highly valued.'*

Equally profound and vigorous are the remarks of John Ruskin, while bewailing the degraded condition of the artizan of our own times through lack of proper art-training.—

> We want one man (he writes) to be always thinking, and another to be always working, and we call one a gentleman, and the other an operative; whereas the workman ought often to be thinking, and the thinker often to be working, and both should be gentlemen, in the best sense. As it is, we make both ungentle, the one envying, the other despising, his brother; and the mass of society is made up of morbid thinkers, and miserable workers. Now, it is only by labor that thought can be made healthy, and only by thought that labor can be made happy, and the two cannot be separated with impunity. It would be well if all of us were good handy craftsmen in some kind, and the dishonour of manual labor done away with altogether; so that though there should still be a trenchant distinction of race between nobles and commoners, there should not, among the latter, be a trenchant distinction of employment, as between idle and working men, or between men of liberal and illiberal professions. All professions should be liberal [Art-Education will make the lowest so], and there should be less pride felt in peculiarity of employment, and more in excellence of achievement. And yet more, in each several profession no master should be too proud to do its hardest work. The painter should grind his own colors; the

---

* Our version gives but faint expression to the mingled sorrow and indignation of the original:—Longini de Sub. Sect. XIIV. 11; edition Oxon.5

architect work in the mason's yard with his men; the master-manufacturer be himself a more skilful operative than any man in his mills; and the distinction between one man and another be only in experience and skill, and the authority and wealth which these must naturally and justly attain.*

With such high authorities before us, we can well afford to smile at those apostles of common-sense (whose sense, by the way, is sometimes very common indeed), with whom enthusiasm calls forth a smirk, and a healthy admiration for things best and noblest, a self-sufficient simper.

From *The Month* edited by F. Fowler) Vol. I pp. 1-6 and Vol. II pp. 71-4, *c.* June-July, 1857

ART EDUCATION IN AUSTRALIA—SECOND ARTICLE

1 i.e. Elkanah Settle (1648-1724), the dramatist rival of John Dryden, who satirized him as Doeg in *Absalom and Achitophel* (1681). Moore's reference here, however, refers to a comment by Dryden in the pamphlet (1674) in which he mercilessly attacked Settle's play, *The Empress of Morocco* (1673). 'For the Latin and Greek authors, he had certainly done them the same injury he has done the English, but that he has the excuse of Aretine for not railing against God—he steals not from them, because he never knew them.' But note that Moore has altered, or misunderstood, the point of Dryden's comment.

2 Père Cahier, Monog. De Bourges; apud (Kenelm Henry) Digby, *Compitum: (the meeting of the ways at the Catholic Church)* 2 vols (1850-51), vol. II, 365 (JSM's original footnote with additions).

3 Idyll XXI: 'crafts' rather than 'fine arts' would be a closer translation.

4 The writer is referring to the recently established University of Sydney.

5 Longinus, the traditional name of the unknown author who wrote *De Sublimata* (On the Sublime), probably in the mid-first century A.D. The criticism of the morals of Longinus's day from which the author quotes is drawn from Section XLIV, the last in the treatise.

James Smith (1820–1910)

Born near Maidstone, Kent, and educated for the church, Smith instead took to journalism and was editing a country newspaper at the age of twenty. In 1845 he published *Rural Records or Glimpses of Village Life;* in 1849 *Oracles from the British Poets;* in 1851 *Wilton and its Associations;* and in 1853 *Lights and Shadows of Artist Life and Character* (1853).

In 1854 Smith emigrated to Victoria and became a leader writer on the *Age*, Melbourne, and the first editor of the *Leader*. In 1856 he joined the staff of the Melbourne *Argus* and wrote leading articles, literary reviews and dramatic criticism for that

* Stones of Venice, vol. ii, chap. 6.

paper for many years. He also wrote for country newspapers. In 1863 he became the Librarian to the Victorian Parliament and during his five years in that post classified and catalogued about 30,000 volumes. But the post was abolished temporarily in 1868 and Smith resumed his duties on the *Argus,* continuing to work for the paper until his retirement in 1896 at the age of seventy-six. He continued his journalistic work, however, contributing valued articles to the *Age* until nearing the age of ninety. He died on 19 March 1910.

Apart from his journalistic work Smith also published *From Melbourne to Melrose* (1888), a collection of travel notes, and *Junius Unveiled* (1909). He also published several tracts on spiritualism in which he became increasingly interested in the later years of his life. Smith contributed to the *Picturesque Atlas of Australasia* and edited the *Cyclopaedia of Victoria* (1903). He wrote a three-act play, *Garibaldi* (produced in Melbourne in 1860), and another play, *A Broil at the Café.* Smith was a member of the Working Men's College and was for many years a Trustee of the Public Library, Museums and National Gallery of Victoria. A good linguist, he took an active interest in both the Alliance Française and the Melbourne Dante Society. Smith was an outstanding journalist and contributed a great deal to the cultural life of Melbourne during his fifty-six years residence in the city.

[MR. VON GUERARD'S NEW PICTURE]

Vor-Raffaellismus had its first, and perhaps its most congenial, home in Germany. It commenced there long before the corresponding art-revolution to which we have given the name of pre-Raphaelitism took place in England. Cornelius,[1] with his co-enthusiasts Veit,[2] and Pforr,[3] and Overbeck,[4] and Schnorr,[5] were the predecessors of Ruskin and the disciples who followed the creed he so eloquently taught. It is not, therefore, astonishing that even in this colony the sole artist of any pretensions who has adopted the new doctrine should be a son of the Vaterland, and a belted knight of Franz Josef.[6] M. Eugen Von Guérard is our local apostle of that microscopism in pictorial delineation which was the extravagance wherein the indignant protest of the German 'purists' first took shape. His landscapes may not present quite fifteen hundred different grasses, as there are not generally so many to be found in the bush scenes with which his pencil is familiar, but they offer a minutely laborious description of almost every leaf upon the gum trees, and of every vein and crevice in the rocks, which would make them delightful illustrations of a treatise on the botanical or geological features of the colony.

It is to be regretted that one who succeeds so well in that patient manipulation which, after all, is but the meaner part of pre-Raphaelitism, should strive so little after the elevated earnestness of feeling with which it was pervaded, and which formed its chief attraction. In Germany, its aim was to bring back the spirit of early Italian art, clothing it in the same [charms?] which it received from the hands of Masaccio,[7] Fiesole,[8] Gozzoli,[9] Lippi,[10] and other masters of the fifteenth century. In England, the object of the 'pre-Raphaelite brethren' may perhaps best be described by saying that they are asserted to do for English art what Wordsworth and the other 'lakists'[11] attempted to do for English poetry. But in both countries it was an awakening from the lethargy into which art had fallen — from the apathy of careless working and commonplace incident to the life, and fervour, and reality of its mission amongst men. The intellectual force and artistic intensity of which it was the expression naturally produced works which startled every spectator into an admission of its power, whether he was pleased with it or not; and men forgot for a moment the graces of Raphael to admire the efforts of those who imitated his predecessors. In Germany, apostates are still living who have long forsworn the vows they pledged in those days. In England, the faith was lost in the natural divergencies of the original minds by which it was inspired, and there is now no more unity of thought or style between Millais[12] and Hunt,[13] Inchbold[14] and Davis,[15] Woolner[16] and Boyce,[17] than between any other two artists of equal note. Nothing now remains of the 'literal manner' but the glory which belongs for ever to the great masters by whom it was first taught and practised. Their greatness, as all greatness in art, has been found to be altogether independent of its manner, and now it is well understood that, as the minuteness of a Van Eyck[18] only increases the feeling of his work, so that of a Denner[19] only brings out with more distinctness the barrenness of idea to be remarked in his productions. If we continue the comparison, in order to show the applicability of these remarks to our present subject, we fear it will be found that Mr. Von Guérard resembles Denner rather more than Van Eyck.

We have just had an opportunity of examining Mr. Von Guérard's new work — a view in the Grampians in the Western district of this colony, a subject that might well inspire as noble an effort as landscape artist ever put forth. The high-priest of pre-Raphaelitism[20] would have told him that these mountains were made 'to fill the thirst of human heart for the beauty of God's working;' that 'they are a great and noble architecture, covered with mighty sculpture and painted legend;' and that 'they are lifted up towards heaven in a stillness of perpetual mercy.'[21] Mr. Von Guérard feels nothing, however, of all this, or cares little about it. He finds nothing more to note in these magnificent ranges, which Mitchell describes as 'truly sublime,'[22] than the ferruginous sandstone of which they consist, or the peculiar character of the trees and shrubs with which they are partially covered. So accurately, indeed, do the latter seem to be made out, that we imagine a botanist would be almost able to discover amongst them the banksia, the casuarina, the xanthorhoea, or some of the other hardy inhabitants of these lofty regions. The view represents the most northern part of the ranges, including Mount Zero and Rose's Gap. Daylight pours down its full blaze over the summits of these hills, and casts strange illusory reflections over the boundless plains of mallee-scrub that stretch away behind them out of sight. The lords of creation are represented by a couple of aborigines, whose attitudes are rather theatrical, but whose presence, while it gives life to the scene, is not out of harmony with the primeval appearances of nature with which they are surrounded. The perspective is correct, the topographical description of the spot is no doubt most faithfull, the elaboration of details merits all the praise due to finished execution, and if the colour were less hard, we should have little fault to find with the technical quality of the picture. There are some other points to which we might allude, but we think it better at present to direct attention merely to the distinguishing characteristics of Mr. Von Guérard's work, and its leading merits and defects. Now that he occupies a position where his example will have more influence than it had before, it is more than ever necessary that just notions should be propagated concerning the principal features and the main tendency of his art. We shall on some future occasion perhaps have an opportunity of entering more into detail. Suffice it to say for the present, that the 'View in the Grampians' is a good specimen of this artist's style; and though it may be wanting in some of the higher qualities to be sought in works of the kind, it has merits not unworthy of its author's reputation.

[From an article by James Smith, the *Argus* (Melbourne) 13 July 1870]

NOTES—JAMES SMITH

1 Peter von Cornelius, (1783-1867), the German painter who joined the group known as the Nazarenes in Italy in 1811. His principal works are his frescoes of mythological subjects in the Glyptothek, Munich, and his 'Last Judgement' in the Ludwigskirke, Munich.

2 Philipp Veit, (1793-1877), a German painter of history and architectural views.

3 Franz Pforr, (1788-1812), a German painter who founded the *Lukasbruder* (Brotherhood of St Luke) with Friederich Overbeck in Vienna in 1809. They became known, at first derisively, as Nazarenes. Pforr's paintings drew their inspiration largely from romantic literature.

4 Friederich Overbeck, (1789-1869), a German painter and co-founder with Pforr of the Lukasbruder. His own work made much use of religious symbolism and minute attention to detail.

5 Julius Schnorr von Carolsfeld, (1794-1872), a German painter who joined the Nazarenes in Rome (1794-1872) and helped them paint the villa of Prince Massimo. In Munich he painted frescoes in the palace of Ludwig I, and became head of the Dresden Academy in 1846 from whence he spread, through his teaching, the ideals of the Nazarenes.

6 Von Guerard was awarded the Cross of the Order of Franz Josef forwarded by the Emperor of Austria to Viscount Canterbury, Governor of the Colony of Victoria.

7 Masaccio (1401-28), the famous Florentine painter who developed the monumental style of Giotto, and was much admired by Raphael and other masters of the High Renaissance. His most famous surviving frescoes are those in the church of the Carmine, Florence.

8 Mino da Fiesole (1429-84), an Italian sculptor, highly esteemed for his graceful representations, both in the round and in relief, of the Madonna and Child.

9 Benozzo Gozzoli (1420-1497), an Italian painter. His most famous work 'The Procession of the Magi' painted for the children's chapel in the Medici-Riccardi palace, Florence, incorporates sumptuousness of decorative colour with the new interest in space and perspective.

10 The reference appears to be to the fifteenth century Fra Filippo Lippi (1406-69) rather than to his son Filippino Lippi (1457-1504).

11 A common term in the nineteenth century to describe the Lake poets, i.e. Wordsworth, Coleridge and their circle, because of their associations with the Lake District of Cumberland.

12 Sir John Everett Millais (1829-96), the artist who with Holman Hunt and D. G. Rossetti founded the Pre-Raphaelite Brotherhood in 1848.

13 William Holman Hunt (1827-1919), the painter and founding member of the Pre-Raphaelite Brotherhood and the one member who throughout his career reminded faithful to the Brotherhood's ideals. His painting 'The Light of the World' toured Australia in 1906.

14 John William Inchbold (1830-88), the landscape painter who was influenced during his youth by the Pre-Raphaelites.

15 Henry William Banks Davis (1833-1914), a landscape and animal painter much influenced during the 1850s and 1860s by the Pre-Raphaelites.

16 Thomas Woolner (see pp. 119-20, Chapter 4).

17 George Price Boyce (1826-97), a landscape and topographical painter, first educated as an architect. His diaries are a valuable source of information concerning the Pre-Raphaelites.

M

18 Jan van Eyck (fl. 1422-41), the Flemish painter famous for the detail and precision of his realistic painting, and for his early use of oil as a vehicle for painting.

19 Balthasar Denner (see p. 111, n. 13).

20 i.e. John Ruskin (1819-1900) who from May 1851 strongly supported their work.

21 The two quotations are from Chapter VII 'The Dry Land' in vol. 4 of *Modern Painters*. Ruskin, *Works* (ed. Cook and Wedderburn), vi, 118, 127.

22 'From the summit of Mount Abrupt I beheld a truly sublime scene', Thomas Mitchell, *Three Expeditions into the Interior of Eastern Australia*, London, 1838, i, 258.

[REPLY ON THE CRITIC OF EUGENE VON GUERARD'S PAINTING OF THE NORTH GRAMPIANS]

[not dated]

To the artist of the above named picture, the name of Vor Raffaellismus is quite a new word, he is only convinced that it had its first origin from the style of painting used in Italy by a great many of Raphael's predecessors which showed a very great tendency to paint saints in religious compositions, other persons in historical pictures and all kinds of things not clad in human forms, so much is possible true to nature, not only in the effect but also in the finishing of details, especially in pictures which were intended to be put in rooms or galleries, not for great distances as it is usually the case with very large church paintings or scene painting for theatres.

Raphael[1] himself made his beginning with very elaborate pictures more so like his great master Pietro Perugino[2] whose works should be seen in its native town to be really able to know the great value of this master's work. He painted more for the effect at a distance, soon as he adopted his second and third style in a time when nearly all his paintings were of a large size but in the same time all his work especially those which were painted for rooms, were highly finished even down to the smallest details, so that it would satisfy the strictest Preraffaelite.

Not only the purity correctness and gracefulness of Raphael's design combined with his beautiful colours entitled this great master to the eternal name which he has, but his being able to keep the correct limits between the extremely conscientious finished paintings of his first style and the more freely painted works of his later days in which we see never a useless darkening of colours or a careless drawing and loose style of painting.

Everyone who has an eye properly educated to see correct, will easily discern that from this highest elevation of art which

Raphael attained the great many artists which followed him down to the beginning of the present century gradually deteriorated and certainly we see that the pupils of Raphael did not exaggerate in finishing too well but exaggerate in finishing too little their pictures, forgetting how careful their great master was to take nature as its only model and rule. It was in the beginning of the nineteenth centry that the great German artists Cornelius, Overbeck, Schadow,[3] Veit, Schnorr, Reinhard,[4] Koch,[5] and others met in Rome and drawing a parallel between the state of the fine arts in the time of Michaelangelo Buonarotti and Raphael with that of their own time, recognised the necessity to begin with a totally new course of studies in order to rectify that careless style of art which was grotesque in the drawing and highly mannered in painting and composition.

More than all the others it was Peter Cornelius which tried to raise the art of drawing and painting but to my belief never he was a follower of that primitive — the Preraffaelite style nor did so his friends (which Mr. G. nearly all had the honour to know personally)[6] but they were convinced that a careful and well finishing style of painting could lead to a reelevation of the art which was so much neglected.

However great Ruskin is in his works on art but the artist whose name and painting give raise to the eluded criticism, thinks for certain that all the above named artists never knew this author's name or in any way were influenced by Ruskin's writing.[7]

If the noble Art Critic which took so much trouble to show his erudition in art literature accuses the style of painting of Mr. V. G. as Preraffaelite this artist can assure the public that it was the first time that he had heard of that school in the year 1854 when he exhibited his first pictures of Australian scenery in Melbourne and that the only reason for which he adopted that so-called style was that he finds nature so infinitely Preraffaelite and with all the existing difficulties he wished to paint so closely as he saw the details and effects of nature; if he fails in it in his want of ability, not in the possibility to arrive near this aim of all the really great artists.

(If the critic accuses the artist to be a belted knight of Franz Joseph he has nothing to reply than that he has the hope that the author of the criticism, so full of disinterested feelings may never have to bear a similar distinction by his sovereign which seem to be so unpleasant to him.) [This comment crossed out.]

As an Apostle of microscopism in pictorial deliniation [*sic*] the artist feels ashamed of his praise because he sees clearly that he is (the author) not a judge of what can be seen in nature and to what use can be brought what we see so well finished in the details of nature, and that an artist should so far as it is compatible with the effect of a picture, imitate nature not only in the masses but also in the details and it is his conviction that a good many which are painting in a different way are not able to finish a picture well and find it a much easier and more profitable work to pay so little regard as possible (to) the details, so as it is well known to keep a painting in a good harmony and finish it well is one of the most difficult operations in painting.

If ever the artist in question could succeed to paint Australian scenes to make them delightful illustrations for treatises of botanical or geological features of the colony then he would be convinced that for the future his paintings would have a greater value, where it will be doubtful if those which can be taken equally well for a misty English or an Australian landscape will have the same future.

If Mr. G. did not succeed in giving such an elevated and earnest feeling to his pictures, as the critic on his painting requires it for his qualities, he is exceedingly sorry as the real artist always shall strive, if possible to satisfy everyone who sees his work. With very few paintings, the artist thinks, to have better succeeded as with the one in question, to explain (?) *so as he sees now* an unmeritted praise from the public in general, owing to the great want of knowledge in the history of art, its rules and perfections, in all his kind admirers; but he hopes that more such learned critics on his paintings will open the eyes and elevate the feelings of those which have made a mistake at present. He is further convinced that from motives which are below the surface the kind author of the art critic, will never be satisfied with his works, and Mr. G. never will attempt to gain his favour with other charms than his careful painting which he executes with the greatest desire to imitate nature as well as in his power, not only in an elaborate copy of her details, but shall do his best to catch now and then a glimpse of the divine poetical feelings which the author of the kind article is so much wanting in his works quite as much as he seems to be full of it himself.

The enemy of well finished works of art, the admirer of careless ones, in taking as examples the great works in the history of art, will find out which of the two styles have lead to a better and more lasting result. The imitation of nature and its effects may be equally well attained in the two styles by artists of equal [strength ?], and each artist will select the style congenial to his individuality. If all artists would adapt the same style, would art have the same charms as it has now? Would it not be in giving up the individuality of the artist that we would arrive at the unhappy point to be only equals and producing equal works to the machine art. Mr. G. wishes to state that he is a great admirer of chromolithography etc. but he thinks that more or less they will be always void of an artistic individuality.

To a certain degree the time produces the want for a certain kind of art, it is very difficult that art will be able to change the taste of the time and unhappily our time is the worst for great historical, religious and even landscape compositions. It is not the want of the proper genius in the artist to create but in our time it is principally the wish for the works of art copied or taken from nature, nearly in all branches of art and especially in landscape painting.

In repeating the words of the author of the critic on his poor painting 'the greatness, as all greatness in art, has been found to be altogether independent of its manner', in Mr. G's painting, besides the want of spirit and elevation in feeling the greatest defect in his work is that poor miserable style to imitate nature in a microscopic way.

He feels very unhappy that he was not able to inspire himself with the greatness of his subject, so as a good many uneducated eyes believed he did, he felt inspired to the highest extent with it as he had the good fortune to look from the high summits of the Grampians into the depths of the forest and far away into the distant plains stretching to the Murray but his wishes were too high for his skill and he feels it now that first it would be necessary for him to elevate his mind at a level with his great judge and kind critic.

Mr. G. did what he could but remained so much behind his great original, if he had the highly educated eye of the learned critic he would probably surpass nature; as to his kind praise that he thinks to be able to distinguish in Mr. G's painting all the different kinds of Australian plants, of whose names he is so cleverly acquainted, very likely he did bestow to the artist beyond his merits. Mr. G. feels very thankful for the kind hint as to the theatrical position of the aboriginies in the foreground and he hopes it shall not be lost for the future and so likewise in regard to the hardiness of the colours he feels equally thankful knowing too well that generally from our enemies we learn better our defects than from our dearest friends, and for that reason he must deeply regret if that not all the paints were cleared up, he feels in the same time that he is too exacting as the criticising article was already too long and very likely the candel of the author too short to extend it any longer. In regard to the fears of the author eluding to Mr. G's new position as a teacher he wishes to allay them with the open promise that as a real artist, which at least he wishes to be, he has not whatsoever narrow views on art, seeing with the greatest delight a good work in any style and he would be too sorry if the few artists in Melbourne would believe that he is narrow minded enough to think less of a work of art which has not the same tendency as his own.

The very kind critic on Mr. G's picture may be sure that never more he will take the trouble to give a reply to his noble criticisms. His time is too precious for that. The trouble that he underwent to give an answer was for the defense of the kind opinion which his former critics and many good friends and patrons entertain of his productions, and which so as he thinks, were treated with a greater contempt than Mr. G's work which he feels it too far away from the high aim before him but he hopes that this feeling of the necessity to improve will enable him to advance in his art.

To conclude he will only add that during his long artistic life in Austria, Italy, Germany, Switzerland, Belgium, Holland, France, and England he had a good many occasions to see the finest works of art and to form his taste and expression and during that time he had also the chance to read a great many art critics but to his recollection never he read an article which expressed a higher opinion of the author's knowledge and learning and a more dictatorial, impertinent and malicious style of writing than in the article of this learned critic. It would be highly interesting for the public in general to know where he accumulated all his treasures of critic knowledge which more than once was so highly amusing in the columns of the Argus.

[From an unpublished letter to the *Argus* (Melbourne) by
Eugen von Guerard, July 1870]

NOTES—VON GUERARD'S REPLY TO JAMES SMITH

1 Raphael Sanzio (1483-1520), one of the most famous Italian artists of the High Renaissance. At the age of twenty-five he was entrusted by Pope Juilius II with painting in fresco the private papal apartments in the Vatican (the *Stanza della Segnatura*).

2 Pietro Vanucci called Perugino (*c.* 1445-1523), an Italian painter from Umbria who worked in Florence and was the master of Raphael.

3 Wilhelm von Schadow (1788-1862), the German painter of history and landscape, who joined the Nazarenes in Rome in 1814. He later became an influential teacher at the Düsseldorf Academy.

4 Johann Christian Reinhart (1761-1847), a landscape painter whose work ranges from 'the idyllic to the heroic, from fresh, unaffected observation of nature to the artificial construction of ideal scenery' (Novotny, *Painting and Sculpture in Europe 1780-1880*, 42). Reinhart is one of the landscape painters whose work may well have influenced von Guerard in the formation of his own style.

5 Joseph Anton Koch (1768-1839), the most important of the German neo-classical landscape painters. His paintings of mountainous scenery may have influenced von Guerard's own style.

6 There is no reason to question this. Von Guerard, born and trained in Vienna (the *Lukasbruder* was formed there in 1809) had also lived in Rome.

7 Ruskin did not write in support of the English Pre-Raphaelites until 1851. The German artists mentioned by both von Guerard and Smith became seriously interested in the work of the Italian artists of the fifteenth century (i.e. before Raphael) well before the English Pre-Raphaelites, Holman Hunt and J. E. Millais. The effective link between the two groups was the Scottish artist, William Dyce (1806-64), who became a friend of the Nazarenes during his study years in Rome (1825, 1827-8) and made their work and ideals known to Hunt and Millais on his return to Britain.

W. C. Piguenit (1836–1914)

William Charles Piguenit, who was born in Hobart, has been described by William Moore as Australia's first native-born landscape painter. His father, who was of French descent, came to Hobart from Kent. His son William studied painting under Frank Dunnett, a Scottish painter who had settled in Hobart.

Piguenit joined the Tasmanian Survey Department in 1849 and remained for twenty-three years before deciding in 1872 to resign in order to pursue landscape painting as a full-time occupation.

He was greatly attracted to mountainous scenery and frequently made long excursions into little-known and even quite unexplored areas of Tasmania. After retirement he made a painting excursion along the Derwent; then, later, explored the valley of the Huon and the Gordon River. His paintings are usually of high mountainous regions, though from time to time he painted the plain country as, for example, his fine 'Flood on the Darling' in the Art Gallery of New South Wales.

In 1892 Piguenit was invited to give the lecture which is printed below to the fourth meeting of the Australasian Association for the Advancement of Science when, in that year, it was held in Hobart. He visited Europe twice in 1898 and 1900, and was included in the Exhibition of Australian Art held at the Grafton Galleries in 1898. In 1903 the Trustees of the Art Gallery of New South Wales commissioned him to paint a picture of Mount Kosciusko. He died in Sydney in 1914.

Piguenit, whose account of his explorations in the Western Highlands of Tasmania is printed below, was a typical late romantic painter who delighted in the scenery provided by high mountains or great open spaces. There is a great and intrepid love of the infinite in his work. His account of his travels reveals a new intimacy in Australia between man and nature in a tone which is objective and unforced, the voice of a 'bushman' who was born in the country and knew it from his infancy.

[AMONG THE WESTERN HIGHLANDS OF TASMANIA]

There are no portions of Tasmania of which so little is known as the wild rugged region lying to the west and south west of the extreme limits of settlement in the Lake Country, nor are there any parts presenting such totally different features both in regard to form and colour. The great obstacle that has always presented itself to the examination of this interesting country has been its extreme difficulty of access. Lofty and rugged mountain ranges, deep ravines, great valleys, more or less precipitous, and covered for the greater part with dense forests and almost impenetrable scrubs, and rapid rivers liable to frequent and sudden floods, are among the chief difficulties which beset the explorer in his researches, requiring him to possess not only stoutness of heart and limb, but also those other necessary qualifications which go to make up what is technically known as a 'good bushman.'

No one with whom I have been acquainted possessed those qualities in a more eminent degree than my lamented friend the late Mr. James Reid Scott,[1] who in past years contributed very largely to our knowledge of the physical geography of the country referred to, and to whom I owed many valued opportunities of placing within my portfolio sketches of the grand scenery which meets the eye on every side.

It is from these sketches that the illustrations I have now the honor of submitting to you for your inspection have been made, and in the selection of them I have kept in view, as far as possible, those most typical of its mountains, lakes, and valleys.

My first acquaintance with the south-western country was made in 1871, when accompanying Mr. Scott and a party of three men on an exploring excursion from Victoria to Port Davey *via* the Valley of the Huon. Our route was along an old track, which, passing close to that river, ended at the Craycroft. From thence we travelled in a north-westerly direction up the Arthur Plains, until we sighted Lakes Pedder and Edgar, the last named being one of the sources of the Huon. Thence south-westerly to Port Davey, passing between the Arthur and Franklin Ranges. For the first 43 or 44 miles of this route the scenery, with the exception of some charming glimpses one occasionally gets of a bend of the river, is for the most part not very striking; but if the landscape possesses but small interest so far, ample compensation is made the traveller by the magnificent view that suddenly bursts upon the eye when the summit of the last hill, overlooking the Arthur Plains, is reached. Mr. Scott, in a letter published in the Hobart *Mercury* shortly after our return, thus described this grand scene:— 'For my part I must confess that the beauty of the scenery, both in the grandeur of the mountain ranges and the brightness and harmony of colouring, far exceeded my expectations. The country is almost destitute of timber, excepting narrow belts along the sides of the streams, and the effect from an eminence is that the spectator is looking over a vast extent of well-grassed fertile valleys, bordered by precipitous rocky mountains rising abruptly from the green plains, and towering up into sharp peaks and fantastic outlines, such as I never saw elsewhere in Tasmania. The mountains being of quartzite or some silicious stone full of quartz veins, the delicate tints of the rocks (from pure white to silver grey, or pink in the light, and a deep atmospheric blue in the shadow) made a splendid contrast with the vivid warm green of the button-grass plain, and the darker green of the timber, kept always bright by the moisture of the climate. The brilliant colours were not due to the temporary effect of sunrise or sunset, but were continuous and ever varying in outline throughout the day. A closer acquaintance with the plains dispels the idea of their fertility, and we found that what appeared undulating, or nearly level country, was composed of many steep narrow ridges and broad spurs from the mountains, covered with large tussocks of button-grass — Gymnoschaenus sphaerocephalus (*Cyperaceae*) — and a jointed rush-like plant — Leptocarpus tenax (*Restiaceae*) — with many patches of ti-tree and various plants of the order of *Epacridae*. The soil is wet and spongy, largely covered with moss at the roots of the herbage. The chimney-like holes of the land lobster abound all over the country, even on the tops of the hills. Towards Port

Davey the ridges are more gravelly and the herbage shorter, the rocky hills assuming a whiter colour, as if snow-clad. We found slate protruding in many places, with a very good cleavage and a purple tinge, like roofing slates. The quartz is generally pure white, and there are many loose masses of it scattered about, looking like huge blocks of white marble ... The plains are well watered by numerous streams of various sizes, each bordered by a belt of thick scrub, chiefly of honeysuckle (*Banksia*) with a dense growth of bauera and cutting-grass, from 8 to 10 feet high, closely matted together, so that it is impossible to pass by pressing it aside. It must either be cut through or trampled under foot, so that much time is required to cross even the smallest creek. The bauera was in blossom, and we saw several of the 'prionotes' with their beautiful pendulous red flowers ... By the streams we found many plants of the Native Plum (*Cenarrhenes*) with ripe fruit, the Native Laurel (*Anopterus*), the *Agastachys*, and the *Hakoea epiglottis*, also the *Persoonia*, the Celery-topped Pine (*Phyllocladus*), and many others met with in the north. In the forests the prevailing fern, as in the north, is the *Lomaria procera*, and two very pretty species of the *Gleichenia*.'

The water of these streams is of a dark brown colour, owing to the peaty nature of the country through which they flow. Singularly enough, they appear to contain but few fish, and those we caught were the small native trout,* none of which exceeded six inches in length. In this respect the southern rivers compare unfavourably with those of the northern side of the island, in which the blackfish often reach as much as four or five pounds in weight.

Resuming our journey, we reached Port Davey, where we camped for five days, experiencing during the whole of our stay very rough westerly weather. We nevertheless managed, with the aid of a boat obtained from a resident, to visit many parts of the port on its weather shore, and among others the grandest bit of scenery I believe to be found in the neighbourhood — that known as 'Hell's Gates' on the Davey River. The 'Gates' are a tremendous chasm between two hills, whose perpendicular sides reach an altitude of from 250 to 300 feet. The river, at the time of our visit, was comparatively low and running at a moderate rate, but in flood time it rushes through the chasm with tremendous velocity. I had much difficulty in making the sketch from which the accompanying illustration has been taken, owing

* Genus *Galaxias*

to the furious westerly wind that was blowing through the 'Gates,' accompanied with driving showers of sleet.

In a subsequent excursion made in 1874, on which occasion my esteemed friend Mr. R. M. Johnston was one of the party, we travelled over much of the same country, but instead of turning to the south-west after reaching the north-west end of the Arthur Range, we continued in a north-westerly direction until we reached the southern shore of Lake Pedder — a fine sheet of water surrounded by hills of a very picturesque character. The country bordering the southern shore is of a marshy nature, with numerous small tarns or lagoons dotted about, filled with the usual dark brown-coloured water peculiar to peaty soils. We camped for two days on this shore, experiencing during our stay the most tempestuous weather, compelling us, in setting up the tent, to seek the shelter of a clump of bushes to screen us as far as possible from the fury of the wind and rain.

After fording the stream connecting Lakes Pedder and Maria (the latter a small lake lying to the south-east of the former) we continued in a northerly direction with the object of striking the Gordon near the Great Bend and of following the Florentine down to its junction with the Derwent beyond Dunrobin bridge. What followed has, however, been so graphically described by Mr. Johnston in his valuable work on the 'Geology of Tasmania' that I gladly avail myself of his kind permission to make the following extract:—'The perilous scrub already described may continuously extend for many miles along the narrow valleys, ravines, and precipitous slopes of the sub-Alps of these regions. The tops of the high razor-back ridges of the schistose rocks bordering the upper waters of the Huon and Serpentine are generally treeless, though extremely rugged, and in traversing long distances it is often preferable to keep upon the crest of these as far as possible, not merely to avoid the horizontal scrub of the steep slopes, and the green innocent looking bauera of the flats bordering the rivers, but also to have the advantage of frequently taking 'trig' bearings of the one or two mountain peaks which may be in sight, such as Mount Wedge, Mount Anne, Mount Picton, and the 'trigs' on characteristic peaks of the Arthur, Franklin, and Wilmot Ranges. It also gives the traveller a great advantage in judging where to pierce a barrier thicket of vegetation at its narrowest point: indeed, no horizontal or other scrub should be encountered in this country before some local eminence has been ascended for the purpose of taking careful bearings of the day's course. It may be imagined, therefore, that progress in such a country is a slow and toilsome one, even to those capable of the greatest physical endurance. The difficulty of progress in the rugged horizontal scrub ravines and slopes between Lake Pedder, Mount Wedge, and The Thumbs, on the Gordon River, may be best illustrated by describing a day's toil of our party when endeavouring to cross the barrier ridges between the lake named and the open Denison Plains along the course of the River Wedge. After four days' fighting and tunnelling among the formidable scrub, we did not succeed in piercing in any one direction more than five miles from our old camp by Lake Pedder. In our final struggles to reach a white-crested peak — rising out of the sea of scrub — which we thought might bridge us over our difficult barrier northward, we were very much disappointed to find, on reaching its summit (only a mile distant from the last camping ground) that it was a solitary pinnacle, standing as a sentinel rock amid dense foliage on every side. There was no help for it but to retrace our steps in order to find a clear space to camp for the night. Only a little patch of green open ground, seemingly a mile below, was visible, and that too in the direction from whence we came. Reduced to one day's supply of food, we also reluctantly resolved to make a forced march back to supplies at the Picton, which would at least give us three days' hard travel. To be without food for at least two days was not a pleasant prospect, but the attempt must be made. Taking careful bearings of our course, we struggled down the steep, bare slopes, over chasms and precipices. Then commenced a most determined fight with the dense scrub. No description can convey an adequate conception of this short but hazardous struggle. At times we were in perfect darkness in the cavernous chambers of the moss-enshrouded branches; nor could we form any idea what height we were above the ground.

'The mode of progress is necessarily single file — the foremost doing all the hard work of cutting and bending aside obstructing branches sufficiently wide to allow the body and knapsack to squeeze through; the rest follow closely, one after another, and render friendly assistance when necessary. The compass has to be consulted every few yards and on one or two occasions such was the darkness in our vegetable cavern that a match had to be struck to show the bearing of the needle.

'One incident alone in this forced retreat produced the utmost merriment to some of our number. In descending through a hole into a dim, gloomy chamber of the scrub, one member of the party immediately in front of me fell, and, striking some

rotten mossy-covered branches of the floor he sank down through
the latter out of sight, and only by his cries could I find where
he had disappeared. I could only see his boot, vainly jerking at
the mossy sheet, which, after he had fallen through, had sprung
back, concealing the deeper recess where he was lodged. In
hurrying to his assistance I attempted to descend a sudden dip
of some twelve feet, but before I could clear my knapsack from
the branches which pressed upon me my foot slipped off a
treacherous moss-covered trunk, and, falling, I found myself
suddenly suspended by my knapsack. Our united cries for help
brought our companions upon the scene; but the ridiculous and
helpless picture we both presented so excited their mirth that it
was some minutes before they recovered calmness to extricate us
from our curious and perilous situation. Minor incidents of this
character were of frequent occurrence on this memorable descent;
but although nearly exhausted with fatigue, steady determination
at last enabled us to emerge upon the small open space of ground
already referred to, where we camped for the night, having been
engaged over twelve hours in piercing a distance a little over a
mile. At the close of the third day succeeding this we managed
to reach our supplies at the Picton, having been two days without
food. Although faint with exhaustion on this memorable journey,
we resisted all temptations to throw away our knapsacks and
collections, and only the abundance of water supply enabled us
to successfully overcome the trials of the weary march, which
reduced all of us to the appearance of skeletons.'

In 1873 Mr. Scott fitted out a party for the purpose of
exploring the country in the neighbourhood of Lake St. Clair,
the Murchison and Eldon Valleys, &c., in which I took part.
Mr. Scott had a boat built expressly for exploring the lake, which
was conveyed by bullock waggon from Hobart, and taken by way
of Hamilton and Victoria Valley to within about a mile of its
destination; from thence it was carried by us on our shoulders
until the shore was reached, where a rough log boat-house was
built by us for its protection. The tourist on his visit to the lake
finds, on reaching its south shore, a noble sheet of water stretched
before him, surrounded for the greater part by high and precipitous mountains, but it is only by the aid of a boat that he can
see its grandest features, notably the views of Mount Olympus
and Mount Ida, from the north-eastern shore. From this point
of view the tourist, on looking across the lake to the south-west,
sees the majestic outlines of Mount Olympus towering up before
him in sombre grandeur, with the slopes at its base covered right

down to the water's edge with a most luxuriant growth of myrtle (beech), fern, and other trees, among which may be seen the palm-like fronds of the *Richea pandanifolia*. Turning to the north-east, a huge rampart of precipitous mountains extends for some miles along this shore, amidst which stands the isolated bare peak of Mount Ida, with the talus at its base covered with a dense forest of Eucalypti. After breaking our way through the scrub and having a look at Lake Laura — a small lake lying at the foot of the mountains — we rowed up the larger lake to its north-west end, where we camped for the night, and next day followed the Narcissus River up its course for about a couple of miles, from whence we could see the rugged mass of mountains forming what is known at the Du Cane Range. Upon our return to the old camping place at the boat-house at Cynthia Bay, a start was made for the Eldon Range. Our course lay up the Vale of Cuvier, along the banks of the river of that name, and passing the southern shore of Lake Petrarch — a very beautiful sheet of water, to which the peaks of Mounts Byron and Cuvier form a noble background. Continuing on our journey we passed to the south of Coal Hill, keeping for some miles on the dividing range overlooking the Murchison. From this standpoint the sketch was made from which the illustration of the Murchison Valley was taken. A most extensive landscape here meets the view. The head of the valley lies at one's feet. On the right hand are the massive heads and peaks of the Du Cane Range; on the left the equally bold and massive spurs of the Eldon Range; while the valley stretches away into the dim distance, in which are to be faintly seen the summits of Barn Bluff, the Cradle, and many other mountains.

It is difficult, without the aid of colour, to show to its full extent the marked change in the features of the mountains of the Lake Country, where the greenstone is the prevailing formation, when contrasted with those ranges lying further to the south-west, such as the Arthur, and the mountains in the neighbourhood of Lake Pedder, where the crystalline rocks with their striking outlines and varied delicate tints take the place of the dark massive-looking greenstone, represented by such mountains as Mounts Olympus and King William, and the Eldon and other ranges; but an examination and comparison of the illustrations of the Murchison Valley and Arthur Ranges will, I think, make this change sufficiently clear.

I should strongly recommend the tourist who does not object to a little mountain climbing, when in the neighbourhood of the

King William Range, to ascend the first peak of that range. If care is taken in avoiding the thick scrub which clothes the base of the mountain, by selecting the ridge or spur on its eastern flank, the ascent is not difficult. Upon gaining the summit a magnificent view will reward him for his labour — for he stands in the midst of a vast panorama embracing almost the whole of the Western Highlands.

Looking over this grand landscape he will see an apparently endless succession of deep valleys and ravines, all densely wooded, and range after range of rugged mountains, all more or less precipitous. Many of these valleys, such as the Loddon for instance, are clothed with the densest growth of myrtle forest I have ever seen, imparting a beautifully soft velvety green to the landscape. Numerous lakes dot the surface of the country, while gleams of alternate sunshine and shadow flitting across it give to it a variety and charm of great beauty; at one time bringing some mountain peak into bold relief and imparting to it, if belonging to the crystalline order or rock formation, the appearance of being snow-clad, while others plunged in shadow are lost in the deep purplish blue of the distance; the whole making up a scene, wild it is true, but of such variety of outline and of such wealth of colour as to make the Western Highlands one of the most charming of the many beautiful landscapes to be found in Tasmania.

[*Report of the Fourth Meeting of the Australasian Association for the Advancement of Science* held at Hobart, Tasmania, in January 1892, pp. 787-94]

NOTE—TO W. C. PIGUENIT, THE WESTERN HIGHLANDS OF TASMANIA

1 James Reid Scott (1840-77), an active member of the Royal Society of Tasmania who spent 'a considerable portion of the latter part of his life... exploring the wild bush lands in the least known portions of the colony'. Elected to the Tasmanian House of Assembly 1866, he later served in the Legislative Council, and was Colonial Secretary of Tasmania 1872-73.

🔲🔲🔲🔲🔲🔲🔲🔲🔲🔲🔲🔲🔲🔲🔲🔲🔲🔲

SEVEN

The Impact of Paris

INTRODUCTION

The establishment of art schools and public art galleries in Melbourne and Sydney, and the immigration to Australia of professionally trained artists, brought a significant change to the local scene. The schools provided elementary training for young people keen to become artists; the collections in the new 'national' galleries, modest as they were, suggested new goals of human endeavour. The immigrant artists found employment as teachers, engravers, lithographers, and cartoonists for the recently-established illustrated press — sometimes supplementing their incomes as photographers. Suddenly the small art circles of Sydney and Melbourne achieved a cosmopolitan air. The new teachers had brought overseas experience with them to Australia; many had spent years studying in Paris which soon became a mecca for Australian art students.

George Moore wrote of this time:

> Everyone must go to France. France is the source of all the arts. Let the truth be told. We go there, every one of us, like rag-pickers, with baskets on our backs, to pick up the things that come in our way, and out of unconsidered trifles fortunes have often been made. We learn in France to appreciate not only art — we learn to appreciate life, to look upon life as an incomparable gift. In some café, in some *Nouvelle Athenes,* named though it be not in any Baedecker nor marked on any traveller's chart, the young man's soul will be exalted to praise life, and it is only through art that we can praise life.

The new milieu that arose among Australian art students was more informal but also more professional than the isolated condition of the artist in colonial times. A mood of conviviality, of comradeship, a positive sense of experiencing the world as artists emerged in Australia for the first time. This new mood is present in the correspondence of the young artists of the 1880s, an enjoyment of the sensuality of life, of life lived to the full, and of art as a way of life. It contrasts strikingly with the moral tone and social earnestness of Victorian critics like John West and James Smith.

John Peter Russell's letters are full of this new enthusiasm and hearty commitment to art. They help us to understand how young Australian artists began to relate their own goals to contemporary English and French art. Russell's attitudes and opinions, transmitted through Tom Roberts and others, were to influence a whole generation of Australian artists.

These letters make it clear that Russell himself accepted the work of the leading French Impressionists enthusiastically. Manet was for him the most original painter of the century, and he greatly admired the work of Monet, Degas, Renoir, Whistler, Pissarro, Gauguin, Guillaumin and Caillebotte. He claimed that Louis Anquetin, one of the *avant garde* leaders in Cormon's studio, had painted the very finest rendering of gas light in a café that he had ever seen, and he was, as is well known, on friendly terms with a more famous rebel at Cormon's studio — Vincent van Gogh.

But there was, nevertheless, a strong conservative side to Russell's taste. Both he and Tom Roberts had trained together in London in the early 1880s, Russell at the Slade and Roberts at the Royal Academy, like so many students of their time, both were admirers of the work of Bastien Lepage, the young French *plein air* realist who had taken over the popular mantle of J. F. Millet. Russell also keenly admired the work of several Royal Academicians, including Millais, Watts and Orchardson; and he participated in the universal admiration of his generation for the work of Puvis de Chavannes.

The conservative side of Russell led him to distrust theory and talk about art; a distrust that became typical of the painters of the Heidelberg School. To the extent that Impressionism was to be understood as painting impressions, swiftly and broadly, *en plein air* in order to record true tonal and colour values it was a thing to be admired. But from his study of Millais' work, he drew pure colours loosely over one another like 'cobwebs' and found that the raw canvas produced the most agreeable results because it soaked up the colour. His description reminds one of the stain techniques on unprimed canvas developed by American colour painters like Helen Frankenthaler and Morris Louis many years later. Yet Russell's eclecticism, his capacity to see virtue in

N

academic as well as *avant garde* work, seems to have produced a sense of uncertainty which runs through his letters and led perhaps in the end to his abandonment of painting as a major activity.

The proto-Impressionist methods, being experimented with variously in the 1860s by Manet, Boudin, Jongkind, Whistler and Monet, which Russell and Roberts and his friends such as Streeton, Conder, Fox and Withers helped to introduce into Australia, reached its climax in 'The 9 x 5 Exhibition of Impressions' at Buxton's Gallery, Melbourne, in August 1889. That both the critics of the time, such as James Smith and James Green, together with the artists themselves, regarded the paintings exhibited as impressionist is clear from the documents published below. But it was, of course, an Impressionism that did not reach beyond the direct, painterly statement; and even that statement was often compromised by the introduction of poetic mood or romantic fancy.

The Impressions Exhibition of 1889 was the high point of Australian Impressionism; after that the desire for poetry and mood, for national themes and national sentiment, began to prevail over the direct visual honesty of the early work of the Heidelberg painters. Nevertheless if the impact of Impressionism was marginal the impact of Paris in general was considerable. This will become clear if we now move on a decade to another and much larger exhibition of Australian art, that held in the Grafton Galleries, London, in April 1898.

The reviews of this exhibition printed below provide a cross-section of opinion as to the nature and quality of Australian painting held by British critics at the turn of the century. The review which appeared in the *Pall Mall Gazette* on 4 April 1898 was written by R. A. M. Stevenson, the nephew of Robert Louis Stevenson and probably the best-informed and most perceptive London critic of his day. Stevenson wrote an important book on Velasquez and did much to win an English audience for French Impressionism.

Stevenson noted that the Australian exhibition was markedly French in character, whereas twelve years before the Australian paintings in the Colonial Exhibition of 1886 were all in the manner of English 'trade' paintings. The French character of the show was noted also by Sir Thomas Humphrey Ward who wrote the *Times* review of the same day. Ward's is probably the most intelligent review of the exhibition. Like Stevenson he realized that the French methods sprang from the influence of French-trained teachers in Australia; and he proceeded to make the important point that Australian painting was closer in spirit to the work of the Glasgow School than to that of any English work. The painters of Glasgow and the painters of Melbourne had accepted French *plein air* painterly and proto-Impressionist techniques more readily than London-based painters who had, among other things, to cope with the strong linear and literary tradition of Pre-Raphaelitism which then dominated academic taste. In this connection, too, it is of interest to note that both Glasgow and Melbourne were new and flourishing industrial cities; in neither were the new artists held back unduly by a well-entrenched and conservative art establishment.

Even the critics who found little to admire were quick to note the French influence. The unknown reviewer for the *Athenaeum* (9 April 1898) who described the show as 'wasted labour' noted the similarity of the work to that exhibited annually by the Société Nationale des Beaux Arts (New Salon) which was held in the Champs des Mars; D. S. MacColl, who wrote for the *Saturday Review* (16 April 1898) and panned the show with the scornful, supercilious comments for which he was noted when things displeased him, noted how Streeton had been influenced, in his view, by 'the poorest French drawing'.

The general drift of these critical comments is worth examining in detail because they reveal the emergence of a British point of view which is broadly analogous to the British image of Australian life as obvious, vigorous and unsubtle. Stevenson found that Streeton's work possessed 'virtuosity' marred by 'raw colour' and 'common sentiment'. He admired Roberts's drawing and observation but found that he lacked 'style and poetry of impression'. Such opinions, and they will be found to be typical, reveal how far even an advanced critic like Stevenson was from appreciating the direct, plastic vision of proto-Impressionism. The impact of this criticism, coming at a time when so many expatriate Australian artists were trying to make their way in London, may have helped to weaken the French qualities in Australian work and bring it closer to English taste.

The last section of the chapter is devoted to extracts from an interesting manual on landscape painting in Australia written by A. J. Daplyn, the friend and colleague of Julian Ashton, and probably an acquaintance of the British artist and critic R. A. M. Stevenson. The manual was written to provide for the growing interest in landscape painting among amateurs following the successes of the Heidelberg school and the kind of painting they popularized. Daplyn taught art for many years, and records the results of his experience, in a pleasant and sensitive way. He encouraged *plein air* methods but like so many British and Australian artists of his time his attitude to Impressionism was ambivalent. Nevertheless it will be noted that all his references, although he was himself a Londoner, are to French teachers and French methods.

John Peter Russell (1858-1930)

John Peter Russell was the grandson of Robert Russell, an iron-master of Kirkaldy, Scotland, who emigrated to Hobart in 1832. His iron foundry was later transferred to Darlinghurst, Sydney, where it was carried on by his sons, the second of whom, John, was the artist's father. The firm, which flourished for many years, built railways, bridges and ships, including gun-boats for the Maori wars. At an early age John Peter Russell visited Tahiti where the family had business interests.

On returning to Sydney, Russell began to study art and paint in water-colour. But his father, intent upon him joining the firm, arranged for him to serve as a 'gentleman's apprentice' in the engineering firm of Robey's at Lincoln. Russell remained in England for three years, returning to Sydney on the death of his father from whom he inherited a private annual income of about $6,000 in contemporary currency. In 1881 he returned to England, having decided to train as an artist. It was at this time that he met Tom Roberts, who became a lifelong friend.

In London Russell studied at the Slade under Alphonse Legros during 1881 and 1882, and then returned to Sydney for some months. In March 1883 he exhibited eighteen paintings at the Third Annual Exhibition of the Art Society of New South Wales. They included several portraits, figure subjects and landscapes. Russell returned to London in the same year and rejoined the Slade. In October 1883, together with his friend Roberts, his brother Percy, an amateur architect, and Dr William Maloney, he made a walking tour of southern France and Spain. In Granada they met Laureano Barrau, then nineteen, who was working under Gérôme in Paris, and Ramon Casas, who was seventeen. It was from these two painters that Russell and Roberts appear to have learnt of Impressionist painting.

In 1884 Russell left London for Paris where he took a studio in the Impasse Hélène, near Montmartre cemetery, and joined the studio of Fernand Cormon. At Cormon's Russell met Vincent van Gogh, Louis Anquetin, Emil Bernard, Toulouse-Lautrec; and became well known among art students in Paris for his prowess in boxing and rowing. His circle of friends also included the Scottish painters, Alexander Reid and A. S. Hartrick, the American Dodge McKnight, and the English sculptor, Harry Bates. It was apparently through Bates that he met Mariana Antoinetta Mattioco, a young Italian girl from Monte Cassino, Italy, who lived in Paris with her two brothers, who played the violin in theatre orchestras while Mariana modelled for sculptors.

Russell joined the Cormon *atelier* at a time when tension was developing among the students against their master's academic methods of teaching. The leaders of the rebels were Emil Bernard and Louis Anquetin, both of whom had been deeply interested in cloissonist theories during 1885 and 1886. Although Russell made friends among this group, he retained a high respect for the methods of Cormon. As a result of the tension developing in the school, Cormon decided to close it for some months. About this time Russell visited Sicily with Mariana and their son Jean and painted there. After their return to Paris, Russell visited Belle-Ile, off the Brittany coast. It was on this occasion that he met Claude Monet. The two painted together and became friends. The following year Russell decided to build himself a house on Belle-Ile and settle there with Mariana, whom he married in Paris in 1888.

Russell lived there with his growing family — five boys and a girl — until the death of his wife in 1907. The family usually spent the winter in the south of France, in Switzerland or Italy. Many painters visited the Russells at Belle-Ile where his house became known as *Le Chateau de l'Anglais*. The young Henri Matisse came twice, in 1896 and 1897, contact with Russell leading him to an increased interest in colour.

The death of his wife disturbed Russell profoundly and he is said to have destroyed a great many of his paintings after her death. He travelled about Europe a good deal, with his daughter, in the years that followed. In 1912 he married Caroline de Witt Merril, an American opera singer and a friend of his daughter, Jeanne. For a time they lived in Porto Fino. During the First World War they resided in England, returning to France and Italy at its conclusion. In 1921 Russell sailed with his second wife and their son, Hereward, to Sydney; and thence to New Zealand in order to settle another son, Siward, on a farm. Returning to Sydney, Russell built himself a house at Rose Bay, and developed a fine garden. It was while at work on his yacht port and swimming pool that he died there in 1931 at the age of seventy-three.

To a greater extent than any other Australian painter of his generation John Russell developed an interest in the principles of Impressionism and the use of pure colour in painting; but he was not by any means a consistently *avant garde* painter, as his friends Claude Monet and Vincent van Gogh were. He continued through life to hold skill in academic draughtsmanship in the highest regard. Perhaps the absence of an academic tradition in Australia enhanced its value for him; for in this respect, at least, he was remarkably similar to all the other important Australian painters of his generation.

[JOHN PETER RUSSELL—LETTERS TO TOM ROBERTS]

Letter 1: probably written in February 1885

This letter was written from Paris to Roberts, then still resident in London but on the eve of his departure to Australia.

Paris,   (Card for McC enclosed)
Monday Night.

Bates[1] was surprised to hear of your going[2] and will write — T'will do you good my lad and JWBK[3] would back this up — Go in, forget style and tackle *our* stuff, for *love*.[4] — Think more than you paint. — So much for my opinion — Now I'll send you two poor drawings — selected by Bates, endorsed by me and backed by Cormon's[5] good opinion especially studies of feet. T'other was too hurried. Astonished to find what a small amount of work I've done. B[6] probably will leave by end of month and so will see you. I'll endeavour to run over too. Thanks for your P.C. Mc.C.[7] wrote from Melbourne.

Should much like to say farewell to you in person but t'will depend on two things pressure of work and money.

If you like rough French Canvas go to Cornellison.[8] Was not obtainable during my last stay in N.S.W.[9]

I can't think of anything else, except Michallet.[10]

Are you bound to go by Orient.[11] If not why not go Messagerie[12] and illustrate the route, properly worked and they would pay a good round sum. Thumbnail sketches — Valley of Rhone, Marseilles, Stra Bonifacio — Messina, Mt. Ida, Suez Canal, Aden, Guardafui, Seychelles, Bourbon, Mauritius &c. — Those ink sketches of yours would fetch the Frenchmen. If this is not to be — work the other — a photo or two of English shipping — Style of that fellow who did Egypt, Thames, Spain &c. for Mag. of Art.[13] Might make £50 to start you.

Command me if I can be of service.

Ever thine is
J.P.R.

G. L. Seymour

You'll remember how we admired his 'Thunder'

NOTES—RUSSELL TO ROBERTS LETTER 1

[1] Harry Bates (1850-99), an English sculptor and painter, and a pupil of Jacques Dalou. He won the Academy medal for sculpture in 1885 for his 'Socrates teaching in the Agora'. Roberts painted Bates working on this sculpture in his painting 'Sculptor's Studio', *c.* 1885. He became an A.R.A. in 1892.

[2] This appears from what follows to refer to Tom Roberts's decision to return to Australia. Roberts sailed on 4 March on the *Lusitania*.

[3] i.e. J. W. Buxton Knight (1843-1908), an English painter who lived at Sevenoaks, Kent. Elected R.A. 1865 but left after two years, preferring to paint out of doors. A member of the New English Arts Club (1888), and a friend of Roberts and Russell, Buxton Knight wrote several books on etching.

[4] 'tackle our stuff for love' refers to Roberts's decision to return to Australia and paint Australian landscapes, 'forget style' indicates the suspicion which Russell had, at least at this time, of a self-conscious manner of painting, and this is linked with his reservations over the Impressionist theorizing which led to *pointillisme*.

[5] Fernand Cormon (1845-1924), the French painter of history and portraits who conducted an important school attended by Russell. Charles Condor and John Longstaff attended Cormon's atelier after Russell left.

[6] 'B', i.e. Bates, who evidently intended to come to Australia. He was a financial member of the Art Society of New South Wales from 1882 to 1886 and exhibited work (sent from London) in the exhibition of March 1883.

[7] Possibly Frederick McCubbin.

[8] Louis Cornelissen and Sons, artists colour men then and now of 22 Great Queen Street, London.

[9] Russell had spent a year in Australia in 1882.

[10] Presumably Michelet paper for water-colour painting.

[11] The Orient Shipping Line to Australia.

[12] Messagerie, the French Shipping Line.

[13] This was George L. Seymour who did a series of illustrations for the *Magazine of Art*, on Egypt (1884, pp. 15-20) and The Thames (1883, pp. 485-92). Russell placed the name in a box at the bottom of the letter.

Letter 2: written apparently late in 1885

73 Boulevard de Clichy Paris. Sunday.

Tomorrow night, my dear T. R. our young friends[1] depart for the Eternal City furnished with such letters as my artistic friends could provide. One valuable one to Veddar[2] — M[3] has not been able to get work in a sculptor's studio here but perhaps his strong feeling that Rome is *the* place influenced his search — Still the lad has passed through some trying times lately and I don't wonder at his desire to arrive on the scene of early hopes/—this is mixed but you'll excuse./

Has the 'Fickle Goddess' been kind to you since we met? Tell me of your doings — particularly as regards the Art.

Do the 'Ducats' come rolling in? If not and you should come to the end of your tether, remember our early talks — So that's disposed of —

Here I'm glad to tell you that I'm getting on in Drawing and for last week's composition[4] 'Bacchus and Ariadne' got first place — Cormon complimentary. I'm immensely in love with the man — really one should succeed with such guidance. His criticising splendid and right to my *main* weakness.

McKnight[5] of ours has done some remarkable water color work — full of genius, all agree. Bates has started a head of me,[6] with much promise, is much interested and I'm trying my best to help him in the sittings by posing as well as I can — Trying work though — He is just now in a rapturous state about a charming Italian girl[7] posing just now for him for a small relief of Dido. very fine!

He is working too hard and I must endeavour to get him up the river now and then. The color round our boathouse has been glorious.

'but it fleeteth, fleeteth, ever'.

Yesterday I gave Joe Mathews[8] a spin over the Champion course[9] — he beat me by three feet, but his sweater was saturated.

Julian's[10] crowded as usual — atmosphere sickening — Met an American girl who knows B[11] well — says he has disappeared no one knows whither — Mrs. M.[12] is now finishing a Greek chiton for me — 4 yds Swiss muslin at 4 frs. — This to be used for decorative panels for screen, having given up 'Poppy' idea — Partly draped females — Sea shore —[13] Not Cold-gravy sea (vide S.M.H.)[14]

in Sincerity,
John P. Russell.

NOTES—RUSSELL TO ROBERTS LETTER 2

1 'Our young friends', possibly Bertram Mackennal and his wife.

2 Possibly Elihu Vedder (1836-1923) an American painter who established himself in Rome in 1867, but exhibited in Paris and received a *mention honorable* at the Salon of 1889.

3 M. i.e. Bertram Mackennal.

4 Cormon held a weekly competition for a history painting among the pupils attending his atelier.

5 Dodge McKnight (1860-1950), the American landscape painter, a pupil of Cormon.

6 Harry Bates exhibited a bronze 'Head of J. B. Russell, Esq.' at the Royal Academy in 1886.

7 It is possible that the 'charming Italian girl' was Mariana Mattiocco whom Russell married in 1887.

8 J. Mathews, an unidentified friend.

9 Russell was a good boxer and athlete.

10 Julian's, a popular 'free' atelier frequented by foreign students, was divided into two studios: the Rue Monmartre which was open to women students, and the Rue d'Uzes, a 'free' informal studio for men only.

11 Brossel, an unidentified friend.

12 Presumably Mrs Mackennal.

13 Russell is evidentally referring to a painting he is proposing to begin.

14 Russell exhibited eighteen paintings in the Third Annual Exhibition of the Art Society of New South Wales, which opened on 19 March 1883. An unknown reviewer in a detailed and generally favourable review of Russell's work wrote of 'No. 145, a Bather, is a study from the nude, the flesh being well treated, but the water has such a cold-gravy appearance that the maiden's reluctance to plunge into it is natural enough'. It is possible that this painting is to be identified with No. 12 described as 'Reclining Figure' signed and dated John P. Russell in the Autumn Exhibition 1973 Recent Acquisitions, Joseph Brown Gallery, Melbourne.

Letter 3:

15 Impasse Helen
Paris
Oct 5, 1887

My dear Tom Roberts,

Your letter was very welcome. I am delighted to hear of your continued success in painting better than ever and nowadays the ducats flow in in close pursuit of merit. When you went out I felt you would do well for in London you were too much taken up with what others were doing and the manner thereof. And now you plug away thinking only of the *matter*.

Happy youth! To have so soon found your road. Here we are all in the dark, too much occupied with style — I wish you could see a collection of some 1200 drawings done by Cormon for his big pictures, not a bit studied for effect, plain working drawing but by heavens the character of the model is there — every bit of him searched. For these qualities he is the first draughtsman in France. Unfortunately as a painter he is most unequal. In his 'Cain' you saw his greatest work.[1] I doubt if he will ever come up to it again on canvas. Perhaps in Clay! His Medaille d'Honneur[2] picture of this year was on the whole disappointing. Overworked and except for drawing and movement as Academic as Bougareau[3] [sic] or Cabanel.[4] The men were fine in feeling for color and the Greeks might have been like 'em but the women simply Paris harlots. Ah me, when I think of work by Millais,[5] Watts,[6] Richmond,[7] Orchardson,[8] E. J. Gregory &c &c I come to the conclusion that with the exception of Delaunay[9] (a notable one) and a very few others, the French can't paint a lady — they get the demi-monde every time. And I'm not at all inclined to believe 'tis for the lack of gentlewomen in France.

Well! my dear T R, I'm about finished with studios and will jump out of Paris as soon as possible. The tone of things don't suit me. With a little bit of reputation I'd return to Sydney — or rather N.S.W. — as it is I am about to build a house in France. Settle down for some five years. Get some work done. It will be in some out of the way corner, as much of a desert as possible. I hope you'll come and stay with us while you are on that 'dig in' trip to Paris.

Friend Buxton Knight will come too. Say for the Exposition Universelle May 1889,[10] and you should send some gems. I've no doubt they would give Australian art a room to itself if important enough — Try! all the world and his wife will be there.

It makes me feel mean thinking and planning for Exhibitions in advance. How differently the old boys worked — Botticelli and the rest right away to the Jap artisan arti(st).[11] By the way, did you like the North Italian school as seen at Luino, Milan, Florence &c?

Did you see Luca Signorelli's[12] frescoes at Orvieto? 'Tis a treat and a preparation for Michael Angelo — Fancy the courtly Luca dragging his splendid guests from the delights of his table to pose for figures in hell. A mild English person and his four lanky daughters (what Harry Furniss[13] calls Chippendale legs) found it all shocking. Could not stand the folks flying from Judgement with legs encased in hose, all so unlike in color and pattern. Still the impression of movement — wonderful.

I've not read Chesneau's[14] book yet. I am too busy with English and American literature. Find I am away behind my friends here. Collecting a great pile of books. Don't know that

I feel much the better. After all, in the Art of Painting, what does all the talk amount to? Not much perhaps. Take a dusty road in sunlight stretching away for a mile or two, then sky. What a job to get the delicate gradation of *values*. Well, a white handkerchief held up is of distinct help when in doubt. Yes! for *values*: But when we get to color — The gorse and heather — Yellow and purple.

> Orange boat sails, blue sea
> Red rocks — green sea.

All a matter of feeling, 'tis *in* the man with brush and paint pot or it is not. There they were all time studying drawing and Values, letting color slide before the advent of Manet, Monet and the impressionists — Now the rage is the other way.[15] Darned fools spotting canvas with small points of pure color. 'Tis as fashionable as gulls wings for hats.

After all, dear T R, isn't great art innocent of style as to the manner of the painting. Look at that dark bearded man by Titian in Louvre.[16] The cuss takes one's attention, not the way 'tis done — that comes after perhaps.

I am about to build a small house on Belle Ile[17] off Brittany. The finest coast I've ever seen. That processional subject will entail another visit to Sicily.[18]

Cost too much money when settled on the tight little island I'll probably commence studies for a picture of the folks thrashing. Got a good chance in the subject. 8 horses at ends of enormous beam. Mill in middle. Chaps and girls rushing in with bundles of grain as gang of horses pass, people raking straw away at t'other end. Tall girls bring corn to barn in baskets. See them, tired, twilight, August moon getting up. Too big a job for me though, just at present. Courage! Courage!

You, apparently, have not had all my letters for I wrote you thanking you for what you had done in Holding affair.[19] You see, if I prosecuted him all expenses would about break my back. So he'll have to slide.

Mr. Fox[20] called once on me here. He is working at Julian's and has passed the summer at Etaples, Picardie.

I hear occasionally from J. W. B. Knight. Been painting at Winchelsea. He sold an eight footer to N.S.W.[21] £400.

Your exhibition will be a success[22] probably as far as British art is concerned. They say art sales are done better now — perhaps the Manchester[23] years will come again and Millais' income go up to £30,000.

Next week we are off to Moret sur Loing.[24] Have a slap at the autumn color. The leaves are changing.

Been trying to push a big one for Sydney. Folks kissing over a gate. Scythe and sea — evening. It has floored me.

Good luck

Yours ever sincerely

J. P. Russell

[Along the left-hand margin of the first page is the following note: Read F. Marion Crawford's 'Zoroaster'.[25] 'Tis full of local colour and fine motifs.]

NOTES—RUSSELL TO ROBERTS LETTER 3

[1] Cormon exhibited this painting at the Salon of 1880, and it gained the Cross of the Legion of Honour for him. The comment suggests that Roberts was in Paris in 1880 and viewed the Salon of that year. 'Cain' was bought by the State and exhibited in the Luxembourg Gallery.

[2] Cormon exhibited this painting 'Les Vainqueurs de Salamine' (The Victors of Salamis) at the Salon which opened in May. The subject of the painting probably referred to the great naval victory of the Greeks over the Persians at Salamis (480 B.C.). It was awarded the Medaille d'Honneur for painting, the highest award the Salon gave. One was also given for sculpture.

[3] William Adolphe Bouguereau (1825-1905), the well-known French painter of history painting in the nineteenth century *Beaux Arts* Style.

[4] Alexandre Cabanel (1824-89), a French painter, mainly of history pieces in the *Beaux Arts* style.

[5] Sir John Everett Millais (1829-96), an English painter, one of the founders of the Pre-Raphaelite movement who later gained much popular success as a Royal Academician.

[6] George Frederick Watts (1817-1904), an English portrait and history-painter as well as sculptor.

[7] Sir William Blake Richmond R.A. (1842-1921), an English history-painter.

[8] Sir William Orchardson (1832-1910), famous for his dramatic scenes of social life and for his portraiture.

[9] Jules-Elie Delaunay (1828-91), a French painter, best known for his decorative paintings of the Pantheon, Paris, such as the frescoes of *Attila and Sainte Geneviève*.

[10] *Exposition Universelle* 1889. For an account of painter-participation in the Paris World Fair of 1889, see J. Rewald, *Post-Impressionism* (1956), pp. 278-80, *et al*.

[11] Russell is almost certainly referring to the print designers of the Ukiyo-E school.

[12] Luca Signorelli (1441?-1523), an Italian painter, and, according to Vasari, a pupil of Piero della Francesca. His frescoes in Orvieto Cathedral display his mastery of the nude in a state of action. See Vasari, *Lives* (ed. W. Gaunt), 1963, vol. 2, part 1, p. 1145, 'into this work (The Last Judgement) Luca introduced many portraits of friends'.

[13] Harry Furniss (1854-1925), an Irish caricaturist and illustrator who contributed to the London press.

14 Russell is probably referring to Ernest Chesneau's *Le Peinture Anglais,* Paris, 1882, which was translated into English by L. N. Etherington, with a preface by Professor Ruskin, in 1885. A third edition appeared in 1887.

15 Russell, who was a student at this time at Cormon's, is probably referring to the *avant garde* group among Cormon's pupils experimenting with *pointillisme.* It included Louis Anquetin, Emile Bernard and others.

16 Probably the so-called portrait of Aretino, now thought to be of Girolamo Adorno (see *The Paintings of Titian,* (Cat. No. 44), II, E. Wethey, 1971).

17 Russell resided in the house for many years. It was eventually converted into a hotel and then demolished in 1950.

18 Russell had visited Sicily in the spring of 1887. Vincent van Gogh refers to the visit in a letter to Russell in April 1888 (see *The Complete Letters of Vincent Van Gogh,* New York Graphic Society, 1959, p. 547).

19 A reference to a personal matter which obviously caused Russell some concern. Holding is also mentioned in Letter 4.

20 Emanuel Phillips Fox (1865-1915), an Australian painter who studied first at the National Gallery School and later in Paris at Julian's and the Beaux Arts (1887-90) under Bouguereau and Gérôme.

21 The painting entitled 'Deserted' was purchased by the Art Gallery of New South Wales for £300 in 1887 and subsequently sold by the Trustees of the Gallery in 1956 for seventeen guineas. It is now in the possession of St. Joseph's College, Hunter's Hill, Sydney.

22 Probably the exhibition of the then recently formed Australian Artists' Association, which Roberts helped to establish as a breakaway group of professional painters from the largely amateur Victorian Academy of Arts. The Association held three exhibitions at Buxton's Gallery, Melbourne, before amalgamating in 1888 with the Academy to form the Victorian Artists' Society.

23 From the 1850s, art patronage in Britain came increasingly from commercial centres such as Manchester, where the Royal Academy and the Royal Manchester Institute staged important exhibitions.

24 Moret sur Loing, a picturesque town about seventy-three kilometres from Paris, and favoured painting spot. Alfred Sisley lived there from September 1882 to Autumn 1883.

25 Marion Crawford was a prolific, much-travelled American-born novelist who favoured Italian settings for her exotic novels. *Zoroaster* was published in London in 1885.

Letter 4:

Paris
Monday
December 26 1887

Dear T.R.

Monsieur Henri Thiebauld de la Crouce[1] turned up and was loud in praise of Blue Gum liniment. What is his little game in leaving Australia? Is it that art is not a remunerative calling in Melbourne or because Madame longed for the gay(?) city? He was improved in health wonderfully.

Yes 'certainly'!! I had your letter and papers with account of that young prig Holding.[2] I thanked you and now do so again.

Young Harrington Mann[3] carried off a prize at the Slade School.[4] Two years in Italy £150 per annum. A few old masters to copy — Good thing for him. Well I saw him off and while trying to get into his hotel a cuss gave advice to me in French about the door — t'was Fox just back from Etaples. Curious to see him in that way.

There is a fine exhibition of work by Puvis de Chavannes[5] — Some really splendid work and I feel more inclined than ever to give him top place in French art of today. Though grey the color is nearly always fine. Perhaps one can class him with our G. F. Watts.[6] Though they both draw grandly and they don't mind leaving out a few ribs or steering wildly in proportion when it suits 'em.

I have been for past two years chasing color — been floored again and again. Do you remember Millais' 'Yeomen of the Guard'.[7] Free it from a little grease and that is my ideal of technique. Pure, or as nearly pure as possible, colors dragged loosely one over t'other — cobwebs. Done in a larger way perhaps than Millais to manage big Canvasses (Decorative). To avoid the smudge that spoils most French painting and renders German stuff damnable, no vehicle Color only on absorbent canvas or better, stiff canvas prepared only with glue. Simple colors but strong Keep pure as long as possible.

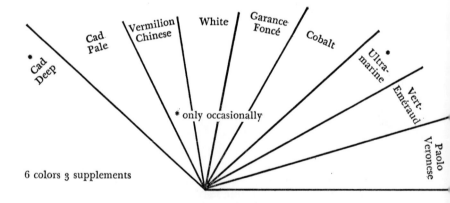

Cad Deep • / Cad Pale / Vermilion Chinese / White / Garance Foncé / Cobalt / Ultramarine • / Vert Eméraud / Paolo Veronese

* only occasionally

6 colors 3 supplements

I find the raw canvas produces agreeable results. It soaks up much color and there is no chance for dexterous br s handling.

Good this last. I find the 6 color palette admirable and almost all one wants. Difficult to get *dirt* or black.

Tis rather expensive in cobalt though. However I am now making my own colors, nights, better than I buy and saving of 60% Try it!!!

Have you seen Maloney since his return to Melbourne? He says in a letter that he is off to an appointment in Albany, W.A.[8]

A letter from J.W.B.K.[9] informs me that his stand off policy is finished — does not pay — and that he is about to change for art's sake and join the *Arts Club*. He thinks my idea of a house and studio in Belle Ile a mad one, 'not enough society artistic.' Just the thing I am wishing more and more to steer clear of. For instance at this time I am busy with studies for a picture Dante and Virgil crossing Styx. Even in this preliminary stage I am much bothered by acquaintances critically inclined. Theyre [sic] opinions are so extremely varied — What it will be when I commence whacking the big canvas. After all my dear, Sir, isn't it to be *my* picture — The fact that you were one of the strongest in Melbourne accounts for your great progress. You didn't pay much attention to what tothers said. Thrown on your own resources like. A splendid thing — Go in and win! I try hard not to let these chaps bother me — but they do — Not alone in Paris or elsewhere in this respect. Many pictures.

Isn't Art a rum business as Turner said?

Cormon mentioned last Sunday that he has another Australian[10] from Melbourne "espece de Prix de Rome" conqueror he thinks. As I don't go to the *atelier* now have had no chance of making his acquaintance. Who is the mysterious stranger?

This pot boiler I've been telling you about. This sticky business. It's all rot of course but most interesting study and the hard work with the models doing good.

For the first time I'm begining to feel what drawing really is.

Pen sketch, at left hand side of page Dante, Virgil, the gay young waterman F Filippo Argenti, being warned off some dozen or so of the miry tribe. Important figures swimming and wading off to give him hell. A multitude away off and all backed by burning city. Simple enough but I'm growing rapidly through my hair.

> Good luck old son
> Yrs J.P. Russell

NOTES—RUSSELL TO ROBERTS LETTER 4

1 An unidentified acquaintance.
2 See Letter 3, p. 191.

3 Harrington Mann (1864-1937), a Scottish painter born in Glasgow; who worked in history painting, genre and landscape. There are paintings by Mann in the Art Gallery of New South Wales ('Nora and her Dolls' 1900) and the National Gallery of Victoria ('Good Morning', 'The Artist's Children', 1904).

4 Where Russell enrolled as a student, first in 1881 and again in 1883.

5 Puvis de Chavannes (1824-98), a French mural painter whose international reputation was very great at this time, both among academicians and symbolists. Today he is best known for his frescoes (1874-78) in the Pantheon, Paris.

6 George Frederick Watts (1817-1904), an English painter of portraits and symbolical paintings.

7 Exhibited in the Royal Academy in 1877.

8 Possibly a reference to Maloney's responsibility for emigrants to Western Australia, during his own return from London to Australia.

9 i.e. Buxton Knight, who in fact joined the New English Art Club in 1888.

10 Unidentified. Possibly Longstaff, who sailed from Melbourne in September 1887 after having won the Travelling Scholarship of the National Gallery of Victoria School and joined the Cormon atelier later in 1887. '"Espece de Prix de Rome" conqueror' would really describe Longstaff's ambitions, but note that Nina Murdoch, *Portrait in Youth* (Melbourne, 1948), states that it was at a dinner party at Russell's house in Paris that it was decided Longstaff should seek entrance to Cormon's atelier (p. 173). Charles Conder (not, of course, an Australian) joined Cormon after August 1890.

Letter 5: written after May 1890

My dear T. R.

Do you owe me a letter or is it the other way? Since writing you last I've been having a Hell of a time with Painting. My hair is mostly all off, and with the other cares of a family and a small property in Belle Ile, I'm all broken up, as inclosed impression will show you. Succeeded in getting some things done in Belle Ile and then had to destroy them for I found that two years alone with (as far as art influences are concerned) nature had so changed my ideas particularly as regards *color* that I could not look at my stuff. Not being obliged to sell — so far — Good!!! Since that have been chasing after broken color. Just beginning to hope.

Another difficulty presents itself immediately. You know how the ordinary grey painting changes in the drying of the color, and consequent loss of brilliancy. Well, when one leaves the colors pure (or nearly so) it changes still more. (A greater proportion of change takes place I mean.) You see I now put the colors on as pure as I can without stirring them up on the palette, so that they are without the protective influence of *the body white*. This gives the lead dryers (which nearly all the color merchants use to make the colors dry equally) the chance to play old Harry with the brilliancy of the work.

[J.P.R. has written along left hand margin the following note:
I fancy the color merchants mix cheap colors with expensive ones say Fr. Ultramarine with Cobalt, Chrome with Cadmium, Lake with Madder &c.&c.]

So I have been experimenting — Making my own color, with more or less success. I am now inclined to favor the grinding of colors with oil to which is added more or less Amber Varnish according to the drying qualities of the different colors. The pigments to be ground to suit the personal taste of the painter liquid or otherwise, to obviate the use of a medium (which can never be thoroughly mixed with the colors without much stirring which makes 'em muddy) so they dry unequally. We agree I think that next to use of lead dryers the worst thing is to paint on top of a former painting which is not thoroughly dry. Oh for the varnish of the old men.

By the way, G. F. Watts has a man to grind his colors — they are perfectly natural — no dryer or varnish. But then he puts the picture aside for perhaps a year. Won't do for outdoor work, or for portraits. Fashionable folk burn to have 'em finished — next week if possible. Climate has a good deal to do with it. You have the pull of us in that. Thanks for Artistic Catalogue.[1] Hope you scooped in the Ducats at the end of the show and Glad to see in the S. Bulletin[2] that you had finished a picture of sheep-shearing — one of a great many magnificent subjects in our country. Long live naturalistic art — though I say no word against the really imaginative — but t'is sickening the way men paint a commonplace picture and pin a sentimental title to it. We are in the throes of a mighty revolution in art. The gropers after truth, men who are searching things for themselves, seeking to render what they *see* and not what they know [to exist] are throwing up most old-time conventions as to rules of composition, sentiment, color &c. They are drifting towards what is best in Impressionism.

Did you see the Manet show at the Beaux Arts?[3] I unhesitatingly place him as the most original painter of our century. This without taking one leaf from the laurels of the other immortals.

Of course, the followers, the rag-tag and bobtail, make Impressionism ridiculous, as the leaders of the movement well know. But what glorious work I have seen by Degas, Claude Monet, (Rodin in sculpture) Raffaelli. Renoir in figure,

o

Whistler, Pissarro, Gauguin, Guillemain, Caillebotte, and a lot of younger men, some of whom have revolted from Cormon's rule.

One of the these last — Anquétin[4] — has done the very finest rendering of gas light in a café that I have ever seen. But, as Degas says of Besnard,[5] there are so many men trying to dance with feet of lead.

Then in decorative art there is Puvis de Chavannes!!! What music in the name.

Rodin is very satisfying. I am happy in possessing several things of his (in trust for Australia): a bust in silver of my wife. He is a white man — Simple — wrapped up in his work, with a head and beard that recalls the great Jove of Michael Angelo. Things seem to be changing in England too. Seems to be so by the papers but I can't say for I've not been there for 5 years.

Been out of the art world of Paris for nearly 3 years and mean to keep out a little longer. 'Tis hard, but does good.

My wife wanted a change, so we drove across France in our cart and couple of horses, intending to winter near Genoa. But when we got there the country did not please me. So we turned back and have taken a small house here for the winter. I bucked at leaving B.I.

'Happy land' No tourists, no villas, no very rich people. Something to eat for all. Very little crime but plenty of evil speaking. Veritable Republic. Each man a piece of land. People on all sides at work in the fields and valleys. T'is flat so the figures are important.

Leaving interfered with work on one or two big canvasses there. That insult to Dante, for instance is very nearly finished. But I mean to paint another canvas same size on returning. Man does not know when he is well off. We changed the pleasant and art nourishing land of Belle Ile for what — Cap d'Antibes peninsula about 3 miles long, the last comparatively quiet spot on the wide Riviera. A few Villas, many nurseries for flowers, blue tiles, market gardens, the rest pine woods. Glorious views. East, Bay of Nice with all the snowclad Alpes Maritimes in view. West, Bay of Cannes and the lovely high foothills of the Esterelles.

But the moral atmosphere is rotten. *Cannes* sacred to bum-suckers and folks whose greatest pleasure is to press the same pavement which has felt the patent leathers of noblemen. Rococo, pretentious architecture. English spoken everywhere. Cocottes, clergymen, journalists, superior cardsharpers, deputies, consumptives, hawks and pigeons jostle one another continually. Distrust is in the air. The way people are swindled is a caution. We live modestly as we do in B.I. It costs us 3 times as much. Why even the peasants are so used to seeing hosts of strangers doing nothing that they say to me when I am off painting — 'Going to amuse yourself with a little painting.' Instead of as at B.I. 'Going to work'. Hell! Fortunately my wife has excellent health. So I am glad in spite of uncongenial surroundings, for she is a treasure to me, all I could ask for and much more than I deserve.

By the bye, when will we hear of a Mrs. Tom Roberts. Don't you know that question and answer from the "Munichandra"

'Who is the happy man? He that sees in his own home little children crown [*sic*] with dust, leaping and falling and crying.'
[Some lines missing here]

In this I send you sketch in Red Chalk, with blessing. Sorry I've nothing in color of a convenient size but will send that later on.

How goes the A.A.A.[6] You asked me to send something out. Will be glad to if you will let me know in time.

We had a delightful six weeks' driving, especially in the Cevennes.[7] We descended the Tarn[8] (It was like Toboganning on water) in long flat boats. Quite exciting at times in the rapids. T'was time of flood. Like the Valley of the Grose in N.S.W. but with old chateaux, villages, Castles, &c. added. Nimes, St. Remy, Les Brux, interesting antiquities Aix fine Van Eyck (?) of King Rene and his spouse.[9] Magnificent carved doors that made Ghiberti take a back seat,[10] to my mind, and old English tapestries originally in St. Paul's, London, Life of Christ but costumes of period when made. Figures full of character. Splendid. Most interesting I ever saw. I drive back, alone, in April.

Ever sincerely yours
John P. Russell

Villa des Pins
Cap d'Antibes,
Alpes Maritimes, France.

NOTES—RUSSELL TO ROBERTS LETTER 5

[1] A reference probably to the Catalogue of the Winter Exhibition of the Victorian Artists' Society of March 1890, the cover of which was designed by Charles Conder.
[2] i.e. the Sydney *Bulletin*.

3 Manet died on 30 April 1883. A large retrospective of his work which included 116 paintings was held in the Ecole des Beaux Arts from 4 to 28 January 1884. It would be a matter of considerable interest to know whether Roberts saw this exhibition. Russell's question at least bears the implication that Russell might have seen the exhibition, that is that he was in Paris at the time. In October 1883 Russell and Roberts were in Spain together, and Roberts is known to have studied in Paris for a period. However, his painting 'Churchyard, Chillingstone' was painted (in England) in January 1884.

4 Louis Anquetin (1861-1932), a prominent pupil at Cormon's who became interested first in Impressionism and then in the divisionist theories of Signac and his friends. His later work was strongly influenced by Rubens.

5 Paul Albert Besnard (1849-1934), a French painter and engraver, influenced by Impressionism.

6 The Australian Artists Association amalgamated with the Victorian Academy of Art in 1888 to form the Victorian Artists' Society.

7 A mountain range in the Massif Central, France.

8 Between Florac and Millau, this river runs in a canyon 1,300 to 1,600 ft deep. Russell compares the gorge to the valley of the Grose in the Blue Mountains.

9 Russell is referring to 'Triptych of the Burning Bush' (1476) at St Sauveur, Aix en Provence, which contains portraits of King René (1442-80), Count of Aragon and Anjou, and his wife Jeanne de Laval. It is now ascribed to Nicholas Froment.

10 Russell is referring to the doors of Aix Cathedral which are carved with relief figures in a late Gothic style. They are dated to 1504.

Letter 6: after June 1890

Cap d'Antibes,
   A.M.,
     France.

Dear T. R.

I find by a paper which Will Maloney sent me describing Melbourne artists' studies, that your address is Grosvenor Chambers.[1] Well, three days ago I addressed a few lines and a sort of study in chalk to 1 St. James. I don't imagine you'll get 'em and perhaps 'tis well. I forgot to inclose this sketch showing how my wife shaved my head with a 'ciseaux-baraquand'.[2]

I am glad to see that you had a success with your naturalistic picture 'Shearing the Rams'.[3] Rational Impressionism and naturalistic art wins in a canter though it does not look like it in Merry England, judging by the recent [academic] elections. Nine tenths of the men have no guts. Don't see nature in a strong way. How can you expect them to paint anything original. Ah it takes courage* to leave the beaten track and hard work to find any-

* What the Iron Duke called Two o'clock in the morning courage and valued so highly.

thing to eat on it. Have you given up the photography entirely now. By the way! How unkind of you not to mention that photographic appointment when you wished my advice about returning to Melbourne.[4] "How beautiful the olive oil jars are, Ethel" said an English dame to her daughter from the cushiony depths of her luxurious carriage /at 8 francs an hour./ Ha! Ha!! The great jars make quite a feature in the landscape. The peasants are saving and use 'em to store what my boy Sandro calls Kac Ka — And so we judge by the outside things in the world.

We have a small girl 3 years — tall for her age. Jeanne Marianna.[5] I tell you, my dear Sir, it brings my hair off in tufts when I try to paint her. Flaxen hair but with a delightful sheen of gold. Eyes sometimes blue sapphire, now like the blue pellucid sea; tomorrow violet. Complexion coming and going. Cream flushed with rose and tipped with carnation. Get her listening to her mother — legends and tales of old Italy. Oh! The Devil and the deep sea — Throw the palette out of the window and let's go for a drive to Clausonne[6] and hear the music of horses' hoofs on the highway. Alas for the poor gamut of a painter. Why don't some scientific chaps invent purer and more puissant colors.
Look at this,

Old rocky garden 35 feet above sea level. Cacti, tamarisk, olives, giant geraniums, needs old pots yellow. Sea a mighty blaze of blues, greens, purple, opalescent lights, distant snow covered Alps, tender green and rose sky. Over all a blaze of sunlight.

And yet folks talk of finish.   What is Finish?

Do you notice how green the sky is in winter?
Goodbye old son and good luck. Like to grip your fist again.

J. P. Russell

Deep digging is the best. Two men working in my garden. One scratched the earth but finished the top beautifully. T'other shoved his fork in half way up the handle and so had no time to smooth the top. I know which gave the best vegetable.
P.S. I think in *studies* one should aim at one thing at a time — say values — anon color, &c. Simplicity and directness.
Next summer we are hoping to visit Granada. Carmona was

I think the name of your host. If the cholera has spared him perhaps I'll abide a time there and try your Roman baths.

[Ink sketch (inn scene with dancer on table)]

NOTES—RUSSELL TO ROBERTS LETTER 6

1 Tom Roberts appears to have moved to Grosvenor Chambers, Collins St., Melbourne, early in 1888 (see *Table Talk*, 28 June 1888). (Grosvenor Chambers, Melbourne, Collins St. East, one built expressly for occupation by artists, the whole of the upper floor being with that end in view arranged as studios, besides which in the basement is the atelier of Mr. Perceval Ball, sculptor. The top floor contains five studios occupied by the following artists:— Messrs. Tom Roberts, J. C. Waite, Walton, Abrahams, and Patterson. Each studio is furnished with an ante-room, and the lighting is expressly arranged on principles laid down by Sir Joshua Reynolds, every room having a direct conglobated light, and all internal objects being blackened in absorbent colours. The middle floor is occupied by Mrs. Eeles, costumier, and contains handsome show rooms, a dark room for the exhibition of silks and the display of gaslight effects; also a large factory capable of accommodating upwards of 40 employees. The ground floor contains handsome showrooms, which were originally intended to be used by Mr. Patterson for his art decorating establishment, also a long corridor and handsome tiled floor leading to the staircase and to Mr. P. Ball's atelier. The front windows on the ground floor have columns and spondrels of cast-iron, the spondrels being filled up with Cathedral glass. This glass work, as well as the stained glass window in the staircase, has been executed by Messrs. Brooks, Robinson & Co., whose artist, Mr. Hughes, has successfully interpreted the purpose of the architects to make these windows illustrative of different features of the fine arts. The basement contains a commodious cellar—occupied by Mr. Ball's—specially designed to enable the sculptor to deal with massive subjects in stone or clay. Rooms upwards of 20 ft. in height.) (From A. Sutherland: *Victoria and its Metropolis*, Melbourne, 1888)

2 *Ciseaux-baraquand*, literally barrack-room shears, perhaps a jovial reference to Roberts's 'Shearing the Rams' mentioned in the following paragraph.

3 Roberts completed the painting in May 1890 (see Spate, *Tom Roberts*, p. 86).

4 Roberts returned to Australia after accepting 'an offer from Baillie and Brown to reorganize the posing, lighting and backgrounds of their photographic studios' (Spate, pp. 31-2).

5 Russell's only daughter.

6 A village in the Hautes Alpes, France.

[THE EXHIBITION OF 9 x 5 IMPRESSIONS, BUXTON'S GALLERY, MELBOURNE, AUGUST 1889]

AN IMPRESSIONIST EXHIBITION

Such an exhibition of impressionist memoranda as will be open to-day at Buxton's Art Gallery,[1] by Messrs. Roberts, Conder, Streeton, and others fails to justify itself. It has no adequate *raison d'être*. It is as if a dramatist should give a performance on the stage of such scraps of dialogue, hints of character, ideas for incidents, and suggestions of situations as had occurred to him while pondering over the construction of a play, or as if a musician should invite people to listen to crude and disconnected scraps of composition, containing the vaguely indicated themes for a cantata, a symphony, or an opera; or as if a sculptor should ask us to inspect certain masses of marble from which he had just blocked out the amorphous outlines of various pieces of statuary. None of these is to be regarded as a work of art. Neither is a painter's 'impression'. It is simply a record in colour of some fugitive effect which he sees, or professes to see, in nature. But, like primeval chaos, 'it is without form and void.' To the executant it seems spontaneous and forcible. To the spectator it appears grotesque and meaningless. The earliest impressionist of whom we have any knowledge was Piero di Cosimo,[2] and he had 'a bee in his bonnet.' Vasari tells us that 'he would sometimes stand beside a wall against which various impurities were cast, and from these he would image forth the most singular scenes, combats of horses, strangely ordered cities, and the most extra-ordinary landscapes that ever were seen.' The modern impressionist asks you to see pictures in splashes of colour, in slap-dash brush work, and in sleight-of-hand methods of execution leading to the proposition of pictorial conundrums, which would baffle solution if there were no label or catalogue. In an exhibition of paintings you naturally look for pictures; instead of which the impressionist presents you with a varied assortment of palettes. Of the 180 exhibits[3] catalogued on the present occasion, some-thing like four-fifths are a pain to the eye. Some of them look like faded pictures seen through several mediums of thick gauze; others suggest that a paint-pot has been accidentally upset over a panel nine inches by five; others resemble the first essays of a small boy, who has just been apprenticed to a house-painter; whilst not a few are as distressing as the incoherent images which float through the mind of a dyspeptic dreamer. Here is an impression, for example, entitled 'Harrowing',[4] which is quite true to its title. It represents a long-legged pig in company with two terribly deformed horses — or are they 'creatures of the slime?' — struggling to get away from one of those scarecrows, which English farmers set up in their cornfields when the grain is ripening, and dislocating their legs — number uncertain — in the process. And here is a mystery, called 'The Milky Way,'[5] consisting of two or three spots of positive colours on what appears to be a sheet of smoked brown paper. Here, again, is something bearing the title of 'Orange, Blue and White,'[6] representing a hydrocephalus doll, with glass eyes, wooden hands and a broken nose, almost buried in a mass of white-lead. And there are landscapes and samples of architecture, belonging to some embryotic world, in which, as Pandulph says, 'All form is formless, order orderless,'[7] and nature herself is either unshapen or misshapen. Some of the impressions, in which sufficient work has been put to entitle them to be spoken of as sketches, show that the artists are capable of much better things. Such is the clever 'Looking over to Williamstown' of Mr. R. E. Falls; the 'Fisherman's Bend,' 'Evening in Richmond Paddock,' and 'Austral Summer,' of Mr. A. Streeton; the 'Treasury,' 'Early and Damp,' 'Good-bye,' and 'Going down to Dinner,' of Mr. Tom Roberts; the 'Dear Lady Disdain' and 'Myosotis,' of Mr. Charles Conder, and the plastic sketches of Mr. C. D. Richardson.[8] These and a few others afford something agreeable for the eye to rest upon; but the exhibition, viewed as a whole, would leave a very painful feeling behind it, and cause one to despond with respect to the future of art in this colony, did we not believe, with Mr. W. P. Frith, R.A., that 'Impressionism is a craze of such ephemeral character as to be unworthy of serious attention.'[9]

[Article by James Smith, *Argus*, 17 August 1889]

NOTES—JAMES SMITH—AN IMPRESSIONIST EXHIBITION

1 Buxton's Art Gallery in Swanston Street, Melbourne, opened by a business-man in the 1880s.

2 Smith's comments on Piero di Cosimo are derived from Giorgio Vasari's *Lives of the Painters, Sculptors and Architects,* particularly the following passage: 'After his death it appeared that . . . in the light of these examples' (Vasari, *Lives* (ed.) W. Gaunt, London, 1963, pp. 176-83). His account of Piero di Cosimo's life and art is Vasari at his best and deserves to be read in full. That Cosimo's work, however, was quite unlike that of the French Impressionists is clear from even the most cursory examination of any of his accepted works, e.g. the mythological subject in the National Gallery, London, usually described as the 'Death of Procris'.

3 In fact 182 exhibits were shown.

4 By F. McCubbin (Cat No. 180).

5 By Tom Roberts (Cat No. 8).

6 By A. Streeton (Cat No. 133).

7 The words are spoken by Cardinal Pandulph in Shakespeare's *King John*, III, 253.

8 C. D. Richardson (1853-1932), a sculptor, and a close associate of Tom Roberts and Frederick McCubbin.

9 W. P. Frith was a highly successful painter of Victorian realistic genre paintings, the best known of his paintings being 'Derby Day' (1858, Tate Gallery, London). The location of the present quotation has not been traced

but in his *Autobiography* (London, 1887) Frith writes: 'A new style of art has arisen which seems to gratify a public ever craving for novelty. Very likely I am posing as an old-fashioned Academician, who declines to acknowledge that eccentricity is a proof of genius, or audacity an evidence of power; and I may be justly, or unjustly, accused of unfairness when I declare that the *bizarre*, French 'impressionist' style of painting recently imported into this country will do incalculable damage to the modern school of English art' (vol. 2, 352); and in his *Reminiscences* (London, 1888) he writes: 'Impressionism, in which neither drawing, colouring, nor truth in any form appears, I pass with the contempt it merits'. The English resistance to Impressionism is discussed in detail by D. Cooper, *The Courtauld Collection* (London, 1954).

Tom Roberts (1856–1931)

Tom Roberts was born at Dorchester, England, on 9 March 1856. On the death of his father his mother emigrated to Australia with her three children when Tom was thirteen. He began work as a photographer's assistant, later becoming the head operator at Stewart and Co., photographers. In 1874 he joined the evening classes of the National Gallery School under Thomas Clark and Eugen von Guerard. Whilst a student at the school he led the move to introduce life classes there. In 1881, at the age of twenty-five, he sold some of his paintings and raised enough money to proceed to London where he studied at the Royal Academy Schools and did some work for the *Graphic* and other London illustrated publications. He travelled with John Russell and Will Maloney to the south of France and Spain; and it was probably whilst in Spain and France that he first heard of the Impressionist painters. Roberts returned to Australia in 1885 and with McCubbin, Streeton, Conder, Davies and others developed a new approach to Australian painting in camps at Box Hill, Mentone, Heidelberg and elsewhere. He helped to organize the 9 x 5 Exhibition of Impressions. In 1890 he painted 'Shearing the Rams' and followed with such subject paintings as 'The Golden Fleece' and 'The Breakaway'. He had established himself at Grosvenor Chambers, Collins Street, Melbourne, as a portrait painter.

In 1891 he came to Sydney and set up a painter's camp at Sirius Cove, and also painted portraits and taught. In 1896 he married Elizabeth Williamson. In 1900 he began a large picture of the 'Opening of the First Commonwealth Parliament' and completed it in London in 1903. Roberts remained in London, although at first he found great difficulty in coping with the English light. He received little recognition from English critics. At the age of sixty he volunteered as a hospital orderly during the First World War and remained for three and a half years. In 1919 he returned to Australia and held a successful exhibition, then returned to England for a few months before settling once again in Australia. He built himself a studio at Kallista, in the mountains thirty miles from Melbourne; and held one-man shows of his work from time to time. His wife died in 1928. He later married Jean Boyes, of Tasmania. Roberts died at Kallista on 14 September 1931.

[CONCERNING 'IMPRESSIONS' IN PAINTING]

To The Editor of The Argus

Sir, — As in your issue of the 17th inst. you have given a notice of our exhibition of impressions and sketches, which is now about to close, and, as that notice or criticism was one taken from a standpoint which was that of strong disapproval, not only of the great portion of the works exhibited, but also of the movement in painting which they, however, modestly, but always seriously, try to represent, we are sure your sense of justice will very willingly allow something to be said from another side, the more so when it is remembered that in the formation of taste in this new country where art is so young and so tentative, every public expression of opinion and every show of works must have a more or less strong influence in the making of that taste.

It will be remembered by those who have at all watched the course of painting in Victoria during the last four years that the works of a few men have been called 'impressionist', the more particularly in speaking of their landscape pictures, and there has been a very general opinion amongst those not intimate with the painters that these works have been more or less 'sketches' rather than finished paintings, that, in fact, they have been rapidly made and of a slap-dash character more than very seriouse [*sic*] well considered efforts to represent effects and moods and thoughts of nature which have impressed the artists very strongly, and which they have tried in turn to impress upon the lovers of their art.

Let us then try to state our case or the principles upon which we have worked, and as well as we can put them in writing. They are these:— That we will not be led by any forms of composition or light and shade; that any effect of nature which moves us strongly by its beauty, whether strong or vague in its drawing, defined or indefinite in its light, rare or ordinary in colour, is worthy of our best efforts and of the love of those who love our art. Through and over all this we say we will do our best to put only the truth down, and only as much as we feel sure of seeing; and it is here that many will say, 'Give us work done faithfully according to such principles, and surely we are ready and willing to admire.' It is here we have our great difficulty.

For the question comes, how much do we see, and how much are our ideas and judgment of works made up by comparing with those we have already known, cared for, and are familiar with?

Without doubt the enjoyment of any work of art depends not only on the innate sense of what is beautiful, but also upon the extent and direction of the education of the eye, through which the aesthetic sense is moved as it takes an artist to paint a picture, so also it takes one to appreciate it.

It is always more or less difficult for the average mind to accept a new beauty or its interpretation.

After the strong light and shade of Rembrandt, or the obvious vigour of such heads as Millais's Simon Fraser,[1] it is difficult to see and value the quality of such a head as Phillip of Spain, by Velasquez, it is so quiet and reticent.[2] It was a long time before any beauty was seen in Corot or Millet, and Whistler's portrait of Carlyle[3] was not always appreciated.

So in judging landscape work in Victoria, the mind is more or less influenced by familiar works. In looking at the works of modern European and American painters, who have in a great measure discarded the studio for their painting ground, and whose aim has been to sacrifice no truth for effect, the spectator may feel a certain want as of finish or arrangement, and here let us leave our mind open, and forget for the moment our own idea of what ought to be in a picture, realise the intention of the artist, then judge if the impression given is true under the conditions represented, leaving the rest to time, for if the work is good it will grow upon and hold us.

In the matter of how much do we see? In a row of cabbages 20 yards from us, how many leaves can we make out? On checking the number, how very few!

In the clumps of reeds or rushes across the river, how many individuals can we distinguish?

On examining our impressions of nature it is surprising how much in single mass objects 'come' at any distance, and how little we really see of detail.

None knows better than we do that in painting a subject of nearly all middle-distance and distance, it is easy to put a strongly marked object in the immediate foreground, and give an appearance of 'finish', but we have to ask ourselves does this spoil our thought? does it hurt the idea? and, if so, we leave it out. In doing so, we believe that it is better to give our own idea than to get a merely superficial effect, which is apt to be a repetition of what others have done before us, and may shelter us in a safe mediocrity, which, while it will not attract condemnation, could never help towards the development of what we believe will be a great school of painting in Australia. —Yours, &c.,

TOM ROBERTS, CHAS. CONDER, ARTHUR STREETON

Aug. 30.

NOTES—LETTER TO THE ARGUS. ROBERTS, CONDER AND STREETON

1 Millais' portrait of Simon Fraser Esq., exhibited at the R.A. in 1885.
2 Phillip IV of Spain. Roberts may be recalling the bust portrait of Philip IV in the National Gallery London, (no. 745) which he would have seen during his residence in London.
3 The reference is to the painting which Whistler called 'Arrangement in grey and black, no 2: Thomas Carlyle' (1872-73) now in the Glasgow Art Gallery.

[JAMES SMITH'S REPLY]

The tripartite letter on 'Impressions in Painting', which appeared in our yesterday's issue, alleges that 'every show of works (of art) must have a more or less strong influence' on 'the formation of taste in this new country.' It was precisely on that very account that we condemned the recent exhibition, because whatever influence it was likely to exercise could scarcely be otherwise than misleading and pernicious. Our correspondents further inform us that their 'impressions' were not, as we hoped, mere sketches or memoranda in colour, but 'very serious and well-considered efforts to represent effects and moods and thoughts of nature;' and, this being so, those serious efforts go to prove either that there is some visual defect, common to the exhibitors, which prevents them from seeing nature as she really is; or that the impressions conveyed by natural objects are distorted and deformed in their passage through the minds of the artists, and are presented in a perverted form upon panel or canvas. Our main objection to their work is that it is wholly foreign to nature, and is destitute of all sense of the beautiful.

As to the contention that it takes an artist to appreciate a picture, the fallacy of the statement is so palpable that it is scarcely worth the trouble of refutation. The Italian princes and prelates to whom the great artists of the Renaissance owed their encouragement and support; the merchants of Venice and Amsterdam, who formed such noble collections of immortal masterpieces; the Manchester cotton manufacturers; the Birmingham steel-pen makers; the Leeds wool-staplers; the Bristol and Liverpool ship-owners; and the STEWARTS,[1] VANDERBILTS,[2] and other wealthy Americans, who have formed private galleries with so much judgment, taste, and discrimination, were certainly not artists. Nor have most of the best art critics in France, past and present, ever handled a brush. It is true that RUSKIN and HAMERTON[3] have done so, and so, we believe, has Mr. J. J. JERVIS [*sic*],[4] one of the ablest of the American writers on this subject. But the last-named gentleman has thus expressed himself with regard to the Impressionists:—

> In them the attempt to define form and expression by great splotches of colour, flatly and coarsely laid on by heavy drag of brush, depending only on sharp contrast for effect, and rude suggestions of things for definite outline and drawing, becomes a brutal realistic failure, conspicuous by the absence of the finest essentials of true art . . . This sort of work stops just where the real difficulties of complete art begin.

Mr. HAMERTON remarks that if the artist — even supposing him to be highly cultivated — 'will honestly put it to himself what his impressions really are, he will find that they have all the characteristics of a sketch, that they may perhaps be clear and vivid in parts, but only at the cost of extreme vagueness and indecision elsewhere.' And this is one of the cardinal aims of all impressionist work. Everything is blurred and indistinct, grotesque and illegible. It is not always even suggestive of the object or scene intended to be portrayed, but perplexes the mind of the spectator by the problems it presents. Instead of a faithful image we are treated to a caricature. Where we look for form and definition we find nothing but confusion and an uninteresting mystery. Instead of the beautiful gradations, the subtle harmonies, and the exquisite finish and perfection of nature, we are brought face to face with something that might be possible under some hardly conceivable conditions of light, atmosphere, and vegetable organisation. At present this something exists only in the imagination of a few young artists who have formed themselves into a Mutual Admiration Society, and cherish the deplorable delusion that the greatest landscape painters the world has ever seen were not only blind to the majesty and loveliness of nature, but were completely ignorant of the true method of interpreting her; while it seems to be believed that a little coterie of painters, in one corner of Australia, is about to revolutionise the entire theory and practice of landscape art.

[By James Smith, 4 September 1889]

NOTES—JAMES SMITH'S REPLY TO THE LETTER FROM ROBERTS, STREETON AND CONDER

1 Alexander Turner Stewart (1803-76), a retail merchant, amassed a considerable fortune and developed a large collection of paintings.

2 Cornelius Vanderbilt (1843-99), a financier and philanthropist, amassed a great collection. William Henry Vanderbilt (1821-85), a financier and railroad operator; left a munificent bequest to the Metropolitan Museum of Art, New York, on his death in 1885.

3 P. G. Hamerton (1834-94), an artist and essayist (see his *Autobiography and Memoirs*, 1897). Smith's later implication that Hamerton was unsympathetic to Impressionism is not supported by the latter's *The Present State of the Fine Arts in France* (London, 1892), which was one of the first sympathetic accounts of Impressionist painting to be published in London. In it Hamerton says of Monet: 'for variety of observation, joined to complete singleness of purpose in each separate work, no French landscape painter is comparable to Claude Monet'; on Renoir: 'the important picture of boating men and girls refreshing themselves by the Seine, is full of healthy colouring, remote indeed from the cadavorous skins that have been common in earthy and bituminous paint; of Degas that he 'sees human nature in his own way, and describes it with a candour that must be shocking to people who have any illusions left; and of Impressionism in general: 'these movements of rebellion in favour of Nature are the refreshment of Art itself, like waters brought from a distant lake or river to the heart of some populous city, some dingy Glasgow, some thirsty and sunburnt Marseilles' (pp. 24-9). But it is to be noted that this was written two years after Smith's own critique, and that opinion about Impressionism was changing.

4 James Jackson Jarves (1818-88), the editor, traveller, critic and pioneer art collector, wrote extensively both on art and travel. His important collection of Italian primitive paintings, the first significant collection by an American citizen, was acquired by Yale University in 1871.

[EXHIBITION OF AUSTRALIAN ART, GRAFTON GALLERY, 2 APRIL-7 MAY 1898]

This exhibition was sponsored and financed by Dame Eadith Walker (1865-1937) the daughter of Thomas Walker (1804-86) a public benefactor who had amassed a considerable fortune as a general merchant. Julian Ashton and Bernard Wise assisted and encouraged her. The exhibition contained 371 works and consisted mainly of the work of the artists and followers of the Heidelberg School in Victoria and the circle of artists associated with the Julian Ashton Art School in Sydney.

Printed below are critical reviews of the exhibition, the first by R. A. M. Stevenson in the *Pall Mall Gazette,* the second by Sir Thomas Humphrey Ward in the *Times,* London, and the third by D. S. MacColl in the *Saturday Review.*

R. A. M. Stevenson (1847–1900)

Robert Alan Mowbray Stevenson was born in Edinburgh, and was educated at Windermere and Sydney Sussex College, Cambridge. He was a close friend of his cousin, Robert Louis Stevenson, who did much to encourage his literary interests. Stevenson studied art in Antwerp and in Paris under Carolus Duran, and later spent several years at Barbizon and Grez. It is quite possible that he knew A. J. Daplyn whom he mentions in his review, who also studied under Duran and worked at Barbizon. In 1882 he taught painting in classes to undergraduates at Cambridge, in connection with the work of Sidney Colvin, then Slade Professor of Fine Art at Cambridge. From 1883 to 1889 he contributed to the *Saturday Review* as a critic of painting and music. In 1889 he was appointed Professor of Fine Arts at University College, Liverpool, resigning that office in 1893 to become for six years the regular critic of the *Pall Mall Gazette.* Stevenson wrote a book on Rubens (1888) and an influential book on Velasquez (1899).

Stevenson championed the aims and methods of Impressionism in England, and was scrupulously fair to tendencies for which he felt less sympathy. He is the 'Spring-healed Jack' of Robert Louis Stevenson's essay 'Talk and Talkers'.

[AUSTRALIAN ART AT THE GRAFTON GALLERY]

Three hundred and seventy-one pictures in oil, water-colour and monochrome, excellently and spaciously hung, should give a fair idea of the aims, tendencies and proficiency of the Australian artists. The exhibition proves that French art, which has swept the European Continent, has almost conquered Australia. This change has been most rapidly effected. The Colonial Exhibition of 1886[1] showed us an Australian art that was still English, or, to speak more correctly, showed us fashions of painting that were founded upon the English trade picture[2] when they were not merely untrained records of nature: mechanical drawings and geological, botanical or topographical diagrams. When they are carefully and scientifically executed I am far from despising these mechanical drawings. They call for patience, skill and certain gifts of observation and eye measurement; gifts only too much discredited by the still more mechanical photographs which one uses and admires as a work of nature rather than as a feat of man's handicraft. A train can beat any animal in a race, and one goes to business in it. Does any one admire coal and iron as one admires the limbs and lungs, the compelling brain and exultant heart of a racer? Now, a photographer is to a draughtsman what a steam engine is to a greyhound. Mere skill of hand and eye may not be art, but it is one of the indispensable legs upon which art must walk. The great difficulty is to get people to take the sportsman's interest in art, to patronize it as they patronize the prize-ring; to admire not only the result, but the noble qualities of the performer.

In 1886 I had to search the Colonial Exhibition for artists,[3] and I found scarce half a dozen artistic handlers of paint; now I found the present show abounding in virtuosity. Men educated in Paris have settled in Australia, and moreover, the Australians have bought for their public galleries one or two fine examples of artistic painting. As early as 1880, Mr. A. J. Daplyn, a man trained at Barbizon and in the studio of Carolus Duran migrated to New South Wales, where I believe he had many pupils. His work in this exhibition is of the older French tradition, quiet, unaffected and without any swagger of brushwork. Though one may find several pictures gentle in effect and handled in a reserved manner, yet quiet, deeply studied work is by no means common. Australia seems in an experimental mood, rather inclined to show off than to think profoundly. Men appear as yet unconvinced of the path, and vary from obedience to nature to the boldest affectation of mastery. Like the Americans, they have no time to waste on the long personal elaboration of an attitude of mind. The slow, unconscious growth of a Corot or a Millet who is scarcely revealed to himself under half a lifetime is uncomprehended by the bustling citizen of the world. To such accomplishment, not self-expression, seems the last word of perfection. I can best convey my idea by saying that they seek just that which Rossetti lacked; which, indeed, he counted a secondary quality. But like the penny wise and the pound foolish, those who make haste to be masters often spoil their chances. Some of these bold handlers and decorative composers give us a raw colour, common sentiment, and even a second-rate comprehension of those very qualities upon which true accomplishment depends — fine drawing, just values, broad but subtle modelling. Handling cannot be considered the first quality in a picture;

the most artistic, the most expressive handling never falls into a perfectly systematic pattern. When a clever man succeeds in forcing such a pattern upon nature even without any apparent sacrifice of quality in his rendering of colour, atmosphere or shape, he nevertheless chills our enthusiasm, weakens our faith in his sincerity, and seems to invite us to regard him rather as a decorator of panels than as a true poet of natural effect. With his reason a man may conceive it possible that a patterned handling covers no insincerity; that a very small niggled execution respects broad masses of tone; but he cannot prevent the character of the style from acting upon his artistic feelings, and suggesting in the one case insincerity in the other laborious shortsightedness.

The spirit of Australian art is far too eager and earnest as well as accomplished to enjoy flattery: for this reason I have tried to indicate two dangers between which it will be obliged to steer. The one is that obedient regard for the structure of nature which tends to blind a painter to the laws which render expression effective in the medium. The second is that exclusive care for style which tends to make the painter a decorative mannerist. Both tendencies seem to me adverse to the creation of profound and lasting poetry in paint. Notwithstanding the high average of this exhibition you look in vain for the crowning work — the picture of Pointelin,[4] a Peppercorn,[5] a Sargent, a Maris,[6] or a Whistler.

But the show contains pictures that would certainly make their mark at the Academy. Mr. Tom Roberts' 'Golden Fleece' (102)[7] shows an excellent power of drawing, much careful observation of certain types of men and the business-like packing of a picture that goes to make a good illustration. When you have seen it, you will know how sheep shearing takes place in Australia; you will know the type of man produced by the country, his tallness, leanness, wiry activity and hard intelligence. But you will know little of Mr. Roberts or his way of seeing. His canvas tells nothing of general effect, of beauty, of the general outlook of the artist; it is a built-up canvas, one to be studied in detail, not to be received as a single view. It lacks beauty of colour, unity of effect and concentration of interest; in spite of its wonderful qualities of observation and human sympathy, it chills one because it utterly lacks style and poetry of impression. Compare it with the works of Mr. A. Streeton, Mr. E. P. Fox, Mr. D. Davies, indeed, with some of Mr. Roberts' other pictures, and you will find 'The Golden Fleece' hard, tight and inartistic, but,

P

as far as it goes, more in sympathy with nature. The cleverest, the most brilliant, the highest toned work in the show is Mr. Streeton's square canvas, 'Early Summer'; but I think I should prefer in the long run quieter work, such as 'Nearing the Camping Ground', by Mr. Ford-Paterson; 'Tranquil Winter', by Mr. W. Withers; 'A Rising Gale', by Miss Cusack; 'The Cook's Gallery', by Mr. Gordon Coutts; 'The Golden West', by Mr. J. Mather; 'Silver Mines, Broken Hill', by Mr. J. S. Diston; 'Portrait Study', by Mr. Longstaff; 'Sketch Portrait of Mrs. Spence', by Mr. Percy F. S. Spence and several other delicate pictures. One has not space to mention all the good things, but I would direct the visitor's attention to work by Messrs. J. R. Ashton, St. G. Tucker, F. McCubbin, H. Fullwood, A. R. Coffey, A. J. Hanson, C. Conder, Hall-Thorpe, B. E. Minns, J. A. Bennett, F. McComas, E. Fitzgerald, Lister-Lister, Howard Ashton, Bernard Hall, A. Loureiro, Llewellyn Jones, and J. S. Watkins and also that by Mesdames A. Musket, M. Drew, E. Meston, J. E. Scarvell, and E. Wright.

R. A. M. Stevenson.

The Pall Mall Gazette, Monday 4 April 1898

NOTES—R. A. M. STEVENSON ON AUSTRALIAN ART

[1] 'The object which the promoters of the Exhibition has in view was to bring under notice the development and progress which had been made in various parts of the Empire, in the hope that more intimate knowledge may be obtained of the vast fields for enterprise and commerce which exist throughout the British Dominions', *Official Guide to the Colonial and Indian Exhibition*, London, 1886, p. 5.

[2] i.e. pictures with a wide popular appeal, many of which were intended for engraving.

[3] See *The Catalogue of the Oil Paintings and Water-Colour Drawings of the Victorian Court, Colonial and Indian Exhibition, Australian Section*, printed at the Chiswick Press, London, 1886. The exhibition included 4 paintings by Tom Roberts (including 'Coming South') all lent by the artist. The largest exhibitors were George Rossi Ashton (5 paintings), Charles Rolando (8 paintings), J. A. Turner (13 paintings) and Frederick Woodhouse (9 paintings). The collection was formed under the direction of Alexander Fletcher, Collins St., Melbourne, who was honorary superintendent of the Arts Section for the Victorian Commissioners.

[4] Auguste Emmanuel Pointelin (1839-1933), a French landscape painter well known for his pictures of the scenery of the Jura.

[5] A. D. Peppercorn (1847-1926), an English landscape painter in oil and watercolours, who met Corot and the other members of the Barbizon school while he was studying in Paris. He exhibited from 1869, and was a friend of Mathis Maris.

6 Jacob Maris (1837-99), a Dutch painter of the figure and of genre. His brothers, Mathis (1839-1917) and Willem (1844-1910) were also painters.

7 Also called 'Shearing at Newstead', purchased by the Art Gallery of New South Wales in 1894 for £275.

Sir Thomas Humphrey Ward (1845–1926)

Ward was a special writer on the staff of the *Times* from 1880, and contributed articles on art and literature particularly. He was born in Hull, was educated at the Merchant's Taylor's School, London, and at Brasenose College, Oxford. In 1872 he married an authoress, Mary Arnold, the granddaughter of Dr Arnold of Rugby and better known as Mrs Humphrey Ward. Ward edited *The English Poets 1881-1918* (1880); *English Art in the Public Galleries of London* (1888); *The Reign of Queen Victoria* (1887); and *Men of the Reign* (1885). He also wrote the authorized history of the Athenaeum Club, London.

[EXHIBITION OF AUSTRALIAN ART]

From today till May 7 the Grafton Galleries will contain an exhibition of unusual interest. It aims at giving an adequate representation of current Australian art, and, as it is organized by the trustees of the National Art Gallery of New South Wales, that object has been fairly secured. Nearly 400 pictures and drawings, with a few pieces of sculpture, form a collection the like of which the colonies have never sent home before; for the best men exhibit and the Galleries of Sydney and Melbourne lend many of their most characteristic pictures. One is tempted to assume in a general way, that colonial art cannot be very good; that the country is too young, and that the talents of its sons generally find other outlets. But in point of fact, the last 20 years have wrought a great change in Australia, and the practice of art has thriven there, if not quite as vigorously as has the practice of literature. These galleries show it, and they show also that the impulse, or at least the mode of expression, has to a great extent come from Paris, through English and Australian teachers who had first learned what the Paris *ateliers* had to teach them. Mr. Bernard Hall,[1] Mr. Daplyn, and some other teachers are instances of this; their work, with that of their pupils, shows the traces of it. In this bright and pleasant display there is very little that recalls anything English; the broad, summary treatment, the firm and yet careful drawing, the manner of laying on paint are in origin French, though they have become in a measure transformed by transplantation. If there is any British work to which the Australian pictures bear a close resemblance, it is that produced by the young men of Glasgow; and we know how strongly French influence has told on them. Mr. Phillips Fox, for example, the painter of a charming portrait of a child in a quaint white frock and sunbonnet (108), might almost have worked with Mr. Guthrie,[2] and the Australian landscapists, in spite of the brightness of their climate, have much in common with their cousins on the banks of the Clyde.

Of the landscape painters, the most noteworthy are Mr. Arthur Streeton, Mr. David Davies, Mr. Lister-Lister, and Mr. Daplyn; while among the painters of combined figure and landscape Mr. F. McCubbin, Mr. Tom Roberts, and Mr. A. Loureiro[3] attract by reason of a certain individuality and force. Mr. Streeton claims our gratitude for giving us impressions of landscape which seem to be distinctively Australian; his 'Hawkesbury River' (62) and his picture in the inner gallery (284), albeit a little too much composed, could hardly represent anything in any other latitude. Mr. Davies, on the other hand, in his tranquil, featureless landscapes, almost suggests the Barbizon tradition filtering down through the New English Art Club.[4] Mr. Lister paints on too large a scale, and does not avoid some approach to the commonplace; but Mr. Daplyn's careful work, if a little old-fashioned, has all the virtue of sincerity. The large picture of Mr. McCubbin (76) bears the quaint title 'In the Wallaby Track';[5] let the unlearned note that the wallaby is a small rodent who wanders from place to place, with no fixed home, and is therefore a kind of *totem* for tramps, two of whom, with the usual baby, are painted in this clever and rather touching picture. This is one of the everyday incidents of Australian life; a tragedy of a more heroic cast is 'The Death of Burke, the Explorer' (69), a large well-painted picture by Mr. Loureiro of Melbourne. Let us add Mr. T. Roberts's vivid and extremely clever picture of bolting sheep, 'A Break Away' (40),[6] some portraits of Sir Henry Parkes[7] and other eminences, by Mr. Julian Ashton and others; some 'heads of aborigines' (143) by Mr. B. E. Minns; some clever pencil drawings by Mr. Lambert (238); and one or two excellent little pictures by Mr. Charles Conder, whose work is well known in London, and we shall have said enough to show that this Australian exhibition is worth seeing. The subjects are fresh, and in technique the average work of Chelsea or Clichy[8] is certainly no better.

[The *Times,* London, Monday 4 April 1898, p. 15, col. 3]

NOTES—THE TIMES ARTICLE: EXHIBITION OF AUSTRALIAN ART

1 Lindsay Bernard Hall (1859-1935) was born at Liverpool, England. He studied at the Royal College of Art, South Kensington, and at the Antwerp and Munich Academies, prior to being appointed to the Directorship of the National Gallery of Victoria.

2 Mr Guthrie, later Sir James Guthrie (1859-1930), a portrait painter and President of the Royal Scottish Academy, was associated with the 'Glasgow School'.

3 Arthur Jose de Souza Loureiro (1860-1932), a Portuguese painter who lived for some years in Australia. Loureiro won a *Prix de Rome* while studying at the Royal Academy, Lisbon, and exhibited for three years at the Paris Salon. He died in Portugal in 1932.

4 The New English Art Club was formed in 1886 by artists outside the Royal Academy who were seeking to revive naturalistic painting in England. It included artists who had worked in France and been influenced by *plein air* methods and Bastien-Lepage. The chief members were George Clausen, Wilson Steer, Stanhope Forbes, J. S. Sargent, H. H. La Thangue and Frederick Brown.

5 i.e. 'On the Wallaby Track'. The painting is now in the Art Gallery of New South Wales.

6 'A Breakaway' is in the collection of the Art Gallery of South Australia.

7 'Sir Henry Parkes', now in the collection of the Art Gallery of New South Wales.

8 Chelsea was then the artists' quarter of London and the Boulevard de Clichy, Montmartre, at that time, the main artists' quarter of Paris.

Dugald Sutherland MacColl (1859–1948)

MacColl (1859-1948), a painter, critic and one-time Director of the Tate Gallery, was born in Glasgow, the son of a Presbyterian minister. He was educated at the Glasgow Academy and University College, London. MacColl won the Gerstenberg Memorial Prize in 1881. He travelled in Italy, Greece, Constantinople, Holland and Belgium.

MacColl belonged to the Westminster group, but did not enter the school till he was in his thirties. He was then acting as art critic to the *Spectator,* defending younger painters against the Academicians. After his mother's death MacColl became financially independent and resigned his post as critic to devote his time to painting. He championed the foundation of a 'Friends of the National Gallery' in 1900. He was appointed Director of the Tate Gallery in 1906, a post he held until 1911. In 1911 he became Keeper of the Wallace Collection in Hertford House. In 1904 MacColl created a stir over the administration of the Chantry Bequest, criticizing the Academy's buying policies as favouring its own members rather than the public interest.

[AUSTRALIAN ART]

It is astonishing how much capital has been expended on picture galleries in London in the last twenty years, and to what ill-directed or badly sustained issues. The Grosvenor Gallery[1] made a splendid start, and proceeded to snub half the great men who made its opening a memorable event in the history of picture galleries and the reputation of modern painters. Then came the New Gallery[2] to take over what remained of the estate, and that has been so innocently directed, has fallen so flaccidly into the hands of Academy and amateur, that if Sir Edward Burne-Jones were to cease exhibiting tomorrow, there would no longer be a reason for its existence. Then came the Grafton,[3] with an exhibition that did not indeed equal the first Grosvenor as a revelation of genius that had been in seclusion, but that did at least collect a number of notable painters from our own country and others, the world outside of Burlington House. Once more all this world seems to have been lost, to have slipped through the fingers of the management. The International Exhibition[4] promised for the summer flits to a skating rink, and the big gallery seems to be derelict, without an object, an idea, a use. A course of absurdly outside categories applied to painting, 'Fair Women,' 'Dramatic Art,' and so forth (we were saved the threatened 'Love in all its manifestations'), included in their haphazard net many interesting pictures; but the course ended the other day in the sands of Mr. Sellar's Old Masters,[5] and the last desperate device is a collection of 'Australian Art'. The importation of Australian meat and wine has its excuse, for those things, though not the best of their kind, are cheap and not unwholesome; but for the importation of the existing brands of Australian painting and sculpture there can be no excuse whatever. There is no Australian art. There are a number of young men who would like to be artists and who do their best to create art on the basis of the illustrated paper and such popular pictures as find their way to Australian public galleries, but there is no evidence of their having ever seen a good picture. They are in the position of the people of Ephesus visited by the Apostle Paul, who had not so much as heard whether there be any Holy Ghost.[6] They have the instinct of art, vague information about its nature, the most misleading examples, and they struggle heroically to produce they know not what.

The present exhibition is the act of a benevolent lady who thought she was doing a good turn to these men in putting their works on the London market. She could hardly have spent her money worse. These dowdy, shallow, glaring pictures merely prove the poverty of the land. How much better to have provided one or two of the most promising students with travelling bursaries, so that they might come over and study in countries where there are pictures. Or better still to have arranged an exhibition of real painting in the Australian capitals, or, best of all, bought one or two masterpieces for the extraordinary 'national galleries' from which a number of these works are drawn. The difference between manufacturing art in so newly manufactured a country and growing it in the richer deposits of the Old World is proved very neatly by the presence in this collection of two works by Mr. Charles Conder, who was in Australia for a few years in extreme youth, but who was lucky enough to escape. We know what he has done since; it would be hard to find the faintest trace of his remarkable gift in the two pictures here; and it is conceivable that it might never have developed at the Antipodes, certain that it would have been hampered, misled, blighted. Take another case, that of Mr. Arthur Streeton. It is quite possible from what is reported of him, that he has the makings of another Conder in him; his pictures here, when the enormous handicap against them is mentally removed, show no little talent, but a talent how badly served by models of the poorest modern French drawing. The same thing is true, very likely, if we only knew of many of these painters, though some are quite definitely and joyfully vulgar for evermore anywhere. And that is all it is possible to say about them.

Saturday Review, London, 16 April 1898

NOTES—MacCOLL ON AUSTRALIAN ART

¹ The Grosvenor Gallery was founded by the banker Sir Coutts Lindsay in 1877, at his own expense, in Bond St., London. Whistler, Millais, Leighton and Watts exhibited there, and Burne-Jones became known from his exhibitions there.

² The New Gallery was opened in 1888 (see *Art Journal*, 1888, p. 221).

³ The Grafton Gallery was opened in 1893 (see *Art Journal*, 1893, p. 145).

⁴ The International Exhibition was held in June 1898.

⁵ The reference is to a Mr D. P. Sellar who attempted to sell a collection of rather poor copies of old masters without success. He then offered the Collection in 1897 to the London Corporation, which declined the offer (*Magazine of Art*, 1898).

⁶ The reference is to *The Acts of the Apostles*, 19, 1-2. ' ... Paul having passed through the upper coasts came to Ephesus and finding certain disciples, he said unto them, have ye received the Holy Ghost since ye believed? And they said unto him, we have not so much as heard whether there be any Holy Ghost'.

Alfred James Daplyn (1844–1926)

Daplyn was born in London and studied painting in Paris under J. L. Gérôme (1824-1904) and Carolus Duran (1838-1917) and worked in the village of Barbizon. Daplyn emigrated to Australia in 1881 and became a friend of Julian Ashton, who had also studied in Paris before coming to Australia. Together they painted frequently in the Hawkesbury River district and helped to pioneer *plein air* painting in Sydney. Daplyn became the first art instructor at the Royal Art Society's School (1885-92), Charles Conder and Sydney Long being among his first pupils. His painting, 'The Moon is Up, Yet Tis Not Night', was purchased by the Trustees of the Art Gallery of New South Wales in 1900, but a later body of Trustees of the same institution sold the painting in 1946, in the ignorant belief that they were discarding a painting of little merit from the collection. Daplyn is represented in the Manly Art Gallery, New South Wales.

[LANDSCAPE PAINTING IN AUSTRALIA]

Introduction
During the last forty years Landscape Art has undergone great changes, so much so that a strict adherence to the old methods would be a mistake in a work having any pretensions to be up to date. In the interval the open air school has arisen, begun by the naturalists and realists, and continued to-day by the impressionists.

The difference between the older and the newer schools is practically this. The adherents of the former are more occupied with the subject, and rely greatly on their powers of composition for the effect of their picture. The latter care little for subject, and disdain all composition as artificial, their great aim being to render on canvas light and air. With Goethe they desire 'Light! Light! More light.'[1]

Formerly pictures often showed miles of country in the style of a panorama; now the artist, instead of taking his *point de vue* from the top of a mountain, and in consequence being obliged to content himself with a slight sketch, to be elaborated afterwards in the studio, makes his studio in the open air. The subject, far from embracing miles of country, is likely to be the corner of the field, his aim not so much to call forth feelings of awe and rapture, by displaying Nature in her grander mood, but to translate for our benefit the beauty that lies in familiar things.

No need for him to scale the mountains or pierce the clouds with eager gaze; his subject awaits him in the cool shade of the forest, by the side of the creek, river, or even in the garden. Perhaps he has chosen the familiar corner that we have passed by a hundred times without bestowing on it more than a hurried glance. There is the old tree whose quaint twisted branches and gnarled trunk have overhung the path since we can remember, a little patch of blue sky, a glimpse of distant houses showing through the trees, long grass flecked with sunshine, perhaps a homely figure, and the picture is complete; not so grand, you will say, as the fifty miles of lake and mountain of the old school, but what a fresh open air effect, and how brilliant are the tones. With nothing to remind us that it is only a picture: no dark heavy foreground, made so to give contrast to the distance, no dirty brown trees to give value to the sky; the eye is not dazzled by shining varnish, and all is bright and fresh.

The school which has cast aside tradition, and devoted itself to investigating the beauty of familiar things, has had a hard struggle, and even now is much misunderstood; it is said to have no appreciation for beauty, and to be low in aim. Now this is surely somewhat illogical, for is it not more reasonable to conclude that those who discover beauty in common objects, are more open to its influence than those who are obliged to wander from country to country in search of it?

Australia being pre-eminently a land of sunshine, which allows of painting in the open all the year round, it is not surprising that those susceptible to art influences should be attracted to the method practised by the *plein airistes,* or painters in the open air, in preference to those of the older school, which are generally heavier in style and darker in tone. Curiously enough, the general public does not share this predilection for colour and light, and often prefers the more sober effects of the old school. The cause of this may be that, as many are from the old country, their taste both for scenery and pictures is coloured by early memories.

There is much to be said in favour of both schools, but writing for Australian students, and considering the character of the scenery to be depicted, the methods of the French impressionist are inculcated, though it should rather be called the open air school, for so many horrors are perpetrated in the name of impressionism that the term is apt to mislead.

Australian scenery has been greatly maligned by writers, tourists, and others; far too much is heard of its sadness, its want of colour, and its monotony; certainly it is not so paintable as the old country, for there are no venerable ruins clothed with ivy, no old churches or castles, or quaint red tiled cottages; in fact, one does not encounter pictures ready made, and that only require transferring to the canvas. But, on the other hand, the scenery is more original, and has not been painted by generations of artists, till one is surfeited by repetition; the intense light makes also for greater finesse of colour; this is especially observable in the tree forms, which require a lighter touch and more subtle tone than the thick foliaged trees of the old country.

Of Australian trees the Eucalyptus is, of course, the most common. We often hear of the 'everlasting gum tree,' but its merits have rarely been acknowledged. Few trees are, in truth, so graceful in form and of such variety. This latter quality is quite lacking in European trees, where the oaks are oaks, and the elms, elms, and are always alike. Now the gum is hardly ever the same, and twenty species may be found growing in the space of a few acres. Some shoot up into the air straight and smooth like a ship's mast; others have rough and shaggy bark, and the trunks twist and turn in endless convolutions; many are of a bright red colour, or spotted like the leopard, while others shed their bark, which hangs round them in weird festoons, revealing, so to speak, the creamy-white flesh.

The branches shoot out from the trunk at all manner of unexpected angles, and go twisting and turning at their own sweet will, seeming to rebel against all laws that control the growth of branches in general.

And the foliage — how gracefully it hangs in feathery clusters, not giving much shade, it is true, being more ornamental than useful, and in this much resembling a fine lady, which the Eucalyptus may be said to personate in the world of trees.

Of course, if we view them in dense masses as they appear on the shores of Sydney Harbour, we are conscious of a certain monotony, but could we penetrate the mass, and note the characteristic forms of the different species, this would disappear.

Besides the different species of Eucalyptus, there are in Australia many trees which add greatly to the picturesque character of its scenery. The Honeysuckle,[2] for instance, would have rejoiced the heart of Corot, could he have seen it; for in most of his pictures you find trees identical in form. How delicate is the tone of its clusters of star-shaped leaves shining in the sunlight. The She-oak,[3] too, as it fringes the creek or river, its feathery foliage only a shade or two darker than the sky. The Tea-tree,[4] with its parchment-like bark; and the various species of Figs, clothed in their mantles of dark green.

All these Australian trees, and there are many more, require in painting a finer and lighter treatment than those of other countries. Painting being comparatively a new thing here, the student has not the help of text-books giving the experience of generations, but has to a great extent to investigate, and trust to his powers of invention for overcoming difficulties; it is for the purpose of helping him that this work has been written by one who has painted for more than twenty years in the open air in Australia.

Choice of subject

The student being able to draw reasonably well, and having acquired some command of his materials, may now think of painting a landscape study from Nature.

Beginners usually choose subjects that would task the powers of an experienced artist, instead of something very simple. They should for the moment put away all thoughts of making a picture, giving their whole attention to placing on canvas the tones seen in Nature; and of course the simpler the composition the more chance of success.

The student when choosing a subject should *half close the eyes,* or shut one of them, which has nearly the same effect. The landscape will now become simplified, the grand masses more prominent, and the thousand and one details which distract the attention eliminated.

Nature paints on a grand scale, and it is manifestly impossible to render on a small canvas all that is seen in a stretch of country perhaps miles in extent; but by the process of half closing the eyes truth to Nature becomes possible and you will learn by it more than any master can teach.

Now observe in the landscape thus seen there is only one highest light (probably the sky) and one deepest dark, and all the other tones are subordinate; this you must reproduce exactly. Observe also that the tones have more finesse and are simpler, and in the distance especially are nearly flat; be very careful to render this, for on it depends whether your picture will possess perspective, or, in the modern phrase, atmosphere.

The analysis of tone obtained by half closing the eyes is of the utmost importance in the teaching of the modern school. As seen thus the choice of subject is greatly facilitated, and the landscape resolves itself into two or three planes — the sky, the distance, and middle distance. The 'motif' will be generally found in the latter, for if there is nothing striking here it will be well to look elsewhere.

It will be observed that the foreground has not been spoken of, and the reason is that in modern pictures it is often conspicuous by its absence; and rightly so, for, if we look at the sky distance and middle distance, we look over the foreground and see it very vaguely, and it should be thus rendered. Let the student realise once for all that a landscape picture is a view from one place only, not half a dozen obtained by turning the head in different directions. For this reason the corners are not painted so forcibly as the middle, where the 'motif' of the picture is generally found. A foreground worked up to the very frame, besides being untrue, is an obstruction to the eye, preventing it from entering. This sensation of entering a picture is obtained by keeping the foreground simple and light in tone, and avoiding any obstruction, such as fences or rows of bushes touching the frame.

Of course, the art of composing a picture cannot be learned by recipes, like puddings; it is the application to special instances of general truths of form and colour, and the laws of perspective. Here are a few of them as laid down by M. Carolus Duran,[5] president of the New Salon:—

1. A subject ought to be complete in itself, without the possibility of adding anything to the sides or top or bottom.

2. Arrange the composition in the mind before placing on the canvas.

3. Art means choice. It is the artist's business to select from Nature — his great difficulty what to leave out.

4. Objects introduced into a composition without necessity damage it.

5. Let not one colour predominate.

6. Repetition of forms is to be avoided.

7. Simplify the colouration and vary the values.

8. The masses must be accentuated, the details contained in them simplified.

9. Never be satisfied with the nearly right.

10. True observation of values is more essential than brilliant colouring.

Many more but for the limits of space might be added. M. Carolus Duran practised what he preached, and his sermons were generally on the observation of values, varied by exhortations not to be satisfied with the *à peu près,* or nearly right. By following these precepts some of his pupils have attained great eminence; John S. Sargent, R.A.,[6] is an instance, and yet, when in Duran's atelier, he was often found fault with by the master for being only 'nearly right.'

The great French painter, Jean François Millet,[7] held the same views, and in an interview with the author, expressed himself strongly as to the importance of No. 2; he went further and insisted on the subject being completely drawn before the canvas was touched with paint ...

An old shanty forms a capital subject, and one not too difficult; so does an old fence overgrown with weeds; an old cart or an old tree is found nearly everywhere, and is generally worth doing.

The traces of age are not only fine in tone, but they harmonise the object with its surroundings and evoke our sympathy. New things do not do this, being often crude in colour and painfully angular in form; neither are they endeared to us by association with man in his daily labour. It is sympathy with all that relates to the lives of our fellow men which makes us seek in landscape signs of his presence; this absent, the beauties of Nature fail in interest. The purple mountain remains to us a purple mountain and nothing more. The primeval forest may stretch before us for miles, and our only sensation be of infinite monotony; but the clearing at once arrests our attention, and we view with delight even the primitive attempts of the savage to make for himself an abiding place in the little hut at the foot of some giant of the forest.

The signs of man's life are in some parts of Australia conspicuous by their absence. The parched land will hardly support the lower animals, much less man, and yet the would-be critic asks why the artist does not seek his subjects in the great 'interior.' He would not find them there if he went, and for the above reason.

The Sky: final drawing in transparent colour

Having chosen a simple subject, it must be drawn on the canvas with charcoal, taking great care with the composition. In France it is usual when the work is of any importance to carry the drawing further in the following manner:— Mix a tone of Ivory Black and Burnt Sienna or Lake, and dilute with turpentine; this tone being perfectly transparent and without any body, may be used as water-colour. Dust off the charcoal, and with the 'rigger' outline the principal lines, at the same time correcting the drawing, and indicating the parts in shadow by rubbing on the tone lightly with a hog's-hair brush. Do not use much turpentine in the shadows; the brush should be nearly dry. We have then a monotone drawing of the subject, with the light and shade indicated.

Should the sky be a prominent part of the subject it is well to commence with it, and the sky being the source of light, the utmost care must be taken to preserve its brilliancy. The painter in the open is inclined to make everything too dark, for the intense open-air light makes his tones seem lighter than they really are, and when seen indoors he is disappointed to find that they are heavy and dark; he should remember this, and at all hazards secure brilliancy.

This is particularly necessary in Australia, and for this reason the painter in the open should make but little use of the darker colours. Leaving the blacks and browns for the studio, let him work with the Light Blues, Lemon Yellow, and Madders; for Nature has no use for strong colours, being, so to speak, a kaleidoscope of coloured greys.

Should the reader be inclined to doubt this, let him look out of the window, and say if there is anything black or brown or any hot crude colour there. Surely he will see nothing but subtle tones of various coloured greys, which unite in perfect harmony.

For example, the black hull of the ironclad becomes a bluish-grey, and the newly tarred fence a greyish-purple; in a word, the clear Australian atmosphere acts the part of a good fairy, and changes the coarse and common into things of beauty.

To secure the effect of light something more is necessary than the employment of light pigments; for brilliancy is obtained quite as much by good technique, i.e., the method of handling the brush and the placing the tones on the canvas. It is not possible to give definite rules for this, being the result of intuition and experience, but it is certain that the more you rub the paint about the more dead and colourless it will become. Mix the tones with the palette knife on the palette, apply them to the canvas with a large flat brush in broad touches; do not rub them together — a slight movement to unite the edges is all that is necessary. If after one or two touches you find the tone wrong, scrape it off and make another, though you should not begin to paint before you are reasonably certain of having found the right one; this done, apply it boldly.

The following tones will be found useful in painting skies, but beware of making them too blue; they are generally of a luminous grey of infinite finesse.

Tones for Skies. — Cerulean Blue and Lemon Yellow, Cobalt and Lemon Yellow, Cobalt and Rose Madder or Vermilion, Emerald Green and Cobalt.

Grey Clouds, &c. — Cobalt and Vermilion, Cobalt and Rose Madder, Cobalt, Vermilion, and Lemon Yellow.

Dark Clouds, &c. — Cobalt and Vermilion, Cobalt and Light or Indian Red, Ultramarine and Vermilion.

Very Dark. — Ultramarine and Rose Madder, Ultramarine with Indian Red.

Very Light Clouds. — Lemon Yellow and Rose Madder and plenty of Flake White, Lemon Yellow and Vermilion, Yellow Ochre and Cobalt.

Distant Mountains. — The same tones as for the sky, but darker.

Smooth Water. — The same as the sky, but a little darker.

Flake White must be used freely with all the above.

With these the student will be able to render an infinite variety of skies, but he will require something more for success than a mere list of tones — viz., intelligence. If he have this he will find no difficulty in apportioning the right amount of colour to each tone, and varying the same according to his needs. It is a thing that cannot be taught by books, experience being the only guide. Let him acquire this by constant practice, and not be deterred by failures, which every good artist has had and profited by. In fact, it is one of the secrets of success, with 'an infinite capacity for taking pains.'

In painting skies it should always be remembered that you are painting air, which is impalpable and transparent and not to be rendered by the ordinary flat tone with which you would paint a house. Sometimes it is well to allow almost imperceptible particles of pure Lemon Yellow and Rose Madder to remain; these serve to break up the flatness of the tones, and at a distance will not be noticeable, but the effect will be much enriched.

This method of the juxtaposition of tones is much practised by the new school, of which Manet, Claude Monet, and Degas are the acknowledged masters. The idea is as follows: Tones of different colours, but of the same value, placed in juxtaposition and viewed at a little distance, are united without the intervention of the brush by the eye alone; and being nearly pure are much more brilliant than those tormented by the brush.

Still another school has arisen in Paris — that of the Pointillistes,[8] who place on canvas points of absolutely pure colour, trusting for the effect to the eye of the spectator and that distance which 'lends enchantment to the view.' The student, however, need not concern himself with these theories, although they will show him how great an importance is attached at the present time to the expression in art of air and sunlight.

Sketching grounds

Some of the finest subjects are to be found on the shores of Sydney Harbour; not for large pictures perhaps, but for picturesque 'bits' it is unequalled. Mosman's Bay is being rapidly spoilt by the builders, but Balmoral Beach will still repay the visitor. Manly too is not to be despised, and Freshwater Beach, a mile or so further on, will afford a great variety of seascapes and studies of cliffs and rocks. In a few miles we come to Narrabeen, where every sort of subject may be found, from the still waters of the lagoon, with its fringe of reeds and she-oaks, to the reefs and sands which form a barrier to the blue waters of the Pacific. Bayview and Newport, a few miles further, are less interesting, but the Hawkesbury River, not far away, should not be missed. The best parts for the sketcher are, however, some thirty or forty miles up, near Wiseman's Ferry. Up the Lane Cove River, near Jenkins' Orchard, are some pretty bits; also on Cook's River, near Tempe. A few miles out, we have Richmond, with its orchards and old farmhouses; and still further, the Illawarra, from Stanwell Park to Wollongong and Kiama. The Blue Mountains cannot be recommended for sketching purposes; the scenery is on too large a scale, and the immediate foreground somewhat barren and stony. One of the favourite sketching grounds in Victoria is the country from Healesville to Lilydale, and particularly the Black Spur and its vicinity. On the coast, Kilcunda, San Remo, and Cape Schank. Nearer town, Heidelberg, and the coast from Hampton to Sandringham and Beaumaris. The river Yarra near Kew was pretty once, but building operations have not improved it. In Brisbane, charming 'little bits' may be sketched along the river bank, partcularly on the North Quay. From the hills surrounding the city, extensive views may be obtained of the winding river and distant sombre forest. A few hours' journey by rail brings one to the Blackall Ranges, or in another direction to the Tweed Heads. Adelaide has many attractions for the artist; in spring the profusion of wild flowers, with their bright yellow blossoms, enlivens the landscape greatly. Fine views may be obtained from the 'mountain summit,' also at the foot of the hills.

[From A. J. Daplyn, *Landscape Painting from Nature in Australia,* Sydney, 1902]

NOTES—A. J. DAPLYN

1 Goethe quote. Light, Light, more Light. A famous last remark, made on his death bed.

2 The popular name for the *banksia*.

3 The popular name for *casuarina*.

4 The popular name for *melaleuca*.

5 Charles-Emile Auguste Carolus Duran (1838-1917), the French artist and teacher, who was the founder in 1889 and president of the Société Nationale des Beaux Arts (New Salon) with Meisonnier and Puvis de Chavannes. Daplyn was a pupil of his and is probably here speaking from a first-hand knowledge of his teacher's methods. Carolus Duran was a leading member of the group of artists who developed a compromise movement between the Academy and the Impressionists. They have been called by Albert Boime 'the *juste milieu*', and he describes their work as follows: 'They deliberately chose the informal technique of the independents (i.e. those artists who associated themselves with the Impressionists) either painting parts of the picture crudely or attenuating and blending the contours of the forms into each other. At the same time, the complete freedom of the Impressionists negated what they considered solid draughtsmanship, and they either gave to their forms a carefully drawn underlying structure or adopted for their subject matter classical and Christian themes. Their solution appealed to the administration of the Third Republic, and many of the artists distinguished themselves through large-scale wall decoration' (*The Academy and French Painting in the Nineteenth Century*, 1971), p. 16.

6 John Singer Sargent (1856-1925), the famous American portrait painter and talented water-colourist. He was a pupil of Carolus Duran in the 1870s.

7 Jean François Millet (1814-75), the famous French painter, engraver and illustrator of idealized peasant life and rural scenery.

8 Pointillism or divisionism was developed by the French painters Georges Seurat (1859-91), Paul Signac (1863-1935), and their followers. It made use of the 'rainbow' palette, and consisted of painting small dots of pure colour which when juxtaposed resulted in 'optical' mixture. This may be the first mention of pointillism in an Australian publication.

Q

🔲🔲🔲🔲🔲🔲🔲🔲🔲🔲🔲🔲🔲🔲🔲🔲🔲

EIGHT

Nationalism

INTRODUCTION

The extracts selected for this chapter have been chosen to reveal how a demand for an art that was expressive of Australian life and the Australian environment came to prevail over other considerations towards the end of the nineteenth century. French realism, French *plein air* painting, French Impressionism and even French symbolism all acted as catalysts in the development of this national art.

Lucien Henry, a Provencal, trained in architecture, sculpture and the decorative arts, was one of the first practising artists in Australia to advocate a national art. National character, he claimed, could be developed if designers would pay attention to the local fauna and flora, and evolve motifs, symbols and patterns from them. In so doing architects, jewellers, wood-carvers and illuminators would both make a name for themselves and help advance Australian civilization. Some work, it was true, he pointed out had already been accomplished along these lines but the quality was poor and most of the work being done in Australia was derivative of European designs.

Most of Henry's essay is taken up with arguing that it is the decorative arts which provide the *formative* base for a national art. What, he asks, are the true guides to national character? Certainly not political institutions, where one need only refer to the imperial control of subject peoples, wherein the institutions of government are foreign to and imposed upon the peoples governed. Nor, he points out, do the Fine Arts provide a reliable guide since they come to maturity only when a society has reached an advanced state of civilization. In the development of societies material needs must first be satisfied, and the *expressive* signs of this satisfaction appears first in the decorative or applied arts. The symbolic forms of decorative art emerge out of daily use, developing in a fashion akin to the development of a language and reflecting without distortion the true character of a people. Archaeologists are aware of this fact and trace from the decorative arts of peoples the emergence of national characteristics prior to the existence of written records. Thus the decorative arts are formative; 'the rich soil from which the other arts draw their sap'.

Few Australian designers paid any attention to Lucien Henry; and his work remains little known even today. For most of the designers of this time the idea of incorporating parrots and kangaroos, wattle and waratah into their designs was as embarassing as asking them to cultivate a broad Australian accent. It was safer, less culturally déclassé, to follow European modes of design — and that is the way, largely, it has remained. Yet in the few years which remained before the impersonal and mechanistic dogmas of modern architecture reached Australia a few architects and designers succeeded in enlivening the Federation style with motifs in terracotta, glass, ceramics and iron-work drawn from Australian flora and fauna. Forgotten for over a century, a very large part of it destroyed, their work is now beginning to be appreciated.

Lucien Henry from France argued the case for nationalism in the decorative arts. Sidney Dickinson from the United States, in the second extract of this chapter, argues the case for nationalism in painting, taking a firmly practical common-sense stand. Australia, he emphasizes, is neither old nor rich and cannot therefore be expected to provide either love or money for the arts. Artists, writers, sculptors and musicians must face up to this fact of their lives and work for a greater public interest in the arts. This they can best do by expressing 'the intimate facts of their own life and environment' for it was in this way that the great schools of painting of Italy, Holland and England attained their eminence.

As we have seen, many colonial artists and critics paid at least lip-service to the academic tradition. Dickinson ignores academic art and champions realism. The realist school had developed in France around the work and personality of Gustave Courbet in intense opposition to academic art. The famous French poet and critic, Baudelaire (in his early life a friend of Courbet), called upon artists to portray 'the heroism of contemporary life' in contrast to the heroism of the scriptures and antiquity. Dickinson calls upon Australian artists to 'present on canvas the earnestness, rigour, pathos and heroism of the life that is lived about them'. He praises Roberts and McCubbin because they sought, despite criticism, to do just that.

Critical comment of this kind coming so shortly after the 9 x 5 Exhibition of Impressions of 1889 helped to turn the painters of the Heidelberg school from concentrating on representing the 'effects and moods and thoughts of nature' as Roberts, Conder and Streeton had put it in their letter to the *Argus* (see p. 206), towards a more nationally-inspired programme. The widespread contemporary admiration for the work of Bastien-Lepage, the French *plein air* realist, encouraged the new mood of realist-nationalist sentiment within which the paintings of bush life by Roberts and McCubbin were conceived.

Both Lucien Henry and Sidney Dickinson *argued* the case for a national art: Arthur Streeton lived it. His letters printed below reveal how a highly talented young artist embraced nationalism as easily and as unselfconsciously as going for a swim on a hot day. His letters resound with his sensuous enjoyment of the light, warmth and colour of the bush. He makes friends with the railway fetlers whose rough outdoor life he admires; feeling at one with the world of man, of work, and of nature. His letters and paintings of the early 1890s reveal the transparent sensibility of the man clearly — perhaps at times even too clearly. For just how dangerously balanced was Streeton's sensibility may be judged by comparing the superbly visual clarity and honesty of 'Fire's On' (Art Gallery of New South Wales), which is a justification if ever there was one of Baudelaire's dictum, quoted above, with 'Purple Noon's Transparent Might' (National Art Gallery of Victoria) where, despite the unrivalled skill and clarity of the aerial perspective, there is a noticeable decline into a popular sweetness.

A sensibility as precariously balanced as Arthur Streeton's was not built for rough roads, despite an ecstasy easily induced by light, heat, life, and labour. And what was true of Streeton as an individual artist was true in large measure of the Australian-ness of the Australian school. In this regard the article by Sydney Long, the eighth extract in this chapter, deserves detailed study; for it is symptomatic of an innocence lost, and it beckons to the thin kine of the lean years. By 1909, when Long wrote his piece, the campaign for the recognition of Australian art had been waged for a quarter of a century. During that period the ideological battle had been won and the economic battle lost. Australian art had achieved a character of its own but Australian artists could not make a living from the proceeds of their work. Only a few of the men who had pioneered the Australian school of painting in the 1880s felt bound to it by deep ties of emotional loyalty. For most of them their art meant more than their country, taking the view that it was better to starve, if one had to starve, in Paris or London (that is to say in cities where the artist was held in some respect and something might always turn up), than remain to starve in Australia, where the artist was regarded as a loafer with a high opinion of himself. But Long spoke, in a difficult situation, for those who stayed.

Although Long's article possesses a specious subtlety — he hedges his opinions with judicious qualifications — a new narrowness of mind now makes its appearance upon the Australian scene. Here we may witness the exuberant and generous nationalism of the 1880s and early 1890s beginning to sour into chauvinism. The narrowness appears at several levels, and wherever it appears the effect is divisive. For example, in the early campaign for the recognition of Australian art no distinction was made between the migrant and the native-born artist. Nor could it have justly been made since the whole campaign for recognition, as we have seen, from the first prophetic utterance of John Lhotsky, through the establishment of the institutional infra-structures, to the creative fulfilment in Roberts and his circle, had been in a large degree the work of immigrant artists. But the campaign for the recognition of Australian art was carried through during a period in which Australia was in an expansive mood, when the wealth and population of the country were increasing and it was in a position to receive migrants, find them responsible positions and absorb them, as it were, into the cultural workforce. But the bank crash and economic depression of the 1890s made things difficult for artists as for everyone else. Between 1895 and 1914 few artists of any consequence immigrated to Australia and the best of the native-born left for Europe.

Written in this tight and reduced situation, Long's article expresses a nationalism stained by adversity; a nationalism internalized by rejection (by English criticism and Australian philistinism), based upon erroneous argument, and highly creative of myth. The myth-making begins with the distinction which Long makes between the 'foreign' and the 'native-born'. The foreign migrant artists, Long asserts, had applied foreign concepts to Australia; they had worn 'foreign spectacles' on their 'academic noses'. The work of Conrad Martens, Long claimed, was entirely unconvincing 'from the Australian point of view'.

Long's argument, of course, cannot bear even a cursory examination of the historic record. From Lewin to Roberts migrants had sought 'an Australian point of view' and some, even in Long's own terms, such as Roberts, Julian Ashton and Conder, had achieved it. Certainly some influential Anglo-colonial critics such as James Smith and James Green had opposed the 'Impressionist' tendencies in the work of the Heidelberg painters but their opposition was based upon aesthetic not upon nationalistic grounds. Despite their apparent opposition to the new painters they were, in fact, echoing reservations about Impressionism which they shared with the artists they were criticizing — and what they said may have been more influential than has been realized. Certainly after the 9 x 5 Exhibition of Impressions no Australian group of painters ever attempted to mount a second 'Impressionist' exhibition. Long was himself unaware of the degree to which Anglo-colonial attitudes were interwoven with the new nationalism. He attacks Conrad Martens's work because it does not suggest the 'weird mystery' of the bush. That influential idea, as we have seen, was not, as Long assumed, an intrinsic quality of Australian nature but a notion elaborated and embroidered by the unhappy migrant, Marcus Clarke. By the time Long received it the idea had become sufficiently acclimatized to appear as a quality native to the bush itself and not, as in truth it was, the distillation of a century of colonial experience of bush life.

Long's dismissal of the importance of the colonial contribution to the emergence of the Australian school of painting was highly influential. By presenting the Australian school as a cultural phenomenon *sui generis,* as the exclusive product of the innocent sensibilities of native-born painters, the historical facts were distorted into myth. The native-born Streeton, who it was claimed possessed the 'Australian eye' par excellence, became the culture-hero of the new myth. To paint Australian you had to be Australian.

Once set upon its course the myth became increasingly chauvinistic. Long's 'foreign spectacles' metaphor soon degenerated into the 'foreign eyes' metaphor. Unless you were born with 'Australian' eyes you could not hope to 'see' the Australian landscape. The physiological absurdity of the argument did not prevent its being accepted universally as *the* distinction between Australian colonial art and the 'true' Australian art. Even today, it is still the most popular generalization seized upon by Australian school-teachers, in discussing the nature of Australian painting. The fault in the argument lies, of course, in the crude and misleading identification of visual perception with the far more sophisticated aesthetic process by which categories (that are supra-national) such as classicism, romanticism, idealism, realism, impressionism, post-impressionism, abstract art, surrealism, etc., etc., have been used by painters during the past century to relate their artistry to things seen. There never was a pure national vision, nor for that matter a pure vision of any kind — except in romantic metaphor.

Long's article was narrowing in another way. Having set up a polarity between the colonial-immigrant European vision which was bad, and a 'native-born-Australian' vision which was good; he proceeds to press a second polarity upon us between 'Sydney-based-national' painting which is good and a 'Melbourne-based-French-grey-technique' painting which is bad. Sydney painting in short is more Australian, that is to say better, than Melbourne painting. It may be noted that Streeton (and he spent many years painting in Sydney) is the only Melbourne-born painter cited by Long in his list of artists who have made a creative contribution to Australian art. Roberts, significantly, is omitted. The subtle process by which Streeton was advanced as the true founder of the Australian school and Roberts relegated to the background — an important feature of the myth for Roberts was born in England — had begun. Melbourne painting was said to be less Australian than Sydney painting because it had succumbed to the French-grey colour techniques, learnt by Australian painters studying in Paris. Long concludes that it is better not only to be born in Australia but to be trained in Australia as well. Long himself had been born in New South Wales and trained in Sydney — by Julian Ashton, who had studied in Paris.

In thus distinguishing between Sydney and Melbourne painting Long gave voice to a rivalry that has continued to the present day. Although the debate has rarely been much more than a contest between artists striving for national recognition it has at least helped to envitalize Australian art by encouraging a competition which has in turn provided variety and alternative choices.

One further aspect of Long's article remains to be considered. Although 'realism in art is the surest of all foundations' there is, he remarks, a need for new trends which will make greater use of symbolism and imagination in Australian art. Long had clearly been influenced by the decorative symbolism then being promoted through the pages of the *Studio*, a trend which possessed both British and Continental sources. His own paintings, one of which, 'The Spirit of the Plains', he mentions in his article, were influential in promoting an interest in *art nouveau* design and a symbolic approach among Australian painters during the early twentieth century.

Long's article is of considerable importance because it foreshadows trends in Australian art that developed during the first three decades of the twentieth century. He continued that process of internalization, first clearly announced by Marcus Clarke, by which Australian nationalism in art was rendered more personal, intimate and subjective. This occasionally helped a personal lyrical temperament, like those of J. J. Hilder and Blamire Young. But a subjective symbolism combined with a stress on the value of being native-born and being trained locally foreshadowed and encouraged the proto-fascist attitudes adopted by many Australian artists and critics during the 1920s and 1930s. Lastly, in his emphasis upon the creation of an Australian mythology and the importance of the interior of the country as a kind of 'emotional heartland' he foreshadowed the work of Hans Heysen, Russell Drysdale, Sidney Nolan, Arthur Boyd and many other painters.

In the last extract of the chapter, Frederick McCubbin also supports a national art, but his approach is warmer, more generous than Long's, and written in the light of greater experience. For it was McCubbin, more than any other painter, who was responsible for the victory of nationalism over *plein air* objectivity in Heidelberg painting.

McCubbin traces the beginnings of national character in Australian art from the 1860s in the work of S. T. Gill, Eugen von Guerard, Louis Buvelot and others — all migrant artists. He then, however, curiously repeats Long's assertion that artists who had lived, studied and worked in Europe produced work that was 'imbued with the spirit of Europe' and 'essentially alien to its new environment'. This is in flat contradiction to his earlier contention that Australian art had begun to achieve its distinctive character in the 1860s. His argument that only the Australian-born could see the Australian landscape is spectacularly rebutted — on McCubbin's own admission — in the case of Louis Buvelot. For it was the work of Buvelot, the Swiss artist who did not arrive in Melbourne until he was over the age of sixty, who taught McCubbin himself, a native-born Australian, to appreciate the beauty of an Australian landscape. Yet he does not seem to realize how dramatically this admission renders the 'foreign eyes' argument worthless.

McCubbin's nationalism is, however, not narrow. He recognizes the importance of the cosmopolitan atmosphere of the 1880s; he stresses the importance of the contribution of Walter Withers, an Englishman, to the Australian school. David Davies, the third artist selected by McCubbin for detailed comment, trained in Europe for several years. Of the four artists considered in detail only Streeton was native-born and locally trained; and McCubbin of course knew that the Australian character of the new school did not depend entirely upon Streeton's achievement. Yet here too the national myth may be seen subtly at work. Streeton's work is compared with that of the French Impressionists; he 'achieved by simplicity of means and spontaneity of utterance, that which they strove for, with mannered conventions and monotonous technique'. The untutored genius succeeds where tradition and sophisticated techniques fail.

It would, however, be both unfair and untrue to charge McCubbin with intentional myth-making. No one, as may surely be seen from an unprejudiced reading of his essay, has put the case for the existence of a distinctively Australian school of painting with such conviction and with such quiet eloquence. Which is fitting. Australian painting may have owed more in the development of its technical methods to Roberts, Conder and Streeton, to Fox, Withers and Davies, and many others. But McCubbin was the one painter wise enough to know in his own heart that an Australian school of painting in order to be valid and in order to endure would have to be built upon the deepest experiences of life and nature in Australia. His was the steady, loyal mind among the 'innocent' eyes and the wayward hearts.

Lucien Henry (1850-96)

Lucien Henry was born in Provence and studied under Viollet-le-Duc, and at the Ecole des Beaux Arts under Gérôme. Henry was sentenced to death for his part in the Paris Commune, but the sentence was transmuted to transportation to New Caledonia. At the completion of his sentence he came to Sydney in 1880, and became an instructor in modelling at the Mechanics' School of Arts, and the first lecturer in art at the Sydney Technical College when the Board of Technical Education took over the Mechanics' School of Arts.

Henry was interested in developing a national school of applied design in Australia. He designed the 'Captain Cook' and the 'Australia' stained glass windows in the Sydney Town Hall and the chandelier of the Hotel Australia; he painted portraits and modelled busts. He was interested in the use of Australian floral motifs for architectural decoration, and designed an Order of the Waratah. Henry returned to Paris in 1889, and published there two years later the *Legend of the Waratah,* dedicating it to Fred J. Bloomfield. He appears to have been associated with the early days of the Labour movement in Australia.

[AUSTRALIAN DECORATIVE ARTS]

In entering on the following essay I am perfectly aware of the difficulties with which I shall have to contend, and I might, perhaps, hesitate were I not actuated by the earnest hope that others will follow me and do fuller justice than I am able to do to the subject in view, viz., the Development of the Australian Decorative Arts.

During the last twenty-five years some architects have not shown themselves averse to the introduction of Australian flora into their work, but, unfortunately, their example has hitherto been followed by few; still we have a right to expect that their successors will imitate them and introduce Australian subjects whenever the designs submitted to them are worth realising in marble, stone, terra-cotta, or wood. If the attention of the architects was turned in that direction, I have no doubt that before the lapse of another twenty-five years we should see in this city and its suburbs public and private buildings decorated with Australian flora and fauna which would present enough original character to form the starting points of a National Art.

A few efforts in the same direction made by the jewellers deserve mentioning and are worthy of praise, not for the results hitherto obtained, but for the tendency they express in introducing aboriginals, kangaroos, emus, emu eggs, and Australian ferns and flowers into their designs. It is only fair, also, to notice that some attempts have been made to apply Australian subjects to wood carving and terra-cotta, but the Decorative Art, which appears so far to have obtained the best results, is that of Illumination. It must be remarked that, as a rule, the designs are lacking in originality, that they are in fact, mere replicas of works which have been in existence for centuries, and that the forced adaptation of their antiquated mode to our modern conception, is anything but satisfactory; nevertheless a few works have been produced in Sydney, which are so remarkable for their originality of disposition, and the perfection of their treatment, as to make it appear certain that for some time to come Illumination will maintain its place in the front rank of the Decorative Arts in Australia.

Illuminators, house-decorators, glass-stainers, cabinet-makers, jewellers, potters, carvers, glass-blowers, iron-workers, either in wrought or cast iron, have before them an almost inexhaustible field, and the first to enter it are almost certain, not only to make a name for themselves, but also to contribute greatly to the advancement of Australian civilization. This last sentence is not a *'lapsus calami,'*[1] I intend it in its fullest meaning.

Were the Decorative Arts to sink lower and lower into the mere handicraft, which has been their limit for centuries, it would be absurd to state that they have anything whatever to do with the advancement of civilization in any country. It is because I think that such will not be the case, and that there are in Australia abundant materials, and ample opportunities for the formation of original Arts, that I introduce the question to the public.

It is my opinion, that in the normal development of civilizations, the Decorative Arts are called before all others to manifest the characters of the races.

It has been repeatedly stated that one can judge of a nation by the Political Institutions which govern it. This may possibly be true in special instances, as for example: in the case of Egyptian, of Athenian, and of Roman civilizations; but it must be granted that such exceptions prove nothing, and that history has, from the earliest ages, been registering the most startling contradictions of such an assertion.

Many races having been precipitated into slavery, have had applied to them, under the pressure of sheer force, the *'camisole de force'*[2] of the political institutions of another latitude, and have suffered for centuries in that abnormal state, until the powerful and irresistible breath of nature forced them into a resurrection. Such being the history of mankind, it would be risky to judge of a race by its political institutions, which are seldom, if ever, now-a-days, the unmitigated outcome of its natural energies.

It has also been advanced that literature in its various forms, sculpture, painting, and architecture, offer in their ensemble a complete manifestation of the civilization attained by a race, embodying in their actual records of the present a reminiscence of the past, and a fore-shadowing of the future. This is an undeniable fact; at the same time, I might point out that these Arts do not arise spontaneously, but are the result of secular efforts, and that their full blooming is always contemporaneous with an already advanced state of civilization; the Minerva

Athene of Phidias[3] has for an ancestor the Minerva Polliade,[4] hidden for centuries in a grove of olive trees, and being nothing else than a square log of wood covered with vermilion; that Homer[5] and Herodotus[6] appeared only as a definite expression of Epic poetry and story-telling, after having been preceded by thousands of poets and *fibsters,* whose very names are unknown to us; suppress the previous efforts of the bards, the Trouvères,[7] the minstrels, and Homer, Rabelais[8] and Shakespeare cease to be in their condensed individualities the perfect expression of an age, the summing up of a civilization; — that the genius of Michael Angelo has its roots in the brain of Dante, and Raffaelle the desired expression announced by Cimabue[9] is only realised by Perugino.[10] Who could imagine a mountain in the vacuum. Aeschylus[11] without Greece, Dante without secular crimes to nail as wild beasts to the land-marks of his Inferno?

Poetry is the embodiment of thought; thought is the definite expression of observations deduced from facts.

Long periods of observations and their unconscious classification in the human mind must elapse before Poetry or true Art can take root, grow, and bloom in a civilization.

The human tendency will be always to attend first to the satisfaction of the material wants; the pastoral, agricultural, and industrial arts will be resorted to and developed in order to supply those wants; as a sign of their satisfaction, we see appearing, in their most archaic forms, the first products of the Decorative Arts; and the path to progress is open for ever.

Language is forming and perfecting itself day by day, its literary expression is as it were stuttering, new words are constantly wanted to cover new facts. The knowledge required for its development is, however, unavoidably the privilege of the few; but the Decorative Arts are there, no longer in the embryonic state, the period of incubation is over, and every day a new symbol is promulgated in a tangible form; they constitute a new language, superposed on the other, intelligible to all, widening its scope day by day, increasing its resources, applying them to everything; till at last, having achieved their destiny, they remain stationary in the subserviency to which they are submitted, when Architecture, that sublime creation of the mind, raises its noble structures, and to give them a human interest embodies in them all the works '*hominis additi naturae.*'[12]

As to sceptic persons, who would accuse me of trying to make too much out of my case, and who are disposed to laugh at the importance I give to the Decorative Arts, which to them are mere

superfluous and insignificant adjuncts of civilized life, to them
I will answer:

When inquiring into the Genesis of great civilization, we are
always unable to reach, with absolute certitude, the initial point
of their departure. It is by the difficult road of logical induction
and slippery hypothesis that we hope to attain it. Philology will,
in a way, determine the origin of the races; but its mission ends
there. This point of origin is undoubtedly one of great importance, still it is only one point of the question, it answers only
to one query of the interest which leads man's mind to the
conquest of the past. The desideratum is to know the life and
social habits of these great nations during their period of infancy,
to realize the value of their mental and physical potentialities,
the combination of which, used as a lever, brought them up to
the pinnacle where it is given to posterity to contemplate them.
The Rig-veda,[13] the Zendavesta,[14] the list of Manetho,[15] the
Bible, the poems of Homer, all belong to the period of written
history: they mirror to us their own time, but when they attempt
to describe preceding ages, their record is wrapped in a network
of legends, the symbols of which are not always clear to our
positive minds. We accept with gratitude the glorious inheritance
they have left to us, but it has proved to be insufficient; we are
anxious to penetrate still farther into the mist of times gone by.
The researches made up to the end of the 18th century proved
archeology to be the mine out of which may be excavated the
most precious documents for history, and during our own century
this archeological work has engaged the attention of legions of
illustrious men who, discovering only the ruins left by time,
Roman prefects, barbarians, Christian fanatics, Mussulmans, and
obtuse Turks, have had to make the best of the circumstances,
to survey carefully the foundations which gave the general plan,
to take a mutilated cap, a bit of moulding, a truncated column,
and for all the other elements of restoration to resort to the
Decorative Arts. A winged kimera,[16] the most insignificant trinket,
a fibula, a bronze halo, a cinerary urn, the point of a wooden
arrow, a stone axe, a decayed fabric, a stone retaining a stain of
colour, a fragment of burnt clay, a golden jug, and thousands of
other objects gathered together and classified, have constituted
a whole, and using these fragmentary elements, the Champol-
lions,[17] the Layards,[18] and all their glorious successors, make us
assist, as interested spectators, at the life of extinct civilizations
which we, in our conceit, had judged as barbarous.

The result of their patient and ingenious work has been not

only to supply history proper with reliable facts of immense value, but also to assign their true place to the Decorative Arts, which have been proved to constitute the substrata of civilization, the rich soil from which the other arts draw their sap, without which they could not rise above the ground and grow and tower into the blue sky.

It would be a great error of judgment for persons engaged or interested in the Decorative Arts to expect that it will be easy to remove the prejudices that are generally entertained against them, not only in Australia but in all parts of the world. For centuries past these Arts have only been resorted to, not from love, but as a mere means to tinsel everything and everybody. The caprice of fashion has been their only dictum, their supreme law. Their theme has, for such a long time, been to copy and repeat always the same thing in the same manner, that every nation in turn has grown tired, *ad nauseam,* of witnessing their apparently eternal sterility.

It does not require a keen eye to understand at a glance the unsuccess of great workers like Lienard,[19] Jno. Leighton,[20] Ruprich-Robert,[21] Dresser,[22] to cite only a few names. We see those would-be innovators start at first on the right track; they go direct to nature and receive its inspiration, but to realise the old saying 'habit is a second nature,' compelled as they find themselves to submit their inspiration to the inveterate habits of their contemporaries in order to be able to live at all; we see with sorrow that their efforts scarcely rise above commonplace works, from the fact that their salient points are sandpapered down to the flush level of Neo-Egyptian, Neo-Greek, Neo-Roman, Neo-Renaissance, &c.

It is everywhere to be found that social and national life is adorned, or rather encumbered, with the products of Decorative Arts which are quite foreign and alien to the people who use them. They do not belong to them, express nothing of them, and are not in any degree the material embodiment of their faith, of their ideal. It is, therefore, easy to understand why people in general are so indifferent to these Arts, which, it must in justice be said, seem to have abdicated all right to express anything.

That such be the case will be readily granted, and no one will care to dispute it. As regards us, however, it does not at all change the prospects of the Decorative Arts. On the contrary it opens to them an incommensurable field and widens their scope in offering to them all the world of today, which, tired of commonplace replicas, is sure to welcome any original manifestation of the human mind.

It is only to be expected that the idea of Australian Decorative Arts will be pooh-poohed by soi-disant connoisseurs, self-appointed aristarchs, who will find it, to say the least, very funny that, having received the few truths sifted out of the dust of the past, we are able to admire an earthenware jug, feeling that there is something more in it than the work of the potter; that behind the wheel, and the compass, and the potter, there is a national spirit which characterises a race and reveals to us its wants and its ideal.

We do not intend to try to convince any of them that a lotus flower or a palmette give a fair idea of the Egyptian and Greek civilizations, literature, arts, sciences, policy.

In their indomitable vanity, which is another name for ignorance, they may attempt their self-glorification by declaring, as their fathers did before them, that 'our century has reached perfection,' that 'it is the century of light,' and not limiting their pretensions to the invention of gas and electricity, look with supreme contempt at the humanity which has preceded them and with distrust, to say the least, towards the one which will follow, and which is advised by 'mad dreamers' to branch off from the barren circle of imitation, as practised in our enlightened age, and to go straight to nature, the inexhaustible fountain of plenty and beauty.

They may say what they like, and pass their own judgements on the Australian flora and fauna, which do not appear to convey much signification to them. According to their dictum the flowers have no perfume,[23] the Waratah is brutal in form and colour, the Banksia is stiff, prickly and like an egret, the Stenocarpus belongs to engineering, and gives a splendid idea of an unsuccessful attempt at perpetual motion, the Kangaroo is stupid and a pest; as for the Lyre Bird, a bad pun with some allusion to press men or politicians and it is dealt with. The word prejudice is far too weak to characterize the feelings entertained towards Australian elements, and it still requires long years of hard and patient work to introduce them into the Decorative Arts.

[From *Australian Art,* February 1888, pp. 9-12]

NOTES—HENRY

1 i.e. a slip of the pen.
2 i.e. a straight jacket.
3 Minerva Athene of Phidias. Henry is referring to the chryselephantine figure of Athene designed by Pheidias, the famous Greek sculptor of the mid-fifth century B.C. for the Parthenon at Athens.

4 Polliade is probably a misspelling for Pallade, and therefore a reference to the Palladion, an early painted wooden image of Athena.

5 Homer, the great Greek epic poet, who lived somewhere between 1050 and 850 B.C. generally regarded (though it has been disputed) as the author of the *Iliad* and *Odyssey*.

6 Herodotus (484-424? B.C.), the Greek historian, known as the 'Father of History', being the first to collect his materials systematically and to check their accuracy to the best of his ability.

7 *Trouvères* or *troveurs*, medieval poets who composed in the northern dialect of Roman Gaul (the *langue d'oil*), a dialect which eventually prevailed over the southern dialect (the *langue d'oc*) to become the French language of modern times. They are to be distinguished from the troubadours, the medieval poets who composed in the *langue d'oc*.

8 François Rabelais (1494-*c.* 1553), the French physician, humanist and satirist.

9 Cimabue (1240-after 1302), the Florentine painter and architect; one of the first painters to introduce naturalistic elements into Byzantine conventions.

10 Perugino, i.e. Pietro Vanucci (1445-1523), famous for the rhythmical character and sweetness of facial expressions of his compositions.

11 Aeschylus (525-456), the famous Greek tragic poet, who is regarded as the founder of Greek tragedy.

12 i.e. man added to nature.

13 A collection of Sanskrit poetic texts of a devotional character of great antiquity. Their origin is ascribed to divine revelation and they form part of the Brahminical system of religious belief.

14 The original document of the religion of Zoroaster, the founder of the religion of the Iranian peoples.

15 Manetho, an Egyptian priest and annalist who lived during the time of Ptolemy I (323-285) and Ptolemy II (309-246). He wrote an Egyptian history in Greek which contains tables of the dynasties of the kings of Egypt with the lengths of their reign.

16 A monster described by Homer, with a lion's head, a goat's body, and a dragon's tail.

17 Jean François Champollion (1790-1832), the founder of Egyptology and translator of the Rosetta Stone.

18 Sir Austin Layard (1817-94), the excavator of Nineveh. He published the results of his work in *Nineveh and its Remains* (1848-49) and *Nineveh and Babylon* (1853).

19 Probably M. J. N. Lienard (1810-   ), the French sculptor and ornamentalist.

20 John Leighton (pseudonym Luke Limner), 1822-1912, a famous English book illustrator; an original proprietor of the *Graphic*.

21 Ruprich Robert (1820-87), the architect and architectural draughtsman of historical monuments who wrote *Architecture Normande aux XIe et XIIIe siècles'* (Paris, 1884-89).

22 Christopher Dresser (1834-1904), the well known English commercial and industrial designer.

23 Cf. Marcus Clarke, p. 135.

Sidney Dickinson

Sidney Dickinson (or Dickenson) was a popular lecturer and art critic. He appears to have been born in Boston and claimed, on his arrival in Sydney from San Francisco by the *Almeda* on 28 June 1888, that he was the Australian correspondent of the *New York Herald,* and that he had lived in Hawaii for five years before coming to Sydney. Shortly after his arrival he read the Declaration of American Independence at the 4 July Celebrations in Sydney, and on 10 August was reported to be lecturing on St Petersburg and the Palace of the Hermitage, 'with dissolving views of the city, St Isaac's Cathedral and the prison of the Nihilists'. His lecture series in Sydney concluded with a 'Night with the People' in the New Masonic Hall, Sydney, on 9 November 1888, 'at popular prices'.

He then moved to Melbourne, where we find him lecturing for the Victorian Artists' Society on Saturday evening 24 November on art 'as he had observed it on the Continent of Europe and America'. His experience in European galleries, he is reported to have said:

> ... went to prove the great falling off of modern painting compared to the time of the old masters. American and Australian art seemed to be developing characteristics of their own, which in time would give them a certain nationality of style, Australian art seeming to possess all the fundamental requirements of becoming similar to the great Italian school. Mr. Dickinson further spoke of the national galleries of pictures in Sydney and Melbourne, saying that no city in America possessed such collections. On the other hand, the colonies had no private galleries such as distinguished American towns. The Victorian Artists' Gallery was one of the best lighted exhibition-rooms he had seen in the course of his travels, and the collection contained many master-pieces, worthy of any art-centre.

In January 1889 Dickinson and his wife were back in Sydney lecturing on art. They then sailed for New Zealand, where he conducted a lecture tour during March and April, and travelled widely. Dickinson appears to have gained a commission from the New Zealand Government to publicize the scenic attractions of the country in London under the auspices of the Agent-General of New Zealand in order to encourage tourism for the Dunedin Exhibition. He took with him a series of views of New Zealand to Paris to be prepared for his London lecture series. Whilst in Paris he visited the *Exposition Universelle* in the Spring of 1889, for by January 1890 we find him back in Melbourne attending a 'smoke night' held by the Victorian Artists' Society in the Old

R1

England Hotel, Heidelberg. A contemporary account of the occasion reads as follows:

> A large number of guests came down by train and marched in a body to the hotel. Mr. F. McCubbin presided, and the evening's festivities were preceded by a simple supper of beef and beer. A large number of art students were present, and amongst others past the student stage were Professor Sidney Dickenson, Mr Perceval Ball, Mr Tom Roberts, Mr C. Charrington, Mr Charles Conder, Mr Withers, Mr W. B. Spong, Mr McKennal, Mr Arthur Streeton, Mr Sanders, Mr Humphries, Mr Altson, Mr Boyd, Mr Gurdon, and Mr Cole. Professor Dickenson gave an interesting account of the various schools of painting represented at the late Paris Exposition, and Mr Ball spoke hopefully of the future prospects of art in Australia. Songs were contributed by Mr C. Charrington, Mr T. Humphries, and Mr A. Altson, and the only draw back to the pleasure of the evening was the early departure of many guests necessitated by the catching of suburban trains.

Apparently Dickinson had also gained other visual material whilst in Paris for on the not altogether inappropriate date of 1 May we hear that he delivered a lecture on the French Revolution, 'illustrated by dissolving views'. The lecture was in aid of the Athletic Association of Melbourne University which was at that time heavily in debt.

Dickinson and his wife became leading lights in the small cultural circle of Melbourne. They played an active part in the creation of the Austral Salon, established in July 1890. Mrs Dickinson was elected the executive vice-president at its first meeting and Sidney lectured on art. The social level and cultural tone of the Salon was much augmented when the Governor of Victoria's wife, The Countess of Hopetoun, graciously accepted the honorary presidency. Lady Clarke and Lady Davies accepted the posts of honorary vice-presidents. Some of the early meetings of the *Austral Salon* appear to have been held at Buxton's Gallery, where the Exhibition of 9 x 5 Impressions had been held the year before. Here on 9 October Mrs Dickinson read a paper on Hindu philosophy and it was agreed that a series of papers on the subject should be given during the remainder of the year 'so that members may have a pleasant way of posting themselves up in one of the subjects which at present is engrossing universal attention'. Mrs Dickinson's paper was followed by a discussion on 'the advancement of the Australian native'.

On 30 October 1890 Sidney Dickinson became the Secretary of the Victorian Artists' Society. His important article 'What Should Australian Artists Paint?' had been published in the

Australasian Critic a few weeks before. During the next two years
he was a frequent and influential contributor to this periodical.
He reviewed exhibitions, and wrote a series of important articles
on the most important private collections of Victoria, including
those of F. W. Armytage, T. D. Wanliss and T. W. Stanford;
many paintings from the last of which were given later to Stanford
University, California. Meanwhile he also contributed articles on
life and nature in Australia to *Scribner's Magazine*.

Sidney Dickinson has more than a fair claim to be regarded
as the first serious art critic to support an indigenous school of
Australian painting. Although he arrived as a visitor and appears
to have remained in Victoria for only a few years he involved
himself deeply in the local art scene. It is clear that he was one
of the important agencies by means of which news of contemporary art in Europe was brought to Melbourne. His writings
reveal an alert, liberal and intelligent outlook. But it is clear also
that his training as a journalist led him to take more interest in
the content than in the style or technique of paintings. It is also
clear both from the article published here and his other articles
that he was a significant influence in the development of national
sentiment in Australian art; and he worked energetically for a
recognition of art in the social and intellectual life of Melbourne's
vigorous but relatively unsophisticated society.

[WHAT SHOULD AUSTRALIAN ARTISTS PAINT?]

A visit to recent exhibitions and to the studios of some of our
leading artists has suggested the inquiry that heads this article —
an inquiry to which subsequent events have given additional
force. Such a question, which might be carelessly asked by the
layman, is of serious import to the artist, who oftens finds that
appreciative reception and sale of his works depend quite as
much upon their subjects as upon his skill in description, or his
strength or delicacy of feeling. In an ideal state of society — and
in the present also, if we may judge by the attitude of many to
whom art naturally looks for support — the true artist is one who
works for the love of his profession, and ignores such considerations as the profitable sale of his pictures. In practice, however,
it is found that he is like other men in having a stomach to fill
and a back to cover, and that, while he may work with all
sincerity and earnestness, he is compelled by necessity to touch
the taste of his public. He may console himself in this by the
reflection that he has plenty of company in the ranks of other

artistic and intellectual workers. How many men there are who smother their ambitions in order to cater to their audience — singers, who fill their souls with the works of the masters of melody, and are obliged to tickle the ears of the ignoble with music-hall ballads and selections from comic opera; instrumentalists, who turn from study of Beethoven and Wagner to execute the jingles of nameless authors in polkas and waltzes; sculptors, who utilise the skill they have gained from studies of the masterpieces of antiquity in perpetuating the features — often far from classic — of men who have been raised to place by some lucky speculation, or the votes of an ignorant constituency; writers, who are compelled to waste in the service of the Moloch of journalism abilities which should produce worthy additions to our permanent literature. Everywhere we see men and women lowering themselves to the level of the ordinary — many of whom, starting with lofty intentions of raising public appreciation of the good, the true, and the beautiful, inevitably lose heart in experience of the magnitude of their undertaking, and lapse into mediocrity themselves.

The difficulties with which artists of all sorts have to contend in a new country are enormous. A nation must be somewhat ripe in years before it develops appreciation of the refinements of life, and it is only when a people become rich that they begin to cultivate art. It is thus that France, Italy, Spain and England have, out of great resources and at various periods, developed almost to their limit the love and practice of art; while Germany, Switzerland, Russia and others have, through comparative poverty, shown a limited interest in this direction, or manifested an awakening only as their fortunes improved. The great progress recently made by the United States in artistic affairs did not begin until after the country had celebrated its centenary, and until the opening up of the vast resources of the continent brought wealth and leisure to a large number of its inhabitants. If, then, we find that Australia, with hardly more than fifty years of settled history,[1] is not so fully awake to the value of art in its various forms as those might desire who have seen the position which it holds in the estimation of older countries, we may be satisfied that it is no more than could be expected, and even congratulate ourselves on recent visible improvements in certain directions.

To increase the public interest in art is the peculiar duty of the artist. However much critics may write, and students of art-history promulgate the principles which have controlled the production of the masterpieces of painting in the past, it is only by visible instances produced in their midst, and by artists of their own time, that the interest of the multitude can be inspired. As we could not expect a child in the nursery to appreciate the epics of Homer, so should we not expect that a public unlearned in art should at once understand the works of Michael Angelo and Titian, Rembrandt and Velasquez; we should rather begin the course of lessons of which these men were arch-teachers with works based upon our own experience, and descriptive of our own intimate life or surroundings. Thus, from the particular and personal, we might hope in time to come to the general and universal, and from the limited art of our own little circle acquire an appreciation of the more expanded practice which maintains in other times and countries.

In what way, then, is this preliminary interest to be excited? Not by encouragement of 'the grand style,' the imitation of the antique, the Renaissance, or even modern schools; but by the expression, with all the power and feeling that the artists can command, of the intimate facts of our own life and environment. Every school of art that has become great attained its position by describing what it found most commonly and familiarly about it. The exquisite art of the early Italian masters — more intellectual and sincere, and thus eternally more satisfying than the hollowly-accomplished efforts of their successors — although dealing chiefly with things celestial and mystical, owes its charming naturalness to its adherence to the facts that were familiar to it in the everyday life of Florence and Siena. The great school of Dutch painting, unsurpassable in drawing, colour and finish so long as it confined itself to descriptions of the inner life of Holland, fell into decay only when its painters began to imitate the allegories of the decadent Italians[2] and the landscapes of Poussin.[3] The chief strength of English art today lies in its intense nationality and its loving description of peculiarly English scenes and incidents in life and history. In short, the records of every school of distinction show a beginning in works by its painters which were based upon their own observation and experience, after which came a wider and more general expression.

Australian life, although in some respects barren when compared with existence in the older countries of the globe, undoubtedly furnishes enough of material and inspiration for any artist who deserves the name. The forests have a character that is all their own; the country, although monotonous in wide and general view, is extremely picturesque in many of its details, and

R2

hardly to be equalled elsewhere in the rich or chastened colours it assumes under the changing seasons; the shores have a melancholy grandeur well suited for description by Art, which, like Poetry, is often most effective when touched with sadness; the mixed life of the city and the characteristic life of the station and bush furnish countless subjects, whose successful description would attract universal attention in the galleries and saloons of Old World exhibitions, but are here ignored because of their familiarity. It should be the ambition of our artists to present on canvas the earnestness, rigour, pathos, and heroism of the life that is about them. These qualities exist if we will but open our eyes to them, and to assist this awakening is one of the highest missions for our painters. Some efforts in this direction have already been made, and if they have not received their full meed of appreciation, they have, at all events, received the approval of many whose praise is most worth the having, and caused a discussion whose effect cannot but be beneficial. It is to be hoped that Mr. Roberts, Mr. McCubbin, and the others who have been impressed with the opportunities for pictorial description which lie in Australian life will not be discouraged either by silent indifference or outspoken criticism, but persevere in an effort which speaks more hopefully for Australian art than almost any other that has ever been inaugurated.

It may not be out of place to remark, in concluding this article, that the writer has no intention of implying that Australian art should be altogether independent of the schools of other countries. It is now and then said of some promising young artist — with full intention of being commendatory — that he is self-taught, or has received instruction only in local schools. Some are even discouraged from foreign study on the plea that the acquisition of other methods would spoil their individuality, their peculiar personal feeling, and so on. Nothing can be more dangerous to a young artist than such commendation and advice — as well might a writer, whose works showed brilliant imagination, but were full of solecisms, bad construction and grammatical errors, be disuaded [*sic*] from adding to his powers by a study of the masters of rhetoric and style. The weak point in Australian art is its general ignorance of the higher powers of painting — powers which are difficult of definition to the tyro, but which he recognises at once on encountering them. If our promising young artists will but acquire the accomplished methods of a school like the modern French, and bring to bear upon them their own individual and national feeling, we shall find art making great progress amongst us; and the more especially as foreign study has the important effect of stimulating observation, which quality alone should show our artists what to paint more surely than any amount of suggestion in words.

[from *The Australasian Critic*, I, 1 (Oct. 1890), pp. 21-2]

NOTES—DICKINSON

1 Dickinson is presumably thinking not of Australia as a whole but of the settlement of Victoria in 1835.

2 Dickinson's knowledge of the development of Dutch painting is faulty here. The emergence of the characteristic Dutch art of the seventeenth century was preceded by a formative period when the influence of Italian mannerism and the followers of Caravaggio in the Netherlands prepared the ground upon which the Dutch masters such as Hals, Rembrandt and Vermeer were to build.

3 Poussin (1594-1665), the famous French painter of 'history' in the classical manner. He lived much of his life in Rome.

(Sir) Arthur Ernest Streeton (1867–1943)

The third son of Charles Henry Streeton, a schoolmaster, Arthur was born at Mount Duneed, Victoria, on 8 April 1867. Streeton studied at the National Gallery School, Melbourne, while he was apprenticed to a lithographer. He met Tom Roberts and Frederick McCubbin while sketching at Mentone in 1886 and they invited him to spend weekends with them at their artists' camp near Box Hill. This association greatly aided Streeton's artistic development and he abandoned lithography for a full-time painting career in 1888. With Roberts and Conder he then established an artists' camp at Eaglemont, near Heidelberg, Victoria. In 1888 he painted 'Golden Summer' and 'Still Glides the Stream'. The former gained him a *mention honorable* at the Paris Salon of 1892, and the latter was purchased in 1889 by the Gallery of New South Wales. He participated also in the Exhibition of 9 x 5 Exhibitions held at Buxton's, Melbourne, in August 1889.

Streeton spent some years in Sydney in the 1890s; and from 1898 to 1906 he was in England where he continued to paint, with little recognition from English critics. This was a period of comparative isolation and hardship for him. An exhibition held in Melbourne in 1907 was most successful, and from that time he gained recognition and obtained many commissions for pictures. During the First World War he served as a private, but after being invalided out received a commission as an official war artist for the Commonwealth. In 1923 he settled in Victoria at Olinda, where he died in 1943.

[ERNEST ARTHUR STREETON—LETTERS TO TOM
ROBERTS]

Letter 1: written probably in August 1890

St. Kilda,
Junction Rd., Summer Hill,
Sunday Evg.

Dear Bulldog,

How are you, old chap? Stretch out your hand to me—shake—
good 'fine thanks'. How are you?

Well where are and where have you been. 'Gippsland Eh'—
How is 'Farmer Aby' coming on?[1] Presume that the Scholarship
Exhbn. will soon take place; he must be nearly complete. Would
very much like to be present at that Exhibition. How also is the
wily old Prof.[2] and his work, and all his pretty damsels 'deep in
Art'?[3]

On my return to our Melbourne, I shall first fill my pipe and
have threepennorth of tram,[4] then scoot away to the studios at the
Gallery, see some of the students, then down to Orchardson,
Graham, Watts and company,[5] and see the Prof., of course; then
up to you. We'll have a good long smoke and think through all
the past 'summer'. The enjoyment of 'the last summer at Eaglemont'[6] was to me more intense than anything I have up to the
present felt. It would surprise you how often I think of it, and,
oh, it is a great comfort. Its suggestion is a large harmony, musical,
rose. Fancy if you could grasp all you feel and condense your
thought into a scheme which would embrace sweet sound, great
color, and all the slow soft movement, sometimes quick with
games, and through all the strength of the great warm and loving
sun. (I feel this very much as I write, so don't read it if you are
in a great hurry.)

Think with me a little, back, say, to that night K.[7] and I were
out on the plateau near the house. We were rather depressed with
the heat of the day, so with only our pants, socks, and shirts on
and blankets and pillows to lie on; you remember, we were on
the dry hill—then you joined us, we smoked, and thought, and
conversed for a long time. I tried to sing 'That Summer Night,
My Darling.'[8] Garonne, you recollect. Went slowly back to the
house very late, about 11 or later, our foreheads finding resistance
in the strong spider webs. And the silent stars, how they make us
think. How they glittered too behind and through the silent,
stately firs and pines. K., I think, had a long drink of water and
lime juice before starting to bunk . . .

Again Queen's Birthday,[9] when the Don[10] and his wife were out and the mass of picnic outside. Jolly hot day, the tank keys in the safe keeping of Bill Peg. Poor K.'s patent arrangement for keeping door of 'Block Hospital' shut. The painful recollections of his suffering. How we made sketches of the girls on the lawn. The lovely pure muslin, and gold, sweet grass-seeds and the motherly she-oak with its swing, spreading a quiet blessing over them all. Behind this splendid tree was the deep gold of summer gates of the west sunset, and the whole gem was framed yes with oleander on the east with the two tropical sleepy round bushes, and on the south pittosporum, and north the big solemn pine. They seemed to keep guard as the silver dusk of night simplified the group of quiet happy boys and girls. The return to the big room, the missing spoons, lost sunshades, and over all the bustle and healthy fun of little 'Topsy'—who seems like 'Cigarette' in some ways.

The uncertain charm of the hill and valley between house and Rly station and 'Auld Lang Syne' on platform and 'farewell' quietly and slowly down the township road with Colonel,[11] and Sonny Pole[12] and Whelan. The two drinks and very, very slow pace up the hill, our home. Don't you remember you and I lay down to rest just below Dr. Bleeck's house? Whelan and Colonel went on — how we thought, smoked and dozed, and woke up about 2.30 a.m. Then up-hill again and oh to rest, after another look at the Southern Cross.

> 'The splendid heavens a shining frame,
> Their great original proclaim.
> In reasons ear they all rejoice
> And utter forth a glorious voice
> For ever singing as they shine
> The hand that made us is divine.
> Addison you know

That is a great thing 'Ode to Creation', I think. So is death of little 'Nell' and 'Sick Stockrider' and also the quiet, beautiful wealth of the 'Bush' that we must still endeavour to work.

A few more men good in their way as our Prof. would cause quickly a big movement.

Well, we can't have last summer again till, well — I'm going to enjoy the coming one immensely if all's well—you will come too Eh. Ah I feel more than I can ever write about this. However, I'm sure it will help my work.

Had a lovely long walk into the bush last Monday — about 18 or 19 miles. Took our lunch and one bottle of beer and flute and terbac Oh I wish you'd been there. An Englishman, Mr. Edwards, and I collected a large bunch of beautiful orchids, 6 or 7 kinds, lovely delightful flowers, hiding their beauty among the grass and ferns—and wattle, wattle, wattle, it would make a fine Garden of Eden; and heath, and gums, broad decorative feeling, masses of shimmering bronze and crimson. Sarsaparilla twisting her purple strength round everything; she is most amorous and sheds her color like blue tears if you pluck her roughly. How sarsaparilla 'loves and is not loved.' I mean by Philistines who sometimes come from the old country, for instance, my brother-in-law — he misses it all.

Varnishing day[13] last Saturday and tomorrow. I was signing a small sketch of McMahon's Point[14] at 4 p.m. Saturday when someone wished to see me. I went outside. A gentleman awaited me with a letter (from Mr. Bevan, amateur artist and critic, I hear) which instructed him to purchase, if possible, the very sketch I was at the time signing. Strange. He had not seen the work. Price £7/7/-.

Have a good deal of work in. But I feel honestly that the Hanging Committee of N.S.W. have not paid my work the respect I feel it deserves.

I came in Saturday morning, was looking round, and one of the Committee asked me if I was satisfied. I had not seen the Exhibition even; in half an hour another, and then another, asked me. Why do they ask me? It is foolish, and suggests a timidity in sticking to the work they have done. One man, Lister (poor work),[15] pressed me to express myself. I said 'No.' I contribute my work subject to your hanging, and, therefore, will abide with, &c. He could see what I felt and pressed me to give my opinion on the hanging of my work, whereupon I slogged into a number of things on the line, tripes. This is of course only to yourself. I feel disinclined to show here again.

No. Barring two or three fellows, the people seem to me to think too much of sales.

No. They can be dam'd, except two or three friends I've met. I like Barnett[16] very much. He is a man of considerable talent and ability and very quick and original. He liked your *Shearing*.[17] His wife is fine looking.

Am afraid the strike[18] will be serious matter. Wish it would come to a head, even if they fight about it, much the best. Saw a procession of union men. Barnet thought there were 10 thousand or more.

I think if it comes to riot or serious strife the Military and

Police would be insufficient. The public then would have to defend their property.

Well final Bye old chap.

Yours very truly
Arthur Streeton

NOTES—STREETON LETTERS

1 Aby Altson (1864-?1937) who won the National Art Gallery of Victoria Travelling Scholarship in 1895, the exhibition for which is referred to here. He studied in Paris, and worked in London as an illustrator, later turning to portrait painting.

2 'The Prof' was a nickname given to Frederick McCubbin by his artist friends because of his 'philosophic' temperament.

3 McCubbin was in charge of the drawing school at the National Gallery of Victoria from 1886 to 1917.

4 A ride on a Melbourne tram?

5 i.e. painters of works in the National Gallery of Victoria that Streeton admired.

6 'Many years ago, when Heidelberg was a park-like stretch of country dotted with a few cosy-looking homesteads, a minister of the Crown purchased the eminence known as Eaglemont. Laid out with rare shrubs and trees as a setting for a mansion the original plan was never completed, an eight-roomed weatherboard house taking its place. The property passed through different hands, till in 1888 it was owned by an estate company of which Charles Davies was secretary, a caretaker named Jack Whelan being the only occupant of the place. David who was the brother-in-law of David Davies, the artist, invited Streeton at this time to live in the house on the hill, which was now crowned with lofty trees. It was here that the Heidelberg School was started, and a dozen or so girl students used to come out and received lessons in landscape and still-life from Conder and Streeton. Roberts was engaged on portrait commissions on certain days in the city.' (William Moore, *The Story of Australian Art*, (Sydney, 1934) I, p. 72).

7 K or Kay, the nickname given to Conder by his artist friends.

8 A popular ballad of the time.

9 The Birthday of Queen Victoria, 24 May, a national holiday.

10 Don Abrahams, see *Smike to Bulldog*, Sydney, 1946, p. 3.

11 The nickname given to Walter Withers by his artist friends, because he was very orderly in his habits and put others on fatigue duty (William Moore, 1, 75).

12 Leon Pole, a caricaturist, mural painter and musician; well-known for his lightning caricatures and skill as a piccolo player. He left Australia for Canada.

13 In 1809 the Royal Academy set aside days when members were allowed the privilege of retouching and varnishing their pictures after they were hung, and prior to the opening of the exhibition. Similar varnishing days were provided by the Victorian Artists' Society and the Art Society of New South Wales.

14 McMahon's Point, a point in Sydney Harbour.

15 W. Lister Lister (1859-1943), was born in Australia, and studied in England, France and Scotland. He returned to Australia in 1888. He was a landscape

painter specializing in large views of sea and shore.
16 Henry Walter Barnett (1862-1928), one of Australia's finest portrait photographers.
17 i.e. 'Shearing the Rams'.
18 The 'maritime' strike (Aug.-Oct. 1890), which involved 50,000 workers.

Letter 2: written about 1891

'Daisy Cottage'
Glenbrook,
Tuesday Evg.

Dear Bulldog,

I firmly believe I'm settled at last. This morning I left my cottage at Penrith[1] and by the 11 train came up here, and I've struck it here, by Jove. Here 'tis about 1200 feet up, and oh so splendid today. Have chosen a fine subject for the W. Color, sitting on the heights of Lucasville,[2] where, without turning the head, one's eye sweeps a great extensive plain fertile with crops and orange groves, and the pure 'Nepean' water running through it, such a grand sight this evening, the sun setting golden behind me and the broad, massive shadow of the mountain (on which I sit like a speck) spreading like a great wing of the night over the great blue peaceful vale. All the air is still, the crowing of cocks, dogs bark and their melody reaches for miles far up to where I rest. Cows look like wee bits of color scraped off your old palette and, man, why!, he's nowhere to be seen; he's just out of it. You just think of him when he blows his train whistle, as it rushes down from the zig-zags[3] and seems to slide slowly down to Penrith, like a tiny worm, and yet perhaps, 'tis a goods of 15 or 20 trucks each containing 8 big strong bullocks which, poor beasts, after being jostled and bruised very much are to be gobbled up by pretty girls with soft delicate cheeks, matrons, and safe old men. Yes, here is a great real drama going on in front of me. To the right sou'-east the plain rises a little, and thousands of strong gum trees stand in a line up to which comes the civilised side of things — crops of maize, lucerne and prairie grass, all so soft and peaceful and yet gradually edging their way into the stately dominion of the Eucalyptus. Looking from here the gums look like thousands of bronzy grey ants coming over the gentle rises — just like that. And then I rise and go back a mile to my lodging at Glenbrook.[4] So interesting and Australian altogether, men and all.

The country between Lucasville and Glenbrook rises and falls a good deal; and there's a sort of canyon, running west into the golden glory of Blue Mountain sunset. And there are about a hundred tents pretty close together (as a rule) — big, strong, young chaps, some with wives and children. On one tent pole was fixed a beautiful waratah, on another a girl's great, big, yellow straw hat. A regular 'Roaring Camp'[5] splendid, and they're cutting a tunnel out of the rock all yellow, and a little machinery to help; shirts and pants hanging out to dry and dozens of fires sending up the columns of blue smoke. Some lovely restful bits something like old Box Hill.[6] Great, well-grown she-oaks, all hairy and soft and full and rich — yes — yes — and I get back to our little cottage — a man who is an invalid, and his wife, both so good and nice, and they're making me comfortable. Oh So nice and quiet here now. One minute from Rly. Stn. Had curried fowl for tea. So glad to leave Penrith. My cottage there was one of a row, and on my left lived a woman with several children and a fearful temper. Three nights ago I was writing in my best room with a cosy fire — and excuse me half a minute — she is chiefly remarkable for a wonderful flow of speech which is not the most select and is carried on with little cessation all . . . day . . . long — mind that. He (the happy husband) came home tight, and she gave him 'hell and tommy.' A tennis match of bad grammar and words. The usual 'bloody' got slapped in the net most frightfully. Well after an hour this harmless pastime gets a bit slow. (She is energetic, large of bone, fleshy, and with a bad-tempered, fiery, amorous eye.) I saw her once from my back yard, and I ran in and bolted the door. She's a daisy, a regular teaser. Well they resumed the business of the second act with a certain amount of muscular exercise (the wall's not thick, so I *had* to hear it all). She seized an axe or stock, or something heavy, and shot at him with it — missed. Then they wrestled, freeing themselves of a healthy oath when breath allowed. She got the gentle instrument again and fetched him a terrible, 'orrible whang on the head, amid great applause from the crockery and furniture. He came to the earth, and then a dead silence — and I shivered. He told her she had cut open his head — that's all. So I revived instantly. Put more wood on my fire, sucked a sweet-smelling orange, filled my pipe, and felt sincerely grateful to Providence that he was not killed.

The other neighbours are very nice. Their little girls and babies and boys came and played about my door, went an errand for 3d., and this morning the eldest, almost 16, good-looking girl (amorous type, Bulldog) swept up for me and whitewashed the hearth and got 2/-, and I gave 'em some wood and the father helped me carry my bags to Stn. So nice — quite sorry to leave 'em.

Well, I practised W. color a bit and I can't cotton on to it very easily. I shouldn't think a sculptor could ever paint a W. color picture. Well must try again. After I've been here a fortnight I'll get a tent and stay, I think, all the long summer — a splendid place.

And how goes it with you old chap?

Yours truly,

SMIKE.

STREETON LETTERS—DAISY COTTAGE GLENBROOK

1 A town thirty-four miles from Sydney. The Nepean flows past about a mile to the west between the town and the foothills to the Blue Mountains.

2 Lucasville, a railway station 172 miles west of Sydney, on the Western line.

3 The zig-zag is a type of railway construction designed to negotiate steep gradients. When the railway across the Blue Mountains was constructed the Colonial Government of New South Wales did not possess the funds required for extensive tunnelling. Consequently zig-zags were constructed on both the eastern escarpment (at Glenbrook in 1867) and the western escarpment (near Lithgow in 1869) of the mountains. The name is given because the lines are laid in one or more zs with reversing points where the line doubles back to enable a train to reverse its direction.

4 Glenbrook, a town on the eastern escarpment of the Blue Mountains, 500 feet above sea-level and about six miles from Penrith.

5 The reference is to *The Luck of Roaring Camp* (1870) by Bret Harte (1836-1902), an American writer widely read in Australia. His work was based on the frontier life of mid-century California and was very popular in the 1870s and 1880s.

6 In 1890 a village near Melbourne, now one of its suburbs.

Letter 3:   Glenbrook
                                                    December 17, 1891.

Dear Bulldog:

This morning, hot, windy, and warm, as I travel down the line, and the mirage sizzling and jiggering over the railway track. I arrive at my cutting, 'the fatal cutting,' and inwardly rejoice at the prosperous warmth all glowing before me as I descend and re-ascend the opposite side up to my shady, shelving sandstone rock, perched high up. I wipe the wholesome moisture from my pale brow, and having partaken of a pull at my billy (like a somewhat lengthy and affectionate kiss), I look up and down at my subject; is it worth painting? Why, of course, damn it all! that is providing I'm capable of translating my impression to the canvas. All is serene as I work and peg away, retiring under the rock a bit when they light any shots, then, 'Up with that b——— waggon, Bill.' 11.30: The fish train struggles over the hill and round to Glenbrook. 12 o'clock: The next shift comes toddling down the hot track with their billies, and I commence to discuss my lunch and tea (of which I consume over a quart every lunch), and now I hear 'Fire, fire's on,' from the gang close by; rest my billy on the rock, take out my pipe, and listen for the shots, with my eye watching the bright red-gum yonder. BOOM! and then rumbling of rock, the navvy under the rock with me, and watching says, 'Man killed.' He runs down the sheltered side, and cries, 'Man killed!' Another takes it up, and now it has run through the camp. More shots and crashing rock, and we peep over; he lies all hidden bar his legs — and now men, nippers and 2 women hurry down, a woman with a bottle and rags. All the shots are gone but one and all wait and dare not go near. Then someone says the last hole was not lit, and they raise the rock and lift him on to the stretcher, fold his arms over his chest, and slowly six of them carry him past me. Oh, how full of dread is the grey, mysterious expression of death — 'tis like a whirlpool for the eyes. Blown to death twenty yards from me and, as a navvy said, it was an ''orrible sight.' By Jove! a passing corpse does chain your eyes, and indeed all your senses, just as strongly as love. All the men followed slowly up the hill, and now all are gone but me and the fatal rocks. I don't feel up to my lunch, so have a smoke and peg away at my gem, but the poor chap, whom I was speaking to only yesterday, haunted me so that I put my gem away, and came away, too, and had a shower and smoke, and thought of him all the while. I asked a navvy if the chap was married. 'No, sir, but one of the Shannon girls is a good bit cut up.' It seems he was engaged to be married.

Thursday: The men didn't go back to work; this sort of thing skeers them a bit: go tomorrow all right, I suppose.

Goodnight, and how are you getting on?

SMIKE

[ERNEST ARTHUR STREETON—LETTERS TO FREDERICK McCUBBIN]
Written probably in 1891

Glenbrook,
Saturday Eve.

Dear old Prof.,

I'm in the Blue Mountains boarding in a wee little cot. for £1 a week. The sun is beautiful in the morning. He rises with me, he goes with me through the dewy forest, and is very intimate with me as I step through all the wondrous wild flowers. Birds

chirp and whistle as I bare my white limbs to the first pure
morning sunlight, and standing on a mossy sandstone rock gaze
around and contemplate as my skin is gently warmed all over
with the flood of sun. All around and above fine tall red gums,
smooth of trunk, as though cast in iron. The bloodwood, grey
gum, turpentine tree, wattle, and all sorts of flowers in their
best summer array. Below me runs a crystal virgin brook with a
rocky bottom and rushes flourishing, tickling me and having
great fun as I step gently into the cold, clear water, one foot,
then the other; I splash the water high over my head; it descends
in hundreds of gems; dry myself with nice towel on the sunny
rock; shake my hair about in the sun to dry, and into my bright
striped pyjamas and back to breakfast. After the meal, boil a
billy of tea, pack lunch — *stacks* of passionfruit; ruby twist,[1]
water-colours and picture — light up and march off at 9.30 to
my work. I follow the railway line for three-quarters of a mile
through a canyon or gully where big brown men are toiling all
the hot day excavating and making a tunnel, which will cost
thousands (about half a mile long), but will save (apparently)
wearing out a great number of engines on the first Zig Zag. I've
past the west mouth and now am arrived at my subject, the other
mouth, which gapes like a great dragon's mouth at the perfect
flood of hot sunlight. There is a cutting through the vast hill of
bright sandstone; the walls of rock run high up and are crowned
by gums bronze-green, and they look quite small, being so high
up, and behind is the deep blue azure heaven, where a crow
sails along like a dot with its melancholy, hopeless cry — long
drawn, like the breath of a dying sheep.[2] Right below me the
men work, some with shovels, others drilling for a blast. I work
on the water color drying too quickly and the ganger cries 'Fire,'
'Fire's on'; all the men drop their tools and scatter and I nimbly
skip off my perch and hide behind a big safe rock. A deep hush
is everywhere — then, 'Holy Smoke!', what a boom of thunder
shakes the rock and me. It echoes through the hills and dies away
'mid the crashing of tons of rock; some lumps fly hundreds of
feet sometimes and fall and fly everywhere among the trees;
and then a thick cloud laden with fumes of the blasting powder.
All at work once more — more drills; the rock is a perfect
blazing glory of white, orange, cream and blue streaks here and
there where the blast has worked its force. Work awhile, then
again 'Fire,' 'Fire's on!' — and off we go, and then work again.
At 12 all knock off and the 'Fish'[3] has just gone over the hilltop
from Sydney with its passengers and mails for Katoomba and

Bourke. I crawl under a shady rock and have lunch and inspect
my arms, which are getting bronzed more and more, with the
flood of palpitating summer sunlight. Prop up my work, and I
think it's coming but just fairly. I'll soon begin a big canvas
(oilcolor) of this. I think it looks stunning. 'Tis like painting in
the 'Burning Fiery Furnace';[4] so beautiful and bright and yet so
difficult to attain. Proff., if you ever come here, beware — beware
of the *tick*. They are hellish insects, shaped like a tick or flat
like a wedge. They get under the skin and make straight to any
vital part, and then, I understand, it's simply hell, you know,
with the *top off*. The bush here's full of 'em, and I got one brute
in the back of my immortal head. Even the invisible halo didn't
frighten him (I'll begin to believe that halo is only a myth). I
felt him boring into my nut like a bradawl and asked the
country wife to look and see what was up. She said '*Tick*,' and as
I sat like a rock on a chair I got a detailed description of the
powers given (Lord knows why) to this little brute. His head and
half his gentle body were embedded in my head, and they applied
kerosene and with a tweezers drew him as you draw a tooth, Sir.
I must admit I felt a little relieved after that and indulged in
a par*tick*ularly lengthy smoke.

Sunday night,
and Oh, such a night.

Today opens with the bright sun and my bathe as usual. After
breakfast, pack up, without coat and vest, just a strap to keep
my pants up, and off I go. How jolly in the 'glowing morn.' 'Tis
very hot, the air is rather thundery and rarefied like that of a
balloon. I don't settle for a while. Soon a darkness fills my soul
as the black demon approaches me and grins as he tightens his
beastly grip on my poor stomach. He is called 'Diarrhoea.' I was
bad all the hot hours of the morning, crawling weakly about the
high hill with my billy of tea and basket containing lunch and
about a dozen passion, on which I looked and sighed audibly.
Even my dear pipe did I relinquish. I came up to the scratch
again, and looking down over the vast Emu Plains behold all the
sweeping grandeur of a thunder cloud suspended over the plain.
The different air currents play round its edges, but the bulk
is the same, and grows angry and purple in its vast strength,
which measures miles. I contemplate, and ejaculate 'Glory,'
'Glory,' 'Glory' — what a sight. 'Tis like the human race, its
crown is beautiful, snowy, happy like a damsel's ivory bosom; and
all peace and smiles as it curls and rolls gently reclining against

the deep azure dome of heaven. Then the other side; underneath it is a lowering sullen color and lightning like a death-agony leaps downward from its heart, and it moans and thunders and then despairingly sweeps the earth with tears. I seize my paints and try. But no, it cannot be today. My stomach fails again, and so my head must stop. I bundle them together; my water color box is almost too hot to touch; and with a long, loving look behind at the spectacle so sublime I pull myself together and tramp the rails toward home. Reviving a bit, I sit down, drink tea and eat a bit, rest and then yarn all the afternoon with my friends, the big, stalwart men. Sitting on a gunpowder keg at the tent door, I hand round the ruby twist; we smoke, and I listen to long yarns and adventures — diggers, prospectors, and so on. One old chap, but energetic; tales of coal, gold, and discussions on the present hard 'bullocking' they have to do in the broiling sun. I like these men. They're like a 'roaring camp,' big and bronzed. I say 'Good-bye' to my big friends and move off. My path lies towards the west, which is a flood of deep gold. I felt near the gates of paradise — the gates of the west.

I'd done nothing all day and the diarrhoea was off for a while, so made a sketch of a row of tents glowing in the last golden light. The men came round and you'd be surprised how they are interested. I'll undertake to say that the love of nature and appreciation of the beautiful is stronger and more apparent in these men — 10 times more so — than in the average wealthy men of the city, who boast a taste.

The night is exquisite, a mellow liquid full flood of twilight is veiling all nature and the soft radiance of the stars getting stronger. It is a lovely, lovely night.

Remember me kindly to all my friends, and the students at the Gallery and Mrs. McCubbin, and write to your poor old

SMIKE.

STREETON LETTERS—GLENBROOK SATURDAY EVE

1 A brand of pipe tobacco.
2 Streeton painted a crow in his water-colour painting 'Fire's On, but did not include a crow in the large oil painting of the same subject. Perhaps the tragic death of the settler described in the letter to Roberts (p. 258) provided him with a more realistic 'symbol' of melancholy.
3 The name given to a train which carried commuters between Blue Mountain towns and Sydney, and said to derive from the name of an early driver of the train, Jock Heron. His name was corrupted to Herring and because of his dominating nature he became known as the 'big fish'. The name was applied to the train in the 1880s and has persisted.
4 A reference to the Book of Daniel, Ch. 3.

Sydney Long (1878–1955)

Born at Goulburn, New South Wales, Long studied under Julian Ashton at the Sydney Art School, later (1907-10) entering into a teaching partnership with him. Long was a member of the first Council of the Society of Artists, and President (1898-1901). He was also one of the first artists practising in Sydney to be influenced by art-nouveau design in his paintings. In 1910 he travelled to London, and studied etching with Malcolm Osborne developing a considerable reputation as an etcher when he returned to New South Wales. Long played an active role in the Sydney art world of his day, as a President of the Australian Painter-Etchers' Society, Director of the art school of the Royal Art Society, and a Trustee of the Art Gallery of New South Wales from 1933 to 1949. *The Etched Work of Sydney Long* A.R.E. (1928) contains a complete catalogue of his etchings to that year.

[THE TREND OF AUSTRALIAN ART CONSIDERED AND DISCUSSED]

The exhibition of Australian Art held in the Grafton Galleries in 1898, moved the Critics to ask where was the Australian School? The cult, which was catholic enough to include Cox[1] and Conder, Scarvell[2] and Streeton, was too broad to lay any claim to distinctiveness, although plentiful indications were visible that the germ of a school was in existence, and that it only required further maturing under our warm Australian skies to justify its claim to recognition.

For almost the first century of our life, we were wholly dependent upon 'foreign' talent. Men with and without established reputations (mostly without), came and looked at our land, saw that it was wonderful and beautiful, and painted it in the manner they had already acquired. Naturally it was not Australian. The foreign spectacles worn on their academic noses made it impossible for them to get away from the conventions and characteristics of their own lands. Conrad Martens is perhaps the earliest and most notable case in point. His work is entirely unconvincing, from the Australian point of view, and suggests neither the weird mystery of the bush nor the dazzling sunlight of our country. His work, therefore, has little or no Australian value, beyond being among the first legitimate efforts at Art in Australia. One has only to compare his work with that of Streeton to see the wonderful advance that has been made in the characterization of our native landscape — to note the change —

from dull grey skies and sunless foliage to the intense blues and golden browns typical of Australia.

The language of the brush is the only universal language after all, and although painters of different schools and countries develop seemingly wide differences of method and colour, they will be found on close inspection to present no wider variants than those which exist between the spoken dialects of a written language.

The man of our back blocks speaks the same language as the Yorkshire farmer, but speaks it with a different accent — a difference, however, no greater than that which will exist between the schools of English and Australian painting. Both are merely the result of a difference in environment, and we shall not revolutionize the methods of painting that are already in existence any more than we have revolutionized our native tongue, merely vary them to give greater and more characteristic expression to our ideas.

It is this difference of environment that will make our Art distinctive. The brilliancy and dryness of the summers and the comparative mildness of the winter give to our landscape a range of hot, warm colour peculiar to ourselves. Streeton recognised this when he painted his brilliant landscapes in such a bright colour key, but, unfortunately, in many instances, he pitched it too high and neglected altogether the more sombre side. But although in his eagerness to get sunlight, he rushed from the blackness of Conrad Martens to the opposite extreme, yet he had a healthy influence on our Art, and it remains for our painters to take the texts of these two men and preach a sermon on Australian painting.

No one painter, however, can hope to play on all the keys. His love for one particular theme in Nature's rhapsodies will eventually colour all his work. And he is a clever man who prevents it becoming a mannerism.

We have, unfortunately, had as yet no painter of such supreme talent as to effectively exercise a wide-reaching influence on his brother artists. And although no one, however able, can hope alone to establish a National School, even in the work of a long life-time, yet every patient seeker after truth may, unwittingly, perhaps, indicate some simple principles, or contribute a word or phase [*sic*] which may ultimately find a place in the National vocabulary. There are, fortunately, many of these patient seekers, earnest and capable men, who are gradually preparing the way to a better understanding of this the newest and the oldest of all the Continents. A great proportion of these are 'Foreign,' but every year marks the appearance of some native-born Australian of more or less talent, who has something to say about his own country.

Up to the present time realism has been the prevailing tendency, the surest of all foundations, and so far has been solely manifested in landscape.

During the last couple of decades, the local exhibitions have from time to time marked the advent of some man who has exercised an influence on those around him. Minns,[3] Fullwood,[4] Lister, Conder, Hopwood,[5] Streeton, Ashton,[6] and others, have each in their turn expressed something individual about Australian landscape, but, generally, from the fringe of coast line, and in the more settled parts of the country where the typical Australian is not. The exhibitions have consequently reflected not the primitive landscape of the country, but bits of seascape, scraps of orchards and blossom that might be anywhere, not forgetting the eternal view of the Harbour. There seems to be as much difficulty in getting the artists farther afield as settling the man on the land. Probably there is the same reason in both cases — lack of encouragement. It is for this reason that Australia loses a big proportion of her artists, unfortunately at the stage when they are beginning to develop a feeling for their native land. If they are strong enough to retain this feeling and return with the knowledge of artistic methods of other countries, it would be a distinct gain, but alas! they return not.

So far, a review of the work of these men show[s] that we are developing a feeling for sensuous colour and brilliant effects of light. And mostly in landscape; the more serious and sombre side of which has not been touched yet.

Pictures of the greyer aspect, if we except Mahoney's [*sic*] 'Cry of the Mothers,'[7] and Streeton's 'Gloucester Buckets'[8] have been very rare. The long weeks of rain after the breaking of a drought, those wonderful winter twilights and sunsets in the bush, are as characteristic as the brilliant sunlight that has attracted the painters so much. Many grey pictures have been produced, but the trouble is they don't look Australian. Withers' picture of a wet road in the Gallery, despite the three-rail fence and the gum trees, might have been produced in a French studio. The same might be said of Heysen's 'Mystic Morn.'[9] The gum trees are there, but the feeling is not Australian. This Australian feeling is not to be got by sticking in a gum tree. Even the universal recipe of the inevitable swagman, given us by some of the critics, will not always answer. If the delicate relation of the colour values is not there, all the swagmen and crows in Australia will not make it Australian. The work of the Victorian artists has always been pitched in a greyer key than those of N.S.W. But it is not the grey of Australia; it rather shows the influence of the 'French Grey' School. Although they are more workmanlike in their methods, due to a large proportion of them being trained abroad, I should say that their work was more unAustralian than any of the other States. Unfortunately, too, they show a strong tendency to stick to the old hackneyed subjects of the European studios.

This is probably encouraged by the set subjects given at the National Gallery Schools for the Scholarship Competitions.

The combination of figure and landscape by which Australia is and probably will be most typically represented, as shown in 'The Black Soil Plains,'[10] 'Rounding up a Straggler,'[11] and in a more imaginative way by 'The Spirit of the Plains,'[12] has not been developed to any very great extent. The figure painters find that the occasional portrait, and black and white work, crumbs that are to be garnered only in the city, lie more to their book than the uncertain masterpiece to be painted at some expense in the bush. We shall have to wait until the wealthy Australian buys his pictures here, instead of satisfying his artistic craving with imitations of the Old Masters, or potboilers by mediocre English artists imported for trade purposes.

We are also waiting for the appearance of an imaginative school.

There is an occasional note struck now and then, but more in an experimental way, and too often founded on some old tradition that is out of harmony with the country. Witness the 'Pan' and the 'Centaurs' exhibited some time ago, whose failure to appear convincing, shows that unlike his brother artists in the older civilisations, the Australian artist will never be able to people the bush with nymphs, or the rivers with naiades, unless he invents a special Australian brand, or forgets his native landscape. They will never look convincing among the gum trees, and men in armour would even be more ridiculous. This lack of any tradition has to a certain extent curbed the imagination of the figure painter. He is brought face to face with the elements that suggested to the Greeks their beautiful traditions, and as he cannot use their symbols, he will have the joy of making new ones suitable to his surroundings. The drover, the shearer, the bullock driver, and even the bush-ranger, to the utilitarian person, seems to be all that is needed as a keynote for Australian land-scape, but yet to me the background calls for something that will better express the lonely and primitive feeling of this country. A feeling more suggestive of some melancholy pastoral to be rendered in music, and perhaps rather beyond the limits of painting, yet given the artist with imagination and a complete knowledge of his materials, he should produce work of the most imaginative kind from his surroundings. Instead of Pans and Centaurs, he will bid the Aboriginal blossom out in all the graceful proportions of manly vigour; when sufficient time has intervened to allow us to forget his failings.

He will be depicted as an heroic figure in his tribal fights. The lonely gullies will be awakened to life with graceful pastorals of native children. The Bell Birds chime, the Curlew's melancholy note will be pictured forms in the dusky maiden's love tragedy. The Gum Tree, with its changes from silver to brilliant yellows and flesh tones, will yield its story, and the flowers and the birds, so quaint and different from those of the old world, will provide graceful and original fancies for the creation of an imaginative school that will be truly Australian.

The vagueness of his motives will render the artist dependent on delicate colour harmonies for the representation of his ideas — ideas which he, perforce, must treat in a symbolic and decorative manner.

In other respects Australian Art will differ very little from that of any other country. We shall always have the inevitable portrait of the inevitable Alderman or Politician. The Swagman will tramp his 'Last Tramp' and boil his billy on the walls of our Exhibitions for many years to come. With the shearer and the man on the land we will develop a fine realistic school of painters, also potboilers, to the great delight of that section of the public which always loves the obvious.

[Sid Long, *Art and Architecture* (Sydney) January 1905]

NOTES—LONG

1 There was no one named Cox exhibiting in the exhibition. This is probably a printer's error for Fox (6 entries) or, more probably [R.S.] Cocks (4 entries).

2 Jessie E. Scarvell, an Australian painter who exhibited in the annual exhibitions of the Art Society of New South Wales between 1894 and 1895.

3 Benjamin Edward Minns (1864-1937), a graphic artist and water-colourist, and an associate of Charles Conder. He drew for the *Sydney Bulletin* and became well known throughout Australia for his 'humorous' drawings of Aboriginals.

4 A. H. Fullwood (1863-1930), an Australian artist best known for his black

and white illustrations for the *Picturesque Atlas of Australia,* the *Sydney Bulletin,* and the *Town and Country Journal.*

5 Henry Silkstone Hopwood (1860-1914), an English artist, born in Leicester, who studied at Julian's, Paris, before coming to Sydney in 1880. Although he remained for two years only he helped to invigorate the small Sydney art circle of the time.

6 Julian Rossi Ashton (1851-1942), an important Australian painter, illustrator, teacher and writer. Through his personality and great influence as a teacher Ashton did more perhaps than any man of his generation to gain recognition for the work of Australian artists in Australia. He was born in Penzance, Cornwall, studied in Paris at Julian's, and arrived in Melbourne in 1878. In 1883 he moved to Sydney, which became his home until his death in 1942.

7 Frank Prout Mahony (1862-1917), an Australian painter and illustrator, best known for his illustrations of Australian outback life. His 'Cry of the Mothers' (1885) is in the Art Gallery of New South Wales.

8 Sir Arthur Streeton's 'Gloucester Buckets' (1894) is in the Art Gallery of New South Wales.

9 Heysen's 'Mystic Morn' (1904) is in the Art Gallery of South Australia.

10 'Across the Black Soil Plains' (1899) is an important early painting by George W. Lambert (1873-1930), who after a career as a black and white illustrator for the press, later became famous for his portraiture in pencil and in oils.

11 By Frank Mahony (1889), in the Art Gallery of New South Wales.

12 'The Spirit of the Plains' (1897) by Sydney Long himself is in the Art Gallery of Queensland.

Frederick McCubbin (1855–1917)

Frederick McCubbin was the son of a baker of West Melbourne. He studied drawing at the Artisans' Schools of Design, Carlton, and later at the National Gallery School, Melbourne. Here he met Tom Roberts and joined him, after Roberts's return from Europe, together with Louis Abrahams, in establishing a camp at Box Hill, for *plein air* painting. McCubbin was one of the painters of the Heidelberg School to paint social history paintings, a series of which he began with his 'Lost Child' (1886, National Gallery of Victoria). In 1886 McCubbin was appointed teacher of drawing at the Melbourne Gallery School, and held the position for thirty-one years. In 1907 he made his first and only overseas trip, having been granted six months travel leave from the Gallery. It was later extended to a year. Both Turner and the French Impressionists exerted a considerable influence upon his work after his return to Australia. Although this later work is intrinsically more beautiful, his reputation as a painter and his place in the history of Australian art resides mainly in his introduction of natural sentiment, often tinged with melancholy, into the plein-airist techniques of the Heidelberg school.

[SOME REMARKS ON THE HISTORY OF AUSTRALIAN ART]

Whilst in conversation the other day with a much travelled Australian, he made the remark that 'There is no Australian Art,' meaning that an Art truly representative of this country had yet to make its appearance. To a man familiar with the Art Galleries of Europe and the highest levels reached by the modern European Artists, it is fatally easy to make this mistake: On the one hand he sees the energy and genius of the great minds of Europe — the exquisite jewels of Architecture, Sculpture, and Painting — a resultant of countless years and innumerable masters: On the other he sees, what he would regard, as the none too brilliant work of a few scattered Artists, ranging over a period of perhaps sixty years — a moment in time compared to the centuries of Europe.

A superficial observer would find logic in his assertion, but a person who has studied the question deeply will immediately discount the truth of it. Having followed the progress of Art here, he will know that an Art truly representative of this country has existed and does exist.

In the following remarks, it will be my earnest endeavour to demonstrate the truth of this, and in establishing the claim that Australian Art possesses to be recognised as national, I hope also to illustrate that to a large extent pictorial art is great, inasmuch as it reflects the life and times of its fatherland. We shall endeavour to follow the history of Australian Art more or less in its historical order.

No distinct manifestations in local Art were apparent in this country till the early sixties of the last century. This date, however, witnessed a vast influx of people from the older countries, drawn hither in the quest of gold. As the Colony rapidly assumed settled proportions, a feeling of permanence began to manifest itself in various ways. One form it lent itself to, was pictorial expression. A group of pioneer Artists sprang into being amongst whom stand out prominently the names of S. T. Gill,[1] Thomas Clarke,[2] T. Wright,[3] N. Chevallier [*sic*],[4] E. Von Gerard [*sic*], Curtis,[5] Johnstone,[6] E. W. Cooke,[7] and lastly, Louis Buvelot.[8]

Views of mountain scenery, though mountains do not play a very large part in the physical aspect of this land, were the class of subjects that seemed to have attracted the greater number of these early Painters. — (There exists, I believe, a curious parallel between our artistic history and that of America, in which country at the commencement of the last century, the artists

s

were greatly addicted to portraying grand and sublime views of rugged scenery.)

We have in our Gallery,[9] examples of this early period of Australian Art — notably, Chevallier's 'Buffalo Mountains,' Von Gerard's [*sic*] 'Mount Kosciusko,' and 'Mitta Mitta Valley.'

It is interesting to note, that these early expressions of Australian Art, contain very little of the human element, and to a very small extent convey a lasting impression of the country or the times. Perhaps it would be asking too much of them to expect these early Artists to give us this. It behoves us to remember that all these men hailed from Europe, that there they had lived, studied and worked. They were all imbued with the spirit of Europe. Hence their Art was essentially alien to its new environment. It belonged to lands of humid skies, of deciduous trees and low toned landscapes; countries so vitally different from our land of strident sunshine, clear skies and dry atmosphere. Our flora which has to resist the fierce rays of a burning sun, and thus possesses a somewhat wan faded appearance, which in a grey light, suggests something subtle, vague, and ghostlike, was a thing beyond their ken. They could not see the exquisite cool blue-green of the Wattles, as it is too peculiarly Australian. Neither could they understand the Gum. The subtle way in which it responds to varying effects of light and shadow was lost on them. Now faintly tinged with the early morning light; now glorious gold in the afternoon sun, each leaf and twig resplendent, and again softly flushed with the warm afterglow, as the twilight awaits the rising of the moon. They did not appreciate the range of subjects, the varieties in shades and colours, the Gum tree presented, from the violet grey tints of the stringy bark to the transparent sheen of the White Gum, upon which colours disport and change in a hundred subtle ways as they would upon a mirror. Yet our trees and our faded flora are such component parts of our Australian landscape. As Monet says, 'Light is the chief sitter everywhere.' Yet it seems, that in no other country does the natural background present such a responsive medium as in Australia, pitched as our landscape is, in a somewhat minor key.

But the early Australian Artists missed all this. They strove to portray in their canvases, that which the tourist so eagerly seeks for; Nature in her grandeur rather than in her homely moods. They ignored, because they did not understand, the effects of man in his relation to Nature — the sun-bleached landscapes, the farm with its neighbouring clump of Gum trees, the fields that merge into wayward forests, the winding road with its bullock wagons, men and women toiling, horses and cattle, and all things that savour of man.

Thus it is that these early pictures do not arouse our sympathies, for it is precisely the pictures of things familiar to us, of homely subjects, 'Things we have seen nor cared to see,' [*sic*] as Browning says,[10] which most appeal to us, and more often therefore rise to true greatness.

All these pioneer pictures leave us cold, they inspire us with no love and with very little interest, beyond the spectacular. They might belong to any country, so little are they Australian. But we must not be ungrateful to their creators. They lit the lamp of Art at a time in the history of this country, when Art was a thing not even dreamed of, and for this their successors should always remember them.

In dealing with this group of Artists I mentioned Louis Buvelot. Yet it is only chronologically that he can be associated with them. He is as distinct from them as Turner is from the conventional Artists of his day. We owe much to him, and we should love him accordingly.

Where Von Gerard and Chevallier went in search of mountains and waterfalls for their subjects, Buvelot interested himself in the life around him, he sympathised with it and painted it. There was no one before him to point out the way; he possessed therefore in himself the genius to catch and understand the salient living features of this country. In a sense he was a forerunner.

All his pictures are reminiscent of Australian life as we know it. Incidents by country road sides, weather-worn farm houses, familiar farm yards, fields in which men are working, fences and wayward Gum trees, the effect of sunlight on a tree or shadow in a forest glade. I remember as if it were yesterday, standing one evening a long time ago, watching the sunset glowing on the trees in Studley Park, and it was largely through Buvelot that I realised the beauty of the scene.

If I chose an example of this Painter's work, which I think thoroughly characteristic of him, it would be 'Summer Evening at Templestowe.'

How poetically he has caught the feeling of the end of a hot summer's day! The long weary afternoon is passing away, and the feeling of the approaching cool south-easterly breeze is suggested. In the sky a big cumulous [*sic*] cloud, that has built up through the sullen heat of midday looms gloomily. Along the dusty road, one sees tired sheep wandering slowly, searching for the scant herbage left by the withering sun. The old homestead is on the right, and nearby the beautifully painted Gum tree. The feeling of closing day, approaching night and rest, the billy fire, and the smoke ascending from the burning gum branches, typify so much of life along Victorian roads. It is thoroughly Australian.

In the Buvelot pictures we have hints of the charm that characterises the Barbizon school[11] of which the Corot we possess is such a beautiful example.[12] He could not have escaped the influence of this movement, living as he did in the French Cantons of Switzerland. That influence, perhaps, helped him to lift the scene from the dreariness of the commonplace to the charm of the picturesque.

Louis Buvelot, the last of the pioneer Artists, is the connecting link between them and that group of young Artists who sprang up in the eighties. The fact that, at that period the National Gallery School, under the guidance of Mr. Folingsbee [*sic*],[13] was just commencing to send its first finished students out into the world, had a great deal to do with the increased interest in Art. It was a period of great enthusiasm — the young native born students began to hold exhibitions; the arrival of young Artists from the old countries served to create a cosmopolitan atmosphere. Newspapers commenced to interest themselves in the doings of the new school; finally people began to talk about 'Australian Art.'

Public opinion was not, however, entirely favourable to the doings of the new school, the newspapers were sometimes caustic and the older Artists openly cynical. So many of the ideas of the new body were in direct contravention to those held by the older craftsmen. The new school believed in painting their pictures in the open air — their war cry was relative values, the necessity to paint everything on the spot, whereas the older Artists for the most part, painted their pictures in the studio, from studies either in black and white or colour.

An exhibition of this new work, held in Melbourne at that time, met with a very severe criticism from one of our leading dailies, in spite of the fact that it merited praise rather than blame, for it was a very interesting collection of studies in relative values, some of which were extremely charming.

In spite of opposition, the group of Painters held fast to their ideals, receiving from time to time fresh recruits. One notable adherent they acquired was a new arrival from England, the now late Walter Withers.[14] Withers' ideals were fully in accord with those of the young school, as they soon discovered on witnessing his work.

Withers settled down at Heidelberg, in which place he seemed to find an abundance of subjects suited to his quiet retiring temperament. It was that season of broken sunlight, soft cumulous clouds, and south-west winds that seemed most to appeal to him. He loved the green, fresh landscape — the approaching shower of rain — the dreamy soft atmosphere of winter. One has only to study the canvas of the Artist — 'Tranquil Winter,' hanging in our Gallery, to realize this. The more you regard this picture, its tone and colour, the more you will feel the truthfulness and poetry of its interpretation.

That sunlight has lost its fierce power of burning hillside and plain, and the absence of the hot wind, drying and withering all things green and fresh, is seen in the delightful tenderness and freshness of the landscape. This sunlight is gracious and friendly. You could work all day on such a day as depicted here, and never feel fatigued. How thoroughly convincing are the trees and the hillside, and how unconventional the subject. The picture possesses that 'happy' element. One feels that in it, nothing has been arranged. Everything is natural and in its place, as though the Artist has come upon some quiet common-place spot, and, magician like, revealed to you and me its tender beauty. In Withers' work, we have the creations of an Artist who thinks; the work of his hand ever responds to his mood. There are many of his pictures scattered in private collections and public Galleries, in which the varying moods of this poetic painter may be studied. There is one beautiful example in the Sydney Gallery called 'An Approaching Storm.'

Heidelberg will ever be associated with Withers. Not the suburban Heidelberg of today, but the remote sleepy Heidelberg of years ago, with its winding country roads, its wooded hills and quiet village life. Eltham, too, he has rendered no less dear to us.

Withers loved the quiet effects of Nature — solitary White Gums, rambling roads, the approach of peaceful evening. In some ways his moods reflected those of Buvelot, though his method of treatment was vastly different. He possessed, in common with the latter, the same intense love of the homely and the picturesque.

About this time David Davies,[15] a one-time student of the National Gallery, under G. Folingsbee, returned from Europe, where he had studied for several years, and settled at Temple-stowe. He soon became known as an earnest Artist of retiring nature, and his work seemed the result of long contemplative brooding over the subdued effects of quiet light. All his canvases seemed to be inspired by evening or twilight effects. The picture in our Gallery, 'Moonrise,' is thoroughly characteristic of him. The beautiful tonality of this picture, the economy of means with which he has rendered the dried up grass and weeds, the quality of its colour, give the canvas a beauty that always delights you afresh when you return to look at it. It is essentially a picture to live with. Though he has since returned to Europe the work he executed here has been of material advantage to Australian Art.

Contemporary with Davies and Withers, and, like the former, a student of the National Gallery School, is Arthur Streeton, the painter of 'The Hawkesbury River.' About the time that Streeton entered the National Gallery, a group of the older students had established a camp at a place near Box Hill, for the purpose of studying both figure and landscape in the open air. Streeton was invited to join this body, and during his sojourn with them, and afterwards at Eaglemont, Heidelberg, he painted a number of pictures that made a deep impression on his fellow students, and the Art world of Australia generally.

It was during a stay at Mosman, Sydney, that he made a trip to the Hawkesbury River district, and there painted that beautiful picture which is one of the gems of our Art Gallery. This picture contains all the brilliancy of light and colour that the French Impressionist, Claude Monet, and his school endeavoured to obtain. But Streeton has achieved by simplicity of means, and spontaneity of utterance, that which they strove for, with mannered conventions and monotonous technique.

In this picture the glorious brilliancy of the noonday sun flooding the landscape with its white light, seems to bleach the local colour with its dominating strength. The picture gives in so striking a manner, the feeling of radiance, that one realises the aptness of its title, 'The Purple Noon's Transparent Light' [*sic*].[16] In what a truly marvellous fashion the Artist caught the golden grey green tones of the gums in the foreground, and reflected the sense of quivering light over the distant hills. You are immediately struck also with the delightful economy of means, with which he has rendered trees and hillside, and the winding river which mirrors the deep blue of the zenith — the latter a little out of the atmosphere of the rest of the picture, if one may be permitted a criticism.

One cannot imagine anything more typically Australian than this poem of light and heat. It brings home to us so forcibly such a sense of boundless regions of pastures flecked with sheep and cattle, of the long rolling plains of the Never-Never, the bush-crowned hills, the purple seas of our continent.

You could almost take this picture as a National Symbol. To read into it that which the Artist has unconsciously expressed, you might say that it typified the strength, beauty and possibilities of Australia.

In the brief notice that I have given of these four Artists, I have confined my remarks to those of their pictures, which hang in our Gallery. There are other notable canvases by all of them, but time will not permit me to refer to them. This same limitation does not permit me to dilate at length on the canvases of other Artists, who have contributed in a like manner to the artistic wealth of this country. The scope of my remarks is limited to pictures hanging in the National Gallery. Some of these are not truly representative of their creators — that is to say, they do not typify as other or more important of their canvases would, the degree in which the Artists have helped the general progress of Australian Art. But in the four examples I have given, Buvelot, Withers, Davies, Streeton, we have a complete history. No one regarding them and appraising them at their true worth, could fail to recognise the fact that as national works of art they take their place with the modern work of other countries. If Art is of any value to the world at all it is as a precious human document of the love and admiration of the workers for that which they express, and it is national in so far as it sympathises with the life and the beauty of the country it belongs to. These four pictures all contain in themselves something of these ethereal qualities. Different mediums of expression, diverse temperaments are there, of course, yet each in its way is beautiful, and each thoroughly Australian. In Buvelot we have the hot summer evening, the tired sheep, the dusty roads, the approaching repose of night after weary heat. In Withers we have the quiet winter scene, that season of temperate weather, and cool green landscape, so grateful to us Australians. In Davies we have the subtle mystery of our twilight. In Streeton we have the startling brilliance of our summer noon.

I could illuminate my point further, by bringing in the works of other, none the less noteworthy Artists, such as E. P. Fox, John Ford Paterson,[17] J. Mather,[18] Hans Heysen,[19] J. Longstaff,[20] but time will not permit us. I pass over for the same reason G. Walton,[21] Tom Roberts, and that brilliant and imaginative genius Conder,[22] who all sojourned here for awhile.

But to return, I hope I have in some degree proved my claim — a claim which my personal experience and observation have ratified to myself — that however much Australian Art owes its existence to other lands, its existence, as a National asset, has depended to a great degree upon its being an unconscious expression in some form or other of the ideals of the people amongst which it developed.

I have no doubt that we will continue to build up a National Art, so long as we respond to our environment. We belong to the same race that produced in the middle of the eighteenth century, that splendid period of British Art containing so many brilliant names. These men were essentially British. They owed very little to foreign training; many of them, indeed, never left their own country. It is therefore not too much to expect of us that we shall ourselves, in our own degree, continue to develop under infinitely better conditions an Art of our own.

One cannot imagine a country more favourable to personal development than our own. Australia presents an infinite variety of motives for pictorial illustration. Through the advances made in reproductive processes, we can possess in our own homes very fair facsimiles of the great pictures of the world. We can grasp their composition, drawing, and colour almost as well as if we were face to face with the originals. Aided by these advantages, it seems to me that the Australian Artist can best fulfil his highest destiny, by remaining in his own country, and studying that which lies about him.

I feel that these remarks on local opportunity cannot be too often reiterated to the young Australian student. Perhaps it is lack of confidence in their own country which urges so many of them to fly at their first available opportunity to that haunt of Artists — Paris. With some, of course, exists a praiseworthy desire to study the technique of the old masters, such as Velazquez [*sic*], or Frans Hals — (this, however, can be done quite as easily at home nowadays) — but to me it appears that the aim of the greater number of them is merely to plunge willy nilly into the great Art World of Paris. Some powerful influence seems to irresistibly attract them there. They read and hear of salons and exhibitions that are dazzling in their variety and beauty; of delightful coteries of Artists; of new movements and new methods. The very name itself — Paris — seems to suggest to them an atmosphere of Art and Romance, whereas their own country seems dull and commonplace. But it appears to me they follow a will of the wisp. Arrived in a strange land, they are thus incapable of understanding or sympathising with the fundamental or true artistic progress of the country. They become mixed up in the life and everchanging thought of studios, schools, and exhibitions, which are, after all, merely the froth or surface of Art. They are caught and dazzled by the fads and fashions of the extremists, rather than instructed by the honest methods of the true Artists, for in this great artistic centre, exist men, very often brilliant in their way, who are ever seeking to create a new sensation. A novel method of expression is to them of more importance than the things to be expressed. Like conjurors, they dexterously play with their new ideas, seeking to dazzle their audiences. New phrases, new catch words — 'Individualism in Art' and the like — cause the wondering student to give a profound significance to their pictorial antics. The student strives to echo and imitate their constantly changing extravagances. He re-acts from one side to the other till he no longer progresses, but merely juggles. 'What then,' one naturally asks, 'has the student gained by deserting his country?' Does it not really seem that he has lost sight of the real significance of Art in following the vagaries of the impressionist, the post impressionist, the futurist, or any other 'ist.'

George Borrow,[23] in 'Lavengro,' gives in a passage of conversation with his brother, a more delightful expression of that which I have endeavoured to point out to you, which I will take the liberty of repeating:— 'Yes, go thy way, young enthusiast, and, whether to London town, to old Rome, may success attend thee; yet strange fears assail me and misgivings on thy account. Thou canst not rest, thou sayest, till thou hast seen the picture in the chamber at old Rome hanging over against the wall: ay, and thus dost thou exemplify thy weakness — thy strength, too, it may be — for the one idea, fantastic, yet lovely, which now possesses thee, could only have originated in a genial and fervent brain. Well, go, if thou must go; yet it perhaps were better for thee to bide in thy native land, and there with fear and trembling, with groanings, with straining eyeballs, toil, drudge, slave, till thou hast made excellence thine own; thou wilt scarcely acquire it by staring at the picture over against the door in the high chamber of old Rome. Seekest thou inspiration? Thou needest it not, thou hast it already; and it was never yet found by crossing the sea. What hast thou to do with old Rome, and thou an Englishman? Did thy blood never glow at the mention of thy native land as an artist merely? Yes, I trow, and with reason, for thy native land need not grudge old Rome her 'pictures of the world;' she has pictures of her own, 'pictures of England; and is it a new thing to toss up caps and shout — England against the world? Yes, against the world in all, in all; in science and in arms, in minstrel strain, and not less in the art which enables the hand to deceive the intoxicated soul by means of pictures. Seek'st models? To Gainsborough and Hogarth turn; not names of the world, may be, but English names — and England against the world! A living master? Why there he comes! Thou hast had him long; he has long guided thy young hand towards the excellence which is yet far from thee, but which thou canst attain if thou shouldst persist and wrestle, even as he has done, 'midst gloom and despondency — ay, and even contempt. He who now comes up the creaking stair to thy little studio in the second floor to inspect thy last effort before thou departest — the little stout man whose face is very dark, and whose eye is vivacious — that man has attained excellence, destined some day to be acknowledged, though not till he is cold and his mortal part returned to its kindred clay. He has painted, not pictures of the world, but English pictures, such as Gainsborough himself might have done — beautiful rural pieces, with trees which might well tempt the little birds to perch upon them. Thou needest not to run to Rome, brother, after pictures of the world, whilst at home there are pictures of England; nor needest thou even go to London, the big city, in search of a master, for thou hast one at home in the old East Anglian town who can instruct thee whilst thou needest instruction. Better stay at home, brother, at least for a season, and toil and strive, midst groanings and despondency, till thou hast attained excellence even as he has done — the little dark man with the brown coat and the top boots, whose name will one day be considered the chief ornament of the old town, and whose works will at no distant period rank amongst the proudest pictures of England — and England against the world! Thy master, my brother, thy at present all too little considered master — Crome.'

It seems to me that this passage contains no small measure of sound advice, and in the same spirit as Borrow I would address the young Australian artists.

This land of yours may appear, sometimes, a very poor thing to you; nevertheless it is your own. If you honour it with a lifetime of unswerving servitude and faithfulness it will in turn honour you. I do not for a moment suggest that you should narrow your point of view merely to what has been done here. You may keep abreast with the finest work that has been done, and is still being done in other countries. Myriad books will keep you in touch with the latest thought in Art. In fact, you may command the best by way of illustration or education that the world can offer you and yet remain here.

In conclusion I would like to state that the remarks I have put before you have been made in all humility.

I have endeavoured to establish a claim that this country possesses a National Tradition of Art, that this Art is valuable, simply because it expresses, in some form or other, the life and feeling of this country. At the same time I am fully aware that there is much to be said on the other side of the question, namely, that Art today has become a very different affair to what it was years ago. Many people claim that the constantly increasing intercourse amongst nations, the nearness of one country to another, has made anything like a local school next to an impossibility. In a word, that Art is now cosmopolitan.

In answer to this I would suggest that one of the reasons why artists nowadays are so completely out of touch with the people as a whole is the fact that what they express has nothing to do with the life of the people. It does not inspire them with sympathy or love. Why is it that all art of all times has expressed either the secular or religious ideals of its country or its times? A living work of art has always been the symbol of some thought, some characteristic, peculiar to its fatherland. Whether the expression has been noble or not has, of course, always depended upon the genius of the artist.

By some profound infallible law those Australian pictures of ours, now in private collections, which stand the test of time and thus evince their true worth, will one day become known to the world. I am convinced that I do not overestimate the matter when I state that future Australians shall have, in the work that has been done and that is being done, a heritage they will be proud of.

May I express, in conclusion, my profound hope in the artistic future of this country.

[From *The Art of Frederick McCubbin*, 1916, pp. 82-95]

NOTES—McCUBBIN

1 Samuel Thomas Gill (1818-80) was born in England and arrived in Adelaide as a young man in 1839. He is best known for his depiction of life on the Australian gold-diggings, and of Australian city and country life in the second half of the nineteenth century.

2 Thomas Clark (1814-83) first taught art at the Birmingham School of Art and was later director of the School of Art at Nottingham. He also taught at the Artisans' Schools of Design, Carlton, and was active in urging the establish-

ment of a School of Art in association with the National Art Gallery of
Victoria.

3 Thomas Wright (1830-86) was born in Sheffield, England, and arrived in
Melbourne in 1852 where he worked for a time as an artist on the gold-fields.
He was an instructor at the Artisans' Schools of Design, and later a Foundation Member of the Victorian Academy of Art. Wright was the first drawing
master of Wesley College, Melbourne. He exhibited work in the Intercolonial Exhibition of 1875.

4 Nicholas Chevalier (1828-1902), the painter, lithographer and cartoonist, was
born in Russia of Swiss parents. He left Russia with them for Lausanne at
the age of seventeen and then studied painting in Paris (under J. S.
Guignard) in 1846, architecture in Munich in 1848, and lithography in
London under Louis Gruner in 1852. Chevalier was the first cartoonist of
the Melbourne *Punch* and is credited with introducing chromolithography
to Australia. An unusually energetic man, he also made woodcut illustrations
for newspapers and painted large canvases of Australian mountainous
scenery.

5 J. W. Curtis. The work of this artist was included in the Intercolonial
exhibition in 1875, where he was described as 'the Australian Gericault'.
This however did not deter the Trustees of the then 'National' Art Gallery
of New South Wales from selling the only painting by Curtis which they
possessed, 'A Winter's Morning', in 1946, in a misdirected attempt to improve
the quality of their holdings.

6 Henry James Johnstone (1835-1907) was born in England. He became a
member of the Victorian Academy of Arts. He studied first under Louis
Buvelot and later at the National Gallery School. Johnstone experienced
considerable difficulties in gaining a livlihood as an artist and established
the photographic business of Johnstone O'Shannessy and Co. to supplement
his income.

7 Edward Wake Cook (1844-1926), a painter who studied first under Nicholas
Chevalier and then at the National Gallery School under Thomas Wright.
Among his fellow-pupils were Tom Roberts, Rupert Bunny, Bertram
Mackennal and Frederick McCubbin. Cook also acted as an assistant to
Chevalier who taught him painting, wood engraving and lithography. He
was a foundation member of the Victorian Academy of Arts. Cook returned
to England in 1873, exhibited at the Royal Academy and became President
of the Langham Sketch Club.

8 Abram Louis Buvelot (1814-88), the Swiss artist who studied in Lausanne, and
in Paris under Camille Flers (1802-68) in 1834. His work was much influenced
by the Barbizon School. Buvelot lived for eighteen years in Brazil. In 1859 he
visited the East Indies and India; and in 1865 emigrated to Australia, where
he made a living as a photographer. James Smith, the critic, was a warm
advocate of Buvelot's work, his fine landscapes became a source of inspiration
to Tom Roberts, Frederick McCubbin and others.

9 i.e. the National Art Gallery of Victoria.

10 A misquote from Browning's 'Fra Lippo Lippi'
First when we see them painted, things we have passed,
Perhaps a hundred times nor cared to see. (11, 301-2)

11 Barbizon School; the group of French landscape painters who took their
name from the small village of Barbizon on the outskirts of the forest of
Fontainebleau where several of them settled in the 1840s. The principal
members of the group were Theodore Rousseau, Daubigny, Diaz and Troyon.

The works of Corot and Millet are often associated with the group.

12 Jean Baptiste Camille Corot (1796-1875), the French landscape and figure painter famous for the fine tonal quality of his work and the naturalism and lyricism of his landscapes. The reference is to 'The Bent Tree' in the National Gallery of Victoria.

13 George Frederick Folingsby (1830-91) was the first Director of the National Gallery of Victoria (1880-91) and Head of the Gallery Painting School (1882-91). Born in Wicklow, Ireland, Folingsby studied under Karl Theodor von Piloty (1826-86) and then practised as a painter in Munich for twenty-five years, exhibited at the Royal Academy and travelled in Europe and Asia Minor.

14 Walter Withers (1854-1914), studied at the Royal College of Art, London, and arrived in Australia in 1882. After working in Victoria for five years he returned to England, married and went to Paris, where he studied at Julian's in 1887 and 1888. In 1889 he returned to Melbourne and in October 1889 joined Roberts, Conder and Streeton at the artists' camp at Eaglemont.

15 David Davies (1862-1939), was born at Ballarat, Victoria. He studied first at the Ballarat School of Design under James Oldham and then at the National Gallery School, Melbourne, under Folingsby, and finally in Paris under Jean Paul Laurens from 1890 to 1893. He returned to Australia to live at Templestowe in 1893 where he painted his 'Moonrise' paintings. At this time he was closely associated with the Heidelberg painters. Davies returned to England in 1897 and lived in Cornwall for twelve years and then moved to France where he lived in Dieppe until 1930, after which he returned to England again. Davies exhibited in Paris at the New Salon and in England at the Royal Academy and the New English Art Club.

16 i.e. 'Purple Noon's Transparent Might'. The mis-reading, natural enough, is frequent. Streeton explained that the title was derived from Shelley's 'Stanzas, Written in Dejection near Naples', 1818.

17 John Ford Paterson (1851-1912), a landscape painter, and a friend of Louis Buvelot. His paintings were both lyrical and romantic, being inspired by Corot and the Barbizon School.

18 John Mather (1848-1916), an Australian painter, etcher and teacher. Born in Scotland, he studied in Glasgow and Edinburgh, arriving in Melbourne in 1878. He is known mainly for his landscape paintings.

19 [Sir] Hans Heysen (1877-1968), an Australian landscape painter born in Germany, famous for his drawings and paintings of the eucalypt.

20 Sir John Longstaff (1862-1941), the portrait painter who studied first at the National Gallery School, Melbourne, and later at Cormon's, Paris. He became a highly fashionable Edwardian portrait painter and occasionally painted large historical subjects such as 'The Death of Burke'.

21 George Walton, a British painter who arrived in Australia in 1890 and was associated for a time with the Heidelberg School.

22 Charles Conder (1868-1909), an English painter who arrived in Australia in 1883, and studied under A. J. Daplyn in Sydney. His 'Departure of the S. S. Orient' (1888) was the first *plein air* painting by a local artist to be purchased by an Australian public art gallery. In 1889 Conder left Australia to study in Paris, at Cormon's. He later became very well known in London as a graphic artist and painter on silk during the 1890s.

23 George Borrow (1803-81), an English writer, mainly of books of autobiographical travel. Through his work he did much to develop in England an interest in the life and culture of the gipsies.

LIST OF SOURCES

Chapter One

The First Encounter. From *A Journal of a Voyage to the South Seas, in his Majesty's Ship, The Endeavour. Faithfully transcribed from the Papers of the late Sydney Parkinson. Draughtsman to Joseph Banks, Esq., on his late Expedition, with Dr Solander, round the World.* London, 1773.

A Land of Romantic Enchantment. A Prospectus for a Set of Picturesque Drawings. Both from *Letters from an Exile at Botany Bay, to his Aunt in Dumfries; giving a particular account of the settlement of New South Wales. With the Customs and Manners of the Inhabitants.* Penrith. Printed by Ann Bell (n.d.) (c. 1794).

The Troubles of an Insect Collector. From the autograph letter by John William Lewin to Dru Drury, 7 March 1803, in the Mitchell Library, Library of New South Wales.

The Extraordinary Insects of New South Wales by Thomas Lewin. Preface to *Prodromus Entomology, Natural History of Lepidopterous Insects of New South Wales,* London, 1805.

Picturesque Views of Australia. From *Views in Australia, or New South Wales and Van Diemen's Land* by Joseph Lycett. London, 1824.

Chapter Two

On Crossing the Blue Mountains. From *Geographical Memoirs on New South Wales,* by Barron Field. London, 1825.

On planning the gardens of the Marine Villas of Port Jackson. From *Lectures on Landscape Gardening in Australia, by the late Mr. Thomas Shepherd, Of the Darling Nursery; Author of 'Lectures on the Horticulture of Australia'.* Published and Sold by William M'Garvie, George Street, Sydney, 1836.

The Beauties of Australia. From *Miscellanies in Prose and Verse* by William Woolls. Sydney, 1838.

Darwin on Crossing the Blue Mountains. From *Journal of Researches into the Geology and Natural History of the various countries visited by* H.M.S. *Beagle, under the command of Captain Fitzroy, R.N., from 1832 to 1836* by Charles Darwin. London, 1839.

Chapter Three

On the State of the Fine Arts in New South Wales. From the letter with that title in the *Sydney Gazette* for 20 July 1829, signed A. B. Mar-ramatta.

The State of Arts in New South Wales and Van Diemen's Land. From the article of that title in the *Art Union*, July, 1839. It is sub-titled: From an MS. on 'Australia, in its Historical Evolution' by Dr J. Lhotsky.

The Fine Arts in their Intellectual and Social Relations From *The Fine Arts: A Lecture, delivered at the request of the Committee of the Launceston Mechanics' Institute.* By the Rev. J. West, Launceston, 1848.

The School of Athens as it Assimilates with the Mechanics' Institu-tion. From the lecture by Benjamin Duterrau published in *Lectures delivered at the Mechanics' Institute, Hobart Town, Session 1849.* Hobart, 1849.

Lecture Upon Landscape Painting delivered at the Australian Library 1856 by C. Martens. From the manuscript by Conrad Martens in the Mitchell Library, Library of New South Wales. This manuscript has been published also in Lionel Lindsay, *Conrad Martens, the Man and his Art*, revised and enlarged edition, Sydney, 1968.

Chapter Four

Von Guerard at the Ballarat Gold Diggings. From the typescript in the Dixson Library, Library of New South Wales. Its provenance is not clear. It was apparently bought by A. H. Spencer, a Melbourne second-hand bookseller (who was acting as an agent for Sir William Dixson) when he was in London in 1937, and sold to Dixson later. On the inside front cover is inscribed in the hand of Sir William Dixson: 'By Eugene von Guerard. The original of this MS is in England; this is the only typed copy that was done. See some original illustrations by Von Guerard at the end'. The half-title reads: 'A Pioneer of the Fifties. Taken from the journal of an Australian digger' with 10 original draw-ings by E. V. Guerard. The typescript is certainly a translation from an original in German, since von Guerard did not possess such fluent English in 1853-4. Compare his letter to James Smith (1870) below. Edward Comstock (M.A. Thesis on von Guerard, Syracuse University, in Syracuse, New York, 1974) suggests that the typescript may derive from a translation of material contained in two or three missing sketchbooks, that von Guerard is known to have kept during his mining days. Von Guerard's other sketchbooks, now in the Mitchell Library, contain diary-like jottings as well as drawings.

Life on the Diggings. From the MS Journal kept by Thomas Woolner. National Library of Australia, Canberra.

Chapter Five

The Bushfires of Black Thursday, 1851. From the *Australian Journal of William Strutt 1850-1862*. Edited, with an Introduction, Notes and Commentary by George Mackaness, privately printed, Sydney, 1958, 2 vols. The original MS is in the possession of Margaret I. Strutt Davies, grand-daughter of the diarist, who has kindly given her permission for the publication of the extract printed here.

The Weird Melancholy of the Australian Bush. Two texts by Marcus Clarke to accompany photographic reproductions of Buvelot's 'Waterpool at Coleraine' and Chevalier's 'Buffalo Ranges' published by the Trustees of the National Art Gallery of Victoria in 1874.

Chapter Six

Art Education in Australia. These two articles were published in *The Month*, vols I (pp. 1-6) and II (pp. 71-74), Sydney 1857.

Mr Von Guerard's New Picture. Article written by James Smith in the *Argus*, Melbourne, 13 July 1870.

Von Guerard's reply to James Smith. Autograph letter by Von Guerard to James Smith inscribed 'Reply on the Critic of Eugene von Guerard's painting of the North Grampians' (n.d.). Mitchell Library, Library of New South Wales.

Among the Western Highlands of Tasmania. From the article of that title in the Report of the Fourth Meeting of the *Australasian and New Zealand Association for the Advancement of Science*, by W. C. Piguenit, held at Hobart, Tasmania, in January 1892.

Chapter Seven

Six Letters by John Russell to Tom Roberts. Mitchell Library, Library of New South Wales.

The Exhibition of 9 x 5 Impressions, August 1889. Review by James Smith, *Argus*, Melbourne, 17 August 1889. Letter replying to James Smith's review, signed by Roberts, Streeton and Conder, *Argus*, 30 August 1889. James Smith reply to the above letter, *Argus*, 4 September 1889.

The Exhibition of Australian Art, Grafton Gallery, London, April-May 1898.

Critical review by R. A. M. Stevenson, *Pall Mall Gazette*, 4 April 1898.

Critical review by Sir Thomas Humphrey Ward, *Times*, London, 4 April 1898.

Critical review by D. S. MacColl, *Saturday Review*, 16 April 1898.

Landscape Painting in Australia. Selected sections from the book of that name by A. J. Daplyn, Sydney, 1902.

Chapter Eight

'Australian Decorative Arts'. From the article by Lucien Henry in *Australian Art,* February 1888 (pp. 9-12).

'What Should Australian Artists Paint'. From the article by Sidney Dickinson in *The Australasian Critic,* vol. I, no. 1 (Oct. 1890), pp. 21-2.

Three MS. Letters by Arthur Streeton to Tom Roberts, 1890, 1891. Mitchell Library, Library of New South Wales. The first three were published, but with some editing and omissions, by R. H. Croll in *Smike to Bulldog,* Ure Smith, Sydney, 1946. For example, in Letter 1 Croll does not include Streeton's quotation of Addison and references to Dickens and Adam Lindsay Gordon; nor the interesting reference to the maritime strike.

A MS. Letter by Arthur Streeton to Frederick McCubbin, 1891.

'The Trend of Australian Art Considered and Discussed'. Article by Sid Long in *Art and Architecture,* January 1905.

'Some Remarks on the History of Australian Art'. By Frederick McCubbin in *The Art of Frederick McCubbin,* Melbourne, 1916.

T

Index